THE RAILROAD TYCOON WHO BUILT CHICAGO

THE
RAILROAD
TYCOON
WHO
BUILT
CHICAGO

A BIOGRAPHY OF WILLIAM B. OGDEN

JACK HARPSTER

Southern Illinois University Press
Carbondale

Southern Illinois University Press
www.siupress.com

22 21 20 19   4 3 2 1

Cover illustrations: *top*, William B. Ogden, circa 1835 (Chicago History Museum; ICHi-39053, cropped and tinted); *middle*, Chicago's first railroad depot, the Galena and Chicago Union; *bottom*, the *Pioneer*, Galena and Chicago Union's first steam-powered locomotive, shown after the company merged with Chicago and North Western (Union Pacific Historical Collection); and *background*, Galbraith Building, Chicago.

The Library of Congress has cataloged the hardcover edition as follows:
Harpster, Jack, 1937–
The railroad tycoon who built Chicago : a biography of William B. Ogden / Jack Harpster.
    p. cm.
Includes bibliographical references and index.
ISBN-13: 978-0-8093-2917-5 (cloth : alk. paper)
ISBN-10: 0-8093-2917-4 (cloth : alk. paper)
1. Ogden, William B. (William Butler), 1805–1877. 2. Chicago (Ill.)—Biography. 3. Railroads—United States—Biography. 4. Mayors—Illinois—Chicago—Biography. 5. Chicago (Ill.)—History—19th century. I. Title. II. Title: Biography of William B. Ogden.
F548.4O34 H37 2009
977.3'1103092—dc22
[B]   2008053404

ISBN 978-0-8093-3736-1 (paperback)

To the citizens of Chicago and to the people of
the Northwest: Would you behold William Butler
Ogden's monument, look around you!
> —A. T. Andreas, *History of Chicago*, 1884

CONTENTS

FIGURES AND TABLES

Tables

PREFACE

The Ogden family is one of the oldest, most distinguished family lines in America. John Ogden, "the Pilgrim," came to the New World in 1641 from Lancashire County, England. A stonemason, he built the first permanent stone church in New Amsterdam, the St. Nicholas Dutch Reformed Church, at the southern tip of Manhattan Island. He also founded the storied commercial whaling industry in America, and, most significant, was the leading founder of the English colonization of New Jersey, one of our original thirteen colonies.

Discovering these facts filled me with enormous pride, as John Ogden was my great-grandfather, nine generations back, through my mother's side of the family. Subsequently, I wrote the first full-length biography on this important colonial American pioneer, *John Ogden, the Pilgrim (1605–1682): A Man of More Than Ordinary Mark*. During my research for that book, I discovered a number of descendants of John Ogden who had also made significant contributions to the growth of our nation. None was as compelling as William Butler Ogden. He was a towering figure in American history during the rambunctious years of the nineteenth century when a new nation was struggling to stretch its boundaries west. But today, the name William Ogden is known only to historians, serious railroaders, or scholars of the great Midwest.

Most Americans have heard of the railroad "robber barons," those Gilded Age men like Collis Huntington, Jay Gould, Cornelius Vanderbilt, Leland Stanford, and James J. Hill, and libraries have many books chronicling their grand but often tainted achievements. Similarly, books about men like Marshall Field, Cyrus McCormick, and George Pullman who built Chicago, America's first great city of the West, proliferate in our libraries. Remarkably, this is the first full-length biography of William B. Ogden, yet he enabled them all. They built on his foundations. When he began promoting railroads in New York, barely twenty miles of track had been laid in America and the cars were still pulled by mules. Collis P. Huntington was still a teenager, working the family's grudging farm near Poverty Hollow, Connecticut; Charles Crocker had not even reached his teens and was helping his father eek out a living in Troy, New York; and Cornelius "Commodore" Vanderbilt, though older, wiser, and richer, was still making his living captaining steamboats on the Hudson River. When Ogden became the first mayor of Chicago in 1837, Field, McCormick, and Pullman had yet to discover this little backwoods hamlet on the shore of Lake Michigan.

Ogden's contemporaries were well aware of his importance. Famed French historian François Guizot called Ogden the man "who built and owns Chicago"; railroad historian Stewart Holbrook called him "a prophet and genius of the first mark; the first great railroad man"; and nineteenth-century politician and lumber baron Isaac Stephenson said of Ogden, "he was one of the most dominating figures of the Middle West during this period. He had as much, if not more, to do with the West's development than any other man."[1]

Perhaps what has kept writers and historians from tackling the story of Ogden's life in the century-plus since his death is the paucity of personal information about the man. His personal papers, letters, diaries, and ephemera were destroyed when his home was razed in the 1871 Chicago fire. He married late in life and had no children, so there were no descendants to pass along family lore about his character or his deeds. His business and legal papers and records abound, but of the man himself, we have almost nothing. To some extent we can look at the published words of his friends or enemies to see into his character, but those are biased sources and can be relied upon only to a point.

In order to look past Ogden's achievements—which were on a heroic scale—and discover the man himself, I traveled to Delaware County, New York, where he was born and lived until he was thirty years old. Although he was a successful businessman there, his most significant contributions to the growth of the nation did not occur until he moved to the hamlet of Chicago in 1836. Yet it was in the Upper Delaware, where he spent more than a third of his life, that I began to get a glimmer of the real William Ogden. It was there, among his large, extended family, his friends, and his fellow Upper Delaware pioneers, that the foundation was laid for the man he became, a man of towering virtues, but also a seriously flawed one.

Old family diaries, local histories, school primers, personal correspondence, and memoirs of people who surrounded the young William Ogden once resided in the Special Collections department in the musty basement of the William B. Ogden Free Library in Walton, New York. My wife and fellow researcher, Cathy, and I spent two delightful weeks in 2004 poring through the material and getting an inkling of who William Ogden was.

Sadly, Walton suffered a devastating flood in the summer of 2006 when the West Branch of the Delaware River reached record highs and overflowed its banks. Hundreds of buildings in the town suffered flood damage, including the basement of the library, and the treasury of ephemera we had perused was destroyed. It seems somehow apocalyptic that all the documentary evidence about who William B. Ogden really was has been taken from us, first by fire and then by flood.

I began to feel more responsibility for telling Ogden's story, since no future researcher would have access to the information we had uncovered in Walton, sketchy as it may have been. In chronicling Ogden's life, my perceptions and attitudes about the man's personal qualities and weaknesses were first forged in that dank basement where I learned about the people and events that shaped his life. I've tried to make use of what I learned to better understand this complex man.

I hope I have done it well.

THE RAILROAD TYCOON WHO BUILT CHICAGO

1

Prelude

---

rief had leveled William Ogden as surely as if he had been struck by a bolt of lightning. It was as if his life had descended into perdition.

It had been three years since his fiancée, Sarah North, died, but the pain was still as raw as the day he received the unexpected news. He had been away on a business trip, much like the trip that brought him here to the Hudson River valley. They had been friends since childhood, playing together in the muddy, rutted streets of Weed's Bridge and Walton, and riding their horses through the meadows of spring and summer wildflowers along the banks of upstate New York's Delaware River. As family and friends had always anticipated, the couple eventually set the date for their wedding for June 1829. Then, unexpectedly, fate took her from him. A sudden onset of pneumonia, he was told.[1]

Hollow meetings to discuss business or politics seemed so unimportant to him now; he couldn't find a place for them in his mind, still so crowded with memories of Sarah and the future they had planned together. He must have known the grieving would eventually pass; he had felt the same sadness when his father died, but it had not immobilized him the way Sarah's death did.

Ogden willed his attention back to the other men sitting around him in the small, cramped room. His brother-in-law, Charles Butler, who had enticed him to come to the meeting, was there, along with Charles's brother Benjamin; but Ogden had probably been surprised at the presence of the other man in the room. Vice President Martin Van Buren was certainly not an imposing man. At only five-feet, six-inches tall, he was trim, erect, and fastidiously dressed. One biographer aptly described him as "a smiling little gentleman, not much taller than the back of his chair, daintily clad and possessed of a wavy golden crowned head."[2]

Matty, as his friends called him, had a reputation of being more politician than statesman. It had been said of him that he soared to the heights on borrowed wings, an indication that he was a master of adopting and adapting the ideas of others. An Albany attorney and Benjamin Butler's law partner, he had become Andrew Jackson's chief supporter in the North, and "Old Hickory" had selected him as his running mate in the 1832 election.

Whatever the vice president's shortcomings may have been, William Ogden knew better than to take his fellow New Yorker lightly. Van Buren was the creator and still the spiritual leader of an organization known as the Albany Regency. It was an effective New York political machine—the nation's first—that controlled the politics in the state and powerfully influenced it throughout the entire nation. His advocacy of New York's right and responsibility to develop its own internal transportation improvements was well known. As a U.S. senator in 1825, he had introduced a resolution that declared, "Congress does not possess the power to make roads and canals within the respective states."[3] He extended that belief to the railroad industry when it began to emerge just a few years later.

It was unusual for the vice president to be in New York during the summer of 1833, attending to what appeared to be a relatively minor provincial matter, when he should have been in Washington at the side of his president, Andrew Jackson, who was fomenting a nationwide crisis over his plan to withdraw all federal funds from the Second Bank of the United States. But Van Buren was nothing if not circumspect. Staying far away from the hearth when the hot coals were being poked just seemed like a wise practice to the consummate little politician. His biographer Holmes Alexander described the vice president's sudden departure from Washington succinctly: "Seeing to what a pass the affair had come, Mr. Van Buren ordered out fast horses in an effort to escape. . . . the Vice President had plans for a protracted tour of upper New York, leaving no address behind."[4]

Charles Butler surely must have explained Van Buren's presence to Ogden. The vice president had plans to meet his good friend Washington Irving so the two could ramble through the old Dutch villages of the Hudson River valley together; so he was conveniently in the neighborhood. More to the point, it was almost certainly at his bidding that the men were even having this meeting with Ogden.[5]

Tall, brawny-shouldered, and handsome, twenty-eight-year-old William Butler Ogden was an extraordinarily successful businessman in his hometown of Walton and in the surrounding Delaware County, New York, towns and villages. He owned and managed a group of thriving lumber and woolen mills and had served his community with distinction in a number of civic posts. He was just the kind of man New York voters would support, which was why the cagey vice president had singled him out for the task he had in mind.

Van Buren peered over the reading glasses perched precariously on the end of his nose and began laying out the reasons why New York's 1835 winter legislative session would be so important. Someone had to be there to champion the important cause that had brought these four men together: railroads. What the vice president proposed was that the Democratic Party run William Ogden for the Delaware County seat in the New York State Assembly the following fall. The party needed someone with eloquence and conviction to address a joint session of the legislature and convince lawmakers to vote in favor of financial aid for the foundering New York and Erie Railroad, lest it fail. It was something the legislature had refused to do in past sessions, and an orator of Ogden's skill was needed for one last try.

The railroad industry was in its infancy.[6] Horses and mules still powered the small handful of short-run lines that operated in a few scattered places across the eastern seaboard. But to visionary men like Martin Van Buren, railroads would be the future of America and the catalyst for the nation's nascent western expansion. One New York journalist, in the *American Railroad Journal*, put a more poetic spin on the economic potential of the New York and Erie: "It will prove a refreshing and fertilizing shower which will unquestionably enable thousands to reap a golden harvest."[7]

Other men disagreed, especially those New Yorkers living along the route of the Erie Canal, in the northern tier of the state. Their towns had prospered from the day the 363-mile-long canal had opened, a decade earlier. Waterborne systems, they insisted, were the answer to east–west transportation, not railroads. This political dichotomy raged in New York.

The vice president straightened in his chair until he was as stiff as a winter cornstalk. He glanced from one man to another and reminded them that state legislators had to be convinced of the value of the New York and Erie Railroad before they would commit funds to the project. He may have locked his eyes on Ogden when he drove home his critical point: it was vital to get legislators to agree on some sort of state aid, or loans, for the railroad, lest another legislative session pass without any action on the project. One big reason this was such a time-critical issue was that neighboring state Pennsylvania was getting dangerously close to approving a railroad from Towanda to Mansfield. That route, if built so close by, would siphon off revenue from the proposed New York and Erie Railroad. Haste was imperative if New York were to maintain its commercial superiority over the fiercely rival state to its south.

State loans to private enterprise for railroad ventures were not unheard of at the time; in fact, they were quite common for financing canals and plank roads. Eight years earlier, New York had advanced a half-million-dollar loan to the Delaware and Hudson Company for one of the country's earliest railroads. States issued these loans in the form of state stock, an instrument backed by a first mortgage on the railroad's property. Railroads' most stupendous boondoggle, federal land grants, would not come into being for another fifteen years.

Ogden knew the problem firsthand. The Erie Canal had hurt his mills badly. It was located too far north to be of any benefit to his numerous lumber and woolen mills, but it certainly aided his northern competitors. But a railroad down in the southern corridor, where Walton was located, would be another story. That would cut his costs of getting his goods to market by as much as 90 percent.

The fact that Ogden had a vested interest in seeing the railroad built had not been lost on Vice President Van Buren. However, Ogden was just not sure he was the man who could sell the idea to northern legislators since they already had their canal up and running. Why would they be willing to help businessmen in the southern part of the state compete with them? Van Buren knew that was one of the chief stumbling blocks. Northern legislators would have to be convinced that the New York and Erie Railroad would benefit the entire state, not just businesses along its tracks in the southern corridor. Another big problem was that many of the legislators had their own money invested in competing technologies like plank roads, canals, and steamships. They had to be convinced to vote their consciences, not just their pocketbooks.

Charles Butler knew Ogden more intimately than the other two men did, and he knew his wife's brother had the intelligence and skills to get the job done, if any man did. He also knew something the others did not: it was Ogden's state of ennui over the death of his fiancée that gridlocked him, not any business issues he faced.

Ogden was skeptical. He certainly realized the importance of the railroad to the southern sector of the state; and he also knew it would be a vital part of New York's emerging transportation system as it, like all the other Eastern states, tried to reach out to the developing lands to the west. But could he convince others of that fact? It wasn't that he lacked self-confidence—that was something Ogden was never short of—but could he do what was required in his present state of mind?

There was another reason for his hesitation, too; Ogden simply did not trust Martin Van Buren. The Ogden family's core business operations, their woolen mills, were being threatened by stiff competition from abroad. A tariff on imports that would help protect their business was passed in 1828 while Van Buren was in the Senate, but the man had seriously waffled on the measure. It was a heavily politicized issue, and Van Buren's true feelings toward it were obfuscated by his political ambitions. Ogden likely guessed that Van Buren's support of state funding for the railroad would never be made public for the same reason.[8] Some members of his Albany Regency held interests in competitive modes of transportation—steamships, toll roads, and plank roads—so the organization had taken no official stand on state aid to the New York and Erie. The vice president rarely took a public stand on *anything* where there was serious opposition. *That* was why Ogden was unsure of the man.

The room had grown silent. To say more might dilute the strong arguments the men had made, so they waited. Ogden likely knew the others were correct in their practical assessment of the situation, and perhaps it might do him good to take on such a task.

He made his decision. He would do it.

Although Ogden did not know it at the time, the plan the men set in motion would profoundly affect the remainder of his life. More important, it would strongly influence the United States' western expansion, the founding of one of the nation's great cities, and the history of railroads in America.

2

The Little Railroad That Could

arlier in 1833, just a few weeks before his twenty-eighth birthday, William Ogden had been ruminating about the nagging torpor that had cloaked him like a shroud since Sarah North's death. He knew he was far too young to be feeling so enervated; or was he? Maybe the fact that he had been forced to become an adult at sixteen had somehow accelerated his life's clock. What Ogden did know for sure was that he had to shake himself loose from whatever malady had hold of him.

As a boy, Ogden had always imagined his life would be an unending series of adventures. He had always been a voracious reader; and the adventures of Cervantes's *Don Quixote*, Lesage's *Gil Blas* or Defoe's *Robinson Crusoe* had filled his mind with ideas of how adventuresome life *could* be. One of his fondest memories was of his father telling him stories. Abraham Ogden had a special knack for making the most mundane experience sound like a grand adventure in his retelling. Among all of Abraham's stories, none likely had a greater impact on the boy than the story of the *Clermont*.

The year was 1807, when William was only two years old. His Uncle Daniel had heard rumors that a new kind of boat, one with a paddlewheel driven by steam, would be making a trial run up the Hudson River from New York City to Albany. The invention of a Pennsylvania man named Robert Fulton, the boat drew all sorts of derisive comments from the citizens of Walton who had heard about her. Daniel and Abraham decided to see it for themselves and set out on their horses for the sixty-mile trip to the Hudson. What they saw that August 11 afternoon was enough to convince both men that a new age was dawning.

A young boy named Henry Freeland was fortunate enough to be standing on the riverbank that day and also witnessed the event: "Some imagined it to be a sea monster while others didn't hesitate to express their belief that it might be the sign of the approaching [last] judgment. What seemed strange in the vessel was the substitution of lofty and straight smoke-stacks rising from the deck instead of gracefully topped masts. . . . the whole country talked of nothing but a sea monster belching forth fire and smoke."[1]

The older and wiser men who watched the strange contraption huff and puff its way past them saw the future: Not just the future of ships that could move upriver by steam, but of wagons that could be propelled in the same way. Abraham shared these stories of a changing world with his young son in the years that followed, and William Ogden never forgot them. But Abraham Ogden suffered a stroke when William was only sixteen, and that ended the boy's fantasies, along with his dream of becoming a lawyer. Still, he adjusted and did his duty. As the oldest son, he took over the family's lumber and woolen mills, and he ran them well and profitably.

Now, about to turn twenty-eight, William Ogden's physical appearance reflected the character and maturity he had gained. His good friend Isaac Arnold, who would come to know him better than anyone else during his Chicago years, described him at about this age:

Portrait of William B. Ogden as a young man, circa 1835. Chicago History Museum; ICHi-39053.

> You might look the country through and not find a man of more manly and imposing presence, or a finer looking gentleman. His forehead was broad and square; his mouth firm and determined; his eyes large dark gray; his nose large; hair brown; his complexion ruddy; his voice clear, musical, and sympathetic; his figure a little above the medium height, and he united great muscular power with almost perfect symmetry of form. He was a natural leader, and if he had been one of a thousand picked men cast upon a desolate island, he would, by common, universal, and instinctive selection, have been made their leader.[2]

A friend-turned-adversary from his later Chicago days, early pioneer Gurdon Hubbard, described Ogden as "a man liberally educated, elegant and soft-spoken."[3]

Ogden had also developed a reputation in the Upper Delaware, indeed throughout the entire northern part of New York, as the kind of man other men looked up to. He had built a reputation as an outstanding business executive, taking those enterprises his father had passed along and improving them, adding to them, making them much more successful than they had been before. With such impressive credentials and the important statewide connections he had made, it was no wonder his name surfaced when Martin Van Buren and his associates began searching for a man to promote their railroad vision in New York.

Railroads were but one of many technological, social, economic, and cultural changes transforming the United States in the early 1830s.[4] Most, like the railroad, were pioneered in western Europe, but they all eventually augured change for the United States as well, as it sought to take its place among the world's advanced nations.

The Industrial Revolution had its beginnings in Britain in the 1780s. However, its full impact was just being realized by the 1830s, the Napoleonic Wars having slowed its progress until about 1815. The revolution's handmaiden, steam power, was just beginning to see broad application by the 1830s too. Canals, improved roads, bridges, and finally railroads enabled trade expansion and made possible the mass movement of people from farms to cities and from city to city. Thus began the process of urbanization in Europe and America. At the same time, Europeans began immigrating to America's cities in significant numbers, driven by high taxes, a series of brutal winters, overcrowding, and a host of other factors in their homelands.

Within America's cities, there was also change. Jobs were plentiful, thanks to new types of industry, and burgeoning industry had also given rise to a new capitalist class. At the same time, there was a growing cosmopolitanism, forged by a renaissance in the arts of music, theater, painting, sculpture, and literature. But this increased opportunity also brought new problems and unrest. American society was heavily stratified, and individuals were seldom able to achieve any upward mobility. There was also a deep and growing division between the Northern and Southern states.

The early 1830s also saw Nat Turner's slave rebellion, which broke out in Virginia but was quelled within forty-eight hours, and the Black Hawk War that was fought between the Sauk and Fox Indians and the U.S. Army and militia over land in the Illinois and Michigan Territories. Andrew Jackson was president of the Union, which included twenty-four states with a population of 12.9 million people; and the demographic center of the nation was only 170 miles west of Washington, D.C. Indians were being removed to the West; Joseph Smith, following the publication of his *Book of Mormon*, was tarred and feathered in Ohio; and the nation's monetary policy was a miserable wreck.

So the decade of the 1830s stood astride huge changes in America, changes that affected the life of every one of its citizens. But of all the changes taking place at the time, none augured as much promise as the railroad. Just the word *railroad* conveyed the same excitement, bordering on public mania, as the word *automobile* in the 1900s, *television* in the 1950s, and *Internet* in the 1990s. It fired the imagination of every young man and woman who heard it.

All the way back to the 1630s, English coal mines had used wagon roads—heavy planks laid end to end upon which carts and wagons were pulled by horses—to move coal and equipment. These were the forerunners of the railroad. In 1758, an Act of Parliament established the Middleton Railway in Leeds, a direct descendant of the same plank-and-wagon technology, that is considered the world's first railroad. Before railroads could progress, however, horse power had to be replaced with a more reliable power source. Over the next sixty-five years, a number of inventors propelled vehicles with steam, constantly improving on the technology that would eventually make the railroad a practical idea.

Although most of the early railroad technology was developed in England, New York is one of a handful of states that can claim top billing in early railroading in America. In 1828, the Delaware and Hudson Canal Company built a sixteen-mile-long railroad from Carbondale to Honesdale in Pennsylvania in an area that was too mountainous for a canal. Like earlier short-run lines in Quincy, Massachusetts, and in Baltimore, horses or mules pulled these cars.

The following year, the Delaware and Hudson took delivery of the first steam locomotive in the country, the *Stourbridge Lion*. Unfortunately, the locomotive was too heavy for the rails and bridges it was to run on, so it lived out its life ignominiously laid up next to the tracks as a stationary boiler. The first locomotive actually built in America, the *Best Friend of Charleston*, also called New York home. It rolled off the line at the West Point Foundry in 1830; but like its predecessor, it died an undignified death the following year when the boiler exploded due to a careless fireman. Each of these events tickled the imagination of William Ogden and thousands of other New Yorkers. However, another event ignited public interest in a big way: *Tom Thumb*.

Peter Cooper, a New York businessman and mechanical tinker who had once been a coach maker's apprentice, built his own steam-driven locomotive in a local coach maker's shop. Because of its diminutive size, Cooper named his locomotive *Tom Thumb* after a traditional hero in English folklore who was no bigger than his father's thumb. The tiny engine was not much larger than a railroad handcar, with a vertically mounted boiler connected to a series of tubes sitting atop. Generating 1.4 horsepower, the little boiler had a revolving fan for draft and musket barrels for boiler tubes. Cooper was trying to prove to the nascent Baltimore and Ohio (B&O) Railroad that his little engine could serve them as well as the imported English locomotives they were considering. Cooper decided to stage a "Great Race" that would capture the imagination of the public and, he hoped, the bosses at the B&O.

Tom Thumb, an early railroad locomotive involved in a "great race" with a horse.

The year was 1830, early autumn; the site, Baltimore. On one side, the steam engine *Tom Thumb*, Cooper at the helm, pulling a carriage filled with passengers on the B&O's iron tracks. On the other side, Lightning, a dapple-gray mare pulling her own passenger-laden carriage on the road alongside the track. The lucky men chosen to ride in the two carriages, lined up right outside Riley's Tavern, were decked out in their Sunday finery. They wore their best woolen suits and white, starched-collar shirts, and each head was proudly crowned by a fine silk stovepipe or beaver hat.

Five thousand people, including most Eastern newspapermen, had gathered to see if this new mechanical carriage could travel faster that the leading ground-based transportation system of the day, the domestic horse. An eyewitness in the midst of this carnival atmosphere later related what happened in the race: "The horse had pulled perhaps a quarter of a mile ahead when the safety valve of the engine lifted and a thin, blue vapor issuing from it showed an excess of steam. [Soon] it was neck and neck. Then the engine passed the horse and a great hurrah hailed the victory. . . . As the gray mare was giving up, the band slipped from the pulley of the boiler . . . and the engine began to wheeze and putt. The horse gained on the machine and passed it . . . and came in the winner of the race."[5]

Many of the onlookers laughed at the outcome and shouted that Cooper's "teakettle on a truck" had no future. But wiser men saw the truth, and the race left little doubt among visionaries of what the future held.

In the months since his meeting with the vice president, William Ogden had rarely slowed down in his quest for a New York Assembly seat. His natural gift for winning over audiences served him well. It would require months of bone-jarring buggy rides along the dusty roads of the Delaware County countryside and dozens of stump speeches in small towns and villages; but Ogden may well have found them a pleasurable distraction. For a young man still in his late twenties, he was in heady company, as we see in an item from the diary of his cousin, George Washington Ogden: "August 4, 1833. Thursday, Walton was honored with a visit from governor Marcey [William L. Marcy]. . . . The next day the Col., Dr. [Henry E.] Bartlett, Wm. B Ogden and John Townsend went to Delhi and took dinner with all the big folks, the governor, etc."[6] Governor Marcy, another leader in Martin Van Buren's Albany Regency, was obviously keeping a close eye on their candidate and guiding him through the political shoals.

Winning the Democratic seat in the state assembly for his district was not too difficult, as it turned out. Now, as a New York assemblyman for a one-year term, Ogden had to prepare his upcoming speech before both houses of the legislature. His passion for the evolving technology of the early nineteenth century would certainly ease the task; but spending some quiet time alone thinking a problem through always helped too. Ogden had descended from generations of millwrights, and the peaceful aura of a quiet mill beside a running brook was a favored place for many millwrights to do their best thinking.

During down times, the Ogden and Wheeler lumber mill in Walton was very still. The sharp, piney sourness of fresh sawdust scented the air and created a thin, filmy veil that delicately danced with every small breeze that chanced by. With the giant saw blades silent, the rippling sound of the West Branch echoed faintly in the distance. Despite the contrast to this serenity, most millwrights could also find beauty and mental clarity in the sounds of a working mill: the angry splash of water as it hurtled down the raceway toward the waterwheel in its stone-lined wheel pit; the crackle and clatter of the wooden gears as they engaged a vertical drive shaft that pierced the mill like a giant spindle; the squeak and squeal of the leather belts that drove the finely honed saw blades; and the creaking and rumbling of the entire mill as it vibrated to the music of its parts. There was an almost religious reverence to the sounds and smells of a lumber mill, whether it was in full operation or silently resting. In a place like this, William Ogden often found clarity in his thinking, and this would likely have been where he retreated as he thought about how best to address New York's legislators.

Self-interest.

Self-interest was something legislators understood and appreciated. Most, however, had little understanding of railroads and even less appreciation for these noisy, smelly, dangerous contraptions that had just begun to shatter the calm stillness of their bucolic countryside. Charles Dickens, England's foremost writer during the Victorian era, visited America during the railroad's infancy. He described an early train ride he had taken:

> There is no first and second class carriages as with us; but there is a gentlemen's carriage and a ladies' carriage: the main distinction between which is, that in the first everybody smokes; and in the second, nobody does. As a black man never travels with a white man, there is also a Negro carriage. There is a great deal of jolting, a great deal of noise, a great deal of wall, not much window, a locomotive engine, and a bell.
>
> The cars are like shabby omnibuses, but larger: holding thirty, forty or fifty people. There is a large row of seats on each side . . . each seat holding two persons. In the center of the carriage there is usually a stove . . . which is for the most part red-hot. It is insufferably close.[7]

Despite Dickens's critical view of American trains, they were here to stay.

Early American railroad building—like canal building before it—was accomplished in small bits and pieces, a few miles here and a few miles there. An early account of railroading on the Atlantic seaboard, *Treatise on Rail-roads*, by Nicolas Wood, was published in 1832. It recorded all the small railroad ventures that were then under way: a number of small roads from Boston inland; a road from the banks of the Hudson River to Paterson, New Jersey; a road from Albany to Schenectady; and another from Schenectady to Saratoga Springs. There was also the Camden and Amboy from New York to Delaware; a road from Philadelphia to the Susquehanna River; another from Delaware to the head of the Chesapeake Bay; and the ambitious road from Baltimore to the Ohio River, the B&O.[8]

Every city and town, and every ambitious entrepreneur, wanted to be first to establish a significant presence with their railroad. At the end of 1830, the year *Tom Thumb* was outrun by Lightning, there were only 40 miles of track laid in the United States. At the end of 1835, there were more than 1,000 miles, and by 1840, 2,816 miles, more than even in Great Britain. But the frenetic pace was just beginning.

New York's earliest railroad was the little Mohawk and Hudson. Chartered in 1826 and running by 1831, the line was using steam locomotive power on all of its sixteen miles of track, except the steeply inclined planes at each end where mules still prevailed.[9] It would later form the nucleus of the prominent New York Central railroad empire. But as its tiny locomotive, the *DeWitt Clinton*, was merrily chugging from Albany to Schenectady, railroad groups from the southern tier of towns in New York were making grander plans.

Bolstered by the earlier promises of then governor DeWitt Clinton to give them their own east–west avenue of commerce to compete with the Erie Canal, individual groups began holding meetings called "railroad conventions" to plan for the project. Each of the groups, acting independently of the others, made its own plans and published its own resolutions in the *Albany Argus*, the New York paper of record. Finally, in December 1831, the individual groups coalesced at a meeting in Owego, just west of Binghamton.

Over two days, the eighty-five delegates fussed and fumed among themselves. Most favored two separate railroad companies, one to build the eastern leg and the other the western leg, that would meet in the middle. Finally, through the leadership of Eleazar Lord, one of the earliest proponents of railroads in New York, the two factions came together, and the idea for the New York and Erie Railroad (NY&E) was born.

Lord recognized the unfavorable position of the southern counties since the Erie Canal had opened; but a report had just been issued in New York favoring a northern route for the railroad, should one be built. In a book about the NY&E in 1855, Lord wrote, "The citizens of the Southern counties . . . encouraged by governor Clinton, and conscious of what was due to their section of the state, concerted and adopted measures to counteract the unfavorable implications and injurious influence of the Report; and to obtain the aid from the Legislature to which they were entitled."[10]

Finally, succumbing to southern pressure and ignoring the report that recommended the northern route, the New York state legislature chartered the NY&E in April 1832 to run from the banks of the Hudson River to Lake Erie. A number of restrictive conditions were added for fear it would compete with the Erie Canal, but railroad leaders were not dismayed. The corporation was capitalized at ten million dollars, but the charter stipulated that it could not organize until 5 percent, or a half-million dollars, was actually in hand. Another restriction required that legislative approval be sought for any connections to railroads in neighboring New Jersey or Pennsylvania. Legislators didn't want their little line wandering too far from home. One thing noticeably missing from the legislative action was any promise of state aid for the venture.[11]

NY&E leaders met in New York the following month to discuss their strategy. Before they could solicit subscriptions, the exact route of the line had to be surveyed and established, but there was no money available for the task. It was a chicken-and-egg situation: they couldn't raise any capital until the route was surveyed, and they couldn't survey the route until they had the money to pay for it. After a lot of gnashing of teeth, and a few failed efforts to solve the dilemma, they went back to the legislature to request a change in the charter. Their efforts were rewarded. They were given fifteen thousand dollars to conduct their survey, and the required subscription amount was lowered to only one million dollars, which at 5 percent meant they needed only fifty thousand dollars in hand to organize the corporation. The group was easily able to subscribe and collect that amount by July 1833. Thus was the NY&E finally—and now officially—born. Eleazar Lord was selected as president of the NY&E.

The railroad was ready to go. Almost. With no tangible assets, and only fifty thousand dollars in the till, the new company lacked enough cash to begin construction. They desperately needed someone to champion their cause with the legislature for some sort of state aid or loan guarantees. But legislators were reluctant to commit themselves any further for this newfangled technology called a railroad. After all, didn't they already operate the most successful canal in the nation?

The 58th Session of the New York Assembly was scheduled to meet from January 6 through May 11, 1835, in Albany. Two new assembly members had been seated from Delaware County, namely William Ogden and Dubois Burhans, a dry goods store owner from Roxbury, in the eastern part of the county. Ogden and his advisers considered the task before them. Most legislators were not focused on the railroad issue; they were more concerned with other problems. To top it off, it was a time of great churning for politics in New York and across the nation. The brand new Whig Party, which was just beginning to make its presence felt, was opposed to President Jackson, whom they had dubbed "King Andrew I" for the strong unilateral actions he was fond of taking. On the other hand, the Anti-Masonic Party was breathing its last breath, its vindictive sentiments too narrow to carry the party forward. State politicians were jumping from party to party like fleas in a pack of dogs, trying to find one that offered both philosophical consistency and strength with the voters. Banking issues were at center stage, as Jackson's credit-tightening fiscal policies were leading the country toward financial catastrophe, according to his critics.

Ogden had to strike a chord that would resonate above all the political and philosophical rumblings on the floor of the legislature. He had to convince the provincially minded legislators that the New York and Erie Railroad wasn't just a boondoggle for southern tier towns but an absolute necessity if the state wanted to grow and prosper. And finally, he had to overcome the voices of the opposition, those with vested interests in canals, turnpikes, plank roads, and steamships who were bent on protecting their respective turfs. He had his work cut out for him.

On March 20, one day before the scheduled speech of Assemblyman Ogden before the legislature, the battle took on a harder edge. Railroad critics within the assembly had manipulated the schedule so the vote on the NY&E would be taken that very day, before Ogden could give his speech. In a 61–46 vote, the assembly rejected the bill to provide state aid to expedite the construction of the NY&E.[12] Thus, when Ogden began to speak the following morning—a speech that would take place over parts of three days and be reported (and often paraphrased with bias) in its entirety in the *Albany Argus*—the assembly had already spoken. But the state senate had not voted, and Ogden knew the assembly would have to reconvene in the fall for their second legislative session. So, undeterred by the setback, Ogden gave a speech that he hoped would give opponents of state aid something to reconsider later in the year.

His speech spared nothing. He spoke of the revenues that might be expected from passenger service and from shipping lumber to market, a subject close to his heart and wallet. He spoke of the costs that would be involved in building the railroad; he answered those who felt the intended grade of the road was too severe to accommodate a successful route; and he addressed those who had voiced the opinion that the NY&E company was seeking only to inflate the value of their stock and had no genuine intention of beginning construction.

He also outlined the threat to New York and its leading cities if they did not keep pace with the rapid transportation developments in neighboring Pennsylvania, warning that New York would no longer be considered the Empire State. "Philadelphia is your great rival," he admonished legislators, "and if New York is idle, [Philadelphia] will gather in the trade of the great West." Above all else, however, Ogden's speech indicated the visionary viewpoint he had of the future:

> The importance of proceeding without delay . . . must be apparent to every one; for if the business of the western states should be diverted from us, it would be difficult, if not impossible, to regain it by any subsequent exertions.
>
> I see continuous railways from New York to Lake Erie . . . and south through Ohio, Indiana, and Illinois to the waters of the Mississippi, and connecting with railroads running to Cincinnati and Louisville in Kentucky, and Nashville in Tennessee, and on to New Orleans. They will present the most splendid system of internal communication ever devised by man.

Finally, he outlined the plans many of the Southern and Western cities and states were already embarking upon to build their own railroads to reach out to Eastern markets: "To look forward to the completion of such a work, may be considered visionary at first view; but should a few years exhibit [it] in full operation, it would only be in keeping with the progress of improvement in this country for the last half century."[13]

Although Ogden had been elected to a full term in the assembly, his work was over after his March speech. He resigned his seat that summer to head for the village of Chicago, unsure whether or not he had found the words to help turn the tide in favor of the railroad. But he needn't have worried. In the fall session in October, both the assembly and the senate passed a bill guaranteeing a loan of three million dollars to the NY&E. Ogden had done his job. As a result, he had also secured for himself a place in history as one of the earliest visionaries of America's railroad future and all that it would mean to the nation's western expansion. Shortly after he left New York for the rough-and-tumble frontier settlement of Chicago, the process he had helped set in motion for the NY&E began. Ground was broken on November 7, 1835, near Deposit in Delaware County amid great fanfare.

Five weeks later, however, in the middle of the night, a watchman on his rounds in downtown Manhattan smelled smoke near the corner of Pearl and Exchange Streets. In only a few minutes, the fire raged out of control in the center of the business district. In the −17° weather, the nearby East River and all the downtown water cisterns were frozen solid, making it impossible to fight the inferno.

Sixteen hours later, when firemen and volunteers finally managed to control the blaze, the most destructive fire in New York City's history had left the business and financial district in smoldering ruins. Miraculously, only two lives were lost because the area was virtually abandoned at that hour; however, more than seven hundred buildings were destroyed. In the aftermath, twenty-three of the city's twenty-six insurance companies went bankrupt, leaving much of the destroyed property uninsured. Among the many fortunes wiped out by the fire were those of many of the NY&E subscription holders, dealing a severe blow to the infant enterprise.[14]

The national financial crisis known as the Panic of 1837 delivered another blow to the struggling railroad. However, like that small engine in the children's story that kept chanting, "I think I can! I think I can!" the NY&E kept chugging uphill, acquiring another three-million-dollar loan from the state in 1838. The first train eventually began to operate in 1841, but shortly thereafter the NY&E was forced into bankruptcy. Nevertheless, construction continued. Finally, in 1851, the line was completed, stretching 460 miles from Piermont on the Hudson River to Dunkirk on Lake Erie, with a few valuable connections to other railroads and canals along the way.

To mark the opening of the historic railroad, a giant celebration was planned. Important men throughout the nation and the state were invited to ride the entire 460-mile length of the road—a "flying trip" it was called in those days—pausing at each whistle stop along the way to accept accolades, make speeches, and enjoy sumptuous feasts. Among the honored guests was William B. Ogden, whose speech before the legislature sixteen years earlier had spurred the event, and who by this time was the nation's leading railroad man.[15]

The final, crowning hoopla was planned for the town of Dunkirk on Lake Erie, the western terminus of the railway. There, in the town's luxurious Loder Hotel, a banquet featuring a surfeit of the area's best meat, seafood, vegetables, and fruits was laid out for the guests. Afterwards, a huge crowd of people gathered in the street outside to hear from some of the dignitaries. Daniel Webster was called upon to speak, and despite his advanced age, the old man teetered over to the window. It was said he had endured the long trip with copious amounts of gin and whiskey, which he alleged were good for his stomach. In a small, brittle voice that not even the other people in the room could hear, he briefly addressed the throng in the street below, waving his bony hand at the crowd. The president of the United States, Millard Fillmore, was next, and he shared his excitement at the opening of the historic road. Finally, William Ogden stepped to the window and shared a few words with the assembled celebrants.[16]

The NY&E line continued to have financial problems, ultimately becoming a pawn in the war between ruthless railroad barons James Fisk, Jay Gould, and Cornelius Vanderbilt. In the early 1860s, it was reorganized as the Erie Railway. For the next one hundred years, it entered and exited bankruptcy a number of times, merged with and split off from a number of other lines, and eventually became the Erie-Lackawanna Railroad in 1960. In 1976 the railroad with the big heart finally gave up, to become just another piece of railroad lore.

Railroad historian Stewart Holbrook called the Erie "surely as unfortunate a line as ever operated in this or any other country."[17] Despite its many struggles—which were not unique among early railroads—the NY&E racked up an impressive list of firsts. It was the first railroad to connect the Atlantic Ocean and the Great Lakes; the first in the United States stretching to four hundred miles or more in length; and the first to construct telegraph lines along its right-of-way. It was truly "the little railroad that could."

Although the NY&E was William Ogden's first serious brush with what many consider to be the nineteenth century's most important technological advancement, it would be far from his last. There were still many adventures awaiting the young man who grew up on the banks of New York's Delaware River.

3

Stately Edifices and Lofty Spires

"I was born close by a saw-mill, was early left an orphan, was cradled in a sugar-trough, christened in a mill-pond, graduated at a log-school-house, and, at fourteen, fancied I could do anything I turned my hand to, and that nothing was impossible, and ever since, Madame, I have been trying to prove it, and with some success."[1] William Ogden is said to have spoken these words to a woman who had recently descended into poverty when she asked what might become of her children. They eloquently sum up the credo of a man who recognized no boundaries on what he could accomplish if he set his mind to something and who assumed that everyone else could also rise above their present position with hard work and determination.

Ogden participated as a key player in three of the most momentous events of the nineteenth century: the founding and development of the great city of Chicago, the birth and growth of railroads in America, and the advent of the nation's westward expansion. Few other individuals made as much of an impact as Ogden on the infant nation as it strove to find its place among the world's leading countries. It was a period in our history that required great leadership, and William B. Ogden fit the bill in every respect. But putting aside his wide-reaching accomplishments, what sort of human being was this onetime rural New York millwright?

First and foremost, William Ogden was an enigmatic man. Because so little of his personal correspondence is known to exist—only two reproduced letters, both about the Chicago fire[2]—we cannot get a clear picture of him from his own writings, normally an important tool for the biographer. His business letters, on the other hand, are numerous, but they are formal and impersonal and tell little except that he was a shrewd businessman.

What can be ascertained from his actions, however, are that many of the qualities he believed in most fervently—honesty, integrity, and fair play—were the same qualities he often breached when it served his purposes. Still, he did not think of himself as a dishonest or unfair man, nor did his many friends—some of the most celebrated and accomplished people of his time—who revered Ogden. He was a man of great sweeping visions, and when he encountered an obstacle to the gaping maw of his dream, he could bend his ethics—occasionally to the breaking point—to get past it. He was an honorable man who occasionally did dishonorable things.

Ogden would be powerfully influenced by four factors during his lifetime, factors that forged the kind of man he became. The first was the unyielding, rock-ribbed Protestant ethos in which he was raised, an ethos that stressed hard work, thrift, achievement, benevolence, and honesty. He followed the first four of these tenets from cradle to grave. That he was gifted with great intelligence and a certain heritage that insured he would not have to start at the bottom rung of life's ladder made it easier for him to believe that hard work could overcome all obstacles. This belief often led him to have little patience with less fortunate members of society, particularly the dirt-poor immigrants who arrived in droves from western Europe during the second and third quarters of the nineteenth century. It was not that he was unkind to the poor; we see many examples throughout his life where his benevolence was unbridled. Yet when people interfered with his business plan by squatting on his land or taking his lumber to warm their shabby hearths, he could be unrelenting.

The last tenet of that Protestant ethos, honesty, proved to be the stickiest for Ogden. He was not a dishonest man. However, he often compromised himself by succumbing to the lax business morality that had swept the nation by midcentury. An extraordinarily shrewd businessman, he firmly believed that destiny rewarded those who were willing to walk the fine line between right and wrong. When he stepped over that line, he easily justified it by comparison to the corrupt business standards that prevailed or in the name of the greater public good that he felt his enterprises served. In these instances, Ogden became a man of his times, rather than rising above the times as he might have done. At one point late in his life, we even see his personal integrity dissolve in a nasty philandering episode.

Finally, Ogden had a deep well of self-confidence to draw upon. Some individuals shrink from confrontation. Ogden embraced it, welcomed it, saw it as a healthy part of human interaction; he never backed down from a fight, especially when one of his "grand plans" was being threatened. But his self-confidence hardened into arrogance as he aged, a fact we see repeated many times over in his dealings with others in his later life.

The second factor that had a profound effect on the man he became was his family. He was taught from his earliest days that family came before all other considerations. Family was everything. This was a tradition from which Ogden never strayed. Throughout his entire business career, he hired blood relatives and extended family members to fill key positions in almost every business enterprise in which he participated. When they succeeded, they were rewarded richly; when they failed, they were given other chances. This practice was a throwback to an earlier, more rural colonial America, when all business was local; but Ogden refused to adjust as he entered the sphere of national, and then international, commerce. He stubbornly held to a practice that had outlived its time, and he often paid a high price for his refusal to change. To Ogden, the thousands of people he employed in his various business ventures were also a kind of extended family. He was a kind, benevolent employer, much loved and respected by those who worked for him.

The third major influence in Ogden's life was his love and loss of one woman, Sarah North. She was the first, and probably the only, woman he ever truly loved. When death took her just before their marriage, it was a crushing emotional blow from which he never completely recovered. He did not marry until he was almost seventy, and then it was primarily a marriage of convenience. Surrounded for most of his life by his large extended family, Ogden took his emotional nourishment from them. This lack of a life partner probably helped to drive Ogden to devote his life to achieving such great heights in the world of commerce.

The fourth factor that molded William Ogden was his sweeping vision for railroads and his unflagging determination to see the vision through. It was in this realm that Ogden's core values were most frequently tested and most often compromised. He was so convinced his vision was correct—and time proved he was right—that he often lowered himself to chicanery in order to advance that vision. As historian Donald L. Miller said, "He had a vision of railroad expansion that transcended personal gain. . . . The driving of the famous 'Golden Spike' [that marked the opening of the transcontinental railroad] made Ogden . . . a nation builder, not merely a city builder."[3] But perhaps the *New York Times* said it best in his obituary:

> In the development of the railroad system of the country, Mr. Ogden has been one of the foremost and most potent of coadjutors. The *Times* has before now had occasion to criticise methods of railroad construction with which he was identified, and may have occasion to do so again. But the most censorious criticism cannot deprive him of the credit of being one of the most enterprising and far-seeing of the railroad magnates who have opened up the virgin lands of the continent to the settler.[4]

Ogden acquired great wealth primarily through his real estate and lumbering enterprises, which provided him the capital to pursue his railroad dream. It was not until late in his railroad building days that tycoons began making vast fortunes from the business, so although he may have profited from his railroad enterprises, it was on a small scale compared to the rewards reaped by those who came after him.

Like many souls who are bigger than life, William Ogden was also a tangle of contradictions. His attitude about wealth was one. Wealth was not important to Ogden, perhaps because he was able to acquire it with seeming ease. Twice during his lifetime he lost much of his fortune, but each time he replaced it with a still larger one. That isn't to say he didn't enjoy his money; he certainly did, and he lived very well, if not extravagantly. But he also gave away a tremendous amount to his beloved city of Chicago and its institutions. This noblesse oblige was part of his Protestant ethos, but it was not always as altruistic as it appeared. It was also a tool used by the rich to insure the solidity and continued growth of their investments.

Another contradiction involved power and influence. Ogden had a hunger to acquire power, but once he had it, he quickly lost interest in it. He resigned from the presidency of three great railroads he founded or cofounded to move on to new challenges. He saw himself primarily as a builder, and once that phase of an enterprise was over, he had completed his personal challenge and moved on to something else. So neither wealth nor power was important to Ogden in and of themselves, but only as tools to help him achieve his objectives.

William Ogden was a person to whom the journey was much more important than the destination. While he was at his personal best building things no one had ever built before, he was at his personal worst toward anyone who sought to derail him in the process. Brilliant, charismatic, and determined—a man of heroic proportions in the nineteenth century—he was not a perfect man.

William Butler Ogden traced his ancestry in America back to 1641 when his ancestor John Ogden arrived in Rippowan (today Stamford, Connecticut) from Lancashire, England. A stonemason by trade, John Ogden learned to take advantage of the opportunities the New World offered, and he became a successful entrepreneur. It was as the leading founder of English colonization of New Jersey, one of the original thirteen colonies, that his chief claim to fame rests.[5]

William Ogden's father, Abraham, was born in 1771 in the family's ancestral New Jersey home, the fifth of ten children. By the time he was eighteen, young Abraham had grown bored with life in Hanover Township, Morris County, and he became determined to seek fame, fortune, and adventure elsewhere. So he struck out for Washington City, the newly adopted seat of government for the United States.[6]

His parents encouraged him but suggested he stop in Philadelphia along the way to visit former neighbors, the Dickinson family. When he arrived, he learned that Jesse Dickinson had purchased a number of tracts of land in Upper Delaware country in New York. Jesse told him that opportunity abounded there for energetic, ambitious settlers, so Abraham threw in his lot with the group that would soon be leaving for New York.[7]

The Appalachian range extends in a broad belt from the Gaspé Peninsula in Quebec to the coastal plain in Alabama. The Catskill Mountains in eastern New York form part of this massive system. On the Catskills' western slope, the Delaware River gathers its headwaters before separating into two branches, the larger one to the west and the smaller to the east, which meander south about eight miles apart from one another. The two branches converge again at today's town of Hancock, which was called *Shehawkan* by the Indians, or "the wedding of the waters." From there the river flows southeast, forming a portion of the New York–Pennsylvania border, before turning southwest to form the border between Pennsylvania and New Jersey. The Catskill region, with its low, wooded mountains, snug little valleys, and beautiful stream-filled meadows, is known today, as it was two hundred years ago, as the Upper Delaware. It is still some of the most beautiful and bountiful land in the eastern United States.

On an earlier visit, Jesse Dickinson had selected a bucolic, pine-studded site for their settlement, where Gannuissa Creek emptied into the west branch of the Delaware, simply called West Branch. Jesse named their new village Dickinson City, envisioning "stately edifices and lofty spires." Now, in 1789, a few years after he had initially purchased the property, he returned with his homesteaders and their livestock, and they began building their town.[8]

There were already a number of other towns and villages settled by this time: Mohawk, Cherry Valley, Schoharie, Marbletown, and Harpersfield to the northeast; and Franklin, Cook House (now Deposit), and Milford closer by. Whenever pioneers planted a new settlement in those days, the routine was much the same. First they raised tents or built lean-tos that would serve as temporary housing until permanent homes could be constructed. Then the men cleared the land. It was a laborious task, chopping down trees, trimming off branches, and cutting them into logs twelve to fourteen feet long. Then stumps were removed for their gardens and planting fields, either by burning them or pulling them out with the raw strength of oxen teams. In this way, they cleared communal and individual plots for homes, farms, stores, and crops, and a small village was born

Abraham and the other homesteaders got busy building their town. They erected a large, three-story gristmill on Gannuissa Creek, which they renamed Trout Creek, and they built large tackles over the water for unloading the boats they all hoped would run regularly between Dickinson City and Philadelphia. They even built a large hotel with an arched room called "City Hall," where public meetings would be held for many years. And they built two lumber mills, one of them owned by Abraham, who had earned his spurs as a millwright working for his father in New Jersey.[9]

Milling was not a yearlong enterprise in the northern latitudes. From late fall until early spring, most rivers and streams either had too little flowing water to operate the mills, or the water was frozen solid. It was during these periods that the pioneers felled trees, wove cloth, and shucked and stored grain, for use when the mills sprang back to life with the spring runoff.

Teenager Abraham Ogden's dreams were more modest than the grandiose schemes of Jesse Dickinson. Still, Abraham's small lumber mill established

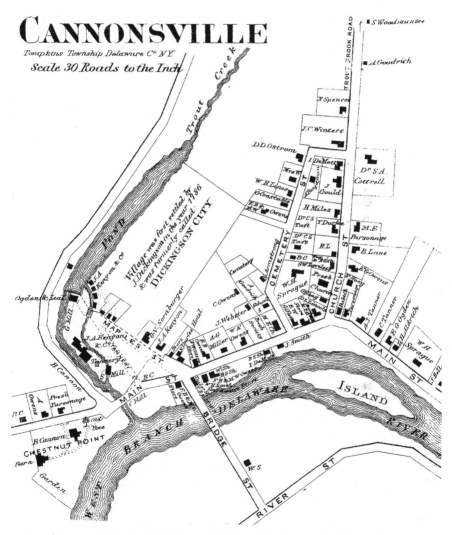

Map of Cannonsville (originally Dickinson City), New York, showing the Ogden and Leal lumber mill on the Trout Creek pond in the 1820s or 1830s.

his foothold in the new village, and he was justly proud of what he had accomplished. Jesse, on the other hand, never could make Dickinson City into the thriving metropolis he had imagined. And so, in 1795 he returned to Philadelphia, where he lived out the rest of his life. Dickinson had sold about 80 percent of his land to Wait Cannon from Sharon, Connecticut, and in the early nineteenth century the town took on his family name, Cannonsville. For the next 167 years, the town remained a peaceful little village hidden deep in a valley, until 1967 when, like a number of other Delaware valley villages, the town was flooded to create a reservoir to slake the growing thirst of New York City. Since the flooding of the small village was done to meet the needs of a grand metropolis, perhaps in some poetic sense Jesse Dickinson's dream of "stately edifices and lofty spires" had finally come true after all.

Within a few years, Abraham Ogden was enjoying the success his hard work had earned him, but he continued to live a frugal life. Alone and with no prospect for a wife or family when he arrived in Dickinson City, he had built a cabin that would meet his minimal needs. It was not unlike thousands of other rude dwellings that housed the brave men and women who pioneered America's frontier in the late eighteenth century. If it was typical of the times, the entire structure was about ten feet by twelve feet, with one small window to let in the light and a deerskin flap to cover the opening. Along one of the longer walls would probably be a bench that served as seating space during the day and as a platform for a straw-filled sleeping palette at night. Two shelves above the bench provided all the storage space needed for a man's meager personal belongings. A small stone fireplace probably sat in one corner, with a hearth and a swinging iron hook for hanging a cooking pot. A few blackened pots and pans sat on a shelf nearby, along with a wooden trencher and a couple of wooden eating utensils. In the corner next to the fireplace was a broom made of twigs and straw for sweeping the earthen floor. The cabin was probably built entirely of logs, although Abraham could have fancied it up with planks once he built his sawmill just down the hill at the edge of the stream. But his needs were simple, and he enjoyed an uncomplicated life. At twenty-six, he knew he had plenty of time for the better things in life when the time was right. In the meantime, he was saving his money because of a promise he had made.

Isaac Ogden was Abraham's younger brother by two years.[10] In 1797, following a long trip from New Jersey, he arrived in Dickinson City to visit Abraham. Isaac was a more serious young man than his brother, but they shared one common trait: they had both yearned for a change in their lives. Their parents, John and Phebe Ogden, owned and operated a gristmill in Morris County, New Jersey, and both boys, along with two younger brothers, had toiled alongside their father as they grew up. An older brother, Daniel, a Revolutionary War veteran

like their father, had also started in the mill, but now he farmed a small piece
of land in Morris County with his own family.

Isaac had come to cash in on the promise Abraham had made to his siblings
when he left the New Jersey ancestral home—the pledge that he would find
a spot for them on his new frontier. Abraham had not forgotten, and he had
been saving his money for this day. He unfolded a plan he had developed for
the two of them and their two younger brothers, Jacob, seventeen, and William, only nine.

He told Isaac about the little village of Walton, about ten miles east of Dickinson City, and a special parcel of land right on the West Branch that was for sale.
The river's fall was perfect for a big mill, and the property was thick with tall,
straight pines. Abraham had been shipping lumber downriver to Philadelphia
for five years, and he knew the people there were hungry for all the lumber the
Ogden brothers could mill. All four brothers had worked in their father's gristmill, and the idea of having their own large lumber mill and infinite supply of
trees was a dream come true. Isaac also had some money saved, so they had the
funds to buy the Walton property and build the mill. They would be fifty-fifty
partners, with the younger boys participating later when they came of age.

So the partnership was struck. Isaac returned to New Jersey to gather his
brothers and all their worldly belongings, while Abraham purchased their land:
two large tracts fronting on the West Branch just north of the town of Walton.
Their tracts totaled nearly five hundred acres in Delaware County, which had
just been carved out of the wilderness.[11] The population of the entire township
of Walton, the county's first, was about twelve hundred people. About half of
that number lived in the village of Walton.[12]

Isaac, Jacob, and William arrived, and the Ogdens built a rugged sawmill
on their new property. The mill was just below a small bridge crossing the West
Branch known as Weed's Bridge, named after Lieutenant James Weed, a Revolutionary War officer who had settled there a few years earlier from Connecticut.
The bridge was about three miles north of Walton village, and was located
along the mail route that was established in 1800 between Kingston and the
small settlements west of the West Branch. Because of the passage allowed by
the small bridge, the community grew up around it and became a hotbed of
activity in the early nineteenth century. A school and a number of log homes,
including those of Abraham and Isaac Ogden, were built. Rounding out the
small Weed's Bridge settlement was a hotel, a couple of taverns, a store, and a
Masonic Lodge, one of the country's earliest. In competition with the Ogdens'
mill there were three mills built by Thomas Griswold.[13]

Abraham, Isaac, and their two young brothers immediately fit into the little
Weed's Bridge community. In 1798, less than a year after their arrival, the two
older men performed their first community service. A "Return of Jurors for

the Town of Walton," dated August 2, 1798, lists forty-eight men who qualified for Delaware County jury duty. Among the names are "Abraham Ogden, Millwright" and "Isaac Ogden, Millwright." Of the other names, thirty-four listed their occupation as farmer. There were also two merchants, two carpenters, two innkeepers, and one each blacksmith, shoemaker, and rafts man.

Abraham and Isaac's business prospered. They had divided the land that was not devoted to their mills or lumber tracts, and each man built his own cabin. The sawmill was busy, and they built a carding machine in the upper floor of the mill, the first one in Delaware County. The new machine, driven by the same water wheel that drove the saw, removed impurities and tangles from raw wool and prepared it for spinning. The wool was passed on to local women, who spun it into yarn on their spinning wheels and then wove it into a rough cloth. This practice usually took place over the long, cold winter months when outdoor activities were at a minimum and the mill was silent.[14]

Seizing another opportunity, the Ogden brothers added a fulling mill and cloth-dressing business to their growing enterprise. Handwoven cloth tended to be of uneven texture and thin in spots, if not finished at a fulling mill. Also, the sheep being raised in America, though hearty and valued for their meat, produced wool of an inferior quality. The Ogdens repurchased the rough cloth from the women, put it through the fulling mill where it was smeared with soap and water, and occasionally animal urine, and pounded with wooden mallets, again driven by the water wheel. Depending upon the quality of the cloth desired, it was fed through the fulling process once, twice, or three times, each time shrinking the fibers of the wool to produce a finer material. The wool could also be dyed in the process. Afterwards, it was stretched on tenterhooks from floor to ceiling and allowed to dry. The final product was then turned into heavy woolen clothing and blankets by the Ogdens, which they sold at their mill. In 1799, Abraham, in partnership with Bailey Foote, started a carding machine operation in nearby Waterville (now Hobart) and shortly thereafter built a fulling mill, carding machine, and cloth-dressing business in Cannonsville.[15]

A portion of one of their Weed's Bridge tracts was so rich in tall, stately pine trees that it was referred to locally as the "Mast Lot." Lumber for crafting masts and spars for the huge sailing ships of the day had to be tall, straight, and well-aged, and the Ogdens' trees qualified on all three counts. The government bought the best of the lot for fifty dollars each, while lesser quality trees brought less money, but were just as quickly sold to private shipbuilders.[16] Local legend says that the Ogdens' Mast Lot provided the masts used on the U.S.S. *Constitution*, "Old Ironsides," which first set sail in 1798. However, according to the ship's museum, original records indicate the masts came from Unity in southwestern Maine, though the Mast Lot trees could have been replacements.

Walton's earliest settlers were educated men, well-read and cultured. The Ogdens, Norths, Townsends, Pines, and Furmans arrived with their saddlebags swollen with literary classics, scientific treatises, mathematical works, and other fine literature. In 1802, well ahead of its time, the early Walton settlers decided to form a library. Fifty townsmen, including a number of the Ogdens, bought shares at two dollars each to purchase books. In 1809 the townspeople funded additional money for expanding the titles, and an act of the state legislature formally incorporated the Walton Library as one of the earliest in the state.[17]

Abraham Ogden and his neighbor James Weed became good friends. Weed, his wife Sarah, and their eight young children had come to Walton in 1791. Now, their youngest daughter, Abigail, only fourteen, caught the eye of their thirty-one-year-old bachelor neighbor. Abraham was a success in business, intelligent, genial, and hardworking. When he asked the Weeds for their daughter's hand, they saw no reason to refuse. Thus on February 2, 1802, in the home of his future in-laws, Abraham Ogden married Abigail Weed.[18]

The happy couple set up housekeeping in the rude log cabin Abraham had built near his sawmill, just below Weed's Bridge. Just over a year later, Abigail gave birth to their first child, Eliza. Two years later, on June 15, 1805, their second child was born, a son they named William Butler. Repeating the two-year cycle, daughter Phebe was born in 1807 and son Albert in 1809. Both of these children would bring heartbreak to the young couple. Phebe died at only four months, and Albert died just before his sixth birthday. Shortly after Albert's birth, the growing family moved into a better, more spacious house. And it was a good thing they did. Mahlon Dickerson was born in 1811, Emily in 1815, Caroline in 1817, and Frances in 1824.[19]

William Butler Ogden spent his early years memorizing his lessons in the little one-room log schoolhouse at Weed's Bridge, cavorting with his siblings and cousins, and learning the ways of the Catskill wilderness. These early schoolhouses were usually about sixteen feet by twenty feet with an open fire-place at one end for warmth. A single window at the opposite end provided the only light. Student desks, roughly hewn slabs supported by four wooden legs, filled three sides of the room. The teacher had a separate table and chair, and the middle of the small room was an open space where the children would stand to recite. Books were few, and goose quills were used for writing.[20]

At home, William was assigned his share of the household chores, but his mother Abigail often had to first hunt for him out in the woods to get him to do a lick of work. It wasn't that William was lazy; quite the contrary, he was an extremely active youngster, robust and athletic, always busy at something. It just seemed to Abraham and Abigail that he had some kind of cosmic attraction to the deep, wooded forests nearby. He was happiest when playing hide-and-seek or feigning a bare-fisted fight to the finish with an imaginary grizzly among the cool, dark sugar maples, beeches, elms, and pines.

When William was about eight years old, the United States entered into another war with Britain, the War of 1812. The three older Ogden brothers,

Abraham, Isaac, and Daniel, were in their forties, which was too old to be called into service, and all of their sons were too young. Still, it was a tense, frightening time for the Ogden family and their neighbors, particularly the early years when most of the fighting was done on or near New York soil. The outbreak of war followed years of angry diplomatic disputes between the two countries, and because the United States had only a small standing army, America's state militias were expected to play a significant role. But many units balked, refusing to fight outside of their own state boundaries. New England states were so opposed to fighting the war that they even threatened to secede.

The war had three theatres of operation—the Great Lakes and Canadian frontier, the Atlantic Ocean, and the Southern States—with the first one most directly affecting New York. Fortunately for the Ogdens and their Delaware County neighbors, the fighting never penetrated too deeply onto New York soil. The action was limited to the extreme northern and western sections of the state, near the borders with Canada. By the time the fighting was over in 1815, America had lost 2,260 men, and another 4,505 were wounded. This did not include those who died of disease, which added another 9,000 to the death total.

Things returned to normal in Delaware County at the end of the war. Life was good for William Ogden growing up in the shadows of the Catskills. One of the best parts was having so much family surrounding him. From his earliest days, his parents taught William that family was the most important thing in life. It was a lesson he would never forget. His social and business life was always centered on family, and even after he left Walton for Chicago, a number of family members followed and continued to be dependent upon him. William never objected; he was the oldest son, and it was expected of him. He always considered his duty to his family as his first responsibility.

Abraham and Abigail Ogden were a constant source of love and support, as were all William's siblings. But it was an added bonus to have so many uncles, aunts, and cousins nearby. Uncle Daniel and Aunt Phebe and their children had arrived in Walton about five years after the other brothers joined Abraham. They established a prosperous farm four miles from Walton, on West Brook, one of three large streams that feeds into the West Branch. Though he had been a millwright like his brothers for a time, Daniel had settled on farming instead and had been very successful at it. To this day, some of Daniel's farmland is still in the family of Ogden descendants. William never tired of hearing stories of Daniel's six years' service in the Patriot militia during the War for Independence, particularly the harrowing anecdotes from the bloody Battle of Springfield in which Daniel had participated.

As a boy, William was large for his age, and he enjoyed hunting, swimming, skating, wrestling, and riding. He excelled at all of them. It was no surprise to either parent when he asked for his first hunting rifle. He quickly became an excellent shot, probably coached carefully by one of his uncles, and deer hunting became his passion. Hunting clubs had come into vogue in Delaware, Ostego, and surrounding counties, and William was eager to join one. Though he was only a boy, his skills were widely known, and he was readily accepted among the older teenagers and men of the area.

The annual autumn hunts were particularly exciting. Men came from more than fifty miles away with their weapons, fine horses, and packs of baying dogs to participate in the sport. William Ogden was also an excellent horseman. Isaac Arnold, in memorializing Ogden before the Chicago Historical Society more than a half-century later, recalled some of the comic verse about his fellow huntsmen that Ogden often recited:

> There is Throop ready mounted upon a fine black,
> But a far fleeter gelding does Starkweather back,
> Cox Morris' bay, full of metal and bone,
> And gaily Skin Smith, on a dark-sorrel roan,
> But the horse, of all horses that hunted that day,
> Was Ogden's fleet charger, and that is a gray.
> Their horses were all of the very best blood;
> They'll make the snow fly, and they'll dash through the mud.

"I've often heard Mr. Ogden describe these hunts," Arnold wrote, "and he said the music of the fox-hounds reverberating and echoing from hill to hill, now the lone cry of a single hound, and then the swelling into the full chorus by the whole pack—with the wild speed of the horses, and the frequent crack of a rifle at the run-aways, was a scene of adventure and excitement never to be forgotten."[21]

Samuel North, a school friend and scion of one of the Upper Delaware's pioneer families, related another story that spoke to the skill and daring of young William. A group of mounted hunters was chasing a deer along the Unadilla River, one of the many small rivers that fed into the Susquehanna, and the frightened beast had taken refuge on a small island, unapproachable except through the deep, swift current. At one point, the island lay close enough to the mainland that a large tree had been felled to serve as a crossing for those with steady nerves and cool heads. William, riding at full speed, slowed only briefly when approaching the tree. Then horse and rider, in complete trust of each other, charged across the makeshift bridge and reached the island. A moment later, North recalled, the crack of a rifle was all the proof needed that William had bagged his game.[22]

Another of William's favorite pastimes was working with the rowdy raftsmen who delivered Abraham and Isaac's lumber downstream to Philadelphia. They were a rough lot and did the dangerous work of fighting the roiling river to float thousands of logs to market. With nothing more than a long peavey and nimble footwork, they danced for hours atop tons of rolling, twisting logs as they moved downriver. Like the huntsmen, the raftsmen too accepted young William into their fraternity, treating him as an equal. Later in life, he told many stories about the rough-and-tumble adventures and dangerous work he shared with these men.

In contrast to his frivolous side, William also had a serious side. His father had to limit his hunting and fishing expeditions to two days a week so his studies wouldn't suffer, but the boy never seemed to resent the time spent with his books. Abraham encouraged him to study so his mind would develop as quickly as his body. Encouraged too by his Uncle Isaac, who had become a judge, he decided as a young teenager to study and read for the law. Nobody who knew him doubted that he would succeed as a lawyer and make an excellent and prosperous life for himself.

In 1820, when he was only fifteen, William left Walton for New York City to begin his studies for a legal career. However, less than a year later that dream ended. Abraham Ogden, only forty-nine at the time, suffered a massive stroke. William's life would be greatly changed.[23]

Abraham had always been a healthy man, vigorous and active in both mind and body. His friends would have guessed him to be the last person inflicted with such a serious illness. Although historical records don't indicate the severity of his condition, he apparently suffered almost complete loss of all physical functions, a total paralysis. If there was a bright side, it was that he retained most of his mental faculties. His memory was impaired, but he retained the quick, agile mind he would need for the task ahead.

Abraham had been an excellent business manager. He possessed all the skills and abilities to make his own Horatio Alger story. Although he and his younger brother Isaac had been business partners from the beginning, Isaac had chosen to pursue a career in community service and law. Both men were content to leave the running of the businesses to Abraham. Now, Abraham knew there was only one person qualified to stand in for him: his sixteen-year-old son William.

Despite all his favorable qualities, including a healthy dose of self-confidence, William Ogden must have been frightened at the prospect of filling his father's large shoes. But it didn't deter him. With his father's wise counsel, doled out in nightly sessions at his bedside, Ogden immersed himself in learning the intricacies of the lumber and woolens businesses. He had participated in both enterprises at some level, so he was not a complete novice; but strategic planning, financial management, inventory control, and the like were new to him. Fortunately, like his father, he had a facile mind. He was intelligent, incisive, and not afraid of challenges, and in time he was performing just as his father had hoped, despite his youth.

Young Ogden began making the business trips his father had enjoyed. They took him to Philadelphia and New York and perhaps as far away as Boston and Washington. Arnold described Ogden's travels as "an efficient educator,"[24] and like most men of curiosity, Ogden's mind and imagination were expanded by what he learned on these trips.

From the moment he had opened his first sawmill in Dickinson City, Abraham Ogden had proven himself to be a shrewd businessman with an instinct for the marketplace. When he moved to Walton and began anew, that innate understanding continued to serve him well. When the New York legislature funded a survey in 1808 to study the feasibility of building the Erie Canal, Abraham watched the process with great interest. When construction finally got under way in 1817, he was already considering what it would mean to the lumber and woolen mills he and Isaac owned and operated. From the beginning, he knew the Erie Canal would be a problem for them. It would be located in the northern tier of the state, so his northern competitors would have easy and cheap access to their markets. His businesses in the southern tier would enjoy no such advantages.

There is no extant record of the strategy Abraham devised to deal with the competitive disadvantage his businesses suffered; but a careful study of his actions make a strong case that such a plan existed, if only in his head. The Ogdens began to diversify. Old-growth forests were abundant for anyone who wished to enter the lumber trade, so the Ogdens concentrated on building their woolens business. They added a number of new woolen mills, all fully integrated with carding and fulling capabilities; and they sold one of their richest lumber tracts to Beers and Stockton, a wealthy and influential Philadelphia lumber company, for the princely sum of eighteen thousand dollars.[25]

Their concentration on the woolens business paid off handsomely. Ogden genealogist William Ogden Wheeler explained: "During the administration of President Monroe [1817–25], the state of New York, in order to encourage the manufacture of woolen goods, offered a silver tea set as a prize for the best woolen goods made in the state. This prize was awarded to Abraham Ogden, and is still [as of 1907] in the possession of his descendants."[26]

Then Abraham fell victim to the stroke, and whatever plans he had put in place were shelved. Once his son William had taken his place and had absorbed the basics of running the family businesses, Abraham knew it was time to get back on track. Most likely in 1822 or 1823, he asked William and his brother Isaac to visit him at his home.

When their grand new house had been built in 1809, Abraham and Abigail selected to have their bedroom on the second floor, in the back of the house. An upstairs bedroom was unusual for the time, but Abigail wanted a vantage point where she could watch the West Branch as it splashed its way merrily past their property. But when Abraham suffered his stroke, they had remodeled a downstairs room into a new bedroom. It was centrally located so Abigail and her children were never far from Abraham in case he needed anything. For him, it would have been a grand location, as he could enjoy the sounds of his family as they went about their daily activities. It was one of the very few delights he was able to enjoy in his severely limited physical condition.[27] The bedroom was likely a cheerful, commodious room, filed with light from the large windows on two walls. We can imagine that a small bedside table held a number of magazines, which one of his daughters would regularly read to their father.

The physical differences William and Isaac would have seen in Abraham were profound. He had been a very physical, active man, but with the stroke he would have become small and frail. Although he could probably still speak with a degree of clarity, his once booming voice had probably dwindled to the chirp of a sparrow. The one thing the debilitating stroke had not destroyed was Abraham's sense of obligation to his family.

Gathering his strength, Abraham described the diversification he had begun before he fell ill. He warned about the opening of the Erie Canal and what he believed it would mean to their enterprises. Abraham did not think the state government had acted fairly in putting southern-tier businesses at such a disadvantage; and he was probably convinced the state would try to make it up to them by building a plank road in their end of the state, a concession most local businessmen did not feel was adequate. Plank roads, sometimes referred to as "the poor man's rail-road," were public or privately built roads made of oak strips fastened to crossties. Often when they crossed private property, the owner would place a substantial log, called a pike, across the road to stop anyone from using it until they paid a toll. The word *turnpike* derives from this practice.

When Abraham resumed speaking, he made a surprising request: Isaac should give up his judgeship and help William run the mills. Isaac had been fortunate: Abraham had done all the work and left Isaac free to pursue his own community service interests. Even after William had stepped in, nothing had changed. But now William needed to get some exposure to community service and to continue the diversification Abraham had begun. There was considerable money to be made in other businesses, like real estate and money lending; and Abraham probably guessed that his eighteen-year-old son would do well if he could devote some time to such endeavors.

Evidence of this plan is clear in the extant records of the family's activities. In 1816 Isaac Ogden had begun a ten-year term as county judge; but in 1823, with three years remaining on his term, he resigned and took control of the family's four woolen mills. His participation is verified by an ad that ran on the front page of the *Delaware County Gazette* in 1825:

WOOL CARDING
And
CLOTH DRESSING
The above business will be carried on at the Mills of the subscriber
in Delhi under the superintendence of experienced and skillful
workmen. The machines have been well repaired with very fine new
Cards, and the
CLOTHIER'S WORKS
put in the best order, the work will be warranted well done, and at
reasonable rates as the public can reasonably desire.
Great allowances will be made for cash, and prompt pay.
ISAAC OGDEN.
Delhi, October 5, 1825.[28]

Although the family had been dabbling in land since Abraham and Isaac's arrival in 1797, William stepped up the real estate and money lending businesses in a big way. An *Index of Deeds* in the Delaware County Clerk's Office for the period 1797 through 1835 shows thirty-seven land purchases and twenty-nine land sales in the family's name. The records indicate that the pace of this activity accelerated greatly after Abraham's stroke. Similarly, the county clerk's *Index of Mortgages* recording the money loaned and borrowed for mortgages during the same time period shows the Ogdens' money lending practices also picked up considerably.[29]

William also continued the diversification, putting the family into the potash business after his father's death. In partnership with Henry Smith, he established a large ashery in the early 1830s on Delaware Street in Walton. Henry Smith had married one of Uncle Daniel's daughters, Julia, so like almost all of the people Ogden would go into business with, Henry was family. The firm was named Ogden and Smith.[30]

An ashery could be a lucrative business. An early fertilizer, potash—obtained from burning hardwood stumps left after a forest tract had been cleared—also had a couple of valuable by-products: lye used for soap and the finishing of woolen cloth, and pearl-ash, used in making glass and ceramics. Ogden and Smith's finished products were stored in bins, put on rafts, and sent downriver to Philadelphia, where a ready market existed for all the products of their ashery.

William also became active in his community. He turned eighteen in 1823 and was expected to spend some time in military service, as were all young men of good health. There was no conscription law in effect at the time, but most young men accepted their duty to become citizen soldiers in their local ad hoc military units. Ogden enrolled in a unit made up of Delaware County men, commanded by longtime Ogden family friend Brigadier General Frederic

Foote. His staff inspector general was Major Selah R. Hobbie, a personal friend of William's from his boyhood. On Ogden's first day in the military unit, he was made a commissioned officer, and on the second, an aide to General Foote. After some time, Major Hobbie left the unit, and Ogden was named to replace him. He discharged the duties of brigade inspector for many years thereafter.[31]

The year 1825 was pivotal for William Ogden and his family. On August 10, his father passed away.[32] Abraham had lived for about five years after his stroke, which had given him plenty of time to pass his counsel along to his oldest son, William. Still, the loss of the man would have been a heavy and sad burden for Abigail and her six children. At only thirty-two, Abigail still had in her care a fourteen-year-old, a ten-year-old, an eight-year-old, and—miraculously—one-year-old Frances, who was somehow conceived despite Abraham's physical limitations. Abraham Ogden was interred in the Walton burying ground, near the log church he had helped build in the earliest days of the village.

The death of Abraham intensified young William Ogden's responsibilities, and as a result he finally became completely his own man. Even while he was bedridden, Abraham had still been an inspiration to his family with his wisdom, counsel, and rarely flagging optimism. Between William and his father, with help from Isaac when called upon, the Ogden family had become very prosperous.

In 1828, at only twenty-three, William was appointed commissioner of common schools for Walton Township.[33] Despite his family connections, his first political patronage came from his own connections the following year. He was appointed postmaster of Walton Township, the primary political patronage plum of the day.[34] The pay he received for the postmaster's job, which he held until he left for Chicago in 1835, was not important, but the job offered a number of benefits. It was a very prestigious position within Walton and Delaware County and allowed him to make a wide range of important local and regional contacts; and it forged a link with officials of the U.S. government, which could be advantageous. The job also allowed franking privileges, and it released the appointee from military service, a perk that Ogden chose to sidestep.

Another event about this time filled Ogden with a great sense of family pride, probably along with a small twinge of personal regret. His youngest brother, Mahlon, was admitted to the New York bar. Having studied at Hobart College in Geneva, New York, and then in the law offices of Chief Justice Swain at Columbus, Ohio,[35] he would later join William as a partner in his land dealings in Chicago, where Mahlon would lead a long and distinguished career. Though his own dreams to be a lawyer had been shelved, William would spend his life surrounded by family and friends in the legal profession.

During these years, William was also involved in the church. The first service of the Protestant Episcopal Church was conducted somewhere in Walton before 1830, and Ogden served as a vestryman and a member of the building committee.[36] He continued to live in the fine house his father had built for the family in 1809. It was a substantial two-story white clapboard house, with ivy growing up one side. The large lot was covered with trees and dotted with his mother's flower and vegetable gardens. The West Branch merrily bubbled by, just to the rear of the expansive lot. Besides William and his mother, his three sisters—Emily, Caroline, and Frances—were still at home, and brother Mahlon, now practicing law in Walton, was still single and living with the family. Nothing pleased William more than to be surrounded by the people he cared for.

A casual observer, or a new resident in Walton, would probably wonder why Ogden was still unmarried as he approached thirty. Handsome, financially comfortable, sensitive, and cultured, Ogden would have been a prize catch for any single young woman. Those who knew him well knew the reason Ogden rarely even dated any of the eligible young Delaware County ladies. His good friend Isaac Arnold wrote eloquently of the broken heart William had suffered a few years earlier in Walton, a tragic separation that he was never able to emotionally overcome:

> I recall a dark, stormy night, in Dec., 1843, when we were living together, at his house on Ontario Street [Chicago]. The wild winter wind was moaning through the trees, which stood close to the building, a great wood-fire was burning upon the old-fashioned andirons. It was late in the evening, we were alone, and had been narrating to each other incidents of boyhood—on the Delaware and the Susquehanna. We had been speaking of schoolmates and early friends.
>
> Earlier in the evening, he had been humming old and half-forgotten ballads. In this way, time passed on, but he took no note of it, and seemed wholly absorbed in his memories. The fire burned low, the hour grew late, but still he kept on speaking of the past, and, finally, he went to his own room, and soon returned with a parcel of carefully-preserved, but long-ago faded flowers; roses, pansies, some old garden flowers,—a ribbon, a glove—some notes, and a little poem,—all tenderly-cherished relics of one from whom, many and long years before, he had been separated by death . . . Half-a-century after her death, when making his last "will and testament" he remembered this romance of his youth, and made liberal and generous provisions for the nearest-surviving relatives of one to whose memory he was still so faithful.[37]

The love Arnold was describing, indeed the love of William's life, was the beautiful young Walton girl Sarah North, daughter of one of the town's founders, who was betrothed to him. Ogden had been in Philadelphia on a business trip when his brother Mahlon arrived on horseback to deliver the sad news of Sarah's sudden death. At least two of Sarah's brothers had already died of tuberculosis, a common killer in those times.[38]

No other single event in the life of William B. Ogden defines him as precisely as his love and loss of Sarah North. That is evidenced by a number of his actions. Sarah died in 1829, and Ogden did not marry until 1875 at the age of sixty-nine, and then it seems to have been primarily a marriage of convenience. When he left Walton in 1835 for Chicago, Ogden deeded a fine house he owned on Delaware Street to three of Sarah North's nieces, her closest and dearest relatives. In 1860, at the peak of his financial fortune, he issued a "Declaration of Trust" that granted mortgage bonds in his Chicago and North Western Railway Company to the same ladies. And in his "Last Will and Testament," he remembered them again with shares of common stock in his companies. In each of these cases, he left one of the three nieces a greater share of the largesse than the others. That young lady's name was Sarah North.

Most tellingly, his will stated that in addition to a large plot of the Walton cemetery being set aside for him and his family members, "I also desire that the descendants of my respected friend Captain Robert North of Walton be buried in my grounds in the same cemetery, and that his remains and those of his wife and children now buried there shall be allowed to remain so."[39] In this, his last wish, William Ogden planned to be reunited with his beloved Sarah North for all eternity. As we shall see later, however, this was not to be.

By 1833 the Ogdens' lumber business was called Ogden and Wheeler. The relationship between the two families went all the way back to the mid-1600s in earliest New England. It is even possible that their earlier ancestors knew each other in England. Various branches of the two families had intermarried on a number of occasions, as early as the eighteenth century. William's younger sister Emily would marry Nelson Knox Wheeler the year after William left for Chicago. At some point in the 1820s the Wheelers had become partners in the lumber mill.[40]

The woolens business, with its numerous mills, was solely an Ogden enterprise. While he was healthy, Abraham had operated the business, along with the lumber mill, and for a time after his stroke, Isaac had stepped in. It appears that by the 1830s William was running all the family enterprises, either alone or in concert with the partners he had brought in.

In the four decades since Abraham Ogden had first headed west, the family had accumulated significant wealth. Now, in the early 1830s, as William Ogden considered their good fortunes, there was only one dark cloud on the horizon: the Erie Canal. They had taken all the steps they could to insulate themselves against their northern competitors, and they had been successful; but they still suffered a competitive disadvantage.

During the first quarter of the nineteenth century, canals had been considered the most efficient form of east–west overland transportation. Most natural waterways ran north to south, while economic development was beginning to run east to west. Canals could effectively connect the natural waterways, creating a nationwide network that would deliver goods and people in any direction. Of course, the railroad could do the same thing, but its time was still beyond the horizon.

The idea to transport goods and people on canals had first taken hold in this country in the late 1700s, inspired by the Dutch and, to a lesser degree, the English and French systems of manmade waterways. However, it was not until the Erie Canal opened in 1825 that America saw what canals could really accomplish. Although railroads would eventually supplant the Erie Canal as the main lifeline to the West, the canal would be profitable for New York until 1883 when tolls were finally abolished. As the University of Virginia's Janet Haven states, "For the dissemination of people, ideas, goods and American national-ism, as well as a model for most subsequent canals, the Erie Canal stands alone in the first half of the nineteenth century."[41]

Those communities that benefited the most from the canal were the ones along its banks, or those with easy river access to it. Many became boomtowns overnight—Utica, Syracuse, and Rochester chief among them. For example, the cost of shipping goods from these towns went from one hundred dollars a ton by road to about ten dollars a ton by canal. Of course, New York City also greatly benefited, as advocates of the canal had long claimed would occur. The mighty Hudson River connected the city directly to the new canal, insuring its position as the young nation's leading city of commerce.[42]

Little wonder, then, that the towns along New York's southern tier, like Wal-ton, were not happy that they could not share in the success of the Erie Canal. Businessmen like William Ogden saw their sales of lumber and woolen products placed at a significant disadvantage because of the high cost of transporting goods to market. More damaging, their products were virtually shut out of the expanding markets to the west, markets like Buffalo, Cleveland, and Detroit, which they could not efficiently reach.

Ogden was savvy enough to know it was not a time to panic. He could still reach Philadelphia cost-effectively, and that market alone would earn his fam-ily's lumber and woolen businesses a tidy living. Their other businesses were prosperous too. But when he considered the worsening transportation situation (mixed in with the persistent feeling of emptiness over Sarah North's death), he realized the call for help from Vice President Martin Van Buren had come at a good time for him.

Little did Ogden realize that an even larger opportunity, one that would change his life forever, was only months away.

4

Go West, Young Man

"**G**o West, young man, and grow up with the country." Indiana newspaperman John Soule's 1851 editorial in the *Terra Haute Express* spoke for an entire generation, perhaps even for an entire century. (Horace Greeley copied the first part for his now-famous July 13, 1865, editorial in the *New York Tribune*.)

If it were possible to put a single label on the nineteenth century, it would be the Age of Western Expansion. Manifest Destiny, which led to western expansion, had its roots in the administration of the fifth president of the United States, James Monroe, who served from 1817 to 1825. In his 1823 address to Congress, which has become known as the Monroe Doctrine, he delivered a straightforward message to European countries: stay out of our continent and we'll stay out of yours. He made it clear that the United States would no longer accept European political influence or meddling over our share of the Western Hemisphere, and that we would not interfere in their wars or internal affairs.

At the time of the Monroe Doctrine, United States territorial boundaries had been set by a series of purchases or treaties with England, France, and Spain to include all of the present-day states east of the Rocky Mountains except parts of Louisiana and Texas. Western expansion would establish the remainder of America's international boundaries.

The term *Manifest Destiny* was not coined until more than twenty years after the Monroe Doctrine. The mind-set behind it was obvious: this land, all the way from the Atlantic Ocean to the Pacific Ocean, rightfully belongs to the people of the United States, perhaps not yet legally but naturally, inevitably. Thus, western expansion—the conquest and settlement of all that territory, and the subjugation of the "savages" that occupied it—was Americans' right, indeed their obligation, to pursue. It encompassed unimaginable opportunities and challenges along the way: the Lewis and Clark expedition (1804–6); the removal of the eastern Indians to the Far West (1829–37); the completion of the Erie Canal (1825); the annexation of Texas (1845); the Mexican War (1846–48);

the Oregon Treaty (1846); the California Gold Rush (1849); the completion of the transcontinental railroad (1869); subjugation of the Plains Indians (1887); and many other signal events.

Western expansion really began long before any of these events. Sometime in 1608, when John Smith and a few of the first colonists at Jamestown ratcheted up their courage and ventured from their small island, they went west on the James River. That was when British America's western expansion began. When William B. Ogden's ancestor John Ogden, "the Pilgrim," led the first English settlers west of the Hudson River into what is now New Jersey in 1664, they were part of the western expansion. And when settlers from the original thirteen colonies—all located east of the Appalachian mountain range—first ventured into Vermont, Kentucky, Tennessee, and Ohio in the late eighteenth century, they too took part.

What led all of these brave men and women to explore new territories beyond the boundaries of their known world was a quest for opportunity and a sense of adventure. Risk was always present, too. It may have been financial risk, as it was with the expansion of the railroads westward; or it may have been more personal, like the threat of torture or scalping. But westward expansion was always about risk and reward.

If we look back to the dawning of the nineteenth century, it's very difficult to comprehend how little our ancestors knew about the continent they called home. The U.S. Census of 1800—only the nation's second—tallied a total population of 5.2 million people in the sixteen states. Yet only an infinitesimal number of those people knew what was west of the established borders of the existing states. An apt comparison may be what we know today about outer space. We know that Mars is out there, and Saturn and Neptune and Pluto, along with galaxies of cosmic places we can't even name. But who among us knows how far each one is from Earth, what matter of things reside there, or what's in the final frontier beyond all that's presently known?

It was the same with our ancestors, until about 1814. From 1804 until 1806, Meriwether Lewis and William Clark, at the bidding of President Thomas Jefferson, traveled from the known world into the unknown, all the way to the West Coast. With the publication of their diaries in 1814, Americans for the first time actually learned something about the West and what was between them and it. It must have been a startling revelation. There were no fire-breathing dragons, no erupting volcanoes. Prairies, yes; wide rivers a person could barely see across, yes; and mountains higher than most people had ever seen before. But the fear of the unknown—the greatest fear of all—was at last tamed. And finally Americans could begin to dream of seeing the vast continent upon which they lived, where there was land and food and clean air and water enough for everybody.

During the first half of the nineteenth century, a number of new towns sprang up in the middle sections of the country, the regions we today call the Midwest and the South. These towns became the gateways between the well-established and well-populated Eastern cities and the unexplored Far West. New Orleans was the first, originally a depot for the French fur trade. It was the only Southern city to grow to significant size by midcentury.

Then came Cincinnati. Sitting on the Ohio River, its strategic location made it the first urban center of the territory known as the North-West, or Northwest, consisting of today's states of Ohio, Indiana, Illinois, Michigan, Wisconsin, and part of Minnesota. St. Louis, another center for the fur trade, emerged as a major hub of waterborne transportation thanks to its location at the confluence of two major rivers. Pittsburgh, Cleveland, and Detroit also began to develop as significant centers of trade and transportation, sharing the common trait of all successful cities of the day: navigable waterways.

Chicago, the last to develop, had the same easy waterway access as the others, yet it eventually outperformed them all, for a number of reasons. Two of the most important were that Chicago secured a huge influx of investment capital from the East to aid its development, and it became the first major railroad center in the country.

The story of western expansion is the story of American capital and American railroads, and that story, in large part, is the story of William B. Ogden.

Two months after Abraham Ogden's death, William Ogden's older sister Eliza became the first of Abraham and Abigail's children to marry when she wed Charles Butler in Walton.[1] Still in mourning for a number of family members, she must have found it a bittersweet time. The bridegroom was a young man, three years older than William. He was born in 1802 in Kinderhook Landing (today Stuyvesant), a small village on the east bank of the Hudson River, twenty miles south of Albany. He studied law with Martin Van Buren, also from Kinderhook where his older brother Benjamin was a junior partner in the law firm. When he finished his studies, Charles declined a number of lucrative offers in order to practice small-town law in Geneva, west of Syracuse in the Finger Lakes region.

In 1829, Charles Butler was toiling anonymously, and quite contentedly, in his modest western New York law office when he discovered a land practice that had plagued local farmers for two hundred years.[2] Title to western New York land belonged to a small handful of English, Scotch, and Dutch land companies that had purchased it from the earliest proprietors, who had been granted the land by English or Dutch monarchies in the 1600s. Early homesteaders were forced into vassalage with the land companies. These farmers had a laborious life clearing the land and preparing it for cultivation, yet they held no title to the land they worked. They contracted to purchase their land on installment, meaning they would receive their deeds only after all the payments were made. Yet because of their stark hand-to-mouth existence, they constantly fell further behind in their payments, and the balance would steadily grow larger due to the interest added.

Charles Butler thought the system was cruel and unfair, and he decided to do something about it in his own Genesee County, which in 1829 had not one single farmer who held title to the land he worked. The answer seemed simple to Butler: find capitalists with ample means to advance money to the farmers on a long term, with reasonable interest. The farmers could pay off the land companies with the cash, acquire their deeds, and work in their own behalf. As the land had appreciated considerably since most farmers or their ancestors had settled it, the capitalists lending the money would have their loans adequately collateralized by attractive farmlands. It was a win-win-win proposition for everyone, Butler believed.

The following year Butler set off for New York City for a meeting with the board of directors of the New York Life Insurance and Trust Company. He met Arthur Bronson, the scion of one of the state's wealthiest and most powerful families that had founded the firm, the first financial services company incorporated in the state. Meeting with the Bronsons, John Jacob Astor, and other leading financial men, Butler convinced them of his plan. After a number of meetings, they consented to the loans and the enterprise was born.

Returning to Geneva, Butler used his extraordinary organizational skills to set up a process to funnel the money. It involved the farmers, the Trust Company and the Holland Land Company, which owned the land in Genesee County. The plan was an unqualified success. As trustee of the plan, Butler eventually loaned out more than a million dollars, and countless thriving farming communities developed thanks to his vision and untiring efforts.

There was one loan he could not approve. Martin Harris, a farmer from nearby Palmyra, wanted a loan so he could publish a bible and start a new religion. He told Butler a fascinating story about another Palmyra man, Joseph Smith, who, following divine guidance, supposedly unearthed a set of golden plates containing the text for the bible and a record of God's promises. He also unearthed two transparent stones that provided clues to interpreting the golden plates' hieroglyphics. They were buried on a hilltop in A.D. 420 by a man named Maroni, the son of Mormon, after a great battle, Harris said. Butler was not able to grant the loan—a new bible was not enough collateral, he reasoned—but the bible, the Book of Mormon, was eventually published and became the foundation for today's Church of Jesus Christ of Latter Day Saints.

Butler and Bronson became friends, and in January 1833 Butler was again in New York City when the two men met Robert A. Kinzie, son of trader John

Kinzie, one of the earliest settlers in Chicago.[3] The Kinzies had survived the Indian massacre at Fort Dearborn in 1812 and fled to Detroit, returning four years later to establish a homestead. When the U.S. government first began selling land in Chicago in 1830, the very first deed was recorded in Robert Kinzie's name, a $109 parcel just north of the Chicago River. A handsome, bearded man, Robert Kinzie bore a striking resemblance to Ulysses S. Grant.

Kinzie offered to sell Butler and Bronson the land he had inherited from his father in Chicago. When he raved about the fabulous future for the area around Fort Dearborn, Bronson and Butler decided to visit that summer and inspect it.[4] Prior to their trip, Bronson did some research. A friend, General Winfield Scott, had been in charge of the campaign against the Indians in Illinois, and Bronson consulted him about the Fort Dearborn area around Chicago. Scott praised the area in glowing terms and encouraged the men to visit it.

William Ogden sat in front of the fireplace in his Walton home, a copy of the October 16, 1833, *Delaware County Gazette* folded in his lap. He had just completed his countywide campaign for the 1834 assembly seat but had yet to make his speech before the legislature. It was snowing lightly outside—kind of early for snow; it could mean a long, bitter winter. But it was of little consequence. It might mean buttoning up the mills a little earlier than usual, but then production could begin earlier in the spring, so it was of no consequence one way or the other.

Ogden unfolded the newspaper and looked at the front page, where he saw an article under the byline of his brother-in-law Charles Butler. "Chicago is a town beautifully situated at the head of lake Michigan, and it is unquestionably destined to become one of the largest cities of the far and great west," Butler had written. "The Chicago River is one of the most beautiful streams I have ever seen" was how he described the muddy, wild-onion bordered river that flowed sluggishly into Lake Michigan.

Ogden probably got a chuckle out of that. Butler and his friend Arthur Bronson were not due back from their trip to the Northwest for a few more weeks; but it would have been typical of the shrewd Bronson to begin promoting any land purchase as quickly as possible. The fact that the article appeared the same day in the *Albany Argus* was further proof of the plan.

Further in the story, Butler described how easy it would eventually be for Easterners to travel west through Chicago and then use the proposed Illinois and Michigan Canal. "When this route shall be established, you may travel from Albany to St. Louis in nine days. . . . it will be the great thoroughfare between Atlantic States and the valley of the Mississippi."

The village of Chicago that Butler and Bronson visited in 1833 was a very different place from the town of Chicago in 1835, and a world apart from the city of Chicago in 1837. Such were the rapid strides the sleepy little village made once it was "discovered." A 1908 speech by one of the area's earliest white settlers, Edwin Gale, made before the Chicago Historical Society, spelled it out:

> When the town first dawned upon us [in 1829] there was not a foot of sidewalk in the place, nor anything to denote a street excepting the stakes of the surveyor, James Thompson, who was appointed by the canal commissioners to survey the section of canal land one-mile square bounded by Chicago avenue, Madison, State and Halsted streets. Thompson reported that he only found seven families in the place outside the garrison [Fort Dearborn].
>
> It was the custom of a few useful water men to drive their two wheeled one horse carts into the river and load their reclining hogsheads with four long handled wooden pails . . . they usually obtained their [water] supply for the scattered settlers from the most convenient places in the stream, delivering to their customers, as a rule, for ten cents a barrel. That the treacherous winds roiled the lake water was the usual plea for furnishing from the river.
>
> . . . neighboring farmers brought hams, bacon, poultry, eggs, butter, lard, cheese and fruits, which they brought in their covered wagons . . . drawn by eight or ten yoke of oxen. These prairie schooners were especially attractive to the boys when loaded with enticing peaches and apples, as was frequently the case. Their sunburnt owners, lank and tall, no more we see today. The snap of their loud-cracking whips, forever's passed away.[5]

Butler and Bronson saw a very different place, but seen through the eyes of the land speculator, it was just as interesting.

Charles Butler was an educated man. He was also gentle and observant, and he wrote and spoke often about the groundbreaking journey he and Arthur Bronson had made to the small village on the Lake Michigan shore.[6] Many of his recollections were recalled in an 1881 talk he gave before the Chicago Historical Society but had originally been captured in his diaries and journals that now reside in the Library of Congress.

It wasn't an easy trip. He related the discomforts the men had suffered in order to reach Chicago, first on the Erie Canal west to Buffalo, then on a steamer down Lake Erie to Detroit. He confessed they found Detroit a boisterous, busy little spot since the opening of the Erie Canal, and one that might be worthy of future investments. There they bought some horses, hired a guide named Gohlsen Kercheval and a couple of muleskinners, and headed on to Lake Michigan.

"If you have never seen a prairie, it is utterly impossible for me to convey to you any idea of the peculiar and interesting aspect which it presents," Butler wrote. "The White Pigeon Prairie [in southwestern Michigan] is an expanse of about fifteen thousand acres skirted or encircled with a dense and noble forest of timber, which is to it like the frame of a picture. If it were owned by a private gentleman, he could not have made a more beautiful park than this."[7]

Butler's first impression of Chicago, however, was not so grand. He described the town as a small, squalid place with fewer than two hundred people crammed together in hastily constructed wooden shacks. His honest opinion of the muddy, sluggish Chicago River also failed to live up to the exquisite description he had penned for the newspaper articles Ogden had read a few weeks earlier.

He described the lodgings he and Bronson had taken in Chicago, a sad little place named the Green Tea Tavern. It had no interior walls, Butler wrote; and to make the room dividers, they just hung some dingy sheets over the bare wooden studs. He related that the wealthy and refined Arthur Bronson had not found the Green Tree Tavern to his liking, so he hired some of the local boys to build him a little house, and in less than a week's time he had his own place. Describing his own accommodations at the tavern, Butler wrote, "the house was crowded with people—emigrants and travelers—many of them could only find sleeping places on the floor which was covered with weary men at night."[8]

He did admit he saw some beauty in Chicago. His window at the Green Tea Tavern looked over Lake Michigan, with Fort Dearborn in the foreground, and he thought it was as pretty a site as a man could hope to see. Wild, too, he recounted; some men actually shot wolves from the windows of their hotel rooms.

Butler explained that most of the land in and around the new town was owned by the federal government and the State of Illinois, and it had not yet been offered for sale to the public, which was why the residents had constructed moveable shacks on the lots. "They could only acquire a pre-emptive right by actual settlement," he explained. Most people were simply squatting on the land, hoping to be able to buy their chosen lot when it went on the market. The village was also crowded with land speculators, all there for the same reason as Butler and Bronson—a quick profit. An English traveler, Charles Latrobe, said the land speculators were "as numerous as the sand."[9]

It was Robert Kinzie's privately owned land on the north side of the river that Butler and Bronson had gone to consider. The only building on that side was an old blockhouse that had once belonged to the fort. Butler explained that they were impressed, certainly not with the order and discipline of the new town, but with the long-range prospects it offered for investors. He wrote that he saw "the germ of a city, destined, from its peculiar position near the head of the lake and its remarkable harbor formed by the river, to become the largest inland commercial Emporium in the United States."[10]

Butler and Bronson then got acquainted with the town's leaders. They knew Robert A. Kinzie from their encounter in New York, but they met the other Kinzie brothers, as well as Gurdon Hubbard, Richard Hamilton, George Dole, John Wright, and other leading men of the village, who were all anxious to interest these Eastern moneymen in their affairs. The local men's chief interest at the moment, Butler said, was to find some outside investment capital to restart construction on the Illinois and Michigan Canal, which they believed would ignite the town's growth.

Butler admitted he and Bronson had taken a keen interest in the scheme. They suggested to the town's leaders that they would study the possibility of forming a company to take on the canal's construction. Based on that promise, a committee of local men was selected to go to the Illinois state legislature in Jacksonville (Springfield would become the state capital three years later) to acquire the canal charter for this new company. The committee's efforts were successful in getting the project kick-started. At the 1834–35 winter session, a bill was passed authorizing the state to take out a federal loan for the project. Although this derailed Butler and Bronson's hope of being granted the project in their favor, it did serve to revive the dormant grant of three hundred thousand acres that Congress had bestowed. The idea was for a canal that would run from the village of Chicago on Lake Michigan southwesterly to the Illinois River at LaSalle, thus opening a route from the Great Lakes to the Mississippi, into which the Illinois River flowed. It was this canal that Butler had referred to in his earlier newspaper article.

Butler and Bronson had planned to travel on to Ohio and Indiana and inspect other opportunities, but Bronson took ill and they had to cut the trip short.[11] On their return home in late October 1833, Butler turned around and left again for the other states they had been forced to bypass. He likely asked William Ogden to accompany him, but Ogden begged off, so he took his other brother-in-law, Mahlon Ogden, William's younger brother. Mahlon had studied for his law license in Columbus, Ohio, so he was already somewhat familiar with the area. They visited a number of the leading towns in Ohio and Indiana, and both men agreed that area too offered golden investment opportunities.

The trips had two unforeseen outcomes. First, they turned the quiet, introspective Butler into an avid risk-taking entrepreneur—he had seen the Promised Land, and he would never turn back. Second, it sparked a previously untapped sense of adventure in Mahlon Ogden that convinced him to join his brother William when he left permanently for Chicago. Butler had been content with his law practice in Geneva, and believed he and William's sister Eliza would make their life together there. But the investment opportunities he had seen in Illinois, Ohio, and Indiana were too great to pass up. Although he currently had no money to invest, he was determined to scratch some together, and he recommended that William do the same.

Although the idea didn't light any fires under Ogden, he said he would consider it. He wasn't convinced he was ready to take on anything more. But the seed Butler had planted germinated, and as Ogden thought more about it, he became more susceptible to the opportunity and to change in general. He had never traveled west of Niagara, and the opportunity to see the emerging Northwest was tantalizing. But in the end, it would be another family tragedy that would finally shake William Ogden out of his lethargy.

On February 17, 1835, Ogden's Aunt Phebe Ogden passed away.[12] It was a blow to the close-knit family, but only the beginning. Two days later, while grieving at Phebe's open graveside, her husband Daniel Ogden had a massive stroke and died only hours later.[13] Their joint death notice in the *Delaware County Gazette* said Phebe died of "a lingering consumption" (tuberculosis) and Daniel died of "paralysis," generally indicating a stroke.[14] Nobody in the family doubted that Phebe's death was the direct cause of her loving husband Daniel's demise.

Soon after his return from the Chicago trip, Arthur Bronson purchased 182 acres on the north side of the Chicago River for twenty thousand dollars from army captain David Hunter who had earlier been stationed at Fort Dearborn.[15] The tract included one-half of the Kinzie Addition that ran from the river to Chicago Avenue and from the lake to just west of State Street; and the whole of the Wolcott Addition, which ran from Kinzie Street to Chicago Avenue, and abutting the State Street–Kinzie boundary, to just west of LaSalle Avenue. The land they had originally gone to inspect, Robert A. Kinzie's parcel, did not impress the men, as it was hemmed in by other parcels; thus the decision to buy Hunter's land instead.[16]

Charles Butler had not found the spare money to invest at that time; but in May 1835, with the aid of some friends to share the financial burden, he bought Bronson's holdings for one hundred thousand dollars, providing a 400 percent profit for the shrewd speculator.[17] Butler put the holdings into the American Land Company, a corporation he established in New York City, and became its president. He and Eliza packed up their belongings and left the small town of Geneva, destined to spend the rest of their years in the city. Butler would open a law firm and find instant success among the important men of New York City, and become one of the most prominent and prosperous financial men in the nation during the era of Western land speculation.

A little-known fact about this incident is the identity of the other seven men who invested with Butler, who had purchased one half of the speculative land for his own portfolio. The others were his brother Benjamin Butler, his brother-in-law William Ogden, Edward Nicoll, Simeon Hyde, John Bussing, Chester Clark, and Barton White. This information is gleaned from the historical files of the Supreme Court of Illinois, from a lawsuit filed in 1862 as an outgrowth of the original partnership.[18]

Butler realized by now that investments in the Northwest were not a one-shot opportunity, but offered long-term investment potential. He also knew that whatever investments he made would require a reliable point man in Chicago to manage the purchase and be alert to additional opportunities. Once again he called on his brother-in-law, friend, and partner in the Chicago land purchase, William Ogden.[19]

Ogden spent many idle mornings in one of his favorite pastimes, riding his big bay gelding Paddy over the Delaware County countryside. It was a habit he had developed whenever the pressures of business or living had begun to get the best of him. After his election to the state assembly, he often rode one of his horses to the sessions in Albany, a leisurely three-day ride that he looked forward to regardless of the weather. With the tails of his long, high-split riding coat blowing behind him like a mad pursuer, he urged Paddy on with a gentle dig of his riding boots into her ribs. After a couple of hours, the ride had worked its magic, and he found clarity in his thinking that he hadn't experienced for many months. He knew why Butler was coming to call—his brother-in-law had sent a letter in advance—and Ogden was ready for the conversation.

Butler got quickly to the point. Someone had to go to Chicago and tend to selling their land. He had discovered while in New York that the federal government would begin releasing some of its holdings in Chicago that coming May, and that fact, he was sure, would ignite interest in the place. Now was the time to sell what they had, he told Ogden, and buy more if possible.

An interesting sidelight to this episode is that most historical accounts describe Butler as Ogden's "wealthy brother-in-law" when he convinced Ogden to go to Chicago. The fact was, Butler was far from wealthy at the time; Ogden was much better off financially than his brother-in-law.

Uncle Daniel's and Aunt Phebe's deaths had taken a lot out of Ogden, and he must have realized that he needed a change of pace in his life. Although he was skeptical about the Chicago investments, he had decided that perhaps he should see them for himself, as Butler, Bronson and his brother Mahlon had done. He told Butler he would go. The men agreed Ogden would leave by late spring.

The history of the Chicago area in its present geological configuration is a relatively short one.[20] During the last Ice Age, most of the northern United States was buried under colossal ice sheets. As these glaciers repeatedly advanced and retreated over the eons, they carved out the Great Lakes, the rivers and smaller lakes, and the terrain we recognize today. About fifteen thousand years ago, the Wisconsin Glacier, which covered northern Illinois, began to retreat for the final time, sculpting the landscape and leaving a limestone bedrock covered by a thick layer of impermeable clay and prairie swamplands in its wake.

Nature, it seems, made only one small error when it carved out *Chicagou*, as the local Indians called the area, after the wild onions that grew along the banks of the rivers and lakes. As the Wisconsin Glacier dug out the valleys that would become rivers on its final retreat, it missed a one-and-a-half-mile stretch of soggy prairie between the eastern end of Mud Lake and the western arm of the south branch of the Chicago River, thus leaving a small land barrier between the Great Lakes and the Mississippi River navigation systems. This one-and-a-half-mile stretch, which sat right on the Oak Park Continental Divide, was known as the Chicago Portage.

If one physical feature defines Chicago from its earliest beginnings to the present day, it is the Chicago River. Before people began tinkering with it, it was a baffling, cantankerous little river—more like a stream—that flowed into Lake Michigan. An 1848 visitor to the area called it "a sluggish, slimy stream, too lazy to clean itself"; while another writer described it as "more than a puny brook, but less than a great waterway."[21]

Tracing the river backward from Lake Michigan, where it terminates, the riverbed came out of the lake and ran due south for about a thousand yards, paralleling the lake and creating a narrow sand bar between the two. Then it veered southwest for about one and a quarter miles until it reached an area known as Wolf Point. Once there, it split neatly in two. The longer North Branch headed north before fizzling out about twenty-five miles upriver, where it was fed by the confluence of three small streams. The South Branch headed south for a couple of miles, then split into two smaller streams. The one we're following continued west for about ten more miles and then stopped. A little further west was a nasty little bog called Mud Lake. It oozed a bit further west and then turned into another little stream that ran smack into the Des Plaines River, which flows into the Fox River, which flows into the Illinois River, which finally flows into the Mississippi River. This mile-and-a-half stretch of muddy open prairie between the end of the western arm of the South Branch and Mud Lake was the Chicago Portage.

Long before any Europeans roamed the continent, the Indians traversed the Chicago Portage to get from one waterway to another. They used the crossing for trade, hunting, trapping, and making war. Six important Indian trails intersected near the Portage, making it a center of pre-European activity.

In 1673, Jesuit priest Jacques Marquette, Canadian explorer Louis Joliet, and their team of voyageurs were returning to Quebec in two birch-bark canoes after their voyage of discovery to the Mississippi River. Their initial route had taken them down Lake Michigan to Green Bay, thence to Lake Winnebago and on to the Fox River. They portaged to the Wisconsin River that took them to the mighty Mississippi at present-day Prairie Du Chien on the Wisconsin-Iowa border. From there the intrepid explorers went down the Mississippi all the way to its confluence with the Arkansas River, southeast of today's Little Rock. From the local Indians, they learned for the first time that this mighty river would eventually flow into the Gulf of Mexico, not into the Pacific Ocean as previously believed. Afraid to venture further they turned back, trying a different route the Indians assured them would be faster. In September they found themselves on the Des Plaines River at the Chicago Portage. They were astounded at the tall-grass prairie that surrounded them, a magnificent piece of American landscape that once covered much of the Midwest but has today all but vanished to the march of progress. Upon their return to Quebec, their description of this undulating sea of blue-green grass, punctuated with wildflowers with its rich soil beneath, would convince their Quebecois sponsors that this was indeed a land worth holding onto. For the remainder of the seventeenth century, French trappers and traders joined the Indians in using the Chicago Portage to extend their reach from the East Coast to the Mississippi Valley and beyond.

One of the earliest maps to show "Chicagou" was published in 1718 by Frenchman Guillaume Delisle, the official geographer to Louis XV and often called the father of modern cartography. Delisle's map clearly showed Chicago at the southwestern bend of Lake Michigan and even indicated the distinctive Y shaped "Chicagou" River that sprang from its shoreline. The nearby Des Plaines River was also called the Chicagou River on Delisle's map. That Chicago would even appear on the map, which was actually penned at the dawn of the century, is surprising, as the only settlement at the time was a tiny French trading post and a few scattered Indian villages.

In about 1779, still four years before England ceded the area to the United States, a black trapper/trader from Saint Domingue, a French colony in present-day Haiti, and his Indian wife established a small fur trading post at the mouth of the Chicago River. Jean-Baptiste and Catherine Point du Sable are considered the founders of Chicago. For the next twenty years, a few other traders arrived and put down roots.

On April 30, 1803, President Thomas Jefferson finalized the Louisiana Purchase from France for fifteen million dollars, which more than doubled the size of the infant nation. It opened the Western frontier and provided Chicago with fabulous opportunities. But by that time, the Point du Sables had sold their Chicago home and trading post to Jean La Lime and William Burnette, having given up hope that the area would see the prosperity they had dreamed of. The La Limes and Burnette, Antoine Ouilmette, François Le Mai, and Louis Pettell, with their wives and families, were the five residents of Chicago when the Louisiana Purchase was made. Early the following year, John Kinzie and family purchased the La Lime/Burnette property and became one of Chicago's foremost families for generations.

Later that year, the development the Point du Sables had awaited in vain finally arrived with the construction of Fort Dearborn. The fort was built in the crook of the Chicago River as it enters Lake Michigan, and brought with it a military contingency of sixty-nine men to join the four families that called the area home. Thus was Chicago born.

For almost a decade, the garrison and the settlers huddled around it were peaceful. The small handful of inhabitants lived in seclusion from the rest of the world in their little Indiana Territory village. Once a year, a schooner was sent by John Jacob Astor to deliver supplies to the outpost and return with its annual supply of furs. This visit was augmented by a bi-monthly mail rider who delivered the tidings of the world to the isolated band of settlers and soldiers. However, the outbreak of the War of 1812 changed all that.

The local Potawatomi Indians joined the British to expel the trespassers from their homeland. It developed into a powder-keg situation, and the garrison was ordered to abandon the isolated fort. On August 15, 1812, a small wagon train with the soldiers and the settlers set out for Fort Wayne in Indiana Territory, after reaching a peaceful agreement with the Potawatomi for their departure. When the garrison destroyed their excess weapons and ammunition, however, the Indians felt the agreement had been breached. They attacked the wagon train, killing about 150 soldiers and settlers and taking many captives. A few, like the Kinzies, who had established friendly relations with the Indians by providing them with weapons and liquor, were spared. Fort Dearborn was burned to the ground.

In 1816, following the war, the fort was rebuilt and occupied by troops until it was finally abandoned in 1837. The fort was eventually torn down in 1856, but the legend of the Fort Dearborn Massacre lived on in Chicago's memory for more than a century.

The Chicago Portage, through all of these events, continued to attract an increasing amount of traffic. If the traffic had remained moderate, and flimsy birch-bark canoes the only transportation across it, cutting a channel through it to connect the major waterways would have been sufficient. However, larger boats with deeper drafts, and lots more of them, were now making the passage. It had become obvious that Joliet's dream of connecting the two waterway systems by canal was inevitable; but the Chicago Portage was not the answer. The sluggish Chicago River, Mud Lake, and the Des Plaines River, even during the wet season when the portage wasn't necessary, were not wide or deep enough to serve the growing needs of western expansion.

In 1809 Illinois Territory was carved out of Indiana Territory, and in 1818 Illinois was granted statehood. The local Indians were reluctant to part with their ancestral lands, and they often clashed with the encroaching whites. Meetings began between the Chippewa, Ottawa, and Potawatomi Indians of northern Illinois, Wisconsin, and Michigan. After a great deal of bargaining, the Chicago Treaty of 1821 was signed, and the Indians were given certain considerations that opened the way for the construction of the Illinois and Michigan Canal.

The following year, Congress authorized the state to build a canal connecting Lake Michigan directly to the Illinois River, bypassing the Chicago Portage.

The federal government also ceded to the state all the land along the right-of-way that was required to build the canal. The governor of Illinois was given the power to negotiate a loan not to exceed a half-million dollars on a pledge of canal lands and future tolls. The General Assembly of Illinois followed with an act creating the state's internal navigation system. But these measures did not spell the immediate doom of the historic passage. In fact, it was a quarter-century before the canal was completed, so the portage continued to be a vital lifeline for trade and traffic between east and west.

Activity on the Illinois and Michigan Canal was slow for the next few years. The route was surveyed and approved, and a decision was made to survey and lay out towns along the route, sell lots, and apply the proceeds to the construction. A civil engineer filed his survey and plat of Chicago as section 9, township 39, range 14, and the area received its first legal description.

The year 1833 was an important one for the settlement of about 150 people. In March an appropriation bill was signed in Congress granting the village twenty-five thousand dollars for the construction of a harbor.[22] Four lake steamboats entered the harbor that first year, sharing the tranquil waters of the Chicago River with birch bark canoes loaded with pelts, maple sugar, and handmade trinkets that the few remaining Indians sold on the streets of the village. Three years later the number of lake steamers would swell to 450. As construction began on the harbor in 1833, a group of men met in the Peter Pruyne and County Drugstore on Water Street and voted 12–1 to incorporate as the Town of Chicago. By 1835 the limits of the town had been expanded and now encompassed about 2.4 square miles.

Chicago historian Donald Miller puts all this in perspective: "In this way, modern Chicago was born, the creation not of the forces of the private market, as some historians claim, but of state planners, who, in laying out canal towns, became what the geographer Michael P. Conzen has called 'urban strategists.'"[23]

In June 1835 William Ogden boarded the steamer *Pennsylvania* on Lake Erie and set off for Chicago, leaving behind his life in Delaware County—permanently, as it turned out, though he would return often for visits. An untitled poem that would be penned years later for the Delaware County Centennial celebration in 1876 honored the early founders of the county, people like his father and his Uncle Daniel, who now rested in peace in their adopted homeland.

> A river dear as life to me,
> From out the mountains finds the sea.
> And oft in thought I wander there,
> Along the banks of Delaware.
> The mountains gaze in somber face,

> Upon the writers in their race,
> As if they watched in constant prayer,
> The dear old banks of Delaware.
> Along those banks on dusty bed,
> There sleeps in peace my cherished dead.
> Unvexed by toil or troublous care
> They rest upon the Delaware.
> And when the race of life is run,
> One boon I ask and ask but one—
> That I with them a grave may share
> Upon the banks of Delaware.[24]

The spring and summer of 1835 had been unusually wet, even for Chicago. Ogden was not initially impressed with what he saw: a soggy prairie bog that smelled strongly of onions. It was true that the little settlement had developed many of the trappings of a real town. The *Niles (Mich.) Register* proclaimed the town's population to be four thousand—up from fifty-four three years earlier—including about forty merchants. It also reported that the town had five churches and bi-weekly steamboat service to Buffalo.[25] There were also log bridges across both the North and South Branches of the Chicago River, and the Dearborn Street drawbridge was operational. Construction was under way on the Chicago harbor; the first slaughterhouse was in operation; the first brick house had been built; and there were taverns and hotels aplenty. The first newspaper, the *Chicago Democrat*, and the second, the *Chicago American*, had begun publication. The town also had its first police force, first jail, and first murder trial. The town's first bookstore had opened, and the first professional entertainment act, by the ventriloquist/fire-eater/magician Mr. Bowers, had been performed, with tickets priced at twenty-five and fifty cents.[26]

For Ogden's purposes, the most important development had occurred a month before his arrival. The U.S. Land Office had opened on the second floor of the store of Thomas Church on Lake Street for the sale of the land it had obtained through an 1833 treaty with the Potawatomi. In its first two weeks, the office reported sales in excess of five hundred thousand dollars.[27]

The entire village was in a frenzied state: "Every inn and tavern was jammed with guests, three in a bed and all across the floor,"[28] one biographer noted. "Immigrants slept in or beside their wagons on the streets, while on the outskirts of the town, circling on the prairie like a gigantic barricade against Indians, stood white prairie schooners with their horses and oxen tethered on the grassy expanse beyond." Despite its progress, Chicago was still a hardscrabble frontier settlement that compared to any that Bret Harte or Larry McMurtry could conceive.

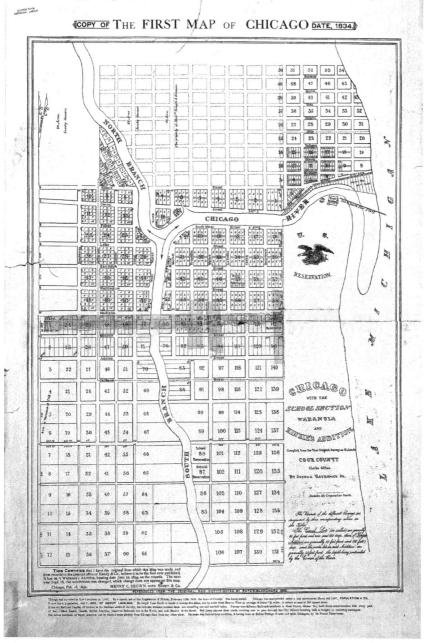

The first printed map of Chicago, 1834, by Joshua Hathaway Jr., which provided real estate information for Eastern land investors and speculators. Very few of the lots indicated on the map had been built upon, however. Courtesy of the Abraham Lincoln Presidential Library, Springfield, Illinois.

Ogden's first task was to find somewhere to stay in Chicago. One of the town's first hotels, and still a gathering place for the rough-and-tumble traders, half-breeds, army officers, Indians, and various riffraff, was Detroit-born Creole Mark Beaubien's Sauganash Tavern. The raucous hotel was located at Wolf Point, the spot just west of Lake Michigan where the Chicago River split into two branches. The hotel, indeed the entire Wolf Point area, was a rollicking place in the mid 1830s: " whiskey, song, and dance were the great democratizers. Visitors from more civilized parts were shocked to see Indian braves spinning the white wives of fort officers around the dance floor of the Sauganash to the frenzied fiddling and toe tapping of Mark Beaubien, or Indian and white women drinking home-distilled liquor straight from the bottle."[29]

By the time Ogden arrived, Beaubien had sold the tavern and its two-story, blue-shuttered clapboard hotel extension to another man. It was now called, grandly, the United States Hotel. This was Ogden's base of operation until the new and much nicer Lake House opened on the north side of the river, near the riverbank opposite the fort, in the following year. The Lake House would be three stories high, built of brick and elegantly furnished. Once Ogden decided to stay in Chicago, he began construction of his own home, a grand affair north of the river.

Ogden's first task was to meet with Frederick Bronson, Arthur Bronson's brother. He held legal title to the Chicago land for his brother and had traveled to Chicago to sell it. But when Butler and his group purchased the acreage, it was arranged for Ogden to meet with Frederick Bronson to handle the title change, which he accomplished. Ogden's next task was to visit the land on the north side of the Chicago River. He rented a fine sorrel mare, crossed the river on a flimsy log bridge, and tied the horse to a tree at the edge of the water. He took about a dozen steps forward before he heard a sharp sucking sound as his leather riding boots disappeared into the mud all the way to his ankles. He stood there with a surprised look on his face and looked around. Stretched before him, he saw an area of hillocks and marsh covered with a coarse growth of scrub oak and underbrush, wet and marshy with coarse grass and cattails poking their heads into the air. Bullfrogs croaked a chorus of insults at him from their hiding places in the reeds, and the strong, earthy scent of rotting humus assaulted the still air. That night, it has often been written, he wrote a note to Butler charging, "You have been guilty of the grossest folly."[30]

In truth, this quote comes not from Ogden, as many historians claim, but from Butler, who wrote, "[Ogden] could not but feel that I had been guilty of an act of great folly in making the purchase, and it was a cause of sad disappointment and of great depression to him."[31]

Despite his misgivings, he was there to prepare the land for an upcoming auction, so he hired some workmen and set about the task. The land had to be cleared and cleaned, platted, laid out in blocks and lots, streets planned, surveys taken, maps drawn, and landmarks established. Fortunately, the summer sun had begun to dry the immense, 182-acre parcel. He accomplished all that had to be done with his usual zeal, keeping his private opinions to himself. He estimated that he spent between fifteen and twenty thousand dollars on improvements in that first year.[32]

His first sale was on June 12, 1835, when he sold a single lot in block 1 to four Chicago men for thirty-five thousand dollars.[33] Ogden was stunned. The planned sale of U.S. government land had brought large crowds to the small town, particularly from the East and Southeast. Ogden built a small wood-framed hut on his property and distributed handbills all over town advertising his private sale.

Harriet Martineau, the noted British writer, historian, and author of the 1837 book *Society in America*, was on a research tour of the United States. Chicago was one of the towns on her itinerary. Although her visit occurred during the summer of 1836, her observations were also reflective of the previous summer when Ogden was preparing for his sale. "I never saw a busier place than Chicago was at the time of our arrival," she observed. "The streets were crowded with land speculators, hurrying from one sale to another. A negro, dressed up in scarlet, bearing a scarlet flag, and riding a white horse with housings of scarlet, announced the times of sale. At every street-corner where he stopped, the crowd flocked round him; and it seemed as if some prevalent mania infected the whole place." Continuing with her description of the buying frenzy surrounding her, Martineau wrote, "As the gentlemen of our party walked the streets, store-keepers hailed them from their doors, with offers of farms, and all manner of land-lots, advising them to speculate before the price of land rose higher."[34]

Early on the morning of June 15, 1835, with this milieu swirling around him, William Ogden arrived at his North Side land to find a clamoring crowd of men awaiting him. He set up a flimsy wooden lectern, tacked a large plat map to the front of the office, and began auctioning off the lots one by one. A large group of men may have caught his attention, hollering and waving fistfuls of money in the air. He discovered they wanted larger parcels, so he began selling three and four adjoining lots together, saving the single parcels for later when the big buyers had been sated. The astonished Ogden took their money as quickly as he could handle it, jamming the cash into every pocket of his breeches. At the end of three frenetic days, he had sold about a third of their holdings for $158,210, which more than compensated the group for their entire original purchase.

Years later, Ogden recounted that by July 1836 his sale of their property had reached six hundred thousand dollars. Blocks he had tried hard to sell in 1835 for three thousand dollars sold for thirty thousand dollars in 1836. However, he related, lots that sold for four hundred dollars in 1835, and for four thousand dollars the next year, dropped to two hundred dollars during the Panic of 1837 that would follow.[35]

Ogden's opinions about Chicago and its opportunities quickly changed as his sharp entrepreneurial senses came into focus, and he saw what Butler and Bronson had seen. For the first time in six years, he became excited about life again. After Ogden concluded his business in Chicago, he had planned to return to Walton. Although he had begun to see the investment opportunities in Chicago, he had yet to commit himself completely to the area. Then he got wind of a land opportunity in nearby Wisconsin, which was then part of Michigan Territory.

Earlier in 1835, a government land office had opened in Fort Howard (today Green Bay), the first one west of Detroit. Ogden took a steamer from Chicago and arrived at the town at the foot of the bay on the west bank of the Fox River. The small town had a long history. It was first settled in 1634 as a French Canadian fur-trading post and incorporated as a town in 1754. The bay itself is a one-hundred-mile-long arm of Lake Michigan ending at the Fox River. As Ogden's steamer slowly made its way down the bay toward the town, he was amazed at the thick forests that lined both sides of the waterway. The lumberman in him saw an opportunity that excited him. This trip was purely for land speculation, but he knew he would revisit this part of the Michigan Territory for its lumber potential one day.

In Fort Howard, Ogden rubbed shoulders with dozens of other land speculators from Milwaukee, Detroit, and Chicago. Most were farmers and working men, there to turn their small savings into a windfall. A few, like Ogden, had substantial money to invest. According to *Life in Territorial Wisconsin*, "William B. Ogden, who in after years was called the 'railroad king,' was the most prominent man among the speculators. He bought largely of land at government prices, and would sell the same property at auction, in the evening. The purchases were very largely made for speculation."[36]

Returning to Chicago on the steamer *Pennsylvania*, Ogden had another stroke of good fortune. He met two men on board with whom he would share lifelong friendships and mutually advantageous business and civic relationships. The first was a twenty-three-year-old fellow with the authoritarian name of J. Young Scammon, who was on his way to Chicago from Buffalo, the boat's terminus.[37] The two men hit it off immediately. Scammon was of Scandinavian ancestry, a tall man, and even at his young age, already beginning to show his weight. He was strikingly handsome, with a kind twinkle in his eyes, and he sported a close-cropped beard. What drew Ogden to him, and indeed drew most men, was his booming voice and quick laugh. Scammon was a jovial man, the type others liked to be around.

When they arrived in Chicago, Scammon had only a few coins jingling together in his pocket. Within a week, he had taken a job as deputy to the circuit court clerk and eventually opened his own law practice. In 1846, Scammon and Ogden would resurrect the Galena and Chicago Union Railroad together, the city's first railroad, and would remain close until death separated them.

The second man Ogden met aboard the *Pennsylvania* was cut from the same cloth as himself. Walter L. Newberry was a year older than Ogden and had discovered Chicago real estate even earlier. In 1830, he was one of the very first speculators to buy land along the proposed Illinois and Michigan Canal route, a forty-acre parcel just north of the Chicago River. In 1833, he returned to Chicago permanently from Connecticut to seek his fortune.[38] Through a combination of good fortune and excellent foresight—he was also said to be a real tightwad—Newberry was one of the few Northwest speculators who retained his wealth through the financial panic of 1837–42. He and Ogden would be neighbors and work together in the future on many of Chicago's most notable commercial and civic enterprises.

Back in Chicago, Ogden began tying up all his loose ends before returning home. During his brief stay, he had made a number of influential friends. This was not the staid, stiff-collared convention he was accustomed to in New York City, Albany, Philadelphia, and the other large Eastern cities where he conducted business. This was a laid-back, informal culture where friendship and trust developed quickly and lasted as long as neither party subverted them. In New York, Ogden had always been "William," or "Mr. Ogden"; after only a few days in Chicago, he became "Will" to all who met him.

In September 1835, the town board passed a resolution establishing Chicago's first fire department and pledged funds to buy two engines and one thousand feet of hose. William Ogden, who had known these men for only a few months, was given the authority to purchase the equipment when he returned to New York.[39]

Before leaving for home, Ogden experienced one more grand adventure. In mid-August, the Potawatomi were in town to receive their final government annuity payment before heading for their reservation. All the tribe's braves performed a ceremonial war dance for Chicago residents, a final good-bye ceremony that few people in attendance would ever forget. Seven or eight hundred braves, dressed in nothing but strips of loincloth with their faces painted vermillion, black, and yellow, danced through the town to the rhythmic beat of tom-toms. One of the men in attendance, Indian historian John Caton, described the scene:

> They were principally armed with tomahawks and war clubs . . . stopping in front of every house they passed, where they performed some extra exploits. The warriors had now wrought themselves into a perfect frenzy. The morning was very warm, and the perspiration was pouring from them in streams. Their eyes were wild and blood-shot. Their countenances had assumed an expression

of all the worst passions which can find a place in the breast of a savage; fierce anger, terrible hate, dire revenge, remorseless cruelty, all were expressed in their terrible features. Their tomahawks were thrown and brandished about in every direction . . . and with every gesture they uttered the most frightful yells, in every imaginable key and note. The dance . . . consisted of leaps and spasmodic steps, now forward and now back and sideways, with the whole body distorted into every imaginable unnatural position.[40]

It has been said that many of the those fortunate enough to see the spectacle feared it might be another Fort Dearborn Massacre in the making, but it ended peacefully, with most of the participants collapsing in utter fatigue on the grassy lawn of the fort.

As he headed home, Ogden probably spent many hours on the deck of the steamer in quiet reflection, listening to the waves lap against the side of the boat and thinking about how he wanted to spend the rest of his life. In a brief stay, he had made a lot of money; however, he made plenty of money in Walton, too. Perhaps not as much, but certainly enough to live a comfortable, contented life. No, if he came back to Chicago, it wouldn't be for the money alone; it would also be for the challenge and the adventure, two of the most magnetic pulls on him.

Ogden spent the winter of 1835–36 at home in Walton with his family. He devoted a great deal of time thinking about the new adventure, and he had long conversations with family and friends about his plans. His biggest concern had been his immediate family, but they made that part of the decision easy. His mother Abigail promised to join him in Chicago as soon as he had built a suitable residence for them, and younger sister Frances, twelve, would naturally accompany her mother. Caroline, nineteen, decided to stay in Walton with relatives for the time; but eventually she too ended up in Chicago, marrying William E. Jones, one of Ogden's early real estate partners. Mahlon decided to make the move, as he had been captivated by the opportunities he saw in the Northwest when he accompanied Butler on their trip. Emily was due to be married later that year to Nelson Knox Wheeler, who had a solid law practice in Delaware County, so she remained in Walton. And Eliza had already moved with her husband, Charles Butler, to New York City.[41]

Ogden went to New York to visit Charles and Eliza in their new home. Butler and Arthur Bronson assured him that there was plenty of ready capital available for investment in the Northwest, and they would continue to funnel money to him in Chicago. Bronson did raise a cautionary note. The deteriorating state of the nation's monetary policy and President Jackson's disapproval of the easy credit policies in effect could spell trouble, he warned. He cautioned Ogden to be watchful.

While in the city, Ogden purchased the two fire engines and one thousand feet of fire hose the Chicago town board had authorized and put them on a steamer headed through the Erie Canal, destined for Chicago.

Ogden returned to Walton. Two letters dated in late 1835, one received by Ogden and one sent by him, reveal an important but little-known facet of his life.[42] A letter from fellow Delaware County Assembly member Dubois Burhans was addressed to "William B. Ogden, Esquire," the latter word used when addressing a member of the bar. Another letter, this one written by Ogden, indicated he represented a client in a legal matter. At some point, probably in the early to mid-1830s, William Ogden had been admitted to the New York bar. He had not done the requisite seven-year internship in a law office generally required to practice law; however, it was not uncommon for a man with political or business connections to gain admittance in that way. This was undoubtedly what Ogden had done; so more than a dozen years after he had been forced to give up his pursuit of a legal career, he had achieved the goal after all. He would also be admitted to the bar in Illinois years later via the same route.

As Ogden made preparations to leave Walton, he took stock of the family's assets. He sold some of their properties and retained others. As for the many sawmills and woolen mills they owned, it is unclear what he held and what he sold. There is a clue in an 1840 letter Ogden wrote from Chicago to attorney Nelson Wheeler in Walton. It states that Ogden is owed a substantial amount of money from a number of Walton companies, indicating that he had held onto some of the family's businesses in that town.

In any event, it is clear that the Ogdens began their new life in Chicago in solid financial condition. However, they would soon discover, as would millions of other Americans, just how temporal material wealth could be.

5

The Benevolence of the Butcher

Three factors, in addition to location, turned Chicago into the leading city of the Midwest and one of the nation's great urban centers: money, men, and railroads.[1] The last would not arrive until two decades after the nascent city began to develop, but the first two were required to get it started.

Chicago certainly had location going for it. That and a liberal national credit policy in the early 1830s were enough to allow William Ogden and others to entice Eastern men of wealth to invest heavily in the town during its infancy. Ogden's brother-in-law Charles Butler, among the most successful of these men with his American Land Company, held property in Illinois, Michigan, Ohio, and throughout the Southern cotton-belt states. The primary goal of Butler and other speculators was not to populate the new frontier, or to foster community development; it was to make a profit for themselves and their investors.

The practice of these speculators—buying government land meant for settlement and then holding it off the market for appreciation—came under heavy criticism in the 1830s and 1840s. But as one speculator of the era said, "If it is wrong to over-bid a settler for a piece of public land, the fault is with those who, by legislation, have ordered lands sold to the highest bidder."[2] Some modern-day economic historians have also decried the practices of Butler and his partners. Paul Gates, in *History of Public Land Law Development*, charged, "American Land Company . . . did nothing to enhance the value except to advertise their lands. . . . It did not identify itself with the welfare of the communities where the lands were located and was a monopoly to the local people."[3]

Much of the criticism, both current and past, is based on the charge that American Land Company's investors and officers were prominent Democrats, men of high political influence, and bankers who were playing loose with federal funds deposited in their banks. Another economist, John Haeger, observed, "Early political attacks portrayed it [the American Land Company] as a voracious octopus grabbing available agricultural land away from farmers." However, Haeger points out, much of that kind of talk was simply political rhetoric by the opposition Whig Party. "The firm was not a conspiracy of Van Buren Democrats to monopolize the public domain. [It] was a business firm which brought together capitalists—some Democratic, some Whig—to make money."[4]

Butler's company was so often singled out for criticism because it was very open about who its investors and directors were, while most other land investment firms kept that information a carefully guarded secret. Even Gates acknowledged that fact, writing that the American Land Company was more vulnerable because the company operated out in the open and on such a large scale. That was Charles Butler's influence.[5]

Although the American Land Company was William Ogden's largest real estate client, Ogden himself was a voracious speculator in Chicago land. It's important to separate Ogden from the Eastern speculators he represented. Economic historian Gates's charge that speculators did nothing to enhance the Midwestern land they purchased was true in the case of most of the Eastern moneymen, but it did not apply to Ogden. He improved the Chicago land he purchased in almost every case before reselling it, contributing significantly to the growth and betterment of the community.

Despite the motives and methods of the Eastern speculators, the money they poured into the Midwest and South, and their self-serving promotion of their investments, did much to grease the skids of Western expansion. Eighteenth-century Scottish economist Adam Smith could have had a town like Chicago in mind when he penned his landmark study, *An Inquiry into the Nature and Causes of the Wealth of Nations*. His theory that the self-interest of individuals ultimately promotes the public interest was never more tested—nor more proven—than in the crucible of early Chicago.

Capital alone, however, cannot build a city. Men of vision, initiative, and perseverance who not only put their money to work but also their hands, their backs, their brains, and their souls are also vital. Chicago attracted these men in spades: William B. Ogden, Gurdon Hubbard, the Kinzie clan, John Wright, Walter Newberry, J. Young Scammon, Cyrus McCormick, Marshall Field, Philip Armour, Potter Palmer, Gustavus Swift, George Pullman, and Louis Sullivan, to name only a few.

These men were the sort that historian Edward Wolner referred to as "imperial city builders." They had a vision for Chicago and were willing to risk everything to make it reality. Their prospects were tied to the city's prospects, and they knew it. As Adam Smith wrote, "It is not from the benevolence of the butcher, the brewer, or the baker, that we can expect our dinner, but from their regard to their own interest."[6] Some of them became known as "boosters," and boosterism is as fundamental a nineteenth-century Chicago phenomenon as the Great Chicago Fire. The boosters blurred the lines between business, politics, and philanthropy, and the three strands became one strong, intertwined cord that bound the city together. Historian Kathleen McCarthy observed, "These men built the city; every aspect of its growth and health was as familiar to them as the lists of their investments. . . . The rite of succoring the poor, like luring new settlers or bargaining for a new transportation route, was merely another component in their overall drive to ensure the city's continued social and economic viability."[7]

Although the boosters' private interests and the city's public interests were often congruent, they just as often involved intolerable conflicts of interest, the sad result of which the city simply learned to endure during its fledgling years. Perhaps what they did was exactly what had to be done to raise a city out of a swamp, a city that eminent Chicago historian Bessie Louise Pierce called the "most American of American cities."[8]

What is undeniable about these two classes of men, the speculators and the boosters, is that they laid the foundation upon which Chicago is built. John Maynard Keynes called risk-taking and innovation the "beasts of capitalism." Chicago had both in abundance. Any number of towns could have done the same, had the right set of circumstances occurred. Michigan City, Indiana, is an excellent example.

Just forty miles east of the Chicago Loop, at the mouth of Trail Creek on Lake Michigan's southeastern shore, Michigan City was incorporated in 1836. Trail Creek's flowing waters afforded good locations for gristmills and lumber mills, and early settlers envisioned a bustling harbor at the creek's mouth. By the time of its incorporation, the town was already home to nearly three thousand people and was a stopping point for stagecoaches. While Chicago was to be the terminus of the Illinois and Michigan Canal, Michigan City held the same distinction with the Michigan Road, a planned, 260-mile road to run from Lake Michigan to the Ohio River. So for all intents and purposes, the two towns began their race for greatness neck-and-neck. Kenosha, Wisconsin, had many of the same attributes as its upstate rivals, Milwaukee and Fort Howard (Green Bay). Milwaukee, founded and incorporated about the same time as Chicago, was actually served by two rivers, the Menomonee and the Milwaukee, and both put the sad little Chicago River to shame. Yet despite the promise of these and other towns along the shores of Lake Michigan and the dreams of their early founders that they would become *the* hub between East and West, it was Chicago that won out.

Chicago became Chicago because it possessed all the vital ingredients: money, men, and railroads. And one man, William B. Ogden, had a deep footprint in all three of these crucial spheres. Perhaps more than anyone else, Ogden epitomizes the image in Carl Sandburg's immortal description in his poem "Chicago":

Hog Butcher of the World,
Tool Maker, Stacker of Wheat,
Player with Railroads and the Nation's Freight Handler.[9]

In the summer of 1836, William and Mahlon Ogden steamed down Lake Michigan aboard the *Pennsylvania*. To the west, like a giant green pincushion, rose the Green Bay Peninsula, today the Door Peninsula, the rugged thumb of land that shelters Green Bay from Lake Michigan. While sea gulls flapped noisily behind their boat screeching for scraps of food, perhaps William told Mahlon the story of his visit to the Wisconsin area the previous year.

One spectacle marveled at by everyone who passed down the lake was the small group of islands at the northern tip of the peninsula that the French had named the *Porte des Morts Passage*, or "door to the way of death." The splintered hulks of a number of unfortunate ships lay scattered on the rocks as mute testament to the accuracy of the warning. Further south along the seventy-five-mile-long peninsula were the magnificent apple and cherry orchards the Potawatomi Indians had planted before they were banished to reservations in the West only a few years earlier. If the *Pennsylvania* was close enough to land, the Ogden brothers might have seen a few of the orchards, now untended but still awash in gentle white and pink blossoms. Although it was impossible for the men to see across the peninsula and the bay to the mainland, William must have recalled the huge, dense forests of pine and hardwood he had seen on his cruise down the bay to Fort Howard, a real lumberman's paradise.

When the Ogden brothers arrived at the Chicago harbor, it was probably hot and muggy, as most June days were on Lake Michigan, and what little breeze there was served only to stir up the natural stench of the place. It certainly didn't smell as sweet as the North Branch of the Delaware.

At the beginning of 1836, despite its promise, Chicago was not without its problems. In fact during those early years, the town probably experienced more problems than any other town of comparable size. But there was also progress. An article from the December 9 edition of the *Chicago Democrat* recorded these impressive figures: "The population of Chicago, according to the latest census is 3279. There are 44 stores (dry goods, hardware and groceries,) 2 book stores, 4 druggists, 2 silversmiths and jewelers, 2 tin and copper manufactories, 2 printing offices, 2 breweries, 1 steam saw mill, 1 iron foundry, 4 storage and forwarding houses, 3 taverns, 1 lottery office, 1 bank, 5 churches, 7 schools, 22 lawyers, 14 physicians, a lyceum and a reading room." If nothing more could be said for the condition of the town at the time, at least its churches and schools outnumbered its taverns four-to-one. Three years earlier it had been three-to-nothing in favor of the taverns.

The brothers checked into the newly opened Lake House, where they stayed at least for a short time while construction began on William's North Side house.[10]

The Lake House sat on the north side of the river, facing the brightly white-washed stockade and outbuildings of Fort Dearborn on the south side. The fort sat amid neatly trimmed grassy lawns and sheltering honey locust trees, presenting a picture of tranquility that belied its bloody past. To the east sat the large residence of the Kinzie family. Their huge lawn sloped gently toward the river, rimmed by wildflowers, and four large Lombardy poplars shaded the house. Had it not been for the smell and the swill drifting by on the sluggish current of the Chicago River, it would have been a scene worthy of an Asher B. Durand landscape painting.

Very soon after his arrival in Chicago, William Ogden sparked a new friend-ship. Harriet Martineau, the very attractive British writer and feminist, was visiting the town during that period. In *Reminiscences of Early Chicago*, Mabel McIlvaine writes: "There was a 'fancy fair' given in Martineau's honor; and Mr. Jones [Chicagoan Fernando Jones] used to speak of going with his sister to meet Miss Martineau at the home of William B. Ogden."[11] Assuming the accuracy of this statement, Ogden must have had a temporary house built shortly after his arrival. His permanent home, Ogden Grove, was not completed until the end of 1836, and Miss Martineau's visit occurred during the summer. Arthur Bronson had had a "quickie" house built for him on his 1833 visit; William and Mahlon may have done the same thing.

Despite the pleasurable distraction of the beautiful and charming journalist, Ogden went right to work. He established the Ogden Land and Trust Agency to manage and oversee his properties and those of his investors, and he opened a small office on Kinzie Street near State Street. He hired a diligent young man, William Larrabee, to assist him as a clerk and bookkeeper.[12] When he began to sell the rest of the land he and Butler had earlier purchased, he discovered the prices had risen by about 300 percent just since his last visit. Due to the federal government's recent opening of the frontier and the building of the Il-linois and Michigan Canal, speculative interest in Midwest land bordered on insanity. Craziness, utter craziness, Ogden probably thought to himself; and he continued to sell more of their land at a huge profit. He also carefully began purchasing more land. The warning of the shrewd Arthur Bronson to be cau-tious was the only factor that kept Ogden from becoming part of the buying frenzy that surrounded him.

From the beginning, Ogden began actively soliciting capital from Eastern investors and making purchasing decisions in their behalf.[13] While Charles Butler's American Land Company would remain his largest client and he even-tually did a lot of business with the wealthy Bronson family, he would ultimately service nearly one hundred other clients as well.

Ogden was torn between the madness of the market and the caution Bronson had entreated. To one of his Eastern investors, he wrote that his North Side property could be resold for at least 400 percent more than he had paid for it and probably "600 to 800 per cent & possibly over a thousand percent."[14] But to another he advised caution, saying the man should not base his expectations on the experience Ogden and Butler had enjoyed.[15]

Ogden was not the only land agent at work in the town. Gurdon Hubbard had been hired by Edward and Samuel Russell of New York to buy and sell in their behalf; and the Bronsons had initially hired Walter Newberry as their land agent.[16] Newberry had met Bronson when Bronson and Butler first visited Chicago and Bronson hired him to handle his original North Side purchase. As the agent for the deal, Newberry made a large profit when Butler, Ogden, and others purchased the land from Bronson the following year. But Newberry was not happy with the 400 percent profit, feeling the land could have been sold for more. In an 1835 letter to a friend, he wrote, "Arthur Bronson has been a perfect marplot in every thing relating to this place. He has had it in his power to make a quarter of a million out of this town had it not been for his timidity." He concluded, "I can't help censuring a man when he acts like an ass."[17] Newberry was correct, as proven by Ogden's sale of the same land for a much higher price. However, since he had been merely the agent for the deal, there was nothing Newberry could do but acquiesce to Bronson.

The structure of the American Land Company provides a good model of how mid-1830s Eastern investors were taking advantage of Western land speculation. Established in 1835, the company was capitalized at one million dollars and managed by a board of trustees, with Butler at its head. From the beginning, Butler's company had the support and participation of the wealthy Bronson family. Their New York Life Insurance and Trust Company had massive liquid funds available for investment. Most speculative purchases at the time were not paid in full; a fractional down payment was made, with the remainder due at some future date. The land itself was pledged as collateral against the loan. The note would be paid off when the land was resold, generally a relatively short time period, since prices were accelerating at such a dizzying pace.[18] Prior to this time, an investor had to funnel his money through local agents in scattered individual markets; but the American Land Company operated more like today's mutual funds. An investor could buy stock in the company and spread his investment over a number of purchases, thus reducing his risk and administrative participation.

The company still had to appoint local land agents to act in its behalf, as it did with William Ogden in Chicago and throughout Illinois. Agents earned their fees by taking a percentage of the net profit from each transaction, a fee that could go as high as one-third in a large deal. Most of Ogden's purchases for Butler's company and for his own portfolio were in Chicago's North Side and in agricultural property along the route of the Illinois and Michigan Canal, land in which Ogden had a great deal of confidence.

The duties of local land agents were many.[19] They negotiated land sales, checked titles, paid taxes, and periodically inspected the land under their management. The more trusted agents also decided when and for how much to resell properties. Some agents, William Ogden foremost among them, also made decisions about needed improvements on the land and oversaw those activities. Ogden, throughout his entire real estate career, eschewed reselling raw land. He bought unimproved parcels, but he believed that improving the land, perhaps even adding a building or two, increased the selling price exponentially. He was correct, and it earned larger profits for his clients and higher fees for his company. At one point in the late 1830s, while Butler was in Europe recuperating from an illness, he even had Ogden travel south to inspect his company's holdings in cotton lands.[20]

Ogden aggressively advertised his services as a real estate agent and property manager by mailing circulars to prospective Eastern investors, a tactic that paid off handsomely. As more and more new lands in the West began to open up for settlement in the 1830s and 1840s, it became increasingly difficult for Eastern speculators and investors to stay current on local conditions in areas into which they were funneling their money. Thus, little by little, they began to entrust decision making on their investments to men like William Ogden who were on the scene. This represented a subtle shift in both power and leadership in the West that reflected a maturation of Western business communities and their growing economic stability and independence.[21] In Ogden's case, he became the decision maker on almost all the Illinois investments he managed; Charles Butler and Arthur Bronson became hands-off clients.

In other words, the Midwest was beginning to come of age.

Ogden's cozy business relationship with Charles Butler was just one of many familial relationships he actively solicited and maintained throughout his life. In a few cases, as with Butler, the two interacted as equals, but in most of these relationships, Ogden's extended family members served as his executive or managerial employees.

Adam Bellow's groundbreaking book, *In Praise of Nepotism*, defines the practice: "The modern definition of nepotism is favoritism based on kinship, but over time the word's dictionary meaning and its conventional applications have diverged. Most people today define the term very narrowly to mean not just hiring a relative, but hiring one who is grossly incompetent."[22] Most modern economists view nepotism as an obstacle to healthy change in business firms; but that was not always the case. When the English gentry first arrived in this country, they brought their multigenerational customs with them. These included the English inheritance practices of entailment and primogeniture. Both insured that the family's wealth was passed on to only one descendant, usually the eldest son, so that the family's estate remained intact rather than being dispersed. It then became the responsibility of the one inheritor to see to the well-being of the remainder of the family.

After the Revolution, the evolving Brahmin aristocracy in Massachusetts society began to replace these practices by weaving intricate webs of familial, economic, and political ties in pursuit of common interests, which often included arranged marriages to improve a family's power and wealth. But they continued to stress the preservation of family wealth and the responsibility of the chief heir to look out for the family. As descendants of these families made their way west into New York in the eighteenth and nineteenth centuries, they brought this ethos along, hand-in-hand with virtues described by Bellow as "a powerful work ethic, an unwavering sense of vocation, a drive to accumulate wealth, and an impulse to swathe their success in the cloak of public virtue and benevolence."[23]

Well into the nineteenth century, as these members of the elite, or the booster-elite as they were known in Chicago, put their wealth to work in larger enterprises, like mills, canals, roads, and railroads, they required capital that outstripped the resources of any single family. So they began to create testamentary trusts and charitable endowments, instruments that served the public good but also pooled their capital for investments and tightly preserved family fortunes.

Hand-in-hand with these customs went another practice that burgeoned along with the evolution of business. Early New England merchant families formed banks that were simply extensions of their family enterprises in order to raise investment capital. The same principle was repeated in the nineteenth century when emerging railroad corporations formed their own construction companies to build their roads. This "keep the money in the family" attitude was not believed to be corrupt until the practice was abused by the "robber barons" following the Civil War.

So as one looks at William Ogden's penchant to invest with and hire from his extended family, it can be seen as a natural evolution. However, the practice would have detrimental consequences for him as he moved from the insular sphere of Delaware County commerce to the tangled, complex world of international commerce. New worlds meant new rules that Ogden was either blind to, or refused to accept.

One thing he was to change was the centuries-long practice of entailment—preserving family wealth by putting it in the hands of one heir. With no children of his own, Ogden spread his wealth at his death, dividing it among the spouses, children, and grandchildren of his siblings and uncles. He could have chosen to preserve the family's wealth, by leaving it intact to his brother Mahlon's oldest son, but the practice must have held no appeal for him. Had this happened—had Ogden passed his entire fortune on to one person—it is probable that in years to come the Ogden family fortune would have achieved the same magnitude as that of the wealthiest families in America.

On the Fourth of July, 1836, a happy event occurred in Chicago. Amid great fanfare, construction officially began on the Illinois and Michigan Canal. Hundreds of Chicagoans journeyed south to Canalport (later called Bridgeport) by boat, horseback, carriage, and on foot to watch the ceremonial first shovelful of dirt being turned. Speeches, a brass band, a cannon salute, and free lemonade (spiked later in the evening, it was rumored) helped create a celebratory mood. Illinois Supreme Court Justice Theophilus Smith (perhaps after one of the spiked lemonades) leaped atop a barrel, read the Declaration of Independence, and promised that in one hundred years Chicago would be "a city of 100,000!"[24]

Work on the canal began, and thousands of men, many of the same Irishmen who had dug the Erie Canal, began to turn dirt. However, the nation's deepening financial crisis put an end to the work in 1841. It resumed a few years later, and the canal was eventually completed in 1848.

Meanwhile, the Irish workers settled by the thousands in Bridgeport, where the South Branch of the river met the canal, eventually creating the largest Irish settlement in America at the time. Wages for the brutal job of grading, digging, and constructing a canal were low; they varied from sixteen to forty dollars a month for hard, lonely work on an unpopulated prairie. Men worked fourteen hours a day, six days a week, and many died of malaria and cholera. These men were a feisty, belligerent mix of transients, immigrants, and Indians, and rowdy fights with pickaxes and rocks broke out among them frequently.

William Ogden saw an opportunity once the canal began work. Contracts were available for construction work on various legs of the canal, and Ogden, in partnership with a man named Harry Smith, contracted to perform two hundred thousand dollars' worth of work.[25] Smith was also from Walton, New York, and may have been a member of Ogden's extended family. Their contract called for constructing part of the Chicago segment of the canal called the Summit Division. The South Branch of the Chicago River was wide and deep enough to serve as the canal for its first five and a half miles. From there new diggings would proceed twenty-nine miles further to Lockport, where the first lock would be built. Ogden and Smith's contract was to begin at the point where the first dredging of the river was required.[26]

This venture did not pan out profitably for the two men due to the gathering economic storm. The State of Illinois, on the verge of bankruptcy by the late 1830s, suspended payments to its contractors. Many, like Ogden and Smith, attempted to continue the work, paying the bills out of their own pockets in hopes of eventually receiving their compensation; but soon they were all forced to stop the work.

Over the years, Ogden would show little patience with the dirt-poor immigrants who began streaming into Chicago in the late 1830s. He was the largest landowner in the city, and these "poor and vicious foreigners" often illegally squatted on his land. As an additional irritant, they cut down his timber to build their shanties.[27] History recorded a number of hostile run-ins between Ogden and the immigrants in years to come.

Despite his penchant for crossing swords with the immigrants, there were occasional exceptions. One was Michael Hoffman, one of the city's earliest German immigrants, who had been left penniless by the Panic of 1837. Hoffman had come to America as a twenty-four-year-old in 1836. He secured work on a digging crew on the canal—perhaps one of Ogden's crews—and during the winter months he peddled water on the streets of the city. In 1840, sensing something special in the young man who was then unemployed, Ogden hired him to work around his house and boarded the man in his home. After about five years, Hoffman got married and moved into his own home, continuing to work as a gardener. Ogden helped him purchase a nice piece of property on the North Side, and he subsequently bought additional land throughout the city. Hoffman became one of the leaders in the German community and developed a solid reputation for the generosity of his benevolent works.[28]

Despite the progress in the little city, it was difficult to ignore the swirling currents and eddies surrounding the country's shaky monetary policy (discussed more fully in chapter 6). The uncertainty did convince Ogden to move even more judiciously; however, it was not in his nature to be too conservative. Like most socially conscious entrepreneurs of his generation—the booster-elite—Ogden was willing to invest money in any kind of venture, as long as it promised profit or provided civic benefit that would enhance his land investments.

He joined with other local moneymen in the formation of a steamboat company to deliver passengers, freight, and mail between Chicago and other Lake Michigan ports.[29] The company was capitalized at two hundred thousand dollars, and two-thirds of the stock was subscribed almost immediately, Ogden personally investing five thousand dollars. The remainder was sold by early 1838, and the company was officially organized as the Chicago and Michigan Steamboat Company, William B. Ogden, President.

Two boats were built, and service was launched, but it did not turn out to be a profitable enterprise. The mail contract was not as large as anticipated, and most of the stock purchasers failed to honor their subscriptions when the Panic of 1837 left them penniless. Ogden and one other investor kept the company afloat for a while, literally and figuratively, but finally, in 1840, they were forced to close it.[30] Ogden wrote to Charles Butler, for whom he had also invested money in the endeavor: "Steamboats I have sold out entirely and have no further debts to pay if further purchasers all pay up and they probably will. If they do our loss is near $6000 . . . a pretty business indeed!"[31] The civic side benefits to this endeavor were the stimulation of shipbuilding in Chicago and excellent steamboat transportation for residents and visitors for three years.

Into this milieu, Abigail and Frances Ogden arrived in Chicago in late 1836 to join William and Mahlon. William's new house, which he named Ogden Grove, stood on four acres in the center of block 35 in the area known as "Kinzie's Addition," to the north of the river and a few blocks from the lakefront. It was bounded by Rush on the east, Ontario on the south, Cass on the west, and Erie on the north. His near neighbors were Walter Newberry, whom he originally met on the steamer returning from Wisconsin; attorney Isaac Arnold; Judge Mark Skinner; H. H. Magee; and the St. James Episcopal Church. The grounds of all these homes were covered with natural forest, giving the neighborhood a rural, bucolic feeling. Ogden's house and one other mansion nearby stood a mile and a half away from any other houses, virtually isolating it among the forest greenery. He had spent ten thousand dollars building it.[32]

Ogden had recruited New York City architect John M. Van Osdel to design the house, the first one in the town to be professionally designed and built by an architect.[33] When Van Osdel arrived on a steamboat, he brought with him not only the plans for the house but also all the necessary windows, stair rails, and trimmings.

Ogden's block was covered with maple, cottonwood, oak, ash, cherry, elm, birch, and hickory trees, with his house in the center. Arnold described it as "a large double house built of wood." The front of the house featured a broad piazza, supported by pillars, which fronted on Ontario Street. Arnold described the remainder of the property: "On the northeast . . . was a conservatory always bright and gay with flowers, also, fruit houses consisting of a cold grapery and a forcing house in which he raised exotic grapes, peaches, apricots and figs. The natural forest, festooned with the wild grape, the American ivy, and other wild wines; and everywhere were ornamental shrubs, climbing roses, and other flowers." Inside, there was an extensive library and a number of paintings and engravings by well-known artists. Despite the money obviously spent on the home and furnishings, Arnold said, there was "no lavish or vulgar exhibition of wealth, no ostentatious or pretentious display."[34]

Perhaps because he was single, Ogden loved to entertain, and his home became a focal point of Chicago society. He was a lover of good books—he *read* them, not simply collected them—and before the Great Fire, he was said to have one of the most extensive libraries in the city. He also loved music, painting, and poetry. Arnold wrote, "He was never more attractive than in his library reciting the poetry of Bryant, Halleck, Holmes, Burns, Moore and Scott; or at his piano playing an accompaniment to his own voice as he sang with expression, if not with artistic skill, the ballads of Burns and Moore."[35]

Another focal point in the North Side neighborhood was the brand new St. James Episcopal Church. A biography of the church described the North Side environs at that time: "Rather than a city scene, there was around it an air of open space and an unfinished quality. The feeling of frontier prairie was still in the place, and although the hustle and bustle of commercial life were fast increasing, the neighborhood was countrified. . . . Even by 1853 . . . the North Side was a lovely homelike place . . . the large grounds, and beautiful shade trees about so many residences gave a sense of space, rest, flowers, sunshine and shadows that hardly belongs nowadays to the idea of a city."[36]

In early 1837, the church was the site of a special event for the Ogden family. Mahlon Ogden had met a young lady, Henrietta Kasson of Columbus, Ohio, and they were married at St. James, with the Reverend Isaac Hallam presiding. William Ogden and his mother were members of St. James, as were many of the most prominent people in the city, including Gurdon Hubbard and John Harris Kinzie.

A few months later, in the same church, Mahlon introduced his brother to another lawyer with whom he had become acquainted, Isaac Newton Arnold. Arnold later remembered his first impression of the man who became his lifelong friend. "As we waited for [Ogden] to come out of the church after service, it seemed that he had a kind word and friendly greeting for every man, woman and child in the congregation. He was evidently a great favorite . . . and everybody stopped to shake hands with him and welcome him home."[37] Later

St. James Episcopal Church on Chicago's North Side, where the Ogdens worshipped.

that year, Mahlon Ogden entered a law partnership with Arnold, and the firm of Arnold, Ogden and Company began handling all of William Ogden's legal affairs in Chicago.

Arnold, like the Ogdens, was from upstate New York, the tiny village of Hartwick, about nine miles west of Cooperstown.[38] During his college days at Hartwick Seminary and Academy (today Hartwick College) he became a dedicated abolitionist. He was admitted to the New York State bar in 1835, and the following year he relocated to Chicago.

Although the Ogdens had been permanent residents of Chicago for only a year, they already felt a part of the community. As William Ogden was to soon discover, they were more deeply integrated into Chicago society than they realized.

6

Mister Mayor

At Chicago's first election of trustees after his arrival, Ogden was elected to the town board.[1] Board members were concerned that their legal designation as the "Town of Chicago" no longer reflected the size and stature of their growing community. A committee, including Ogden, was appointed to study the matter. It petitioned the state legislature, and on March 4, 1837, Chicago received a city charter. From north to south, the new city extended from North Avenue to 22nd Street, and from the shore of Lake Michigan west to Wood Street. The charter also created a mayor and city council system of government, so an election was scheduled for the first Tuesday of May to elect the first mayor and council of the City of Chicago.

Along with his furniture and personal possessions, Ogden had shipped his favorite riding horse, Paddy, to Chicago from Walton. In early April 1837, he and Paddy likely cantered from his house on the North Side down muddy, rutted Dearborn Street, clip-clopped across the floating three-hundred-foot wooden Dearborn Street drawbridge, and stopped in front of Cook's Coffee House on the southeastern corner of Dearborn and Lake Street. Draymen rattled by, their low wagons piled high with goods, and the muddy street bustled with men and women carefully picking their way across, trying to avoid the wagons, horse droppings, and mud puddles. The small building had been one of the town's earliest hotels but was now a favorite gathering place for town leaders.

Ogden went inside and entered a small room facing Lake Street. A light but cold breeze was blowing off the lake, and the white curtains at the open window billowed out like a spinnaker. There were three other men present. Francis Sherman, from Connecticut, had a prosperous brick-making business and was running for the new city's common council in the first ward. Ogden had met him during his first visit.[2] Peter Pruyne owned the town's drugstore and was running as a Democrat for the state legislature.[3] Then there was "Long John" Wentworth, all six feet, six inches of him, the editor of the town's first newspaper, the *Chicago Democrat*.[4]

Wentworth was at once both Bunyanesque and Runyonesque, huge in stature and just as large and colorful in life. He was one of those characters that Chicago became famous for, and if he hadn't already existed, some creative journalist would have invented him. It was said of Wentworth that he had walked into Chicago barefoot, boots in his hand, so they wouldn't get caked with mud. Over his shoulder was slung a jug of whiskey to bathe his sore feet. He hailed from Sandwich, New Hampshire, and it was said that he didn't have a humble bone in his body.[5]

All four men had one thing in common: they were Democrats in a town that was fast becoming Whig territory.[6] Wentworth got right to the point. He told Ogden the men would like to run him for mayor of Chicago. Though Ogden had only been in town for a little over a year, this was a city of newcomers like himself. He disliked politics, but he realized that politics and business were inexorably intertwined on this Western frontier, and it would be to his benefit to be the city's first mayor.

The Whigs would be running John Harris Kinzie, son of one of the town's earliest settlers.[7] Kinzie was a good man, but he believed Chicago would be best served by building more plank roads out into the countryside. The other men were all convinced the "iron horse" was Chicago's future. Wentworth vowed he would throw the support of the *Democrat* behind Ogden's candidacy. It's likely he warned them that T. O. Davis, owner of the *Chicago American*, the town's second newspaper, would back his fellow Whig, Kinzie.

When Ogden accepted the men's offer, they laid out a bare-bones strategy for the next four weeks.[8] Most municipal elections were ideologically nonpartisan; the parties sought victory primarily to enjoy the spoils that went to the winner and his friends. The Whigs promptly dubbed Kinzie "the first born of Chicago,"[9] a campaign slogan they were confident would insure his election. That it was untrue was but a minor point. Kinzie did have the backing of most of the "Old Settlers," as the old-timers were known, including the popular and influential Gurdon Hubbard. He had served as the second president of the town board, ran a successful hardware and variety store, and had been popular years earlier with the fur traders, the Fort Dearborn crowd, and the Indians. At first blush, it appeared the Whigs had a big edge.

Fortunately, time was too short and relationships too tight in the small city to make this the kind of acrid political race for which Chicago later became infamous. The Whigs did take one serious shot at Ogden in the *American*, calling him "a transient speculator," a strategy that ultimately backfired.[10]

There were six wards in the city, thus six polling places. Three inspectors were appointed for each.[11] Voting was done *viva voce*, with each person approaching the table where the votes were recorded and announcing his choice for all to hear.[12] When the final tally was made, Ogden won handily, 489–217. He had won the count in all six wards, even Kinzie's own ward, where he won by one vote. However, future friends J. Young Scammon and Walter Newberry both cast their ballots for the losing Kinzie.[13] The vote count was low in part because only men could vote and also because many of them were newcomers and had yet to take a civic interest.

Long John Wentworth was still repeating one story about election day more than forty years later. Wentworth was a young man at the time, but it seems he appeared even younger. When he went to cast his vote, one of the inspectors at his polling place charged him with being under twenty-one years of age and thus ineligible to vote. After some effort, and perhaps with the aid of some other men who knew him, he convinced the inspector he was of legal age.[14]

On May 3, 1837, William B. Ogden took the oath of office as the first mayor of the City of Chicago: "I do hereby swear that I will support the Constitution of the United States, the constitution of the State of Illinois, and I will fully discharge the duties of the office of Mayor for the City of Chicago according to the best of my abilities."[15]

Early government in Chicago was a mishmash. In 1833 there were eight major and nineteen minor rump governments in the town, each with its own officials and state-approved powers. By 1837 the system had been simplified, but there were still two major governing bodies, the board of trustees, a holdover from township days, and the mayor and common council, created under the city charter. This first term for Mayor Ogden and the Chicago Common Council members was for only ten months to allow the date of the next election to catch up with the effective date of the city charter. Thereafter, mayors and aldermen served a full one-year term. Although the mayor held somewhat more power than the president of the trustees, it was not the absolute power that later mayors would wield.[16]

On his first days in office, Mayor Ogden began to take stock of his new domain. Population was 4,170, and they were an industrious lot. Each person was required to list his or her occupation on the city census, and only one man identified himself as a "loafer."[17] Chicago was now a city and had a good mix of merchants to serve its residents. There was a brand-new harbor; a channel had been cut through the sandbar that divided the Chicago River and Lake Michigan to aid navigation, and the city was on its way to becoming an important Western port. Construction on the Illinois and Michigan Canal, with its northern terminus in Chicago, was under way. New capital to expand the infrastructure had so far been readily available. Finally, there was a "can do" attitude that would have been the envy of any fledgling community.

Unfortunately, Ogden never finished his list, nor did he have a chance to balance it with some entries on the negative side of the ledger. Scarcely one week after his election, the bottom fell out of Chicago's world and that of the United

States as well. It was known as the Panic of 1837, and it was the young nation's most serious depression yet. The panic was caused by a number of factors, chief among them the long-running feud between President Andrew Jackson and the president of the Second Bank of the United States, Nicholas Biddle, and the steps they took to counter one another.[18]

The early 1830s had been a time of expansion and prosperity. The government opened up vast tracks of Western land for sale, spurring a frenzy of speculative buying. The huge volume of cash that was raised, along with all the other money in the U.S. Treasury, was deposited in Biddle's bank. But in 1833, because of fraud and corruption in the privately owned bank, Jackson had all the federal funds removed from it and redeposited in state banks.

With so much money coming in, state banks and wildcat banks grew rapidly, adopting reckless credit policies and fueling even more rampant speculation. A giant economic bubble was created. In July 1836, in order to curb the speculative fever, President Jackson issued an executive order called the Specie Circular that mandated all government land offices to accept only gold and silver specie, or coinage, for land sales. Since state banks did not have adequate specie backing, land sales immediately plunged and speculators began defaulting on their payments. What little gold and silver there was that was not being hoarded began to flow from Eastern banks to the West to continue the land-buying boom.

Banks were clearly in trouble, and some began to close. Others stopped making new loans altogether and called in existing ones; and credit contracted across the nation. Depositors rushed to their local banks to withdraw their funds. Finally, in May 1837, the bubble burst when every New York bank stopped payment in specie, and banks across the nation followed suit. Ultimately, 40 percent of the nation's banks failed, and another 10 percent faltered.

In Chicago, Ogden and his constituents were thunderstruck. Real estate prices plummeted and Eastern capital instantly dried up. Land that had been valued at one thousand dollars before the collapse was now worth fifty, yet the speculator's debt on the near-worthless property did not decrease. For Ogden's ten-month-long first term, only a small handful of records exist in the Illinois Regional Archives, but they paint a picture of a brand-new city in dire financial straits. The Treasurer's Report of May 17, 1837, indicates that the town treasury turned over $2,947 to the new city treasury, from which $954 had to be paid out for bills due.[19] That left Ogden and his aldermen with a budget of $1,993. It appears the city's only funding sources were property taxes and business licenses, and those would apparently not be due again until the following year. Other than that bleak news, and because of it, the extant records reveal only a few actions taken by the mayor and the common council.

On May 9, a committee appointed by the earlier town council to study the condition of the Dearborn Street bridge reported, "we believe that the same may be repaired so as to be done without much delay . . . with an outlay of from eight hundred to one thousand dollars."[20] No further record states what action, if any, was taken; but since the job would have demanded half of the city's resources, it was probably not undertaken. In the early days of cities like Chicago it was not uncommon for the residents themselves to pitch in and do the work, with donated supplies, on such projects. Two days later, a similar report on the "North Bridge over the North Branch" also warned of necessary repairs, and this action was passed. However, no specific dollar amount was included in the report.[21]

In early Chicago, the biggest threat was fire. The entire city was built of lumber, and the buildings huddled together like frightened sheep. A fire would be disastrous. In late May, an ordinance was passed with a number of dos and don'ts for the citizenry: "No ashes . . . shall be kept or deposited in any part of the City, unless the same be in a close and secure metallic or earthen receptacle . . . under the penalty of three dollars for each offense."[22] The same subject spurred more action in July. The previous month the council had requested a loan of twenty-five thousand dollars from the state—"Denied"[23]—but they now moved forward with the purchase of two fire engines anyway. In a July 5 letter to the supplier, Seely and Porter of Rochester, New York, Mayor Ogden wrote in spectacular understatement, "would not larger wheels . . . be better for us as our streets are not paved and are often muddy."[24]

The company's response promised, "we have now finished 2 of our Best fire engines which you can have at a moment's notice—the wheels of these engines are wider on the tread than usual & will suit your muddy streets." In response to Ogden's request for a discount, Seely and Porter said, "we'll deduct one per cent if payable in the city of New York—this is the Best we possibly can do."[25]

Other "important" issues decided or discussed during Ogden's term involved the relief of the city's poor, which the common council decided was the county's problem; an ordinance to restrain and punish drunkards and vagrants; and an ordinance concerning disorderly houses of ill fame: "Any person guilty of open lewdness or other notorious act of public indecency tending to debauch the public morals . . . shall be fined in the sum of twenty five dollars."[26]

During his term, Ogden also appointed the first permanent board of health in the city, oversaw the election of the board of school inspectors, and authorized the city's first census. According to an early history of Chicago, the population of the new city was collared into a relatively small area:

> The inhabited portion of Chicago [in 1837] consisted chiefly of Kinzie Street on the North Side with a few scattered residences on Clark, Dearborn, Wolcott and Rush; on Lake and South Water Streets on the South Side; and on those portions of Clark, Dearborn and LaSalle streets between South Water and Washington

streets there were small farm houses surrounded by gardens. State and Madison Street was then way out in the country. The West Side was more sparsely settled and plover and snipe abounded from Clinton Street to Union Park.[27]

As mayor, Ogden authorized the issuance of city scrip to be used for all the city's internal transactions in order to keep the commercial wheels spinning. A "we're all in this together" mentality developed that helped the city weather the storm for the next five years. Given the hard times and the fact that his term was only ten months, Ogden's achievements as mayor were necessarily limited. Without a doubt, his most significant contribution to the city occurred in the fall of 1837.[28]

The dockets of both the municipal and circuit courts were jammed. The city was full of debtors, and they were nervous—how would they pay off their debts when the property that backed them was now worth only a pittance? It was said there were lawsuits worth two million dollars against citizens of the city, much of it against some of the area's earliest pioneers. Ogden later wrote about the situation to a friend in New York: "The town's ancient dynasty have mostly fallen. . . . it seems as if there was scarce one left to escape the blight and mildew of 1836."[29] It was, nineteenth-century Chicago historian A. T. Andreas said in marked understatement, "a time of great pecuniary distress."[30]

A bitter fight developed between those who wanted all debts to be repudiated and those who believed the debtors should stand behind their obligations. The state legislature had just established a superior court, and it was to convene in Chicago for the first time that winter to take up the issue. Those favoring repudiation called a meeting in Chicago; their goal was to have the superior court session suspended so they could appeal directly to the legislature for a new law that would release them from their obligations. Chicago was a tinderbox, and unless something was done, Ogden's term as mayor could witness a bloodbath in the streets.[31]

The night of the public meeting arrived. It was held at a wood-framed hotel, the New York House, on the north side of Lake Street near Wells, in the long, low dining room. Despite heavy snow falling outside, the room was filled with men and women sitting on benches and straight-back chairs, their angry faces dimly lit by tallow candles surrounding the room. Chairing the meeting, state senator Peter Pruyne stood at the wooden lectern banging his fist for order. Those who favored repudiation, including their leader, state supreme court judge Theophilus Smith, sat on one side of the room; their opponents, far fewer in number, including J. Young Scammon, Isaac Arnold, and Mahlon Ogden, sat on the other side. There was very little talk across the aisle, save for a few angry exchanges.

When there was order, the meeting began. James Curtiss rose to speak in favor of repudiation. A politician and former lawyer who had given up the practice of law, he thundered his message at the crowd, ending by saying, "No one will be benefited by the forced collection of these debts but the lawyers."

To argue for staying the course, attorney E. G. Ryan took the podium. The large, broad-shouldered Irishman challenged Curtiss's arguments point by point, pounding the lectern and scolding the repudiators. In closing, he pointed directly at Curtiss, and spitting the words at him like a man proclaiming a curse, cried, "Demagogues and designing men you all are, and if this is the kind of lawyer you expect will save you, you are in for a long and bitter winter of regret." The entire crowd broke into a chorus of caterwauling, until someone shouted above the din that they should hear from the mayor.

William Ogden strode to the podium. He was a tall man—over six feet—and he rose to his full height as he began to speak. In a calm voice, he admonished the crowd that he too had debts, and that like many of them he had been badly strapped by the unfortunate panic. But, he told them, the bad times would pass, and they would all recover. He painted a verbal picture of the bright future he saw for Chicago and the bountiful financial opportunities that would be available to all but those who dishonored themselves by shirking their obligations. "Conceal your misfortunes," he told the crowd. "Make the best of a very bad time, and avoid the self-fulfilling prophesy of financial doom. Don't commit the folly of proclaiming your own dishonor," he exhorted, pounding the lectern for emphasis, "and above all things, do not tarnish the honor of our infant city."

"The speech created a profound impression, and turned back the tide of repudiation and dishonor which threatened to overwhelm the infant city," the *Chicago Inter Ocean* said years later.[32] Had repudiation occurred, it might well have damaged any future attempts at obtaining funds to expand the city. Ogden, along with many other debtors, quietly weathered the bad years as best they could.

When Mayor Ogden turned the reins of the city over to his replacement, Buckner Morris, in March 1838, it was a big relief to him, as he could now return to his real estate practice. However, there was one additional story of the city government from the period, probably somewhat exaggerated, that reflects just how bad the hard times were. In February 1839, a "people's meeting" was held at the Lyceum Hall to select a People's Choice candidate for the upcoming mayoralty election. The depression was nearing its worst; it was a trying period for the nascent city. Who would want to be mayor at such a time? Apparently, nobody did. But the people selected local merchant Benjamin Raymond as their candidate. Raymond had not sought the nomination and was obviously not pleased when he learned of it.

Ex-mayor William Ogden was chosen to deliver the news to Raymond. He walked down the muddy wooden sidewalk, greeting everyone he passed, until he arrived at 122 Lake Street. He glanced at the painted sign on the window, "B.

W. Raymond, Dry Goods and Groceries," and entered the store. Raymond was standing behind the counter, and Ogden approached, hailing him in greeting. When he told Raymond the purpose of his visit, Raymond "leaped over the counter, [and] knocked Mr. Ogden prostrate with a bolt of factory-cloth." It created a disturbance, so the story went, that shook Lake Street as it had never been shaken before. "Excited citizens came rushing, and everybody wondered where in the world Sam Lowe, High Constable, was, that he should not be on hand when he was wanted." Despite the brouhaha, Raymond eventually agreed to accept the people's nomination, and the following year he was elected Chicago's third mayor. He and Ogden remained friends despite the ruckus.[33]

Many years after the financial panic was over, Long John Wentworth delivered an address before the Sunday Lecture Society. He described what Chicago commerce was like in the late 1830s and early 1840s:

> The banks all failed, and corporations and individuals issued certificates of indebtedness, which were interchanged as currency. States, counties, and cities paid their debts in warrants upon an empty treasury. The canal commissioners paid contractors in scrip, and the contractors paid their laborers in a lesser scrip, redeemable in the scrip of the commissioners.
>
> Nearly every man in Chicago doing business was issuing his individual scrip, and the city abounded with little tickets, such as "Good at our store for ten cents," "Good for a loaf of bread," "Good for a shave," "Good for a drink," etc., etc. When you went out to trade, the trader would look over your tickets, and select such as he could use to the best advantage. The times for a while seemed very prosperous. We had a currency that was interchangeable, and for a time we suffered no inconvenience from it, except when we wanted some specie to pay for our postage. In those days it took 25 cents to send a letter east.
>
> But after a while it was found out that men were over-issuing. The barber had outstanding too many shaves; the baker too many loaves of bread; the saloon-keeper too many drinks, etc., etc. Want of confidence became general. Each man became afraid to take the tickets of another. Some declined to redeem their tickets in any way, and some absconded. And people found out, as is always the case where there is a redundancy of paper money, that they had been extravagant, had bought things they did not need, and had run in debt for a larger amount than they were able to pay.
>
> Of course, nearly everyone failed, and charged his failure upon President Jackson's specie circular. In after times, I asked an old settler, who was a great growler in those days, what effect time had had upon his views of General Jackson's circular. His reply was that General Jackson had spoiled his being a great man. Said he, "I came to Chicago with nothing, failed for $100,000, and could have failed for a million, if he had left the bubble burst in the natural way."[34]

William Ogden was not insulated from the damage. The Ogden Land and Trust Agency had a number of Eastern clients whose loans came due during the depression. Ogden required them to secure their defaulted mortgages with property, realizing that eventually the economy would recover and the land would regain much of its value. He wrote to his brother-in-law and largest client, Charles Butler: "I am sure I am lessening debts on some of last year by taking farms and in other cases I am busy strengthening securities. I have done a great deal in that way already and shall do more. The condition of forfeiture in our bonds works admirably in doing this but the trouble is I have to grant more or less extensions when additional security are given." He continued, "You must not fear of my taking lands where it is not advisable to do so. I have an aversion to doing so except where I know the case is desperate. I have already greatly strengthened securities upon near $110,000 of our most uncertain debts and shall add some $20 to $50,500 more."[35]

While Ogden's real estate firm did not prosper during the Panic of 1837, it was not bled dry either. He owned all of his personal land investments outright, free from encumbrances, and many of his clients did as well, so he was not forced to sell in a falling market. Although the flow of investment capital had slowed to a trickle, it did not evaporate. Ogden was able to find sellers—lots of them—but he was also still able to find a few buyers during the panic.

He continued to counsel his clients to hold on to their land; he assured them Chicago would be among the first Western cities to recover. He told them to improve the land they owned, to build on it. That would insure rent and position the property for a quicker sale when things improved. With so many unemployed in Chicago, he told his clients, cheap labor could easily be found to make those improvements.[36] To one client, he wrote that he could rent his river property if he would construct a warehouse on it at a cost of only $750 to $1,000.[37] To Charles Butler, he wrote he had purchased four lots in two days for only $200 and was able to immediately resell the poorest of the four for $1,000. He joked with Butler, "What would New Yorkers say to this with their notion of Western property now."[38]

As the financial crisis deepened, Ogden became liable for obligations he had incurred by endorsing the financial notes of others. Some were friends, and he could not abandon them or his legal obligation to stand behind their debts. He had already paid out ten thousand dollars for others, and another twenty-five thousand dollars was rapidly coming due.[39] In a letter to a friend, John Coster, he lamented, "I have been obliged already to mortgage nearly all my property & all this when I have not owed a dollar on my own account for the last 2 or 3 years."[40]

Despite the damage done to the real estate market by the Panic of 1837, other businesses sprang up to keep Chicago's economy rolling, though at a much-reduced pace. When his real estate business faltered, Ogden continued to seek other opportunities like the canal contract and the steamship business. One was a particular success.

Chicago's first beer brewers, William Haas and Konrad Sulzer, had arrived in Chicago in 1833 with some small apparatus, a lot of malt, and 150 barrels of ale. When Ogden auctioned off some of his and Butler's land in 1835, the two German immigrants purchased a one-hundred- by two-hundred-foot lot from him and established the Haas and Sulzer Brewery. They built a forty- by eighty-foot frame building and began brewing "the finest beer in Chicago."[41]

Despite the town's small population, the business was an immediate success, and the first year's production was six hundred barrels of ale. Water was supplied by an artesian well the men had bored, an idea that Ogden would follow up on years later. In early 1838, Ogden bought Sulzer's interest in the brewery and immediately financed the erection of a larger brewery at Pine (now North Michigan) and Chicago Avenues. East Coast beer was very expensive, and taverns were favorite spots for men to gather and grumble to one another about the sad state of the economy, so the business prospered. Ogden was the silent controlling partner in the brewery, and he handled the finances. He doggedly hounded late-payers and was a tough negotiator when dealing with suppliers. In 1840, ordering four hundred thousand pounds of hops from his New York supplier, he wrote, "My brewery is the only thing that makes money without trouble."[42]

In 1839 Haas sold his interest to English immigrant William Lill. Another German immigrant, Michael Diversey, rented space in the brewery to operate a dairy—a common practice, as both products required ice for product storage. In 1841, as the economy was beginning to recover, Ogden sold his interest to Diversey. The business became the Lill and Diversey Brewery.

Another business that germinated during the depression was grain forwarding. The first shipment of Midwest wheat was sent from Chicago to Buffalo in 1838, a paltry shipment of seventy-eight bushels, an inauspicious beginning for a city that eventually became the grain trading capital of the world. The wheat was divided into thirty-nine sacks and dispatched on the steamer *Great Western* by Charles Walker, owner of C. and A. Walker on South Water Street. Stores like Walker's and that of his competitor John Kinzie were known as "forwarding companies" because they forwarded grain and other products to the East, and their boats returned with other goods.[43]

Tuesday afternoon, July 23, 1839, was a bright, sunny day in Chicago; but neither the heat nor the ongoing financial panic could put a damper on one of the few chances Chicagoans had to celebrate.[44] An estimated four thousand people gathered at the north end of Rush Street, on and about the wharf that reached out into Lake Michigan, to see the huge new steamer *Illinois*, tethered at the end of the dock. Fort Dearborn, just across the river, and all the ships in the harbor were gaily decorated with streamers and flags hanging from every flagstaff and masthead. Hundreds of gulls perched on the shrouds and ratlines of the sailing vessels, adding their cawing chorus to the voices of the happy crowd.

Walter Newberry's older brother Oliver, then of Detroit, along with his partner George Dole, had started one of the town's earliest businesses, Newberry and Dole. A storage and forwarding company, it had gained wharfing privileges in 1835 and had just completed construction of a large, wooden, two-story grain elevator—the city's first—on the wharf. The wealthy Oliver Newberry had commissioned the building of the lake steamer to be used in the nascent Chicago grain trade.

The steamer *Illinois* was impressive, and the men and women in the clamoring crowd elbowed forward for a closer look at the fine ship. On its forward deck was a gleaming brass cannon that was used to alert people to its arrival. The cannon had once stood guard at the first Fort Dearborn and had been dredged from Lake Michigan's muddy bottom quite by accident in 1833. After one look at it, Walter Newberry had purchased it for his brother's ship.

To celebrate the arrival of the steamer, and what it and the new grain elevator would mean for the city, Newberry had asked his friend Will Ogden to make a speech and present a fine set of colors to the ship's skipper. Ogden stood on the ship's deck alongside his friend General Winfield Scott, the Newberry brothers, and George Dole and looked down at the sea of anxious faces on the wharf.

His voice boomed, welcoming the huge crowd and noting what a special day it was. He recalled the day, only a year earlier, when Charlie Walker had dispatched thirty-nine sacks of wheat through the Great Lakes to Buffalo, the very first shipment of grain from the city. The crowd let out an appreciative roar, turning toward Walker who stood among them. The handsome, bespectacled Walker grinned and waved his acknowledgement. Ogden praised the beauty of the *Illinois*, calling it "a splendid specimen of naval architecture," and described the rapid strides the city had made bringing the East and the West together. He paid a glowing tribute to Robert Fulton, saying, "the lake and the prairie around us would have still remained in the wild solitude of nature . . . but for Fulton."

Ogden turned to Captain George Blake, and with a flourish he handed him the fine silk flag. "We present to you our country's flag. . . . Stand by it in peace; stand by it forever." In a final prayer, he beseeched, "For this noble craft, we would ask of Him who rules the raging storm and bids the rising waves be still, to save her from storm and tempest, from rocks and shoals, and bring her in safety to her destined haven." At the end of the celebration, the *Illinois* steamed north with dignitaries and invited guests to Gross-Point, near present-day

Evanston, and then south to the Calumet River, before returning to Chicago, putting an end to a splendid day.

Later that year, 3,768 bushels of grain were hoisted from farmers' wagons to the top floor of Newberry and Dole's grain elevator and piped down into the waiting hold of the two-masted *Osceola*. A new industry was well on its way.

The year 1840 saw Ogden reenter politics on two occasions. First, he ran for and won a seat on the city's common council as alderman for the sixth ward. Chicago was still tightly held in the grip of the depression, and little business of any importance was conducted that called an outlay of funds. In fact, saving every penny possible was the mantra of the day. The council voted to dispense with the office of city marshal and failed to pass almost every ordinance that came before it that required expenditures, unless absolutely necessary. Petitions for new sidewalks and street grading, for instance, came up at almost every meeting but were immediately quashed. The aldermen also had to consider numerous applications from citizens asking to borrow money from the school fund; but those were all denied. There was one item of special interest to Ogden that arose during this council term: the Dearborn Street drawbridge (discussed later in this chapter). But all things considered, it would have been a long and tedious year for those trying to serve the city.

That same year, Ebenezer Peck, an avowed critic of the Illinois and Michigan Canal, announced his intention to run on the Whig ticket for the Illinois House of Representatives.[45] Illinois Democrats formed the Canal Party and entreated Ogden to run against Peck. He agreed to run—against his better judgment—because he was convinced the Irish would control the election. He was correct in his assessment, and he lost the election to Peck.

In business, Ogden did obtain an advantage during the depression. On February 6, 1841, he was admitted to the Illinois State Bar, thanks to the many influential contacts he had made since moving to the state.[46] Although he did not seek out clients to represent, he did offer his legal representation in Illinois to some of his better real estate customers. One client he served locally for many years was the wealthy Bronson family of New York.

During this entire tight-money period, the city's pioneers—those who came to Chicago prior to 1840, later known as the Old Settlers—remained determined to build their city's social infrastructure, despite the hard times. The Chicago Lyceum for Social and Intellectual Pursuits was the young city's first cultural organization. Described as a group of "book-oriented intellectuals," it was formed in 1834. From its inception, it met successively at the Presbyterian Church, Cook's Coffee House, and on the second floor above John Johnson's barbershop. By January 1840 the group had acquired its own Lyceum Hall on the third floor of the Saloon Building at Clark and Lake Streets. William Ogden was an enthusiastic member.[47] Among the Lyceum's primary projects was collecting books for its reading room. By the mid-1840s, however, other diversions having surfaced, the organization faded quietly away. Its library was given to the Young Men's Association, of which Ogden was the president. Ultimately, the books would be passed on again and form the foundation for the Chicago Public Library.

One historian wrote this about the Old Settlers' charity and cultural philanthropy in early Chicago: "William Butler Ogden was a model civic steward. During the crucial decades between Chicago's inception and the Civil War, he conscientiously volunteered for a welter of public and private positions, personally helping to shape the city's government, economy, charities, and cultural institutions. Nor was his example uncommon. During the antebellum years, men and women instinctively volunteered their time and talents to deal with the city's changing needs, moved by religious injunctions, the desire to protect their investments, and a sharp sense of noblesse oblige."[48]

Though times were difficult for Chicagoans, for the most part they were an optimistic lot, and their lives went on. Ogden's North Side home had become the social center of the city's gentry. His mother and younger sister Frances quickly adjusted to Chicago and became enthusiastic and genial hostesses for William's parties and gatherings. The house became an unofficial inn for famous and important visitors to the city. Martin Van Buren, Ralph Waldo Emerson, Samuel J. Tilden, journalist and early feminist Margaret Fuller, and Daniel Webster were counted among the overnight guests. Ogden reveled in taking important people on a carriage tour of the city, extolling its virtues. "He would make the longest day short," his friend Isaac Arnold recalled, "by his inimitable narration of incidents and anecdotes, his graphic descriptions, and his sanguine anticipations of the future."[49]

Like most effective orators, Ogden was also a gifted conversationalist. He loved to talk, and he was very good at it, and as a result friends and guests at his home enjoyed his company. "As a conversationalist, I have hardly ever known his superior, or even his equal," said his friend E. B. Washburne, a future U.S. secretary of state and American minister to France. He claimed Ogden's powers of narration and description were unrivaled and said, "If a public speaker is to be measured by results accomplished, there were few men ever . . . more successful."[50]

Urbane, quick-witted, and charming as Ogden was, portrait artist G. P. A. Healy, who painted a number of Ogden portraits, said, "I found him in conversation a worthy rival of the three best I ever met . . . Louis Phillippe [last king of France, 1830–48], John Quincy Adams and Dr. O. A. Bronson."[51]

During his time alone, astride a fine horse, Ogden enjoyed recapturing the adventures of the hunt he had loved as a boy. He and Paddy were a frequent sight galloping along the lakeshore between Twelfth and Eighteenth Streets. Informal horse racing began in Chicago as early as 1834, and by 1845 the Chicago Racing Club was in operation.[52] Ogden was the president of the group and often participated in the races. In 1845 when Dr. William Tichnor of Kentucky took a ten-year lease on the Chicago racetrack, the sport became even more prominent in the city. Tichnor erected bleachers for spectators and fenced the entire course, and his summer and autumn races attracted large crowds. Purses occasionally reached as high as six hundred dollars, and race day was a spectacle, with marching bands and colorful parades.

In late 1840, Ogden was struck with "bilious fever . . . and ague," known today as malaria, which he suffered for more than three months. The swampy conditions in and around Chicago were ideal mosquito breeding grounds, and many in the city suffered from the disease at one time or another. We learn of Ogden's condition from a November 1840 letter he wrote to Robert North, the brother of his deceased fiancée Sarah.[53] In it, he noted his ongoing interest in the affairs of his original hometown. Ogden had been shaped by the Upper Delaware. It was in the marrow of his bones; and although the remainder of his life would be spent in urban environments, he was forever connected to the hills, meadows, and rivers of Delaware County by some visceral thread: "Every incident connected with my native town & village interests me deeply and I am happy to say that time makes slow progress in easing my attachment for all that belongs to it and particularly for the friends I have left there and for the prosperity of your little board of Episcopal brethren & their church."

North had asked for a donation for the Walton church's building fund. Ogden offered fifty dollars, but in a somewhat petty gesture, told North to get the money from one of the Wheelers in Walton who owed him a substantial amount. Despite his wealth, Ogden was obviously watching his pennies throughout the depression.

Charles Butler did not weather the economic storm as well as Ogden. He did not yet have his brother-in-law's wealth, so he had used the easy credit that was available to finance most of his speculative land purchases. Regarding Butler, Ogden wrote to a friend, "Charles's affairs, I fear, are desperate & the Bankruptcy law his only relief. He probably carries me & many others with him."[54] This dismal prophecy did not come to pass, as Butler did survive the panic, poorer but wiser. Ultimately, he was forced to surrender much of his Chicago property. His friend Arthur Bronson picked up many of the mortgages, as he did for a number of others who were struggling. It was not benevolence that triggered Bronson's gesture; he knew he would ultimately make a nice profit.[55] Toward the end of the depression, and now a significant Chicago property owner again, Bronson turned this time to Ogden's firm to manage his Chicago investments.

The University of Chicago Press published Homer Hoyt's *One Hundred Years of Land Values in Chicago* in 1933. The book is awash in statistics, charts, graphs, tables, and narrative about its subject matter. One of the statistical tables provides a stark look at how the nation's periodic financial panics affected Chicago's real estate values (see table 6.1). When the financial crisis and its lingering effects finally ended in 1843, Ogden was one of the few moneymen who emerged still intact, if poorer. He paid off every obligation he had incurred, including those he had assumed for others.

Table 6.1
The effect of financial panics on aggregate land values in Chicago, 1833–1879

Year	Aggregate Value ($)
1833	168,800
1836*	10,500,000
1842[†]	1,400,000
1856*	125,000,000
1861[†]	60,000,000
1873*	575,000,000
1879[†]	250,000,000

Note: The data show the aggregate value of the 211 square miles of land within the 1833 corporate limits of Chicago.
* Beginning of financial panic.
[†] Ending of financial panic.
Source: Hoyt, *One Hundred Years of Land Values in Chicago*, 470 (table 80).

With the 1837 panic behind them, Chicago's citizens were ready to take their city to the next level. By 1842 when city leaders first began to see a little daylight on the horizon, the largely unfinished Illinois and Michigan Canal became their foremost priority. The State Bank of Illinois had failed earlier that year, and with state debt nearing fourteen million dollars, it was obvious the private sector had to step in if anything was going to happen. Completion of the canal seemed the only thing that might insure the state's future.

In June, a self-constituted, ad hoc committee initiated by William Ogden began quietly discussing the project.[56] Ogden had recruited his friend and client Arthur Bronson, his attorney Isaac Arnold, Chicago attorney Justin Butterfield, and state senator Michael Ryan to counsel with him. Bronson's reentry into the Chicago land market during the panic was a blessing.[57] He brought the city both political clout and broad financial contacts. He was a large holder of canal bonds too, so he had a very personal interest in seeing the canal succeed. His bonds had required only a 25 percent down payment, with the balance to be paid off in three annual installments, plus 6 percent interest on the outstanding balance, so he was anxious to see the project move forward. Ogden too held some of the state bonds, which were given to him and other contractors who had continued work on their canal construction contracts in lieu of cash.

The men met in a small room, likely at the Lake House. It was a hot, humid day, and all the windows would have been open so they could enjoy whatever small breeze chanced through. Arthur Bronson had traveled all the way from New York City to attend the meeting. Bronson was a tall, thin fellow, immaculately groomed even on the rugged Midwest prairie. Although he had the haughty bearing of a man raised with wealth, there was also a surprisingly genial tone to his voice when he spoke. He and his family had invested a lot of money in canal bonds but also in speculative land along the proposed canal corridor, so he was anxious to see the project have new life breathed into it.

The men discussed how the fallout from the panic had affected all Midwesterners, and they talked about the hesitancy of the current state legislature to restart the canal project. A soft-spoken lawyer with penetrating eyes and a heavy drooping moustache, Isaac Arnold had spoken to a number of legislators and found no appetite in their ranks for the project. Justin Butterfield, another attorney, had arrived in Chicago in 1835, as Ogden had. He sat on the board of trustees of Rush Medical College with Ogden and was his North Side neighbor. He was a handsome man with a full head of wavy black hair, a prominent aquiline nose, and a direct glance. His deep voice resonated throughout the small room when he spoke. He believed there *was* enough sentiment to get the work restarted, if the legislature could only be nudged a wee bit.

Ogden told Bronson the Chicago men had come up with an idea that might do the trick.[58] The state had already spent a little over five million dollars on the canal, and it would cost another three million-plus to finish it. But if the legislators could be convinced to convert the remaining work from a deep-cut channel to a shallow-cut channel, the canal could be finished for as little as one and a half million dollars. A shallow-cut canal would be forty feet wide and four feet deep; a deep-cut canal would be sixty feet wide and six feet deep. Most canals were of the shallow-cut variety, but Illinois had originally chosen the more expensive deep-cut in order to insure that all Mississippi River steamboats could use the waterway. To cover the necessary sum, the men in the room hoped the present bondholders would advance the state the additional amount, to be repaid by the canal's future revenues. Bronson said he believed the idea could be sold to the bondholders in New York, if the Chicago men could sell it to the Illinois legislature. The other men murmured their assent, and the decision was made to go forward.[59]

Michael Ryan visited the New York bondholders, after Bronson had provided him with the necessary letters of introduction.[60] Most were amenable to the plan, as it offered them a chance to recoup their original canal investments for only a small incremental amount. A few of the other men went to the legislative session in Springfield the following year and presented the scheme. Legislators were delighted; Illinois businessmen were raising a hue and cry to restart the work, and now the politicians had a way to make it happen without committing themselves too deeply. They passed the necessary legislation, which involved another round of bonds, and work began once more. When completed in 1848, the Illinois and Michigan Canal became one of Chicago's and Illinois's greatest assets.

By the time the 1837 depression bottomed out, Chicago real estate values had plummeted by as much as 90 percent, and in many cases lots could not be sold at any price. But by the mid-1840s Ogden and a few other visionary businessmen knew that a second spurt of growth was on the horizon. The basic strengths of Chicago—its location foremost—had not changed, nor had America's hunger for spreading west. If anything, the value of Chicago's location had improved. What had once been the tallgrass prairie was well on its way to becoming America's breadbasket, aided by the invention of plows with sheet-steel faces built by frontier blacksmiths like John Deere. The products of these farms still had to find their markets; and the growing population of Midwest farm families had to buy supplies, equipment, lumber, household products, and thousands of other necessary items. As the emerging hub between East and West, Chicago was primed for its role.

William Ogden began buying real estate again. One parcel of particular interest he and his brother Mahlon acquired was a large piece of land near the old Chicago Portage site at Mud Lake. The property abutted another large parcel owned by Long John Wentworth. Mud Lake was a nasty little place; Chicago pioneer Gurdon Hubbard, who made a passage through it in the late 1820s provided an apt description:

> We struck camp and proceeded up the lagoon, or what is now known as the South Branch . . . preparing to pass our boats through Mud Lake into the Aux Plaines [Des Plaines] River. Mud Lake drained partly into the Aux Plaines and partly through a narrow, crooked channel into the South Branch, and only in very wet seasons was there sufficient water to float an empty boat. The mud was very deep, and along the edge of the lake grew tall grass and wild rice, often reaching above a man's head, and so strong and dense it was almost impossible to walk through them . . . only at rare intervals was there water. Those who waded through the mud frequently sank to their waist, and at times were forced to cling to the side of the boat to prevent going over their heads; after reaching the end and camping for the night came the task of ridding themselves from the blood suckers. The lake was full of these abominable black plagues, and they stuck so tight to the skin that they broke in pieces if force was used to remove them; experience had taught the use of a decoction of tobacco to remove them, and this was resorted

to with good success. It took us three consecutive days of such toil to pass all our boats through this miserable lake.[61]

Where others saw only mud and blood suckers, Ogden saw gold, though he and Wentworth would become the center of contentious debate years later, battling the city over the strategically located land.

Ogden also bought more lots on the North Side, at deeply distressed prices. He wrote in his notebook: "I purchased in 1845, property for $15,000 which, twenty years thereafter, in 1865, was worth ten millions of dollars. In 1844, I purchased for $8,000, what eight years thereafter, sold for three millions of dollars, and these cases could be extended almost indefinitely."[62] Ogden did not hold all this land and realize the full profits mentioned because he was continually buying and selling.

Over the years, a vast amount of real estate passed through his hands as the city grew. Despite this turnover, he never shed his philosophy of improving property before reselling it. He built, at his own expense, more than one hundred miles of public streets upon which he planted shade trees, and a number of bridges, and he poured millions more into the infrastructure of the city. He was also among the most vocal advocates for public parks.

Ogden was not the only real estate man to spend his own money on land improvements. Gurdon Hubbard had petitioned the town trustees in 1835 to repay him in the form of tax abatements for some improvements he had made on his investment land. When he succeeded, Ogden and others quickly lined up at the public trough; but the well had quickly run dry, despite Ogden's persuasive arguments.[63]

A number of Ogden's clients owned land on the North Side, as he did. One of the main impediments to the North Side location was the Dearborn Street drawbridge, the city's first bridge and still the only north–south passage across the river. It had been built in 1834 and was a primitive timber affair with two movable leaves that were lifted with chains to provide a sixty-foot opening for the passage of vessels. At each end of the movable section was a gallows-frame that "stood like instruments of death to frighten the timid stranger at night."[64] But the three-hundred-foot-long wooden structure was unreliable and required frequent repair. Ogden realized a new bridge would enhance North Side property values and position the area to compete more aggressively with burgeoning South Side commerce.

In 1840 while Ogden was serving as a member of the common council, the issue of the bridge's deteriorating condition arose again. Over the strong objections of South Side businessmen, Ogden convinced his fellow aldermen to approve three thousand dollars in city bonds at 7 percent interest to build a new bridge at Clark Street. When it appeared the deal might fall through for lack of bond buyers, Ogden subscribed one-third of the bonds for himself and off-loaded them to his Eastern clients without their knowledge.[65] The aggressive move paid off, however, because property values did increase, and Ogden's clients never questioned his judgment.

With the money allocated, Ogden moved forward with one of the most audacious moves of his career: he designed the new bridge himself.[66] It was a steam-powered swing bridge, pivoting 90 degrees on a floating central pier in the middle of the river. The design allowed the bridge to easily swing open, allowing the passage of boats. When it was necessary to open it to allow vessels to pass through, a chain anchored at the shore was wound up on a capstan on the float end of the bridge. It was an ingenious design. Ogden had either seen a picture of such a bridge in one of his books or he simply made it up. Regardless, it proved so serviceable that similar bridges were built over the next few years at Wells, Randolph, and Kinzie Streets. Upon completion of Ogden's new bridge, delighted townsmen immediately tore down the old Dearborn Street Bridge.

With his real estate business growing again, William Ogden took in his first partner, a young man named William Edwin Jones, and renamed his firm Ogden and Jones.[67] Jones had previously worked for Charles Butler's American Land Company in New York City. In 1845 Jones married Ogden's sister Caroline, who had since come to Chicago to rejoin the family. The partners also established the North-Western Land Agency and contracted with other agents in Illinois, Wisconsin, and Michigan to make and manage investment purchases in those growing areas.[68]

The Dearborn Street swing bridge, designed by William Ogden.

Now that the leaders of Chicago—the booster-elite—were all making money again, they returned their attention to the social infrastructure of the city, thus insuring the safety and growth of their of land and business investments. The Chicago of the 1840s was dramatically different than the city and town of the previous decade, when the population was mostly New Englanders and New Yorkers. European immigrants were arriving on a large scale. First to come were the Irish, who were driven out of their homeland by the enormous crop failure that came to be known as the Potato Famine, or the Great Hunger. The first wave of Irish had begun to arrive even before that disastrous period to work as diggers on the Illinois and Michigan Canal. On their heels came the Germans, trying to escape the democratic revolutions in their country; they were followed by smaller waves of Scandinavians, Welsh, Scots, and English.

With Chicago located near the geographic center of the fertile plains between the Appalachian and the Rocky Mountains, East Coast cities had to reach out to this rich hinterland with new canals and roads, which made passage to Chicago relatively cheap for the new immigrants. When the first rail connection was forged between New York City and Chicago in 1853, the pace of immigration accelerated.

The majority of these new citizens had one thing in common: poverty. They huddled together in their own sequestered enclaves, building ramshackle houses and taking whatever menial jobs they could find. They also worked to preserve their group identity and cultural heritage, further shutting them off from the remainder of the Chicago community. Although more than half of Chicago's 1860 population of 119,000 was foreign-born, the social problems of the poorer immigrants were largely ignored until after the Great Fire in 1871, with one notable exception.

In 1850, with city and state governments turning their backs on the problem, a group of private citizens founded the Chicago Relief Society. Although it showed promise, it was abandoned less than two years later when the county began making relief payments to the poor. But most of the effort still remained with the private sector, chiefly the booster-elite and their churches. According to historian Kathleen McCarthy, "William B. Ogden had a hand in every worthy undertaking."[69]

Paradoxically, Ogden, like many of the Old Settlers, was very charitable to the less fortunate on a one-to-one basis but very unforgiving to the poor as a class. He seemed to understand how an individual or family could fall upon hard times and require a hand up; but he saw the poor as a group as lazy and unwilling to help themselves through hard work. His attitude toward the poor is reflected precisely in his statement that appears at the beginning of chapter 3.

Often, anti-Catholic sentiments went hand-in-hand with anti-immigrant sentiments, most especially those with anti-Irish roots. Most rock-ribbed Protestants had a difficult time accepting the tenets of the Catholic Church, and they made no secret of the fact. Evidence suggests that William Ogden had no such religious prejudices. When an Irishman, the Right Reverend William J. Quarter, was put in charge of the Chicago Diocese in 1843, his first task was to clean up the financial mess left by his predecessors. The diocese owed nearly four thousand dollars, and the faithful were too poor to be much help. Quarter accomplished the task and then turned his attention to education. He received a state charter for the University of St. Mary's of the Lake, "to confer . . . such academic or honorary degrees as are usually conferred by similar institutions," and began seeking funding for his new school.[70]

Ogden donated an entire city block of land to the school, bordered by Chicago Avenue, Cass, Superior, and Wolcott Streets, just a few blocks from his home. Then he, Walter Newberry, and J. Young Scammon provided cash toward the construction of a campus on the property, now renamed the University of St. Mary of the Lake. St. Mary flourished until 1866, when financial difficulties forced it to close. However, in 1921, under the same charter originally granted to St. Mary's College, a new seminary was opened forty-five miles northwest of the original campus. The seminary is still actively operating today.[71]

Despite the problems with the burgeoning immigrant class, the remainder of Chicago society was moving forward. One of the city's first theaters, the Rialto, later renamed the Chicago Theater, opened on the west side of Dearborn, just below the river on the South Side. Originally constructed as an auction house, the wood-framed building was refurbished as a theater. Two hotels, the Tremont House and the Eagle, were on the same block, with the Refectory, a fine restaurant, across the street. The first season at the theater included a performance by the Jefferson Family, a group of comedians and actors.[72]

Ogden and others founded the Young Men's Association of Chicago. For more than thirty years the organization maintained a reading room and conducted lecture courses. Chicago was indeed growing up. Even today some students of early Chicago history consider it to have been a crude and illiterate frontier town with no intellectual and artistic culture. Nothing could be further from the truth.[73] At its incorporation as a city, it included a bookstore, a theater, two newspapers, and three debating societies. By the time of the fire in 1871, there were sixty-eight bookstores, regularly scheduled exhibits of fine art and painting, and a score of active theater groups. From its incorporation, Chicago was a cosmopolitan city with a degree of refinement that was belied by its rabid commercialism.

In the fall of 1835 or 1836, a twenty-three-year-old man arrived from Philadelphia on horseback. He had recently completed his medical studies at the Jefferson Medical College, and he proudly introduced himself as Dr. Daniel Brainard. He rented office space, hung out his shingle, and became one of a number of practicing physicians in Chicago. But Dr. Brainard was not just another young doctor; he had big plans in mind and the tenacity to see them through.[74]

Within two years he sought and gained a charter for Rush Medical College, named after the Philadelphia physician under whom he had trained. Brainard's timing couldn't have been worse; but he maintained his practice during the depression and doggedly continued to pursue his dream. In 1843, with the financial panic behind him, William Ogden donated a piece of his land at Dearborn and Indiana Streets for Brainard's college. He also gave Dr. Brainard money to build the first classrooms on the campus and was rewarded by being named president of the board of trustees of the fledgling institution.

The college officially opened on December 4, 1843, with twenty-two students enrolled in the sixteen-week course. During the first century of its operation, more than ten thousand physicians received their training at Rush Medical College. The college was even affiliated for a time with the University of Chicago. By the earliest days of the twenty-first century, the modest college had grown into the Rush-Presbyterian-St. Luke's Medical Center, one of the premier academic medical centers in the nation.

The mid-1840s marked a turning point in William Ogden's life. He began to gradually pull away from the day-to-day operations of his real estate business, leaving most of the work to his young partner, William Jones, and then to a series of other partners he brought in over the years. He already possessed wealth beyond a lifetime of needs, and he no longer had anything to prove as a businessman or city booster.

With a less crowded calendar, Ogden began to spend more time with his family. A young man named Edwin Sheldon married Ogden's youngest sister Frances in 1846.[75] The couple lived in the Ogden's North Side home for the next quarter-century, a common practice at the time. Ogden Grove was a huge home, and everyone had plenty of private space. Sheldon once remarked about their life together as a family, "These years brought to each of us, as they do to all, days of trial, of suffering, and of sorrow, and yet in all that time, looking back with careful scrutiny, I can not recall one harsh or unkind word received from [Will Ogden] . . . his friendship [was] steadfast; and his good will unbounded."[76]

Ogden spent a great deal of time in his library with his treasured books, or in his large experimental fruit orchard. In 1847, *The Prairie Farmer*, a Midwest agricultural magazine, ran an article called "Private Gardens of Chicago" in which they toured three of the city's outstanding private gardens, including the Ogdens':

> The garden of Wm. B. Ogden, Esq. comprises about four acres. In it, taste and means
> have combined to produce the agreeable both for the outward and inward sense.

Mr. Ogden has planted a great variety of others [trees]: evergreens of pine, larch, balsam, and the American arbor vitae.

Of grapes there are a considerable quantity, all in fruit. A part of these grapes are growing in the open air, and a part in a grape house. Under the glass we also saw a few nectarines, and a specimen of apricot. We saw some rhubarb of very fine quality . . . gooseberries to a considerable extent . . . Berberry in fruit for the first time in the West. . . . plums . . . currants . . . raspberries, &c.

Flowers smile upon the visitor from every side in this garden. Balsamine Impatiens . . . in all conceivable colors . . . of such size as would make the mere growers of Ladies' Slippers stare.

A right pleasant stroll it is through these shady walks.[77]

Ogden was interested in the landscape ideas of his fellow New Yorker Alexander Jackson Downing, one of the nation's earliest prominent landscape designers and horticulturists. Much of the landscape work done at Ogden Grove was based upon Downing's ideas.[78]

But despite the beauty and serenity of Ogden Grove, it couldn't retain William Ogden's interest indefinitely. During this entire period of domestic bliss, Ogden's fertile imagination was at work on his next big project.

When it came, it changed the face of an entire continent.

7

Harnessing the Iron Horse

lthough he loved his home life, William Ogden's innate restlessness eventually got the best of him, and he began to pursue his dream of putting into place Chicago's final linchpin for success, the railroad.

Nearly a decade earlier, when the city had been struggling to establish its roots, North Side residents coveted the South Side's commercial growth. All roads entering Chicago from the south and the east terminated on the South Side, so it had become the commercial hub of the city. The North Side nabobs decided that to compete more effectively they needed a railroad into Illinois's lucrative lead region, with its terminus in their back yard. It would not only increase their land values but also secure for them a leading position in the development of Chicago railroading.

At the time, St. Louis had what Chicago wanted: the dominant position in Midwest trade. From its enviable location on the Mississippi River, St. Louis controlled the steamboats' most prosperous route to the lead mining regions of northwestern Illinois and southwestern Wisconsin. Galena, in the extreme northwestern corner of Illinois on the Galena River, just before it empties into the Mississippi River, was the regional lead mining trade center. St. Louis had the Galena trade; Chicago wanted it.

What was probably the first published mention of a railroad for Chicago appeared in the *Chicago Democrat* on December 3, 1834. A small item, reprinted from the *Peoria Champion*, listed several subjects for the consideration of the Illinois General Assembly at its upcoming session. Among the subjects was "the incorporation of a railway from Galena to Chicago, to facilitate the business which must of necessity be carried on between those places."[1] At that time, Galena, which had been laid out in 1827, was a larger, more important place than Chicago, and it would produce more than eleven million pounds of lead the year after the notice appeared in the newspaper. Its market for the product was in the East, and among the time-consuming and expensive routes to get it

96

there, one was through a Lake Michigan port, either Milwaukee or Chicago; but the first wagonload of lead sent through Chicago a few years earlier had taken eleven days for the trip. That explained desirability of a rail route.

At the urging of Chicago's North Side businessmen—who recognized an opportunity when it was right in front of them—the Illinois legislature initially chartered the Galena and Chicago Union Railroad (commonly called the Galena) on January 16, 1836.[2] Illinois had granted a number of other railroad charters, but only one, a small, financially troubled line called the Northern Cross that planned to bisect the state from Meredosia on the Illinois River to Danville on the east, had laid any track. A few of the men associated with that initial Galena charter joined William Ogden ten years later to revive the dormant charter. These included Thomas Drummond of Galena and Justin Butterfield of Chicago. Another prominent name on the early company's roster was Elihu Townsend, a wealthy New York investor who played a mysterious hide-and-seek role in the resurrection of the railroad a decade later.[3]

We are indebted to one man, Ralph William Marshall, for the bulk of what we know about the early years of the Galena, from its initial chartering through its years of dormancy. His 1937 master's thesis for the University of Chicago is the only written account of those earliest days of the West's first railroad. His work was taken from a number of primary sources, many of which are no longer extant.

The original charter included a number of attractive provisions.[4] The railroad could be operated by animal or steam power, and the company was given the right to merge with other railroad companies already chartered. It was also granted the right to determine its own tolls and to build arterial lines, two unusual concessions for early railroads. It was even allowed to use the charter to build a turnpike rather than tracks on any portion of the road the company deemed advisable. In that case, however, the tolls were set by the charter: "for each mile . . . of travel . . . for a man and horse, two cents, or for a single person, one cent; for four or six horses or a wagon and driver, loaded, three cents, and for same empty, two cents . . . for hogs, goats and sheep, one mill per head." Under the charter, the company was granted three years to begin construction, and in a condition that would later become crucial to Ogden and his reorganizing group, it had ten years to complete the railroad from Galena to Chicago or forfeit the charter. Capital stock was set at one hundred thousand dollars, with a right to increase that amount up to one million dollars, and shares were priced at one hundred dollars each. The promoters had expected local and Eastern investors to finance the business and believed the federal government would donate the necessary land for the right-of-way from the public domain, as it had done with most successful canals. And it just might have worked, save for the financial panic that followed.[5]

The company initially issued 1,975 shares of stock.[6] On November 20, 1837, thirteen individuals held shares in the company. However, two days later the records indicate that while thirteen still held shares, six of them were different owners. More telling is the fact that several now held as little as one share, the minimum necessary to sit on the board of directors. This group included the mysterious New York investor Elihu Townsend. One man, Elijah Kent Hubbard, now held more than three-quarters of the stock, or 1,519 shares. On the surface, this doesn't appear curious; one wealthy person often controlled such enterprises. It becomes suspicious because Hubbard, who was also now the president of the board, was only twenty-four years old and had no money.

The corporation's stock records contain no evidence that anyone else held an interest in Hubbard's block of shares. In spite of that, it is certain that he held the stock in trust for someone else. Although two other men later held this block in their names, the shares really belonged to the elusive Townsend. He had bought controlling interest in the company from most of the original charter holders, but why he chose to hide his ownership behind this ruse is not known. We do know that Elijah Kent Hubbard was a cousin and business partner of Gurdon S. Hubbard, one of Chicago's earliest settlers and most important men. This cloak-and-dagger scenario resurfaced eight years later and played a vital role in William Ogden's takeover of the Galena and Chicago Union Railroad.

Despite Hubbard's youth and his position as a front man for Townsend, he had taken hold of the enterprise and began moving it forward. He supervised the driving of some piles on Madison Street, the first step in railroad construction. Then his untimely death at age twenty-six in 1839 put a stop to everything. Lacking a driving force and facing the devastating effects of the Panic of 1837, all work ceased on the Galena. It slipped into a period of industrial cryonics, like so many other business and civic projects during the slump. At his death, Hubbard's estate contained only the 1,519 shares of stock in the Galena, valued at a mere eight hundred dollars.[7] In a macabre twist, Hubbard remained the president of the company until it was resurrected in 1846.

After work stopped on the railroad and for the next seven years, Chicagoans were reminded of the Galena whenever they strolled or rode their buggies down Madison Street, where Hubbard's pilings stood like lonely sentries keeping watch over the sleeping enterprise.

It was a crisp November afternoon in 1845 at Ogden's North Side home, Ogden Grove. With most of the leaves stripped from the trees, it was far too late in the year for Ogden to graft and cultivate his experimental fruit trees or grape vines. During this season, he most enjoyed entertaining guests in his library, with a warming fire glowing in the hearth. This day his guests were his attorney, Isaac Arnold, and friends J. Young Scammon and Walter Newberry. William E. Jones, Ogden's new brother-in-law and real estate partner, was also present.[8]

Ogden had invited the men to his home to talk about one of his favorite subjects, railroads, and about one of the city's Old Settlers, Gurdon S. Hubbard. An anomaly among Chicago's leaders, Gurdon Saltonstall Hubbard alone had bridged the city's time warp from French Canadian fur trading post to future metropolis.[9] Arriving at age sixteen in 1818 as an employee of the American Fur Company, he was quickly promoted to superintendent of all Illinois River trading posts and married the niece of a Kankakee Potawatomi chief. By 1827 he had purchased the Illinois trading posts from John Jacob Astor's American Fur Trading Company.

In the early years, Hubbard established his headquarters at the trading post in Danville, Illinois, but he was a frequent presence in Chicago. One of his contemporary admirers, Henry Blodgett, described him thus: "Splendid in physique, six feet and something more in height, he rode a splendid horse, and dressed in just enough of the frontier costume to make his figure a picturesque one. He wore buckskin leggings, fringed with red and blue and a jaunty sort of hunting-cap. In a red sash about his waist was stuck,

Gurdon S. Hubbard, one of Chicago's earliest pioneers.

on one side, a silver-handled hunting-knife, on the other, a richly mounted tomahawk. . . . altogether he made a figure ever to be remembered."[10]

When the city began to grow and the Indians and fur traders were replaced by a more sophisticated citizenry, Hubbard discarded his buckskins and his Indian wife for appropriate business attire and a "proper" wife, and he went on to acquire substantial wealth and community standing as a land investor, merchant, meat packer, and civic leader. Years earlier, Hubbard had been the driving force behind getting Chicago designated as the terminus for the Illinois and Michigan Canal. But now, like Ogden, he saw the opportunity railroads offered, not only to the city but also to the men who built them. His cousin, Elijah Kent Hubbard, had been the second president of the Galena when the charter was new. Now Gurdon Hubbard was setting a plan in motion to purchase the majority of outstanding shares and meager assets of the company, which had spurred the meeting in Ogden's library on that cold November evening.

Gurdon Hubbard and the other men had been amiable competitors in a number of other ventures.[11] In fact, Hubbard and Ogden had been partners in some land deals, and Ogden had even become his lawyer after acquiring a law license in 1841. But now, Ogden and his associates realized that if they were going to obtain the moribund railroad charter, they would have to outmaneuver Hubbard and any other potential buyers that might be lurking in the wings.

The importance of railroads to the future of Chicago and to the westward expansion of the nation had never been out of Ogden's mind since his move from New York. While many men of vision continued to believe canals or plank roads were the answer to the growing nation's transportation needs, Ogden never wavered in his belief in the future of the railroad. He had simply been waiting for the opportune moment.

While the Galena railroad was blissfully sleeping for eight years, a few things had changed. In northwest Illinois, thinning veins and new tariff regulations had damaged Galena's lead mines, and lead was no longer the city's chief product. Galena was now a major Mississippi River shipping center for wheat and agricultural products. So the town's passion for a railroad had cooled considerably since earlier days when a sturdy wagon, pregnant with lead ore, could take up to eleven days to reach Chicago, and if it rained, many more. But now, connecting Galena to Chicago by rail would strengthen Chicago's position and weaken their own port, Galena's civic leaders reasoned.

Many Chicago businessmen were also skeptical of railroads. The Illinois and Michigan Canal, though it would not be completed for another two years, had already been a boon to them; they suspected that a railroad would only prove to be injurious competition. Also, earlier railroad debacles had drained state coffers of a significant amount of money when they failed. Finally, most Chicagoans were still dazzled by plank roads and the opportunities they seemed to offer.

At the beginning of 1848, as Ogden was still struggling to get his railroad up and running, an average of two hundred big wagons a day lumbered into Chicago with their cargo over the system of plank roads that reached out north, south, and west of the city.[12] Road companies were taking in significant cash in tolls, and most men believed this revolution in transportation would insure the future prosperity of their city. Professional teamsters, rough-and-ready men practiced in the art of forcing amateur drivers off the road and into the prairie mud, ruled these roads. They were joined by farmers driving their own crops to market, who were quick to learn the survival-of-the-fittest road rules. So many teamsters and farmers arrived daily that a tent city was set up for them on the lakeshore at the foot of Randolph Street. Here, gamblers, sporting women, pickpockets, bunco artists, and assorted hooligans competed for attention and for the almighty dollar. What money wasn't squandered on this mélange of riffraff was spent in the city's saloons and retail establishments.

All of this led to a prevailing wisdom in Chicago that business was great, real estate was booming again, and the population was swelling, so why tinker with a good thing? Very few of Chicago's business elite saw the railroad as anything but a threat to their prosperity. The consensus of opinion seemed to be that if William Ogden and his friends clung to such a pipe dream, they certainly weren't going to find much enthusiasm for it in Chicago or anywhere else in Illinois.

But entrepreneur Ogden, grain shipper Newberry, J. Young Scammon, and a few others knew otherwise.[13] They realized that struggling little towns like Elgin, Freeport, and Rockford sat astride the rich farming lands of the Rock River Valley in northern Illinois and southern Wisconsin. Farmers along the railroad's proposed route had two ways to get their crops to market, after they were loaded into wagons: they could take the short route, a week or more, to Galena, or if their loads were larger, the longer but easier route on a plank road to Chicago, a two- to three-week jaunt. Neither option offered them much profit. The Illinois and Michigan Canal, when it opened, would offer farmers in the Rock River Valley no relief as they still had to get their crops to Galena or Chicago on their own. Ogden appreciated this plight better than most; it was exactly the situation he had been in with his New York mills when the Erie Canal opened.

A few weeks before the meeting at Ogden's home, Rock River Valley farmers had met to discuss this problem. They decided to call for a railroad convention on January 7, 1846, at Rockford.[14] Their goal was to find somebody who would pick up the charter that had been granted and restart construction on the Galena and Chicago Union Railroad. Ogden became aware of their plan, which was what had spurred his meeting with his friends to lay out their strategy for controlling the Rockford meeting.

More than three hundred delegates from ten counties in Illinois and Wisconsin showed up for the Rockford convention, including sixteen representatives from Chicago, who, as everyone realized, would have to carry the ball if the project were to succeed. Included in the group was Ogden's team: Jones, Arnold, Scammon, and Newberry. Revealing that they were currently in negotiation to buy the charter, Ogden's team pointed out that if each farmer bought but one hundred dollars in the railroad's stock, the venture would raise five hundred thousand dollars and be assured of success. Newberry proposed a resolution calling for his company to be granted the charter if they could purchase a majority of the existing stock. After a lot of agitated debate, it was passed almost unanimously.

Although most of the men at the convention were in favor of resurrecting the railroad, a tavern keeper from Marengo spoke strongly against it, denouncing railroads as "undemocratic aristocratic institutions that will ride rough-shod over the people and grind them to powder. The only roads that the people want," he growled, "are good common plank-roads upon which everybody can travel."[15]

There was already an extensive system of plank roads in operation in northern Illinois. One, the Northwestern Plank Road, had its terminus in the West

Side of Chicago and extended all the way to the town of Maine, seventeen miles distant. The road was planned to eventually reach Elgin. Another, the Southwestern Plank Road, began in the city in an area known as Bull's Head and ran sixteen miles to the town of Brush Hill, from whence it extended another fourteen miles to Naperville. But plank-road advocates were in the minority at the Rockford convention.

Gurdon Hubbard was incensed when he heard of Ogden's scheme, as he had planned to resurrect the railroad himself.[16] He believed he held first rights to purchase the charter, perhaps because of some wording in his cousin's will. But Ogden and his team knew that Hubbard's rights, even if he held them, would be forfeited in one week because of the charter's original condition that all work had to be completed in ten years.

Ogden did not attend the railroad convention. The cagey entrepreneur was in New York meeting with Elihu Townsend, the man who controlled the majority of stock in the company.[17] Ogden's plan to beat Hubbard and any other interested charter buyers to the punch had worked, although as it turned out, Ogden had a big advantage. Townsend had been a board member of the New York and Erie Railroad when Ogden was promoting that route to the New York legislature a dozen years earlier, so the two were old acquaintances. After some negotiation, but not until the following year, Townsend agreed to sell his shares to Ogden in return for two hundred shares of stock in the new enterprise. A second man, Thomas Mather of Springfield, Illinois, was in partnership with Townsend on some of the shares he held, but Townsend represented both interests in the sale of the stock. In addition to the charter and the few miles of work already accomplished by Elijah Hubbard, Ogden's group received title to 940 acres of timberland on the Des Plaines River—the enterprise's most valuable asset—that could furnish ties and timber for fuel for the road.[18]

Ogden probably had long been aware of Townsend's hidden ownership and was simply waiting for the ten-year term to expire before making his move. Although Ralph William Marshall states that Ogden visited Townsend in order to purchase his shares *after* Ogden's group had secured the charter, almost certainly Ogden had at least one visit with Townsend *before* they acquired it to insure that the deal could be made. Marshall indirectly verifies this, writing that Ogden's group "had come to Rockford with a definite plan of action."[19]

Marshall gives another indication of their plan when he notes that only nine days before the Rockford railroad convention, the shares of Galena stock that had been held in the Elijah Hubbard estate were transferred on the Galena's books to one Francis Howe, again shielding Townsend's ownership. Six weeks after that, and following the Rockford meeting, the records show six shares were transferred from the Howe account, one share each to William Ogden, William Brown, Walter Newberry, Thomas Dyer, J. Young Scammon, and Charles Walker.[20]

The day after the Rockford meeting, the early stockholders met in Chicago and elected a board of directors, including the six men who now qualified by virtue of their single shares. Ogden was elected president of the board. Gurdon Hubbard was left out in the cold. The friendship between the two men was over, and Hubbard would play only a minor role in the emergence of Chicago as the railroad capital of the nation.

Another interesting facet of the buyout of Townsend's interest is that no money changed hands.[21] He received ten thousand dollars in Galena stock immediately and another ten thousand dollars in stock after the first thirty-five miles of the road had been built. Ogden and the other directors were not out-of-pocket one cent so far. One fact we do not have access to, and apparently Marshall did not either, is the number of shares Ogden and each of his partners/directors ended up with after all the shakeouts.

The next order of business was to resubmit the charter to the Illinois legislature under the new names, and it was approved on February 24, 1847. The new group asked for two changes in the charter: first, to increase the capital stock to three million dollars, and second, to increase the number of directors to thirteen. Both provisions were approved. William Ogden and his team were now in control of a company with three million dollars in stock, and still they had not spent a penny on it.

In 1847, as busy as he was with his railroad, Ogden again served a one-year term as an alderman on the Chicago Common Council, now for the ninth ward, as the city had been redistricted.[22] There were few significant activities during the year, according to the Common Council Archives, just the normal minutiae associated with running a city. These include the council's considering such mundane issues as an ordinance to prevent cattle and swine from running loose on the streets; appointing bridge tenders, schoolteachers, firemen, pound masters, and other city employees; and remonstrating against the evil smells from Charlie Cleaver's soap and candle factory. There were, however, two issues that affected Ogden during his term.

The first involved education. Because of his success in helping to stage the River and Harbor Convention, Ogden was asked to take on the same task for the Western Educational Convention, to be held in Milwaukee. During the meeting, the Northwestern Educational Society was formed to provide better training for Illinois teachers. Ogden was named its president. The group recommended the organization of state societies, with county and town auxiliaries, for the advancement of common school education, more training for teachers, and the hiring of more female teachers in order to reduce costs. "Out of it," wrote Chicago historian Thomas Wakefield Goodspeed, "grew the state's admirable system of normal schools and colleges."[23]

The second common council issue involving Ogden was the railroad. It is likely his decision to run for alderman in 1847 was sparked more by his railroad interest than any sense of civic responsibility. Within the year, construction was due to begin on the Galena, and the initial stage called for laying track from the outskirts of the city into the city itself, an action that would require some deft political handling if Ogden and his associates were to gain their desired route.

Bearing this out, at one of the early council meetings Ogden introduced an ordinance proposing that the city grant a right-of-way to the railroad from the city boundary eastward into the city on a line with Kinzie Street.[24] The ordinance would grant the company permission to lay the necessary track and to build the required drawbridges and depot. The track would end on the North Side at the site Ogden had chosen for the city's first railroad depot. It was a contentious issue for two reasons. First, many of Ogden's fellow aldermen simply did not want any railroads coming into the city; these men were still pledged to other transportation options. Second, even those who did favor railroads were spilt on where they wished to see the depot located; each man wanted the terminus and its promise of commercial growth in his own ward. As a result, Ogden's ordinance did not pass. As we'll see, however, Ogden would eventually get his way.

By August, Ogden's team had opened subscription books in ten Illinois counties.[25] Ogden, Scammon, and Newberry were actively soliciting subscriptions from investors in the East and in Chicago, even though they suspected it would be a futile endeavor. Another member of the board, Thomas Drummond of Galena, was doing the same thing in his hometown.

All three efforts failed. Galena investors saw the railroad as a threat to their emerging commerce, and Chicago investors remained unmotivated because they would soon have their canal open. As J. Young Scammon remarked, there was no man in the city who "could conveniently or was disposed to subscribe for more than $5,000 in the stock."[26]

Eastern investors also saw little hope of the venture getting off the ground; they were aware that seven Illinois railroad ventures had failed during the Panic of 1837. Nevertheless, board member E. B. Washburne wrote a long, impassioned letter to one of Boston's most illustrious Brahmin businessmen that was published in the newspaper, inviting their interest: "Can you not, my dear Sir, bring your citizens to a proper consideration of this matter, in which they are so deeply interested? New York is awake for the accomplishment of this great work. Will Boston be behind her?"[27]

Ogden and Scammon followed up by visiting a group of bankers and lawyers in Boston who had put a significant amount of money into building the successful Michigan Central Railroad. The bankers looked down their patrician noses at the two men and told them bluntly to go home, raise what spare change they could from their farmers, and build their little road. Then when the railroad went broke, as it most certainly would, the Boston bankers told Ogden and Scammon, they would pick it up for a song and complete the line.[28]

Undeterred by the failures, Ogden and the other directors pushed forward. They now realized that with no state or federal aid and no interest on the part of big-money investors, they would have to sell their stock subscriptions to "the ordinary man." They lowered the necessary startup capital from five hundred thousand to four hundred thousand dollars and embarked on a new plan that called for keeping expenses as low as possible and offering their stock to as many people as they could reach.

Richard Morgan, an engineer who had been hired to plan the road, told Ogden that it would require about $2.6 million to build the entire 182-mile road. As they were struggling to find the money, Morgan came forward with another idea. The Michigan Central Railroad had successfully built their route across that entire state, from Detroit to New Buffalo, on Lake Michigan. Morgan suggested the Galena also build east, around the southern end of the lake, and meet the Michigan Central. Tying these local and regional lines together was every railroad builder's vision, and Morgan's plan was very attractive. But once Ogden saw the costs—an additional $328,000—he was forced to abandon any hopes of going east. That was just as well; the idea of enriching the Boston bankers who owned the Michigan Central held no appeal for Ogden.[29]

However, the idea of building eastward did not disappear completely. On April 5, 1848, in Ogden's report to the stockholders, he mentioned it again. More significant, in the same report, he hints about his "grand plan" for the little railroad: "It cannot have escaped the observation of all acquainted with the region of the country to be affected by the construction of this important work, that, if constructed now and extended east from Chicago around the head of Lake Michigan till it meets the Michigan Central Railroad, as it soon will, it secures to the country through which it passes *the Great North-Western railroad thoroughfare for all time to come*"[30] (italics in the original).

What had transpired with the Michigan Central since Ogden had initially nixed the plan to tie in with that railroad was an interesting bit of good fortune. The Galena board had discovered that a moribund charter existed for a road called the Buffalo and Mississippi River Railroad. Its charter granted the road the right-of-way from New Buffalo to the Illinois border. The Galena group bought the old charter, and by holding it over the head of the Michigan Central, encouraged that road to eventually extend into Chicago, completing the rail link from Chicago to New York.[31]

Clearly, William Ogden had much more in mind for the Galena than a small granger railroad, even at this early date. Giving birth to the little railroad, however, was a frustrating time for Ogden and his team, but they never wavered in their belief in its future. They turned their attention back to Chicago for selling stock, not to the businessmen and investors, but to the man on the street. Chicago had nine wards, and a two-man team was appointed to work each ward, supported by newspaper ads promoting the venture. A giant public meeting with a festival atmosphere was held at the courthouse. Ogden and Scammon made speeches, and all the ward teams were introduced. The same plan was carried out in all the towns along the route of the railroad. On September 1, 1847, the *Rockford Forum* reported on "$250,000 to $300,000 having been subscribed" in these small towns and villages.[32] These included $1,500 in Hazel Green, $3,700 in New Diggings, $9,600 in Shullsburgh, and $6,000 to $7,000 in Fair Plan.

For two years, Ogden devoted almost all of his time and energy to selling stock in lots of one or two shares, often on credit, to the farmers along the railroad's 182-mile route. He realized these men and women couldn't afford to come in from their fields to attend meetings, so he visited them on their own turf. He spent his nights in small, mud-spattered inns, abandoned cabins, and crude rural farmhouses. On occasion he even wrapped himself in a blanket he carried in the back of his carriage and slept under a tree by the side of the road.

J. Young Scammon, one of Chicago's "Old Settlers." Chicago History Museum; ICHi-39052.

During the second year, J. Young Scammon joined him on the road. Scammon had established a law firm, Scammon, McCagg and Fuller, with two other attorneys, and one of his partners, Ezra McCagg from Hudson, New York, would become William's sister Caroline's second husband in 1854.

Ogden and Scammon bounced along Illinois's narrow, bumpy dirt roads in a two-horse business buggy, tall stalks of wheat and corn forming a canopy over their heads. For Ogden, it was a blessing to have someone to talk to over the long, lonely days and to share the burden. They spoke at public meetings at every stop, often addressing only the half-dozen farmers who could be encouraged to come in from their fields. They chatted with anyone they could corral at general stores and on small-town streets. Dust sticking to their teeth, they trudged out into furrowed fields to try to sell just one share of stock to a weary farmer pushing a plow. They even met with farmers' wives, trying to talk them out of butter-and-egg money for one share of stock. The cheapest down payment on one share was $2.50, and Ogden often gladly proffered the small down payment as a loan to any farmer or his wife who seemed sincere in their desire to help launch the project.

A bit of Galena folklore, probably at least partly true, also spoke to Ogden's success as a salesman during this period.[33] It was said that he secured twenty thousand dollars in subscriptions in one day on the streets of Chicago from farmers who were selling the wheat they had hauled into town in wagons over the abominable roads that entered the city. Ogden seemed to feel that if it had to be a citizens' railroad, paid for by the citizens themselves, then by God, so be it. Scammon remembered their grassroots sales effort years later: "Many farmers and other persons, be it said to their credit, did come forward and subscribe, though they had to borrow the first installment of two dollars and fifty cents on a share and get trusted 'till after harvest' for the same. When it is remembered that it cost five bushels of wheat and often from four days' to a week's journey to Chicago, with a load of grain, to get the first installment of a single or few shares of stock, none can doubt the public interest in the enterprise."[34]

The *Prairie Farmer*, the state's leading agricultural publication, saw the advantage of the railroad for Illinois farmers, and in an 1847 editorial it urged readers to help make the project a reality: "We trust no farmer residing within ten to thirty miles of the proposed route, will refuse to take stock," it said. "If unable to take more than one share, then take that, and show by action that you desire the work to be built, and think the project expedient."[35]

Selling stock was only one of Ogden's and Scammon's objectives as they bumped along the dusty trails of northern Illinois. They also had to negotiate with the property owners along the route to obtain rights-of-way for the Galena's tracks. Since the operation was still cash-poor, they avoided paying for track rights whenever possible, bartering with shares of the railroad stock instead. Since most property owners were desirous of having the railroad pass their property, negotiations were not normally difficult, but they were time-consuming. Of course, it was better yet when they could obtain the right-of-way at no cost at all.

DuPage County is directly west of Cook County, Chicago's home. When the Galena engineer Richard Morgan initially planned the route, he had intended that the rails through DuPage County follow the well-established wagon and stage road through Stacy's Tavern (today Glen Ellyn) and Gretna until it reached the Fox River. However, a group of citizens from Milton Township met with Ogden and Scammon and offered them a free right-of-way through Milton if they would bend the intended route slightly south through their town. Always looking for a cheaper way to build the road, Ogden agreed. According to a history of DuPage County, as a result of the alteration in the train's original route, "the small communities which dotted the wagon trail quickly became virtual ghost towns, [and] among these were Stacy's Bend [Tavern] and Gretna."[36] This speaks loudly to the importance farmers and landowners put on having a railroad run directly past their property and through their town.

There had been talk about staging a convention to discuss and debate the status of rivers and harbors and their special needs. Ogden recognized that this subject resonated with people throughout the nation whose cities faced such issues. He saw such a convention as a grand opportunity to advance the progress of water transportation; but he also recognized that it would allow him, Scammon, and Newberry to mix with hundreds of Eastern moneymen who might be potential investors in their railroad. So he took the lead in organizing the Chicago River and Harbor Convention, an event scheduled to begin on July 5, 1847, in Chicago.[37]

The event was a staggering success. The city held over its annual Fourth of July festivities by a day so visitors could see how Chicagoans celebrated. There was a grand parade with floats, marching military units and bands, and thousands of cheering Chicagoans lining the streets. For the meeting itself, an immense tent, covering about two-thirds of a block, was made by a local sail-maker and erected in the courthouse square. Seats for four thousand people were installed. Ogden, as head of the arrangements committee, nominated the convention chairman.

It has been estimated that as many as ten thousand delegates and visitors attended, including Horace Greeley, publisher of the *New York Tribune*; Thurlow Weed, editor of the *Albany Evening Journal*; Erastus Corning, president of the New York Central Railroad; and a newcomer to Congress, its only Whig member, Abraham Lincoln, from downstate.[38] The delegates approved pressing for more federal aid for water-based transportation projects in the West and protested President James Polk's veto of a river and harbors appropriation bill.[39] Although Ogden, Scammon, and Newberry were still unable to overcome the Eastern investors' skepticism of their railroad plan, the event did have its historic significance: it was the first national gathering in the city that would eventually become the convention capital of the nation.

The most immediate problem was still finding the money to build the road. Despite many failures and primarily through the grassroots sales efforts of Ogden and J. Young Scammon, enough money was finally raised to begin construction.[40] On April 5, 1848, the first annual meeting of the new company was held in the Merchants Exchange Building. Ogden reported that 1,206 people had subscribed $351,800, of which $20,817 had been paid so far. It was enough to get started. Ogden hired a young man named John Van Nortwick to be chief engineer for the road.[41] Also from upstate New York, Van Nortwick had spent a number of years in the engineering department of the New York canal system before moving to Batavia, Illinois, in 1846. Astutely, he had purchased land in Batavia that was covered with hardwood trees, knowing that a ready market existed for the lumber in nearby Chicago, which was trying to expand its shipbuilding industry.

The board decided to grade and lay only the first forty-one-mile segment of track, which they could afford to complete with the cash in hand. This section, when completed, could generate immediate traffic and cash, a big advantage. Ogden also saw other advantages in tackling this first leg only: "The grades on that portion of the road between Chicago and Elgin are scarcely equaled by any other road in the country," he commented in an April 1848 report, "the maximum grade going east, being but six feet, and going west, but twenty feet to the mile."[42] The forty-one-mile stretch was also straight and would require no costly bridgework.

This first leg also included the trackage within the city itself that so far had been denied by the common council. After what must have been more intense politicking, the company was given the right to build a temporary track from the city boundary at Kinzie and Halstead Streets east to the river so that the locomotives that were due to arrive via Lake Michigan could be off-loaded and driven out of town.

Keeping expenses as low as possible without compromising the railroad was important to the board. Early iron tracks were available in two styles. The newer, safer, and more costly style was T-rails, manufactured in Great Britain, and still used to this day. The older style was called strap rails, and they were just that: straps of iron. The board was told it would cost about $14,500 per mile to build with T-rails, but only about $8,500 per mile with strap rails. It was an easy decision for the cash-poor railroad to make.[43] By 1852, when the enterprise had become profitable, the railroad began using T-rails on new construction and replacing the old strap rails with the safer T-rails.

A railroad track's superstructure was composed of thick wooden crossties, about nine feet long, laid thirty inches apart from center to center. Across these were six-inch-thick wooden rails that were secured to the crossties by triangular knees that were spiked in place. Atop the rails were thinner oak ribbons, and the iron rails were secured atop those.

Chief engineer Van Nortwick's responsibilities included laying out the course of the road and overseeing the construction by private contractors. In June 1848, on the outskirts of Chicago, a worker drove the first peg into the ground at the corner of Kinzie and Halsted, and grading the roadbed began.[44] One of Van Nortwick's early decisions involved a heavy dose of self-interest. When construction began, the population between Chicago and the Fox River, about thirty-eight miles distant, was sparse. But along the river there were a number of small, thriving communities. The land between the two places was low and marshy; a stagecoach trip took sixteen grueling hours, while a wagon laden with farm products could take many days, depending upon how much rain had preceded the trip. So the citizens of the small communities desperately wanted the railroad from Chicago to go through their towns. These communities included Elgin, Aurora, St. Charles, Geneva, and Van Nortwick's own hometown—and the home of his lumber interests—Batavia.

Over the objection of Van Nortwick and the river towns' leaders, the Galena board approved laying the first forty-one miles of track directly to Elgin. The citizens petitioned the board to reconsider, even volunteering to pay for a survey to their towns. Ogden saw an opportunity to reap additional revenues, and he suggested to town leaders they could build their own railroad spurs to connect with the Galena.[45] They agreed, and the St. Charles Branch Railroad, the Aurora Branch Railroad, and the tiny 1.8-mile Geneva Branch Railroad were born. The Aurora Branch ran right through Batavia, so in the end everyone was appeased.

Like Ogden, another Galena board member, John Bice Turner, was from New York, and the men had probably been acquainted there. Turner had moved to Chicago in 1843, and with money he had earned as a contractor on the New York and Erie Railroad, he bought three thousand sheep and became a sheep farmer. When the Galena was restarted, Turner bought ten thousand dollars' worth of stock in the company and was named to the board of directors.[46]

In May 1848 Ogden and Turner traveled East to purchase a used engine, passenger cars, iron, and other necessary materials. The key piece of equipment, the locomotive *Alert*, had toiled for nine years along the tracks of the Utica and Schenectady Railroad in New York and then put in another two years of service for the Michigan Central Railroad.[47] On October 10, the brig *Buffalo* delivered the locomotive, renamed the *Pioneer*, to Chicago. The little engine had been refurbished like new: "its fresh black paint gleamed; its brass and

copper facings . . . polished to mirror-like reflection; its wheels and smokestack
. . . sandpapered till they resembled steel."[48] Technically, the little engine was a
six-wheeler, a 2-4-0, with two leading wheels followed by two coupled driving
wheels and no trailing wheels. It was a wood-burning steam locomotive and
had been originally built in 1837 by the Baldwin Locomotive Works. Within
two years, the *Pioneer* was joined by the *Whittlesey*, a feisty twelve-tonner with
four drivers, built by Norris and Brothers of Philadelphia, and by the muscular *Pigeon*, a fourteen-tonner also built by Baldwin and originally run on the
Detroit and Pontiac Railroad.[49]

The scrappy little *Pioneer*, the Galena and Chicago Union's first steam-powered locomotive,
purchased by Ogden in 1848. This photo was taken after the Galena and Chicago Union and
the Chicago and North Western merged. Union Pacific Historical Collection.

Galena railroad folklore has passed down a story about the railroad's first
customer. After the first three or four miles of track had been laid heading west,
board members decided to take a ride to the end of the line, at Oak Ridge. The
gleaming little *Pioneer* was pulling an empty freight car and a makeshift passenger car, and the dignitaries and their guests clambered aboard. They happily
waved at gawking spectators who lined the track, cheering as the little train
chugged past. At Oak Ridge the board and their guests enjoyed a round of refreshments before heading back to Chicago. As they prepared to depart, J. Young
Scammon noticed a farmer at the back of the crowd perched atop a wagonload
of wheat. Scammon walked back to the man and asked in his booming voice if
the farmer would like to have his wheat be the first in history to enter Chicago
by train. The old farmer hesitated, uncertain. He pulled a dirty red kerchief
from his back pocket and wiped his brow, while considering whether or not

to entrust his valuable cargo to the noisy, smelly little train. When Scammon told him the delivery would be free, and he could even accompany his wheat into Chicago, the old man couldn't resist. The crowd helped load the sacks of wheat into the freight car—which was no more than a simple wooden box sitting on a flatcar—and the old farmer and his wheat happily headed off into history. (Other versions of the oft-told story had the first shipment be dressed hogs, while another said it was hides and pelts.)

By November 21, 1848, ten miles of track had been laid. The board of directors invited a number of stockholders and newspaper editors to take a "flying trip" over the new rail line. A couple of baggage wagons were provided with seating, and at about 4:00 P.M. the train, bearing about one hundred brave souls, chugged out of town with a huge crowd of onlookers cheering them on.[50] As the *Pioneer* chugged westward, William Ogden probably had a clear mental picture of another flying trip, eighteen years earlier, when the *Tom Thumb* sputtered its way down the tracks in Baltimore in its mighty race against Lightning the horse. What a fine moment it must have been for him!

Edwin O. Gale, one of the earliest settlers in Chicago, spoke of the early years of the Galena in 1908 before the Illinois State Historical Society:

> The Galena . . . was chartered . . . when railroads were hardly known, and about the time when no one could pay five miles fare. It is true that we were greatly afraid of railroads and the city council made the terrible thing go outside the city limits, clear out to Halstead Street [in 1848] . . . to protect us from probable catastrophes. It was treated as dangerous as shooting prairie chickens would have been on State and Twelfth streets a few years before. How we hurrahed when the engine Pioneer showed that it could actually move, and on October 26, 1848, drew two cars seven miles.[51]

Despite its early success, the Galena was still chugging and clattering its way into Chicago on tracks that had only been granted "temporary use" status. However, a three-man commission was appointed in early 1848 to assess that matter. The railroad had proven its worth and had silenced all but its most skeptical critics; it seemed that everybody was now on the Galena's bandwagon. In order to overrule the common council's initial decision against the railroad, it was decided that those individuals and businesses along the de facto right-of-way must be paid for damages to their properties. The commissioners realized those entities had gained more than they had lost by being located next to the tracks, so they assessed damages at a nominal amount of six cents per landowner. The offer was accepted without dissent, the necessary quitclaim deeds were made to the company, and the roadway into Chicago was secured.[52]

Meantime, the railroad progressed westward. By the time the railroad tracks reached Cottage Hill, about halfway to Elgin, it was generating receipts of sixty dollars a day; and when it reached Elgin on January 22, 1850, business was booming. The company logged $22,529 in freight receipts and $22,802 in passenger receipts between June 1849 and May 1850, and operating expenses were $18,520, producing net earnings of $26,812.[53]

These were such encouraging results that Ogden and the board approved adding additional rolling stock to the line. By the end of that year, it was reported that the Galena had the following rolling stock in inventory: three new fifteen-ton locomotives, one used ten-ton locomotive, thirteen double covered freight cars, and sixteen double platform freight cars. Also there were three single covered freight cars, six single platform freight cars, eleven gravel repairing cars, and four handcars. To accommodate the growing passenger business, there were two new passenger cars, one of fifty-six seats and the other of sixty seats; two used forty-seat passenger cars; and two baggage and accommodation cars.[54]

In a business where most companies were struggling for survival, the Galena was a model of success. For better or for worse—and the future would bring more of each—the first railroad west of Lake Michigan was off and running. Ogden stuck to a pay-as-you-go formula for building the line, never going into debt to advance the road beyond the dollars on hand. As each rail leg was completed, new customers were added—the farmers who had bought their stock in the railroad one share at a time. In each village or town, lean, hardened farmers, their sunburned faces resembling old cracked leather, passed rough, heavy sacks of wheat from hand to hand onto the freight cars of "their" railroad. Normally taciturn men, they smiled broadly and congratulated one another as the little train chugged out of their village on the way to its next stop. The Galena was profitable from the beginning, Scammon himself describing it as "eminently successful."[55] The *Chicago Daily Journal*, on November 21, 1850, proclaimed the accomplishment: "The 'Iron Horse' is now fairly harnessed in the Prairie land."

When Charles Dickens visited America in early 1842, many things he witnessed amazed him, but he was particularly taken with the emergence of railroads on the prairie frontier. In the travelogue he published upon his return to England, he wrote about the spectacle of a little steam engine pulling its cars through small, sparsely populated frontier towns and villages, similar to the ones that now lined the Galena's route.

> The train calls at stations in the woods, where the wild possibility of anybody having the smallest reason to get out is only to be equaled by the apparently desperate hopelessness of there being anybody to get in. It rushes across the turnpike road, where there is no gate, no policeman, no signal; nothing but a rough wooden arch, on which is painted "WHEN THE BELL RINGS, LOOK OUT FOR THE LOCOMOTIVE." On it whirls headlong, dives through the woods again, emerges in the light, clat-

ters over frail arches, rumbles upon the heavy ground, shoots beneath a wooden bridge—dashes on haphazardly, pell-mell, neck-or-nothing.[56]

Chicago's first railroad terminal, the eastern terminus of the Galena, was built in early 1849 on a triangular parcel on Kinzie Street, just north of the river, as Ogden and his co-directors had long advocated.[57]

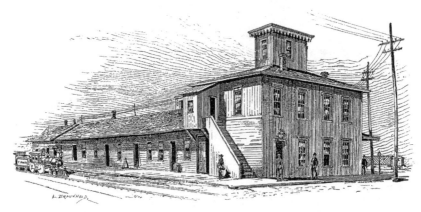

The Galena and Chicago Union Railroad depot, Chicago's first, which opened in 1849 on Kinzie Street, on the North Side.

One of the city's Old Settlers, John S. Wright, had been another of the early proponents of a railroad in Chicago.[58] Although he failed to invest early in the technology, he had purchased the real estate that eventually became home to the Galena's first depot. He had bought the land from Arthur Bronson for $37,500—probably through Bronson's real estate agent, William Ogden—and sold it to Ogden and the Galena for $60,000 just a few years later. He would have preferred to hold onto the choice piece of land, knowing it would continue to escalate in value; but he was still in debt to Bronson for the purchase and had to sell the property in order satisfy that debt.

That initial depot was a crude little affair, costing only $1,200 to construct, and was reminiscent of a building from Al Capp's colorful little backwoods village of Dogpatch. It was a plain, one-story wooden shack facing the tracks, with room to house two engines. But as time passed and more money became available, it was improved and enlarged, with provisions made for handling freight and then passengers. A second story was added for offices, and atop that, a small wooden cupola with windows—an Ogden brainchild—from where station agents could spot incoming trains and alert the waiting passengers on the platform below. It was such a good idea that within a few years most of the city's major hotels had installed cupolas on their roofs. When an incoming train was spotted, horse-drawn omnibuses were dispatched to the appropriate terminal to pick up the hotels' guests.

With a predominantly Irish crew grading the road, installing ties, and laying rail ahead of her, the little *Pioneer* clattered along the tracks carrying construction supplies and workers. It reached Belvidere in December 1851 and Cherry Valley in March 1852, despite severe winter weather. Finally, "Amid cannon and the ringing of bells, the *Pioneer* proudly snorted into Rockford on August 2, 1852."[59]

During the building of Chicago and the West's first railroad, William Ogden suffered a profound personal loss. His life had been a flurry of productive activity throughout the late 1840s and the early 1850s; but on October 9, 1850, it came to a virtual standstill when his mother Abigail, only sixty-two years old, passed away.[60] Except for very brief periods, Ogden and his mother had lived under the same roof since the day he was born. When his beloved Sarah North died, Abigail saw him through it. During his father's five-year illness, the two were the primary support for one another. When he moved to Chicago, she followed and ran his household, entertained his guests, and continued to be his cheerleader as he became one of the leaders of Chicago business and society. Like many unmarried men, Ogden's attachment to his mother was especially strong, as was hers to him.

Granting her final wish, William, Mahlon, Caroline, and Frances escorted the body back to Walton, where she was buried in the new cemetery in the southeast part of the village. Her husband Abraham was disinterred from his resting place in the old burying ground and reburied by her side. Earlier that year, William's Uncle Will had died in Walton; less than two months after his mother's death, his Uncle Isaac died; and only four months later, Caroline's husband and William's partner, William Jones, died. The early 1850s were a sad time at Ogden Grove; and although the family carried on, much of the house's gaiety was lost forever.

Ogden immersed himself in his job as president and guiding light of the Galena railroad. But in 1851, he was caught completely by surprise. A few of his fellow board members charged Ogden with conflict of interest and demanded his resignation as president. Specifically, their charge involved railroad ties.[61] Ogden had become a silent partner in his brother-in-law's lumbering firm, McCagg, Reed and Company.[62] In its earliest days, when the Galena was struggling to gain traction, Ogden asked McCagg, Reed to furnish a large number of ties on credit. They would be paid, he told his brother-in-law Ezra McCagg, when the railroad began to generate some cash. McCagg knew Ogden was good for the money, and he agreed to the terms. Although a couple of years had passed since the incident, and the Galena was producing handsome profits, the invoice had never been paid. When McCagg, Reed presented it again for payment, a few board members charged that Ogden had in effect made a tainted contract with himself, and they demanded his resignation.

The majority of Galena board members supported Ogden and told him to ignore the politically motivated charge. However, Ogden tendered his resignation and insisted they accept it. Grudgingly, the board acquiesced, and John Bice Turner was selected to replace Ogden, who also resigned his seat on the board. Since none of Ogden's personal papers survived the Chicago Fire, it can only be surmised why he chose not to fight for his job, a fight he could easily have won. The Galena had achieved a level of success few other early railroads even approached, and it was running smoothly and profitably. But the personal challenge for Ogden was over. History would show on two other occasions that he had no particular interest in running a railroad; he wanted simply to build railroads. It was the journey that mattered, not the destination. Ogden was ready to move on to something else, and although the circumstances of his departure were not what he might have hoped for, that didn't seem too important to him.

On the other hand, despite the best of motives, Ogden's nepotistic tendency was bound to catch up with him eventually. This was not the Upper Delaware, where as the scion of a pioneer family he was free to mix business and family interests together as he pleased. It was a lesson in controlling hubris that he was slow to learn.

If giving up the presidency of the railroad he had built was not important to him, paying for the railroad ties certainly was. Meeting a commitment was a badge of honor, and Ogden planned to see that his promise to Ezra McCagg was fulfilled before he completely moved away from the Galena. Ogden had his attorney, Isaac Arnold, file a lawsuit against the Galena for nonpayment of the McCagg, Reed invoice. The case was bitterly contested, but ultimately the court found against the railroad. The court's decision stated that not only were the ties sold to the Galena below market price but that the railroad, in its crippled financial condition, could not have secured the materials elsewhere. It was complete vindication for Ogden.

Marshall's study corroborates the court's findings that very little money was available to the Galena when they began construction: "The total cost of putting the First Division in operation, including rolling stock, was $405,382.36 and on March 5, 1849, only $365,000 of stock had been subscribed, and while fifty per cent of the subscription price had been called for, only $106,041.27 had been paid in. But by using stock for money wherever possible, by purchasing rolling stock on extended credits . . . by borrowing, and by advances on the part of the directors when every other means failed, the road was put through. Chicago had its first railroad."[63]

Ogden's attorney and friend Isaac Arnold later wrote of the affair, "Mr. Ogden . . . had given his time, his money and his credit to push on the Road, and had risked in it his private fortune. I remember few, if any, cases in my professional life in which I felt a deeper personal interest. A verdict against him would have left a stain upon his character."[64]

Given the court's findings, Marshall's corroboration, and the shrewd and effective leadership Ogden had provided, it's difficult to understand why a few board members would have demanded his resignation. Galena and Chicago Union board minutes do not identify these few members, or their reasons. The only account that throws some light on the situation is a rather garbled explanation given by J. Young Scammon, one of the board members and Ogden's good friend. According to Scammon, there were a few board members who objected to " a trait in Ogden's character and conduct [that] presents him in very bold and advantageous style."[65] But more important, they were unhappy with Ogden's placement of the Galena terminal on the North Side of Chicago. They believed he was trying to feather his own nest by putting it close to where he owned a great deal of land. The city was divided into three parts, the North Side, the South Side, and the West Side, and each board member's interests were tied primarily to one of the city's three division.

These unhappy few decided to unseat Ogden as president and started a whispered smear campaign that Ogden and Scammon were attempting to unseat each other on the board. Unfortunately, each man believed the rumors that the other man was out to get him, despite their close friendship. The fur flew for months between the two sides, while the instigators stood aside and watched the once cohesive board fall apart. Finally, when nobody trusted anybody any longer, the instigators—still unidentified—stepped in and ousted Scammon from the board and made the exaggerated charges against Ogden for his purchase of the railroad ties.

All in all, it was a nasty mess. Still, under John B. Turner's leadership the railroad continued to grow and prosper. It reached Freeport in 1853, but then the board decided to change the final terminus of the line from Galena to Savanna, another Mississippi River port. The people of Galena who had invested were outraged. They felt the board was acting in bad faith and ingratitude in bypassing their town. William Ogden, although no longer part of the board, supported the people of Galena, telling the board that a promise had been made. In the end, there was a compromise. The Galena and Chicago Union established its terminus in Freeport, and the Illinois Central Railroad eventually built a continuation of their route into Galena.[66]

Despite the cloud that hung over some of the Galena's earliest dealings, none of the principals involved in the West's first railroad venture ever denied that William Butler Ogden was the man primarily responsible for building it. Chicago railroad historian David Young points out one more by-product of the Galena's influence on Chicago: the incorporated stock company. "That corporate form of governance was essentially unknown in Chicago before William B. Ogden and his partners settled on it as a way to finance the revival of the moribund Galena & Chicago Union charter," he wrote. "Chicago's first railroad was also its first important corporation and became the model for those that followed."[67]

The immediate success of the Galena dissolved the drought in Eastern capital that had plagued Ogden and his partners. As table 7.1 shows, Galena's passenger count alone, not even considering its freight business, opened the eyes of investors as to what a well-run railroad could accomplish. Its freight haulage was equally impressive. Table 7.2 shows the amount of wheat the Galena carried for one year alone, compared to its chief competitors.

Over the next few years new short-line railroads, most feeding only a few local markets, sprung up like weeds across the Midwest prairie and throughout

Table 7.1

Galena and Chicago Union Railroad passenger traffic, 1851–1856 (fiscal years)

Year	Passengers
1851–52	91,920
1852–53	140,016
1853–54	238,296
1854–55	471,325
1855–56	553,777

Source: Galena and Chicago Union Railroad Company, *Ninth Annual Report* (1856), 21.

Table 7.2

Bushels of wheat transported by competitive carriers, 1853

Transportation System	Bushels of Wheat Carried
Galena and Chicago Union RR	901,366
Illinois and Michigan Canal (all shippers)	352,103
Lake [Michigan]	62,031
Rock Island RR	44,115
Eastern RRs	15,081
Illinois Central RR	14,789

Source: "Rail-roads, History, and Commerce of Chicago: Three Articles Published in the *Daily Democratic Press*," 1854. Chicago History Collection, Chicago Public Library.

the woodlands and mining districts of Wisconsin and Michigan. Farmers, mine owners, and lumbermen wanted a route past their businesses so they could easily and cheaply take their products to market. Chicago was the market most of them wanted their products to reach. Over the next decade, dozens of new railroad companies formed, gained charters, and began construction, only to find the economics of the business much different than they had anticipated. Some failed, but most merged or were purchased by other, more successful lines. The financial panic of 1857 derailed many of these roads. The Galena took advantage of the downturn by buying, leasing, merging, consolidating, or simply signing advantageous business agreements with many of the failed or failing roads.[68] These included the Dixon Air Line; the Beloit and Madison Railroad; the Chicago, St. Charles and Mississippi Air Line; the Rock River Junction Railroad; the Chicago, Burlington and Quincy Railroad; the Fox River Valley Railroad; the Chicago and Aurora Railroad; the Iowa Central Air Line; and the Chicago, Iowa and Nebraska Railroad.

When the Panic of 1857 struck, the Galena had 56 locomotives and 1,200 pieces of rolling stock that ran over its 260 miles of finished track, which had been built for slightly more than $8 million. Gross earnings for the year preceding the panic were $2.8 million. It was a very robust carrier.[69] And although the Galena fared much better than most railroads during the panic, it did not come through unscathed. John Turner clung tenaciously to the company's credo of fiscal caution. When freight and passenger revenues began to dip, he began cutting the workforce, dropping from 1,904 employees to only 722. Despite that, the Galena began laying a second track to handle additional traffic, a move that was unimpeded by the financial crunch. Overall, the company's ratio of expenses to earnings remained at a comfortable level until the panic ended.

Looking down on the United States from outer space during this period, one would have sworn that a giant cobweb was being spun, with Chicago as its nexus. Each time one of the Galena's growing stable of engines rolled into a new town pulling a string of freight cars, a few grizzled men stood hunched over on the wooden sidewalks, looking on in disappointment. They were the stagecoach operators, and the plank-road entrepreneurs, and the freight-wagon builders; and as they watched their livelihoods literally disappear in a puff of smoke, they shook their heads in disbelief.

Chicago suffered from a number of infrastructure problem in the 1850s. The city's emergence as a rail junction, which caused a massive clog of rail lines from the hinterlands into the central city, was certainly one of the larger ones. Looking at it from a railroader's perspective, the Galena's chief engineer John Van Nortwick solved the problem. He was keenly aware of how much money was being wasted by each railroad building its own tracks into the city. When he saw the underfunded Aurora Branch Railroad on its way to town, he made a suggestion to them: rail sharing. Through a system of negotiated track rights, the Aurora Branch used the Galena's rails. They operated their own trains with their own crews over the Galena's iron by paying 70 percent of any revenues they earned on that thirty-mile stretch they shared.[70] It was a brilliant idea. Within a few years, not only in Chicago but also in major rail centers that followed, Van Nortwick's idea sparked a spate of expense-sharing measures that included connector lines, bridges, and even terminals in smaller markets.

Although he no longer ran the Galena, William Ogden was still one of its largest shareholders, so he watched all this growth and prosperity with great interest. He was not finished with the Galena. When he was ready—and he had his own timetable—he would once again take charge of the railroad to which he had so lovingly given birth.

8

The First Businessman

Robert McCormick never liked farming.[1] In 1810, at age thirty, he inherited his family's estate, Walnut Grove, which sat smack-dab in the middle of Virginia's beautiful Shenandoah Valley. Fortunately for Robert, there were plenty of slaves to labor in the fields, so as the master of the estate he was free to do as he pleased. What pleased Robert more than anything was tinkering. He had a knack for mechanical things, and he pleasantly passed his days in his farm's blacksmith shop, a small, square log cabin perched on a high stone foundation. At his littered workbench with an old stone anvil attached to one end, he toiled for hours on a variety of gadgets: a device for breaking hemp and flax, a blacksmith's bellows, and a hillside plow, among others.

It seemed to Robert as he watched his muscular, glistening slaves swing a scythe all day long during harvesting season that there had to be a more efficient way to harvest grain. So in 1815 he began working on a horse-drawn grain harvester, or reaper. The walls of his blacksmith hut were black with the soot of a thousand fires, and for inspiration Robert gazed through the one small window at the branches of the tall maples and sycamores that surrounded his homestead, to the misty summits of the Blue Ridge Mountains in the distance. When he finally finished the first crude prototype of his reaper, his wife Polly suggested he turn the project over to their son Cyrus, an assertive, business-minded young man who shared his father's talent for mechanical things.

Cyrus Hall McCormick was a stern-faced fellow who seldom spared a smile. Thick black hair, black sideburns, and a neatly trimmed black beard made a hairy halo surrounding his face. Even in his later years, when the sideburns and beard had turned white, the thick hair on his head remained black as a starless Shenandoah Valley night.

By 1831, Cyrus had a working model of the grain harvester.[2] He continued to work on it and finally obtained a patent in 1834, making Robert and Polly very proud. Over the next thirteen years, he perfected the design and began building the machines, slowly at first, then at a pace that quickly outstripped his small Virginia machine shop. In a highly unusual move for the times, he licensed manufacturers in New York City, Cincinnati, and other large cities to build the machines for him. He also contracted with agents throughout the Midwest to sell his product, and in 1845 he sold 143 bright red Virginia Reapers.

Cyrus McCormick's original 1831 grain harvester, the Virginia Reaper.

Two years later, succumbing to the lure of big city life, Cyrus moved to Chicago. He saw that Chicago "with all its mud and shabbiness, was the link between the Great Lakes and the Great West. Here he could best assemble his materials . . . and best ship his finished machines to both East and West," according to one of his biographers.[3] McCormick had only one problem: he had neither money nor credit to build his own manufacturing facility.

Among the companies he had licensed to build his reapers was Gray and Warner, a Chicago manufacturer of grain cradles and scythes. McCormick entered into a contract with Gray to manufacture five hundred machines for the harvest of 1848 in a factory they built on three lots in the Kinzie Addition, just north of the Chicago River. But when a quarrel arose over the terms of the partnership, Gray sold his license to Ogden, Jones and Company for seven thousand dollars. A new company was formed called McCormick, Ogden and

Company, and McCormick was quick to ask Ogden to help him finance a larger, grander factory.[4]

Ogden recognized the significance of McCormick's machine.[5] Up to that time, grain had been harvested by the same methods for centuries. Farmers wielding one-handed sickles or two-handed scythes spent hundreds of hours in the hot fields cutting the grain, and then it had to be collected and stored within a very short time—perhaps five to ten days—or it would rot on the ground. Most farmers never finished harvesting all of it and would turn out their hogs and cattle to feed on the crops they were unable to reap. It was a wasteful process, but it was all the farmers could do, given the tools available to them. Ogden had become familiar with the problems of these farmers, first as a mill owner in New York and later while canvassing the rural Illinois countryside selling Galena railroad stock subscriptions.

When McCormick sought him out for a new partnership, Ogden immediately agreed. He proposed to loan McCormick one hundred thousand dollars and to invest an additional twenty-five thousand dollars himself, for a half interest in the new factory. A deal was struck. "This partnership helped McCormick greatly. It gave him at once capital, credit, prestige and a factory. It enabled him to escape the tyranny of small anxieties," McCormick's biographer asserted.[6]

McCormick continued to improve the Virginia Reaper and obtained new patents on it. In 1848 he applied for a patent extension on the original Virginia Reaper, but it was denied. It was a bitter pill; many other companies

Cyrus McCormick.

had copied his machine and were competing with him using his own invention. A less-driven man might have given up; it just encouraged Cyrus McCormick to work longer and think harder.

Unfortunately, the partnership with Ogden did not work out well. "[Ogden] possessed a strong temperament, too strong to harmonize with the fiery zeal of McCormick's nature. Also, the one was absorbed in his reaper, while the other had wide interests in every activity that touched Chicago," wrote McCormick's grandson.[7] Thus, in 1849 they agreed amicably to disagree, and McCormick bought out Ogden's portion of the business for fifty thousand dollars. They had sold fifteen hundred machines that year, providing McCormick with enough money to pay Ogden's high asking price and to repay the loan.

McCormick's four-story brick factory, built with Ogden's money, was Chicago's first, and for a long time its largest, industrial building. Competition remained intense for McCormick, mostly from companies putting their name on products derived from his original design. But he was more than just an inventive genius; McCormick was also a shrewd businessman. His company was revolutionary for its time. It was among the first to offer a free trial of its product, a money-back guarantee, a credit payment system, and a flat-priced product ($120), with no bargaining or hidden pricing scheme. He established an agency system throughout the country and was a pioneer in early advertising.

One contemporary account of McCormick's success comes from Ogden's friend J. Young Scammon, who said that it was at Ogden's suggestion that the first reaper was sent to England for the great London Exposition of 1851. The machine was a huge hit, and it spurred sales of McCormick's Virginia Reaper worldwide.[8]

The McCormick reaper, more than any other single product before or after it, revolutionized farming. Where it had once taken nearly 90 percent of the population to feed the nation, the number eventually fell to about 2 percent. Its value to Chicago cannot be overstated either. With the railroads and the canal providing the means to move grain products to Chicago, and the grain elevators in place to handle the product, the reaper provided the product itself, in an abundance that nobody could have dreamed possible. By the early 1850s, Chicago passed St. Louis as the grain exporting capital of the Midwest, and by the mid-1850s it passed Buffalo as the largest in the nation. Eventually, it became the world's largest grain exporter. International Harvester, now renamed Navistar, the company that grew out of McCormick's Virginia Reaper, was Chicago's first industrial giant; and like almost everything else of importance in the burgeoning city, it had William Ogden's fingerprints on it.

By 1848, Ogden and a number of other city leaders recognized the need for an organization that could administer, standardize, and promote the burgeoning grain trade in Chicago, which had grown exponentially since Charlie Walker sent his thirty-nine sacks of wheat to Buffalo ten years earlier. Newberry and Dole had continued to make improvements in their grain elevators, and many privately owned warehouses now stood along South River Street, where grain could be stored until shipping time. Up to this time, grain had arrived in Chicago by steamship, barge, or oxcart. The volume and the price of the product could change dramatically from day to day, depending on the weather and the fluctuations of supply and demand. In an unregulated, open-market environment, products were sold in baskets or sacks between hard-bargaining farmers and merchants. It was obviously time to develop a more streamlined system.[9]

Ogden and about twenty-five other businessmen rented rooms above a flour store on South Water Street and began to plan. Thomas Dyer, a meat packer, was selected as president of what they were calling the "Commercial Exchange"; Charles Walker was appointed vice president; and twenty other founders, including Ogden, were named directors. Soon they had drafted a statement of purpose: "to maintain a Commercial Exchange; to promote uniformity and equity in trade; to facilitate the speedy adjustment of business suits; to acquire and to disseminate valuable economic information; and generally to secure to its members the benefit of cooperation in the furtherance of their legitimate pursuits."[10] In the years to come, the Chicago Board of Trade, as it would be renamed, took on one more very important task: the regulation of the futures trade in grains and other agricultural products. Thus was born the nation's first agricultural exchange, which today remains one of the world's largest.

Chicago had changed a great deal in the decade-plus since it had become a city, but in many ways it was still the same bedraggled place it had been on the day of its birth. Author John Lewis Peyton visited the burgeoning city in 1848 and described it in his 1870 book *Over the Alleghanies and Across the Prairies*:

> The city is situated on both sides of the Chicago river, a sluggish slimy stream, too lazy to clean itself, and on both sides of its north and south branches, upon a level piece of ground, half dry and half wet, resembling a salt marsh, and contained a population of 20,000. There was no pavement, no macadamized streets, no drainage, and the three thousand houses in which the people lived were almost entirely small timber buildings painted white, and this white much defaced by mud . . .
>
> Chicago was already becoming a place of considerable importance for manufacturers. Steam mills were busy in every part of the city preparing lumber for buildings which were contracted to be erected by the thousands the next season. Large establishments were engaged in manufacturing agricultural implements of every description for the farmers who flocked to the country every spring. A single establishment, that of McCormick employed several hundred hands, and during each season completed from fifteen hundred to two thousand grain-reapers and grass-mowers. Blacksmith, wagon and coachmakers shops were busy preparing for a spring demand, which with all their energy they could not supply. Brickmakers had discovered on the lake shore near the city and a short distance in the interior, excellent beds of clay, and were manufacturing, even at this time, millions of bricks by a patent process, which the frost did not hinder, or delay. Hundreds of workmen were also engaged in quarrying stone and marble

on the banks of the projected canal; and the Illinois Central Railway employed large bodies of men in driving piles and constructing a track and depot at the beach. Real estate agents were mapping out the surrounding territory for ten to fifteen miles in the interior, giving fancy names to the future avenues, streets, squares and parks. A brisk traffic existed in the sale of corner lots, and men with nothing but their wits, had been known to succeed in a single season in making a fortune—sometimes certainly it was only on paper.[11]

From the beginning in Chicago, Ogden had made it a point to entertain important men and women who visited the city. Peyton, a Virginia gentleman and popular writer, would be no exception.

While staying at the Tremont House, Peyton received two visitors: "I found the gentlemen were William B. Ogden, one of the earliest settlers in Chicago, and now one of the solid men . . . [and] his friend . . . the Honourable Stephen A. Douglas, a distinguished senator from Illinois, whose fame was rising every day."[12] Ogden invited Peyton to join him, Douglas, and a group of friends for dinner the next evening at Ogden Grove. "I found that he was a bachelor living in a sumptuous establishment, and entertaining *en prince*," Peyton remarked.[13] The dinner party included thirteen other distinguished gentlemen, many of the leading men in Illinois politics, commerce, and the military. Peyton was particularly taken by Stephen Douglas. Standing just over five feet tall with a broad chest and strong features, Douglas, like Ogden, was a brilliant conversationalist and a "hale fellow well met," according to another friend, Isaac Arnold.[14] "During and after-dinner," Peyton wrote in his journal, "much interesting conversation took place."[15]

It's unknown how Stephen Douglas and William Ogden became acquainted. Douglas moved to the city in 1844 with his new bride and immediately began purchasing land along the Illinois and Michigan Canal. He also bought a significant parcel of lakefront land on which he planned to build his residence. It's very possible he made his purchases through Ogden, but if not, they may have become acquainted through mutual friends. Douglas's biographer said he was "close" to Long John Wentworth, a good friend of Ogden's.[16] It's easy to visualize the two men—two of the most accomplished orators of the day—sitting comfortably at the dinner table debating the great issues while the other guests silently enjoyed the repartee.

Peyton's observations on Chicago that appeared later in his book were on the mark too; Chicago and Illinois were making rapid commercial progress. On April 16, 1848, another grand celebration held in Chicago proved the point.[17] As the cool evening approached, a large but relatively tame crowd watched as the passenger packet *General Fry* was pulled into the dock at Bridgeport, just south of Chicago, by a team of mules. She was the first boat to leave the steamboat basin on the Illinois River at LaSalle, Illinois, at the western end of the Illinois and Michigan Canal, and arrive at Bridgeport on Lake Michigan at the eastern end. It had taken her one day to make the ninety-six-mile trip.

To complete her historic journey, the *General Fry* had to pass through fifteen locks and one aqueduct to compensate for the forty-five-foot height differential between the Illinois and Chicago Rivers. The canal on which she made her journey was sixty feet wide and six feet deep on some portions, and forty feet wide and four feet deep on others. Paths were cleared along both sides of the canal to permit mules to tow the boats and barges along the waterway. The engineering masterpiece had cost just over $6.1 million to complete. It was paid for by the sale of lots of federal land along its route, plus loans taken out from Eastern and British investors.

Many in the large crowd were the Irishmen who had dug the canal and now lived in Bridgeport with their families. They were rugged, hard-used men, normally raucous and celebratory; but they were quiet on this day, perhaps thinking of the thousands of their number who had died of cholera and other waterborne diseases during the project.

A few days later, the merit of the new canal was proven again when the *General Thornton* steamed from LaSalle to Chicago with a cargo of sugar from New Orleans, bound for Buffalo. Rates on the canal in its early days were six cents a mile for passengers, three and a half cents a mile for freight, and three cents a mile for coal. Lumber was charged one cent per mile per one thousand board feet. Early cargoes contained some curious products: beeswax, wood ashes, sumac, marble dust, and ginseng.

The useful life span of the Illinois and Michigan Canal was seriously eroded by the coming of the railroads, just like that of the Erie Canal before it. Still, it made a valuable contribution to the future of Chicago and Illinois, allowing boats to travel all the way from the eastern seaboard to the Gulf of Mexico. Grain from Illinois, lumber from Wisconsin, coffee from New Orleans, and dozens of other vital products from other stops along the way were soon being shipped through Chicago to Eastern ports, and in many cases, on across the Atlantic to Europe.

Canals and railroads were very different transportation systems. On the one hand, they were competitive with each other, but on the other hand, they were also complementary. Together, they helped establish Chicago as the transportation hub of the West, insuring a very bright future for the city that only fifteen years earlier had been nothing but a scruffy mudhole.

An interesting footnote to the opening of the canal was the fate of the geographic landmark that started it all, the Chicago Portage. What Louis Joliet had envisioned in 1673 had now become reality, though not at the site he had recommended. Today, the Chicago Portage National Historic Site preserves one small piece of this birthplace of Chicago. It is one of only two National Historic Sites in Illinois and can rightfully be called Chicago's "Plymouth Rock."[18]

The completion of the canal in the late 1840s would do much to hasten Chicago's rise to preeminence among Midwest cities, but it would be the railroads that would give Chicago its final nudge to the top in the mid- to late 1850s. J. J. Ampère, a scholar, author and son of the French scientist who gave his name to one of the measurements of electricity, visited Chicago in 1851. In his two-volume work, *Promenade en Amèrique*, he published impressions of what he experienced in America. "Chicago is not a great city like St. Louis," he wrote, "but [it is] . . . very curious in the rapidity of its progress."[19] His talent as an author would surpass his ability as a prognosticator, however; he completely failed to grasp the importance of the railroad to Chicago's future because he assumed that "the dangers of navigation on Lake Michigan and the small number of ports which its shore offers will always be a serious obstacle to the population of Chicago."

Ampère, like so many notable men before and after him, was entertained by William Ogden during his stay in the city. "No one can better inform me regarding Chicago than Mr. Ogden; no one is better acquainted with the city," he wrote. "As we were walking in his garden, [Ogden] showed me a tree, a survivor of the primitive forests, and he told me, 'Fifteen years ago I came here; I tied my horse to this tree, which was in the depths of a forest.'"[20]

Although most of William Ogden's wealth came from real estate and lumbering—his later railroad ventures would not add greatly to his fortune—he was also involved in a wide variety of other enterprises, like McCormick's harvester. However, the acclaimed American historian, Pulitzer prize-winning author, and librarian of Congress, Daniel Boorstin, probably came closest to summing up Ogden's range of interests and activities. "The American businessman—a product (and a maker) of the upstart cities of the American West between the Revolution and the Civil War—was not an American version of the enterprising European city banker or merchant or manufacturer," Boorstin wrote in *The Americans: The National Experience*, the second book in his trilogy that interprets American history.[21] Boorstin points out that the very term *businessman* seems to have been of American origin and emerged during the early 1830s when new Western cities were being founded and developed. To make his case for the historical development of the American businessman, Boorstin singles out William B. Ogden: "He was destined to be an upstart businessman on a heroic scale," Boorstin wrote. "Here was a new breed: the community builder in a mushrooming city where personal and public growth, personal and public prosperity intermingled." Boorstin's comments tab William B. Ogden as the archetype of America's businessmen.

The First Bank of the United States was chartered for twenty years in 1791 by the U.S. Congress following the adoption of the Federal Constitution in 1789.[22] The charter was not renewed; but a Second Bank of the United States was chartered in 1816, again for twenty years. Again, the charter was not renewed, and there were no other federally chartered banks in the country (except two small ones in Washington, D.C.) until 1863. Into the void came state banks, private banks, and individual lending practices.[23] With no federal bank, U.S. Treasury revenues were funneled into the state banks. As Western land speculation heated up and funds became readily available from a number of sources, loans were indiscriminately showered in all directions. Rampant mismanagement and fraud caused the Panic of 1837 (see chapter 6). Numerous other panics followed over the next thirty years, until a national banking system was installed in the 1860s.

In Illinois, the first state bank was chartered in 1819 but soon failed.[24] The second one was chartered in 1835, but by 1842 it too had failed. Three years later, the state had had its fill of banking, and a state law was passed prohibiting Illinois from engaging in the banking business. The federal government and the state government had both failed, so it was now the turn of private banks to play the game. Taking advantage of the language in the new state law, George Smith opened the Chicago Marine and Fire Insurance Company, which was similar to a bank in some ways but offered more safety to its borrowers and savers. However, insurance companies like Smith's and the larger Wisconsin Marine and Fire Insurance Company also began illegally issuing their own currency. One Chicago historian pointed out that, "Without state banks, businessmen were forced to depend on a motley array of currency which included fluctuating paper money of other states, city script, Cook County warrants, Canal Script, Michigan Script, Railroad Script, Indian Land Script, and miscellaneous business paper such as warehouse receipts."[25] Other, more conventional local banks, all under private ownership, also prospered in Chicago during the period.

Although Ogden was not a major player in Midwest banking, he was marginally involved in it, as he was in almost every major segment of nineteenth-century commerce. Perhaps because his real estate, railroad, and lumbering interests were so overshadowing, very little has been recorded about his activity in the banking industry. He was president of the Chicago branch of the State Bank of Illinois at some point in its history. Nineteenth-century Chicago historian Andreas says that during the mid-1850s, Ogden was a trustee (and probably also an investor) in the Illinois Savings Institution, which was strictly a savings bank, as opposed to a more lucrative but less stable commercial bank. He was also a trustee and an investor in Chicago's Merchants' Loan and Trust Company.[26] Both William and Mahlon Ogden were partners and directors in George Smith's Chicago Marine and Fire Insurance Company, chartered in

Illinois in 1849.[27] It is probable that most of Ogden's banking affiliations came about through investments in those companies.

By this time in his busy career, Ogden had become a wealthy man for the second time. He asked his financial manager to determine his personal wealth and report the findings back to him. After a full investigation—a difficult task given all the diverse investments Ogden held—the financial manager reported that he was worth about a million dollars. "My God, Quigg," he is reported to have said, "but that's a lot of money!"[28]

According to Kevin Phillips's *The Politics of Rich and Poor*, there were only forty-eight millionaires in the United States in 1848. A scholarly review of wealth in early Chicago based on city tax rolls, which comprised only real estate owned within the city, states that in 1849 William Ogden was the city's wealthiest resident.[29] Using the same criteria, the article states that the wealthiest 1 percent of the city's population owned 52 percent of Chicago's wealth, and the wealthiest 10 percent owned 94 percent of the wealth. Given how quickly men who started with money were able to earn much more in the city, it's little wonder that the inequality in wealth was greater in Chicago than in any other city of its size.

In 1847, Mahlon Ogden left the law firm he had helped found with Isaac Arnold and joined his brother William in his real estate business. Three years later, Mahlon and Edwin H. Sheldon, who was married to Frances Ogden, the youngest sister of Mahlon and William, were made partners in Ogden, Jones and Company.

During his years in the law partnership, Mahlon had never done much courtroom work, preferring to work on the research side of the business. He especially enjoyed real estate title work, which Arnold, Ogden and Company had handled for his brother's company. In true booster fashion, he had been elected to a four-year term as a probate judge in 1841 and as a city alderman following his term on the bench. He would serve two additional one-year terms as an alderman, in 1871–72 and in 1872–73 while the city rebuilt after the Great Fire; and he was a trustee and director in a number of Chicago commercial and civic organizations over the years, becoming an influential figure in the community in his own right.

Mahlon lost his first wife, Henrietta, in 1852, and two years later he married Frances Elizabeth Sheldon, who was possibly related to his brother-in-law, Edwin Sheldon. Although he was an able, intelligent, and honest man, Mahlon Ogden lacked his brother's charisma and leadership qualities; but he seemed perfectly content in a secondary role.

When William Ogden's partner William E. Jones passed away in the mid-1850s, the company name remained unchanged. But in 1856 Stanley H. Fleetwood, Ogden's longtime New York City friend, joined the firm, and the name was changed to Ogden, Fleetwood and Company. The firm continued doing

a grand business investing for its clients. Just before the Panic of 1857, its estimated sales averaged more than one million dollars a year, a staggering sum
at the time.[30]

Between his railroad building, real estate, banking, and civic responsibilities, William Ogden was physically and mentally worn out by the early 1850s.
In 1853, he decided to join his sister Eliza and her husband Charles Butler on a
grand tour of Europe. The Butler's three children, Abraham, twenty-one, Emily,
fifteen, and Anna, twelve, joined their parents and their Uncle Will. In London
the group was invited to attend the Lord Mayor's banquet in Guild Hall. Charles
Butler wrote to a friend, "The places assigned to us were at the top of the table
and directly opposite to the Lord Mayor and his lady and the cabinet ministers
so that we were within a few feet of the speakers. All were seated according to
rank, William Ogden, as ex-Mayor of Chicago, being placed among the distinguished guests, next below the foreign ministers. All the guests appeared in
uniform, making a splendid spectacle in the finely lighted Guild Hall."[31]

The travelers experienced a close call in a desolate mountain pass near Vitero
in central Italy.[32] They were traveling in two carriages, the second one having
fallen some distance behind the first, when the lead carriage was attacked by
banditti. As Butler related the story, the bandits plundered the first carriage
and were about to set upon the second when two mounted horsemen, one a
priest, came upon the scene. The priest galloped off for help and aroused some
nearby military guards, who arrived in time to drive off the troop of bandits
before anyone in the party was harmed.

After the first summer on the continent, Butler was forced to return to New
York; but Ogden, his sister, and her three children stayed on for the remainder
of the trip, which eventually lasted about eighteen months.

William Ogden's interests, both personal and professional, were far-reaching and diverse. There were very few things that didn't interest him, and when
he sunk his teeth into something, he gnawed it, shook it, and savored it like
a dog with a fat, juicy bone. Europe was a brand new bone for Ogden, and he
relished every moment.

In Holland he made a discovery that especially excited him.[33] He made a critical study of the canals of Holland, especially the great ship canal at Amsterdam,
and he was struck by the huge size of the ships passing easily through the Dutch
canals. He compared what he had seen to the narrow and shallow Illinois and
Michigan Canal that could only accommodate small, shallow-draft boats. He
became convinced that the large steamboats plying the Mississippi River from
New Orleans to St. Louis and Cincinnati could be redirected to Chicago via a
more navigable Illinois and Michigan Canal.

From the continent, Ogden wrote a series of letters to the *Chicago Democratic Press* advocating a ship canal connecting Chicago with the Mississippi

River and the Gulf.[34] His words would eventually be heeded, but not until many years later when the work became part of the city's Sanitary Drainage and Ship Canal project.

Another idea he developed on his trip also took many years to germinate. He noticed that most major European cities employed tunnels under the rivers at major streets to accommodate pedestrians and carriage traffic. Such a system, he reasoned, would benefit Chicago, and he recommended it to the aldermen when he returned. The city did finally utilize such tunnels, but not until New Year's Day, 1869.[35]

Ogden also took an interest in artesian wells while visiting Paris. In an 1854 letter to the *Chicago Tribune*, he discussed in great scientific detail the possibility of using artesian wells to supply Chicago's water. The letter demonstrated the depths Ogden would plumb if a subject grabbed his interest:

> Among the many things of interest in and around the City of Paris, its Artesian Wells can not fail to arrest the attention of the traveler, especially if disposed to enquire into the nature, structure, and philosophical phenomena which the Interior of the earth represents.
>
> The first important Well of this character was sunk, I believe, in Artois, in France, which gave the name *Artesian* to wells of this description. . . . the deepest and most interesting Artesian Well ever made is "The Artesian Well of Grenelle," situated in a suburban quarter of Paris. . . . at a depth of 1,700 feet, the borer struck water, which spouted up in such force as to break through all the machinery surrounding the top, and deluge the place with water, sand, and a peculiar black mud, said to be unlike anything found on the surface of the earth.[36]

Ogden went on to describe how the well was capped and the water controlled, the rate of flow of the water from deep within the earth (550 gallons per minute), the temperature of the water, and how it was purified and used in Paris, among a mountain of other scientific and technical minutiae. Finally, he referred to the Galena and Chicago Union Railroad's experimental effort "to supply their Depot at Chicago with a fountain of soft and superior water, by means of an Artesian Well, which they have been boring for many months past." He suggested that Chicago should begin studying the feasibility of using this method for its drinking water.

For lighter diversions, the family visited major museums, and Ogden loved scouring the art galleries for works of expatriate American painters. He purchased a number of their paintings and other art objects, which later adorned his home in Chicago. They also visited the great libraries of Europe. From Paris, Ogden wrote to William Bross, encouraging a movement to raise funds to establish a free library in Chicago. "If you do any good toward the securing of such an object on a liberal and permanent scale, you may pledge me $1,000 in aid, if the subscription should reach $50,000, or for $3,000, if it shall reach $100,000."[37]

As the family prepared to return to America, the travelers were shaken by a dire premonition, recalled years later by Anna Ogden West.[38] While the group was waiting in Paris for their ship to sail, Eliza Butler came down one morning visibly disturbed. She said she had dreamed that their ship had sunk on the way home. When the omen was repeated the next two nights, she begged that the group return on another ship. Eliza Butler was normally a calm, matter-of-fact woman, so these dreams bothered the entire party; and they did reschedule their trip on a different ship. According to West, the group thus "escaped the lot of those who sailed by the ill-fated *Arctic*."

On September 21, 1854, around the time the Ogdens would have been returning from Europe, the 2,800-ton, wooden-hulled, three-masted steamship *Arctic* did indeed ram another vessel, the passenger ship *Vesta*, and sank off Cape Race, Newfoundland.[39] A member of the Collins Lines fleet, the *Arctic* was one of the finest ships sailing the North Atlantic at the time. Transatlantic passenger service was relatively new, and the Collins Lines was making a run at supplanting the leading company, the British Cunard Lines. Of the 368 people aboard the *Arctic*, 300 perished in freezing seas, the disaster spelling the doom of the Collins Line. The questionable part of this story, however, is that the *Arctic* was on its way *to* Europe, not returning, at the time of the shipwreck. Thus, whether Anna Ogden West got part of the story wrong, or it is just a fascinating Ogden family legend, is uncertain.

The eighteen months Ogden spent abroad with the Butlers—the longest period of uninterrupted familial time he had spent since his boyhood—refreshed and reinvigorated him. It became especially important when his nephew Abraham, with whom he had established a strong bond on the trip, drowned the following year while away at college. The young man was only twenty-three at the time.

Soon after his return to Chicago, Ogden had a visit from one of his cousins from New York, Eliza Ogden Mead, a daughter of his deceased Uncle Daniel. She had traveled to Chicago by train and remarked in her diary that the trip cost $19.83. She also wrote about Ogden's European purchases, saying "I spent the morning looking at the nice things that Cousin William brought from Europe with him. He has the greatest variety of pictures that I ever saw in oil paintings, water colors, photographs and common engravings, it is as good as a museum to go through the house and see."[40]

That December, in New York City, the Ogdens attended another family wedding. William's sister Caroline had first married his real estate partner William E. Jones; but the marriage lasted only six years because Jones died unexpectedly in 1851. On December 12, 1854, Caroline married Ezra B. McCagg.[41] McCagg was from Kinderhook, New York, and had secured his law license in 1847. Moving to Chicago, he entered into practice with J. Young Scammon. Eventually he headed his own firm, McCagg, Culver, and Butler, and went on to become one of the wealthiest and most prominent men in Chicago.

In the fall of 1855, Dr. Daniel Brainard, the recipient of Ogden's financial support a dozen years earlier when he had opened Rush Medical College, had recently returned from his own trip to Europe.[42] On his visit he had met an accomplished French portrait painter, George P. A. Healy, in Paris. He invited Healy to visit the United States to paint his portrait and those of William Ogden and Isaac Arnold. Healy accepted the commissions. He had not anticipated a long stay, but Ogden invited him to stay over the winter of 1855 as his guest at Ogden Grove, and Healy accepted the offer.

During the winter, the two men became friends. Ogden introduced Healy to many of Chicago's leading men and women, and the painter soon found he had more commissions than he could handle. Photography was still in its embryonic stage, and people of wealth loved to have their portraits painted. As Ogden had done some years earlier with architect John Mills Van Osdel, he convinced Healy to stay in Chicago permanently. Ogden realized that bringing cultured, talented men like Van Osdel and Healy to Chicago was the surest way to enrich the city, and he never passed up an opportunity to do so.

Today, Healy's work hangs in the Metropolitan Museum of Art in New York City, the National Gallery of Art, National Portrait Gallery, and Smithsonian American Art Gallery in Washington, D.C., and numerous other national and state galleries. He painted Ogden's portrait a number of times, but all those paintings were lost in the Great Chicago Fire of 1871.

Despite serving as Chicago's first mayor and as an alderman for two terms, Ogden was never much inclined to politics. He had considered himself a Democrat for as long as he could remember. His friends claimed that party labels did not define him, his beliefs did. In 1848 the new Free-Soil Party had been established in opposition to the extension of slavery into the new territories acquired from Mexico and in support for the total abolition of slavery. For all intents and purposes, the party died with the Compromise of 1850 that supposedly settled the slavery issue, although some die-hards hung on for a few more years. But during the very few years the party existed, it created quite a stir.

The party was comprised primarily of antislavery Democrats and Whigs and abolitionists from the defunct Liberty Party. When a group from Illinois went to the party's convention in Buffalo in 1848 to organize and nominate a slate for the upcoming presidential election, Ogden joined the delegation. His role as president of the Free Soil League of Chicago demonstrated his commitment to the cause. The party nominated Ogden's fellow New Yorker Martin

Van Buren for president and Charles F. Adams for vice president. The platform supported a homestead act, federal government-sponsored internal improvements, and a tariff on revenues. Ogden was chosen to lead Illinois electors for the national election.[43]

The antislavery issue resonated with Ogden, as it did with most of Chicago's New York natives. Perhaps his feelings about it can best be illustrated by something that occurred a few years earlier that involved his brother Mahlon; because on this issue, the two men shared identical sentiments, as did all of Abraham Ogden's sons and daughters. Edwin Heathcock, a black man, was working as a laborer on the north side of the Chicago River when he became embroiled in a noisy argument with a fellow white worker. The white man insisted Heathcock be arrested when he could not produce his proof-of-freedom paper. Heathcock was an industrious, churchgoing member of the community and had never been in trouble. But he was arrested anyway and jailed for six weeks while his likeness was posted around the area as a troublesome runaway. When nobody claimed him, an item ran in the newspaper saying he would be sold to the highest bidder at auction.

A large crowd was assembled on the morning of the sale, buzzing with excitement. A small stage had been hastily thrown together, and Heathcock stood on the stage for inspection, stripped to the waist. He glared defiantly down on the audience, occasionally nodding and smiling at friends or coworkers he spotted among the crowd. The sheriff asked for an opening bid, and the crowd grew silent. These were friends, neighbors, and acquaintances of Heathcock, and they had come to see that justice was done for the man, not to purchase him. Again the sheriff asked for an opening bid, and again the crowd stared mutely at him. Finally, exasperated, the sheriff loudly announced that the prisoner would be returned to jail and another auction scheduled.

"I bid twenty-five cents." Everyone in the crowd turned and craned their necks to see who had spoken. Standing in the back of the crowd with his hand upraised was Judge Mahlon Ogden. Angry now, the sheriff asked for another bid, but the crowd was silent. Finally, with no recourse open to him, the sheriff handed Heathcock over to his new "owner." Ogden handed the sheriff the coin as the crowd cheered.

Ogden smiled at Heathcock and said, "Edwin, I have bought you. I have given a quarter for you; you are now my man—my slave. Now, you go where you please."[44] Such was the attitude of the Ogden family toward slavery.

When the Free-Soil Party merged with the antislavery Republican Party a few years later, William Ogden and other like-minded men followed. He would remain a Republican for the remainder of his life, although he always considered himself a moderate Republican.

Although slavery was primarily a national issue, it found its way into Chicago's local elections in 1856. The Anti-Slavery Extension candidate for mayor,

Francis C. Sherman, had been mayor in 1841, and he would serve two additional terms, in 1862 and 1863; but in the 1856 race he was pitted against proslavery extension candidate Thomas Dyer. Both candidates, despite their philosophical differences over the slavery question, were Democrats. William Ogden and most of his friends and business acquaintances were fervently opposed to the extension of slavery. On March 3, one week before the hotly contested election, the antislavery forces assembled at a huge rally. It was covered by the *Chicago Tribune* in the unabashedly partisan fashion of newspapers of the day:

GRAND RALLY OF FRIENDS OF FREEDOM.
ELOQUENT SPEECHES—GREAT ENTHUSIASM.
VICTORY! VICTORY! VICTORY!

... the Metropolitan Hall was crowded to excess by an immense assemblage of the untrameled [sic] voters of Chicago, to ratify the election of the Hon. FRANCIS C. SHERMAN, as the Anti-Slavery Extension Candidate for Mayor.[45]

Ogden was unanimously elected president of the meeting and was its principal speaker. In his speech, he deplored the introduction of the slavery issue into a municipal contest, denouncing it as wrong and uncalled for; but he said that the Pro-Slavery Party had forced it upon the election. "Mr. Ogden's effort," the *Tribune* story related, "was an eloquent one, and frequently interrupted with hearty applause." Despite the rhetoric, Dyer won the election and was sworn in as Chicago's fifteenth mayor on March 11, 1856.

On the slavery issue, Ogden and his friend J. Young Scammon also turned up as contributors, albeit small ones, to a Chicago-based organization called the Committee for Relief of Fugitive Slaves in Canada.[46] The organization was championed by a local newspaper, the *Western Citizen*, and its editor, Zebina Eastman.

By the end of 1856, Ogden's heavy work schedule had again taken a toll on him. He decided to spend the Christmas holiday resting in Walton with family. His cousin Eliza noted his arrival in her diary: "William B. arrived in town this morning and came out here this afternoon, he looks very natural and says he feels better than he did when he left home, but I tremble for him, he looks to me like a fit subject for apoplexy."[47]

Chicago's population jumped from 4,170 in 1837 to 29,963 in 1850, and to 109,260 in 1860. While Chicago provided a model for the world on transporting goods into and out of the city, transportation within the city itself was archaic. It had become increasingly difficult to move about, interfering with the citizenry's ability to get to their jobs or to transact normal business and leisure activities. Crude wooden sidewalks were installed only when the public outcry was too great to ignore, and the problem of the mud only worsened with the increased traffic.[48] William Ferguson, a Scotch scientist and author, visited Chicago in 1855 and described his impression of the streets: "In wet weather, all is mud, which the vehicles, rattling over the loose planks, splash up on the passers-by plentifully; and in dry weather, all is sand, which the gusts from the lake blow into eyes, and mouth, and ears in a provoking way."[49]

Modernization of Chicago's outmoded infrastructure was agonizingly overdue. The mud and the water also created another problem: standing sewage. The city was literally an open cesspool. In 1849 a cholera epidemic killed hundreds, and in succeeding years the city was struck by typhoid and dysentery. In 1854 another cholera epidemic struck with devastating force. Sixty people a day died. Finally, a public hue and cry of such proportion arose that the city was forced to act. In 1855 a three-man Board of Sewerage Commissioners, headed by ex-mayor William Ogden, was appointed and charged with the unenviable task of cleaning up Chicago.[50] In an epic drama that lasted nearly a half century, Ogden would become both hero and villain in the antisewage crusade.

The commission hired an eminent engineer, Ellis Chesbrough, to tackle the issue. After a great deal of study, his innovative solution called for a sewerage system that would drain by gravity into the river. The city's flatness was the major impediment to drainage, however, and to solve that problem Chesbrough came up with an audacious plan that left people shaking their heads in disbelief. His solution: raise the level of the city.[51]

There is little doubt in the mind of most Chicago historians that the city's capitalist oligarchy, including Board of Sewerage Commission chairman William Ogden, were behind Chesbrough's plan. They had long fought stricter sanitation laws that could have ameliorated the problem, fearing it would harm their businesses.

The plan called for raising the street grade as much as sixteen feet above its present level. The space underneath the new streets would provide room for sewer pipes and also for new water pipes and gas lines. Long walls would be built at curb level to hold the dirt-filled core in place. The audacious plan left one obvious problem: the buildings along the streets would either sink below the new street level or have to be raised to match it. Concurrently, the river would have be dredged and widened to handle the increased flow of sewage. The resultant dirt, Chesbrough suggested, could be used to pack around the sewer and water lines as they were laid.

The first problem solved, theoretically at least, who could now solve the second problem, raising the buildings? Enter twenty-eight-year-old George Pullman.[52] A nice-looking fellow who sported a fine crop of chin whiskers and sideburns, Pullman was a well-dressed, courtly man. He later gained fame and fortune as the leading innovator and manufacturer of railroad passenger cars, but in 1859 he was still seeking his first fortune.

When the Erie Canal had been enlarged in his native New York, Pullman had devised a technique for raising buildings, but his business there had begun to ebb. He wrote to his mother that he was leaving for Chicago, "on urgent business connected with a contract for raising the Matteson House, which I am endeavoring to secure."[53] To be on the safe side, he shipped one thousand screws-jacks ahead of him so he could begin the job immediately if he was selected.

While he was awaiting word on the contract, and to make ends meet, he began moving houses. Many people who still lived in what had become the business district were beginning to move to the residential areas, transporting their wooden homes with them. The vacant land could then be developed or sold for a handsome profit. Pullman had devised an effective way of moving these smaller buildings, using skids to slide the structures along the ground. After a short time he learned he had received the contract to raise the five-story, brick Matteson House when it was announced in the *Chicago Press and Tribune*.[54]

The process of raising a large building was elementary.[55] First, a crew of workers dug under the existing foundation and placed heavy timbers under the building. Next, hundred or even thousands of screw jacks were spaced evenly under the timbers, and hundreds of workmen, each tending up to ten jacks, ratcheted up the building a quarter-turn at a time. Once sufficient elevation was achieved, a new supporting foundation was built beneath the raised building, and the structure was lowered down upon its new foundation.

Pullman hired some local workers, and with eight hundred of his screw jacks under the Matteson House, they lifted it, built a basement, and lowered it back down.[56] The job was finished by April 3, 1859, and it was the largest building ever elevated at the time. Contracts followed to lift the buildings housing the *Chicago Democrat*, Jackson Hall, the Tremont House, and the New York House. By the end of the summer of 1860, the firm of Pullman and Moore he had formed with his new partner was joined by two competitors, Brown and Hollingsworth, and Ely and Smith, and everybody's business prospered.

The pièce de résistance came when the three building-raising companies banded together to lift an entire block of buildings at once, each company handling a different section.[57] It was estimated that the block, comprising the north side of Lake Street between Clark and LaSalle, weighed thirty-five thousand tons and measured 320 linear feet. Six hundred men, manning six thousand screw jacks, lifted the entire block four feet in four weeks.

The entire process in the city took two decades to complete. Some owners chose not to pay to have their buildings raised, and the business district took on an otherworldly appearance. Newer brick buildings rose majestically skyward, while the building right next door sat in a hole. Plank sidewalks followed the rise and fall of the buildings, going up and down, up and down, like a crazy stairwell. Only a city like Chicago could have contemplated such an outrageous scheme and made it work. What it may have lacked in aesthetics, it made up for in practicality, and Chicago became the first city in the nation with a sewerage system.

Noah Brooks, a well-traveled and well-respected newspaper journalist of the mid-1800s, did a brief stint at the *Dixon (Ill.) Telegraph* in 1855. While at that job, he visited Chicago and penned his unfavorable impressions of the city, which would be published ten years later. Of his 1855 visit, he wrote:

> The sloppy, low, and neckbreak streets appeared to be sinking in the ooze of Michigan's shore, and squalid shanties, vile saloons, and dens of infamous resort spread all over the margin of Chicago river and its branches. A few large grain warehouses were regarded as mighty monuments of Chicago's rising prosperity, and wooden stores clustered thickly about some of the bridges that connect the various "sides" of the city, subdivided by the river and branches. The raising of the grade of the streets has been just begun, and here and there were ambitious buildings rising up with the streets, while the majority of the blocks were below the new grade, and dangerous steps and slopes—a terror to near-sighted people—afflicted the wayfarer from one end of the city to the other.[58]

On Brooks's return visit in 1864, he would be much more favorable in his opinions.

As often happens, the solution to one difficulty—in this case, the sewage problem—created a new problem. By the 1850s, the river was so polluted that during the rainy season it carried its deadly cargo all the way to the city water supply intake, a large pipe that extended two miles out into the lake. Again the Board of Sewerage Commissioners approved a risky proposition: reversing the course of the river so the waste would be sent down the Illinois and Michigan Canal to the Illinois and Mississippi Rivers where, according to advocates of the plan, it would be diluted and deodorized. A three-million-dollar bond issue was floated, the canal was deepened, and powerful pumps were installed at Bridgeport that helped to reverse the river's flow—but barely.[59]

In 1871 the project was completed, and Chicago's sewage became the problem of the canal's downstream communities. Newspapers in every town along the canal vilified Chicago, along with Ogden and the other sewerage commissioners. But this paled in comparison to what his fellow Chicagoans would have to say about Ogden a few years later.

As the reversal of the river was nearing completion, it occurred to Ogden that it would increase the value of his Mud Lake property, twelve miles west of the city, that he had purchased some years earlier. But to maximize its potential, he realized, he would have to drain his reedy swamp. So he dredged a twenty-foot-wide canal five miles long from the Des Plaines River to the Chicago River for the purpose of draining his property. The new canal bordered the property of "Long John" Wentworth, and he too stood to gain by draining his land.[60] However, it is not clear if he participated in dredging the canal or simply gave his approval. In any event, the canal became known thereafter as the Ogden-Wentworth Ditch, so he shared in the blame for what was to follow just the same. A number of unforeseen consequences cropped up that made villains of the two Chicago icons.

Spring rains caused the Des Plaines River to flood. Since it was five to ten feet higher than various parts of the city, it backed up into the Ogden-Wentworth Ditch, channeling floodwater—sewage and all—back into the Chicago River, in turn making the river backwash into the lake. In effect, it re-reversed the entire waterway back to its original source.[61] Besides the obvious health problems that resulted, the malodorous river was so offensive that the *Chicago Tribune* sarcastically claimed, "passengers who were stopped by an open bridge used to walk over the river on the stench."[62]

There were other problems as well. The height of the water in the ditch caused it to flow rapidly, eroding the sides and sending thick deposits of sediment back into the South Branch and the Illinois and Michigan Canal, negating the purpose of the entire deepening process the city had paid for so dearly. Another danger was that a sunken ship or ice flow could clog the river during the wet season, producing a massive flood in the middle of the city.

Cholera struck again in 1873, and smallpox and dysentery epidemics continued to occur. Public outcry grew against the Ogden-Wentworth Ditch. Ogden, the thicker-skinned of the two men, had moved back to New York, having lost his home in the Chicago Fire two years earlier. He paid little heed to the uproar, refusing to believe that his ditch had caused the damage. At one point, he was reported to have said, "I'm not posted about the situation, though I know something has been done in the way of ditches out there."[63] He vaguely promised he would look into it, but apparently he never did.

Like many strong-willed men, William Ogden's self-confidence had hardened into arrogance as he grew older. Nowhere was that more evident than in his handling of the Ogden-Wentworth Ditch crisis. His hardheaded stonewalling of the facts, and his refusal to accept blame for the damages caused by the ditch, would have seriously tarnished his image in earlier years. Now, it was simply regarded as a sign of the corrupt political and business climate into which Chicago had sunk.

John Wentworth's attitude, on the other hand, hardened into defiance. In 1873 a mob invaded his farm and attempted to fill in a section of the ditch. "I bought a certain tract of land of the Canal Trustees," he thundered, "and I propose to keep possession under all circumstances, and to dig ditches and plant wherever I please."[64] Wentworth did divulge one additional piece of information that partially explained why he and Ogden were so adamant about maintaining water flow into their ditch.[65] Apparently they had discussed the possibility of building grain elevators, docks, and warehouses on the Mud Island property, turning it into a valuable income-producing asset.

Finally in 1877, after Ogden's death and following years of pleas from the city and the state, those handling the Ogden estate agreed to build a dam at the Des Plaines River end of his canal. The *Tribune* reported, "Mr. Ogden, who was the most obstinate in the matter, is now dead, and it is not probable that his heirs have inherited his personal prejudices."[66] Wentworth, still defiant, was opposed to the dam, but as it was on Ogden's property, he had no recourse. Though the dam helped somewhat, it did not alleviate the problem altogether. The ultimate solution did not come until 1900 when the city bought the property from Ogden heirs, and the Chicago Sanitary and Ship Canal was finally completed. Clearly, the Ogden-Wentworth Ditch crisis was not one of William Ogden's finer civic moments.

Another parcel of land Ogden purchased in 1853 for six hundred dollars became another cause célèbre.[67] In the late 1840s, during the Potato Famine, a large number of Irish peasants immigrated to Chicago and became squatters on a piece of land then on the outskirts of the city. Located a couple of miles up the North Branch of the Chicago River, roughly between Chicago Avenue at Halsted Street and North Avenue at Magnolia Avenue, this 160-acre thumb of land surrounded on three sides by the river was called Goose Island, after the geese the Irish kept, although it wasn't a true island. From earliest days, the northern end of the island had been home to industrial businesses like lumber milling, soap making, and shipbuilding. The southern end was a grassy, pleasant area, and that's where the Irish had built their ramshackle shanties, calling the area "Kilgubbin" after their Irish homeland.

When Ogden purchased the property, he set about "straightening" the river by digging a canal up the remaining landlocked side of Goose Island. When his North Branch Canal was finished, the property was truly an island, surrounded on all four sides by the river. Ogden used the clay dirt dug from the canal to make bricks for the brick-hungry builders in the city, and the island became unofficially known as Ogden's Island.

Over time, other industry joined the brickworks, the mills, and the shipbuilding yard, and the island became home to tanneries, grain elevators, lumberyards, and eventually a gas and coke company. At some point, it took on the nickname "Little Hell" for all the foul-smelling, smoke-belching businesses it harbored. Eventually the city built wooden bridges at Halstead, Division, and Weed Streets to access the island. Sometime in the late 1860s, Ogden sold the land, which by then had become one of Chicago's most notorious slums. In 1902 the city council officially changed the name to Ogden Island, but that name is now obsolete, although apparently still legally recognized as the name of the historic spot.[68]

While all of this was going on in Chicago, William Ogden had continued to nurture his dream of building a railroad empire. When he was finally ready to act, in the mid-1850s, he set a course that changed American history.

9

The Best of Everything

William Ogden was not directly involved in the railroad business during the years immediately following his resignation from the Galena. He observed the railroad from afar or through friends who remained on the board, and he allowed his partners to run the bulk of his real estate business. But he had a number of grand plans that were slowly germinating, plans that would ultimately make him wealthier and more powerful than ever.

One event he did attend in 1850 was the National Pacific Railway Convention in Philadelphia. By this time, Ogden was so well known nationally for his vision for railroads and their expansion across the entire country that the delegates elected him presiding officer. It was an exhilarating four days for attendees. Most were ardent railroad supporters, but there were also a few detractors. The convention's main agenda, like that of similar meetings that had been held in both Eastern and Western cities, was to propose routes to the West and promote a transcontinental railway bill in Congress. Ogden issued a follow-up report on that meeting to Congress, which Secretary of War Robert T. Lincoln referred to many years later in his own report to Congress on the history of the transcontinental railroad movement: "In 1850 William B. Ogden of Chicago, convinced of the practicability of a transcontinental railway, gave the aid of his powerful influence to the agitation of the measure."[1]

Laying more than two thousand miles of track across rugged wilderness and through mountains of granite was beyond the ability of private enterprise to finance. Heavy federal subsidy would be required if the dream were to be realized. But so far, provincial rivalries over which route the railroad should take had kept the project from finding majority support in Congress. The first ray of hope peeked through late in 1850. In the fall, President Millard Fillmore signed the first railroad land-grant bill. The law, proposed by Illinois's Stephen A. Douglas, gave more than 2.5 million acres of right-of-way to two railroads. The Illinois Central Railroad planned to go from Chicago to Cairo, Illinois, at the confluence of the Mississippi and Ohio Rivers, while the Mobile and Ohio Railroad, operating in Mississippi and Alabama, would go from Columbus, Kentucky (across the river from Cairo), all the way to Mobile on the Gulf of Mexico. The two companies would thus provide a continuous rail link from the Great Lakes to the Gulf.

Although the railroad land-grant program would lead to a number of abuses, in theory it was well designed. By giving away public land along a railroad's right-of-way in a checkerboard pattern, the U.S. government immeasurably increased the value of that half of the land that it retained. The idea was that the railroad would sell their half of the land in the checkerboard to pay for building the road, and the government would hold its half until settlement increased its value. The land-grant program proved to be the kick-start to develop a transcontinental railroad, although its realization was still many years in the future.

After attending the National Pacific Railway Convention, Ogden spent the remainder of the early 1850s traveling. He spent eighteen months touring Europe with his family, and undoubtedly he visited every European railroad executive he could find along the way. Upon his return, he repacked his grips and headed out again, this time with serious business in mind. Traveling alone aboard boats and trains, in buggies and on horseback, Ogden visited every corner of the nation's heartland, through the vast Midwest and into the Great Plains, probing, scrutinizing, and thinking.[2] He visited the rich iron and copper region at the farthest stretches of upper Michigan. He drank dark lager beer with mine owners and talked with them about the problems they faced being so far removed from the rest of American society. He went back to central and northern Wisconsin, waded through tamarack swamps, admired vast pine and hardwood forests, and talked with sawmill operators about getting their lumber to market. Astride a fine horse, he marveled at Iowa's tallgrass prairie, and he chatted with farmers in their rude sod houses after visiting their waving fields of wheat, corn, and barley. In Nebraska Territory he waded calf-deep in the foul-smelling muck of a pig farm, and he saw sweetgrass curing on the ground that provided hay for huge herds of dairy and beef cattle. He stood in the freezing wind that blew across Lake Superior, watched magnificent sunsets on the plains, joined a Sunday picnic of prairie farm families on the bank of the muddy Missouri, and spent two days fishing the North Platte River with a dairy farmer and his son in southwest Nebraska Territory.

He also visited the leading cities of the Midwest: Milwaukee, Duluth, St. Paul, Sioux City, Des Moines, and Omaha, where he took lunch and dinner with leading businessmen. He discussed their opportunities and their challenges and listened while they spoke wistfully of the day when, the good Lord willing, the first train might clatter through their town.

When he finally returned to Chicago, Ogden spent days organizing and cataloging his thoughts and observations. As he surveyed his work, he felt a growing excitement. For the first time, he was able to actually see the manifestation of his railroad vision in black and white. It was all there before him as a cohesive whole, not floating loosely through his mind as detached thoughts and ideas. And as it took shape and form, he became more and more convinced of the viability of his vision and committed to seeing it through, regardless of the obstacles he might face or the actions that might be required to overcome them.

In June 1855 Ogden turned fifty years old. Many years had passed since he had piked logs down the raging waters of the Delaware River with the raftsmen or sat by his father's bedside struggling to learn about his family's businesses. His beloved Sarah had been gone for twenty years, and his mother for five years. Although often accompanied to important social events by elegant ladies, he had never had any serious romances since Sarah's passing. He couldn't deny that time was creeping up on him.

To celebrate his birthday, he invited a number of good friends to join him for dinner. J. Young Scammon, Isaac Arnold, Charles Butler, John Turner, his brother Mahlon, New York railroad attorney Samuel J. Tilden, and a few others all showed up bearing small gifts to honor their friend. Ogden and Tilden had first become acquainted during the brief Free-Soil Party movement of the late 1840s and early 1850s, when both men were helping to establish the antislavery organization that eventually metamorphosed into the Republican Party, although Tilden eventually reverted to the Democratic Party. He was another native New Yorker, and he and Ogden would be involved in a number of pursuits together over the years, both men earning substantial money from these joint ventures. He also served as Ogden's attorney on most of his complex railroad deals.

Ogden had an agenda for the get-together that exceeded just a few celebratory toasts to his half-century mark. But first, they would enjoy cocktails and dinner. The Lake House, where the celebration was most likely held, had one of the finest bars in the city, and mixed cocktails were all the rage. Their waiter took orders for knickerbockers, sling flips, stonewalls, pig and whistles, and perhaps even a few mint juleps. A couple of the men smoked cigarettes with their libations, another fad that was just beginning to catch on in civilized society. Beautiful tin boxes of Three Kings, Vanity Fair, Old Judge, and even Ogden's London-made Guinea Gold cigarettes would have been available for men of means.

After cocktails, the guests dined sumptuously.[3] The Lake House was the first restaurant in the city to offer amenities like napkins and printed menus, and they shipped in fresh ingredients by rail, like oysters, oranges, and New England lobsters. When dinner was finished and the dishes cleared, the waiter probably offered fine aged sherry or port and passed out hand-rolled Caribbean cigars. Then the gas lamps were adjusted for more light, and Ogden rose to speak.

We can imagine that he probably endured a long string of toasts, both serious and frivolous, to his health and his age before he finally tapped on his snifter for quiet and then thanked his friends for helping him celebrate the landmark birthday. Then his tone turned serious, and he told his guests the real reason he had asked them to join him. He wanted to lay out his vision for a grand new railroad. It was a vision he had nurtured for almost a quarter-century, the vision that had carried him forward during the dark days when few men wanted to align themselves with his Galena and Chicago Union Railroad.

No doubt he described in some detail, often relying on his travel diary, the places he had visited over the past couple of years and the folks he had shared dreams and ideas with on his "voyage of discovery." He probably spoke about the iron mines in Michigan and the huge herds of cattle in Nebraska Territory and about the waving fields of wheat and the sweet smell of clover. Ogden the orator was at his best in settings like this.

The centerpiece of his story was a large, hand-inked parchment map he had commissioned, which he hung on the wall behind him.[4] On the far right it showed Lake Michigan, shaped like a long, fat sausage, with Chicago prominently noted on its southwestern shore. From Chicago, delicately drawn hatched lines radiated north and west into remote regions where some of his guests had never ventured. Along the northern line were carefully labeled the towns of Kenosha, Milwaukee, Sheboygan, and Green Bay. Upon entering Michigan's Upper Peninsula, the line passed Escanaba and then turned west, all the way to Duluth at the southwestern tip of Lake Superior. The western line out of Chicago was equally ambitious, touching Moline, Iowa City, Des Moines, and Omaha, with a number of smaller towns noted along the way. From each of these two main trunk lines, smaller ones radiated off in many directions into the countryside, passing through dozens of small towns and villages that most of them had never heard of.

When Ogden finished sharing his vision, the people in the room must have been thoughtfully silent while they tried to fully grasp the implications of what they had just seen. Ogden's plan, presented so clearly on the large parchment, was truly visionary: a totally integrated rail system throughout the entire Midwest and Great Plains. Ogden explained what everyone in the room realized, that eventually a nationwide rail system would be built. His proposed system would serve the middle of the nation—the heartland—and connect Chicago to the westward rail network, just as Chicago was currently connected to the Eastern rail network. In fact, Chicago would be the nexus of a national rail system that covered the entire country from coast to coast. Ogden explained that his Midwest rail link would be called the Chicago and North Western

Railway System. Significantly, in an 1848 report he had issued to Galena and Chicago Union Railroad investors, he had referred to Chicago as "the Great North-Western railroad throughfare for all time to come," indicating how long he had nurtured this railroad vision.[5]

Throughout the 1850s and 1860s, William Ogden was president and/or director of a dizzying array of railroads, more than two dozen in all.[6] Many were simply separate divisions or corporations of what would later become his two primary railroads, the Galena and Chicago Union and the Chicago and North Western. But others were independent roads, and Ogden sat on their boards as a major investor or bondholder.

In 1853 he was named president and a director of the Chicago and Fort Wayne Railroad, but the company became insolvent in the Panic of 1857, and Ogden was named its receiver. He brought in his friend, New York attorney Samuel J. Tilden, and together they drew up a plan for the railroad's reorganization by merging it with the Pennsylvania Railroad. The consolidated road was renamed the Pittsburgh, Fort Wayne and Chicago. Since the road had been an interstate line, it had to be incorporated in Pennsylvania, but "permissive" laws also had to be enacted in Ohio, Indiana, and Illinois. On February 10, 1860, Tilden wrote to N. H. Swayne of the Pennsylvania Railroad advising him of the steps under way to legalize the merger: "Mr. Ogden is to-day in Pittsburg with authority to have a settlement effected if it can be."[7] Ogden was offered a twenty-five-thousand-dollar fee as retainer for his part in the venture, but he turned it down, saying the railroad could not afford it. He finally accepted a ten-thousand-dollar fee when it was pressed on him.

At about the same time, from his position in the Illinois state senate, Ogden was appointed to head a committee to organize the chartering of the Chicago and Alton Railroad (more about this in chapter 11).[8] Today, more than a century and a half after Ogden's participation with the Chicago and Fort Wayne and the Chicago and Alton Railroads, it is impossible to deduce how those two events fit into his grand plan for the Chicago and North Western. What is certain, however, is that somehow they did. When he had a plan, Ogden was single-minded to a fault; everything he did was somehow related to the primary goal. Studying the development of the Chicago and North Western reveals that truth again and again.

Over the next couple of years, Ogden continued to refine his dream and to polish it. One of the keystones of his new enterprise would be the state of Wisconsin. The railroad had to pass through Wisconsin to reach the rich mining regions of Michigan's Upper Peninsula, so he was particularly keen on developments there. But due to unfortunate timing, the first step in his grand plan turned out to be precarious and came dangerously close to financially ruining him.

Two small, inadequately funded railroads, backed mostly by Eastern investors, were struggling to gain a purchase in Wisconsin.[9] The Madison and Beloit Railroad was chartered in 1848 and renamed the Rock River Valley Union Railroad two years later. By some unknown machination, Charles Butler, Ogden's brother-in-law, became president of that railroad. Meanwhile, the Illinois and Wisconsin Railroad was chartered in 1851. These two lines planned to join up in Janesville, Wisconsin; but when the roads teetered at the edge of bankruptcy, authorities approved a consolidation, and in 1855 the new road became the Chicago, St. Paul and Fond du Lac Railway, commonly called the "Fond du Lac."

Ogden purchased a significant position in the bonds of the new enterprise and became a personal endorser for nearly $1.5 million of the company's floating debt. He was appointed president and took a seat on the board. Communities throughout Wisconsin were ecstatic at the prospect of finally having a railroad operated by an established leader in the industry, someone they could count on: "the affairs of the Chicago, St. Paul and Fond du Lac Railroad are now in a most prosperous condition . . . there is no doubt that the subscriptions along the line will soon be completed to the amount of $1,000,000. This will put the road on a perfectly responsible basis," crowed the *Milwaukee Daily Sentinel*.[10] However, the jubilation was premature.

When the Panic of 1857 hit, the company slipped into bankruptcy. It could no longer meet the interest on its bonds, and Ogden was called upon to provide payment for the debt he had underwritten. Creditors and banks agreed to put Ogden in charge of liquidating the debt, including his part of it. Despite the fact that most of the Fond du Lac bondholders were from New York City, there didn't seem to be a high level of concern in that city. "Mr. William B. Ogden has been set down as . . . the richest man in the West. His embarrassments are caused by the failure of the Chicago, St. Paul and Fond du Lac Railroad to meet its payments promptly. It is only a temporary affair, and as soon as Mr. Ogden can realize the cash on a portion of the immense property which he holds, everything will be made straight," wrote the *New York Herald*.[11] Using much of his own personal fortune, Ogden did retire the outstanding debt to everyone's satisfaction. Some of the debt he negotiated away, and the remainder he paid himself.

Ogden's vast enterprises included real estate, railroads, lumber, finance, and banking, all hit hard by the depression. Settling the Fond du Lac's debt took a big bite out of his resources and put him in a precarious financial condition. A testament to the trust and respect in which he was held throughout the world is shown by the number of people who came forward with offers of help. On an earlier tour of the continent, Ogden had spent a couple of days traveling with a Scottish lord, and the two had remained in touch. He received the following letter from the lord: "My Dear Mr. Ogden: I hear you are in trouble. I have placed to your credit in New York, 100,000 pounds. If you get through I know you will return it, if you don't, Jeanie [his wife] and I will never miss it."[12]

Other friends also offered loans or outright gifts. Matthew Laflin, a wealthy Chicago Old Settler and successful industrialist, offered him one hundred thousand dollars; Robert Eaton of Wales, eighty thousand dollars; Colonel E. D. Taylor of Chicago, one hundred thousand dollars, and Samuel Russell of Connecticut, whose investments he had handled for many years, placed his entire fortune of five hundred thousand dollars at Ogden's disposal.[13] Ogden had not asked any of these people for help, and he declined them all, but their offers do indicate the high esteem in which he was held. According to one source, "he was often heard to declare that it was worth while to become embarrassed in order to experience the generosity of such friends."[14] During the 1857 panic, Ogden traveled often to New York City to secure loans to tide him over. To assist him, he hired his railroad attorney Samuel J. Tilden to be his personal attorney, because Tilden's New York City contacts went very deep.[15] By this time, the Fond du Lac railroad had completed laying just a little over one hundred miles of track. However, it had reached a sweet deal with another road, the Milwaukee and Mississippi, insuring it track rights all the way to the Mississippi River at Prairie du Chien, Wisconsin.

The Fond du Lac's story was not unusual for the period. Throughout the 1850s, due in large part to the success of the Galena and Chicago Union, new railroads popped up throughout the Midwest like a prairie fire. Most were underfunded, fraudulent operations, or their owners were ignorant of the business. Like a field of wheat, they swayed in the wind between their rich promise and harsh reality. When the panic swept through the land, it was like a giant scythe leveling the dreams of hundreds, if not thousands, of investors, farmers, and small businessmen. For William Ogden, it turned out be a bonanza, despite his financial scare.

Where other investors would have seen the financial panic as an insurmountable obstacle, to Ogden it was simply a small bump in the road. He secured legislation in both Illinois and Wisconsin permitting the reorganization of the Fond du Lac, and on June 2, 1859, Tilden bought the railroad at auction. Five days later, it was chartered in Illinois as the Chicago and North Western Railway (C&NW), William B. Ogden, president, and Tilden legally conveyed the Fond du Lac to the new company. It was a start—a very hard start to be sure—but Ogden's dream had taken its first step.

Shortly after Ogden finalized the purchase of the Fond du Lac, he took a rail trip to the small village of the same name at the southern end of Lake Winnebago to check out the tracks and equipment. Upon his arrival a small crowd of well-wishers greeted him, including one lady who insisted on a moment of his time. She introduced herself as Mrs. Delia Ward, and when a graciously smiling Ogden extended his hand for hers, she slipped a small booklet into it. "This is dedicated to you, President Ogden," she told him.[16]

Ogden looked down and discovered he was holding a song sheet. The handsomely lithographed cover proclaimed it to be the "North Western Railway Polka, composed by Mrs. Delia B. Ward." Tall, stately pine trees braced an engraving of a gleaming train, pulled by an engine that closely resembled the little *Pioneer*. An oval inset at the bottom of the page showed men and women in their best finery dancing at a grand ball. Inside the song sheet was the music—sans lyrics—to a catchy polka tune, staple fare for the heavily German population in every Wisconsin town. Ogden was deeply touched, and he treasured the precious gift until the Great Fire of 1871 destroyed it and every other valuable memento of his life.

With new money now available for the railroad, the line immediately pushed from Fond du Lac north along the shore of Lake Winnebago to Oshkosh and then over the next two years to Fort Howard (Green Bay.)[17] The C&NW now had another foothold in the valuable Great Lakes shipping corridor, and it became the first railroad to serve the state's vast lumbering interests.

Ogden also bought, as part of the Fond du Lac purchase, the small Ontonagon and State Line and the Marquette and State Line Railroads, both of Michigan, and the Wisconsin and Superior Railroad. In addition to the charters and the railroads themselves, Ogden was after the generous land grants that had been awarded some of the Wisconsin lines by Congress. However, a squabble ensued in the Wisconsin courts over the land grants, and many were withdrawn. Still, the C&NW emerged with a seven-hundred-thousand-acre grant for the land traversed by the Wisconsin and Superior.

All of these early developments were funded primarily from the personal fortunes of Ogden and his close associates, in the form of loans backed by company stock in the C&NW Corporation or by a direct swap of stock between the two railroads. In 1861, the C&NW was authorized by the Wisconsin legislature to extend its road sixty miles northward from Fort Howard to the Menominee River, at the Michigan border.[18] This was a crucial part of Ogden's plan to reach Upper Michigan's rich iron and copper mining district. Building this short leg, however, would take a decade and have cataclysmic repercussions for William Ogden and the people of northeastern Wisconsin.

Ogden had not lost his oratorical power or his persuasiveness during the time he was building and consolidating the Wisconsin railroads amid the Panic of 1857. Almost every single Wisconsin railroad—and there were a great many—slipped into bankruptcy during the panic when they were unable to meet the interest payments on their bonds. Thousands of hardworking Wisconsin farmers and businessmen lost money on the deals.

While cobbling together the Fond du Lac road, Ogden had obtained a large stock-subscription from the farmers and townspeople along one of the routes. But when hard times descended, many subscriptions had not been met and construction ground to a halt. The people who had met their obligations were angry; they felt they had been swindled. They feared that this road would also go into bankruptcy, like all the others, and they would lose their money. In a fury, some declared they would shoot Ogden if he ever came into that part of the country again.

Ogden sent a notice to all the citizens along the route, calling a public meeting and announcing that he would address them about the issue. His friends tried to dissuade him from going, but he insisted he was in no danger. Isaac Arnold recounted the story:

> A great crowd of excited men gathered. Believing themselves wronged, they were ready for any violence. [Ogden] was received with hisses, and groans, and denunciation. . . . In his own clear and candid way, he detailed the facts; told them of his own sacrifices and losses for the Road, and by what unavoidable disasters it had been delayed; and then . . . he painted its success in the future, pointed out that it would double the value of every farm, and when he concluded, instead of Lynching him, they appointed a committee . . . which said—"Mr. Ogden: we are authorized by the farmers, and other stockholders along the road, to say, if you wish it, we will double our subscriptions."[19]

Ogden saw each of these challenges as an opportunity. They were all part of a greater vision.

Throughout the late 1850s, Ogden was constantly on the road. He was either traveling the Midwest bringing his Chicago and North Western Railway to fruition or in New York trying to cover his financial losses suffered as a result of the Panic of 1857. In mid-August of 1858, however, he did return home to Ogden Grove to take a brief respite from his activities. There he was greeted by a surprise that must have gladdened his heart.

"A deserved compliment to our fellow citizen, W. B. Ogden, Esq., on the occasion of his return to this city, after an absence of several months," the *Chicago Journal* reported. The story went on to say that a large number of Ogden's friends and prominent citizens, accompanied by a small musical band, marched unannounced upon his house at 11:00 P.M. on Saturday night. Dr. William Egan, serving as spokesman for the group and on behalf of all Chicago citizens, congratulated Ogden on his success in bringing the C&NW to Chicago: "[Ogden] pledged a princely fortune—sixteen hundred thousand dollars—toward constructing a line of road which is second to no other in importance to Chicago." With Ogden obviously beaming with pride, Egan added that all the difficulties of the railroad "had not whitened a hair or added a wrinkle to his brow." The entire entourage was invited inside Ogden Grove for "refreshments and a general interchange of kindly feelings" before ending the evening.[20]

While Ogden continued building his railroad into the early 1860s, the Civil War began tearing at the fabric of the nation. President Lincoln's government was moving forward as best it could, but it was a hard time. In 1862 Congress finally passed, and the president signed, the first Pacific Railway Act. It established a framework for the construction of a transcontinental railroad route. Two years later, a companion piece of legislation specified the details. Under that act, two new railroad charters were approved. The Union Pacific Railroad was to begin construction in Omaha, on the Missouri River, and build westward, while the Central Pacific Railroad would begin in Sacramento and build eastward. William Ogden advised President Lincoln and leading congressmen that he had long believed that a route through the central part of the country—the route ultimately selected—was the most appropriate. Southern states had been lobbying for a southern route, but when they seceded from the Union, their pleas became moot. A northern route, espoused by the Northern states and territories, never had a serious chance, as everything west of Wisconsin was virtually unpopulated.

The two new companies were given a right-of-way two hundred feet wide for the roadbed and telegraph lines, and they were granted checkerboard sections of land along the right-of-way for each mile of track completed. The government also agreed to provide low interest loans to both companies to assist with construction costs. These loans would range from sixteen thousand to forty-eight thousand dollars per mile, depending on the terrain.

The Central Pacific Railroad already had a head start on the project, thanks to a Connecticut-born engineer named Theodore Judah. Judah had traveled to California, and he thought it would be possible to build a railroad from Sacramento eastward, over the seemingly impenetrable Sierra Nevada Mountains, for the western leg of a transcontinental rail line. It was a dream that earned him the moniker "Crazy Judah." When he tried to raise funds for his dream in San Francisco, he was laughed out of town, so he returned to Sacramento and met with about a dozen men whom he thought might finance his vision. Among the dozen were a dry goods merchant named Charlie Crocker, a wholesale grocer named Leland Stanford, and two partners in a hardware store, Mark Hopkins and Collis Huntington. These four men, thereafter to be known as the "Big Four," agreed to finance Judah's venture. Soon, however, it became apparent that Judah's vision of a transcontinental railroad and the four merchants' vision of a quick buck were at odds. They bought Judah out; and before he could raise money to repurchase the company, he died of yellow fever.

Meanwhile, back East, the original Pacific Railway Act had authorized the creation of a board of commissioners consisting of 163 men from twenty states and territories to work out the organization of the Union Pacific Railroad and Telegraph Company.[21] William Ogden was one of the commissioners. A meeting was called for September 1862 at Chicago's Bryan Hall. When chairman Samuel Curtis convened the meeting of the "Board of Special Commissioners for Construction of a Railroad and Telegraph Line from the Missouri River to the Pacific Ocean" with a roll call, more than seventy-five members were in attendance, a good turnout considering a war was in progress. There was also a large contingent of Eastern moneymen and engineers who had come to follow the proceedings, as well as newspaper reporters from around the country.

The commissioners elected three officers and determined when and where the company's one-thousand-dollar bonds would be offered for public sale.[22] When two million dollars' worth of these bonds had been sold, with a required 10 percent down payment, the officers would supervise an election for a thirteen-man board of directors, which would be augmented by two directors appointed by the president of the United States. Thereafter, the commission would be disbanded, having finished its work.

William Ogden was the natural choice to be the first president of the Union Pacific. The commissioners realized that his name and reputation, in railroad and public circles as well as with Eastern investors, would enhance the Union Pacific's chances of getting off to a strong start during the initial subscription drive. It was not a job Ogden had sought, nor one he was particularly inclined to accept. He had his hands full building his own Chicago and North Western road, with plans to drive it westward to the Missouri River for a connection with the Union Pacific in Omaha.

Although the Union Pacific/Central Pacific was commonly referred to as a "transcontinental railroad," that was not an accurate description. As one of the earliest written histories of the Union Pacific said, "This road was not to begin where the roads from the East then ended . . . so the initial point of the Pacific railway was located on the Missouri River, at Omaha . . . until December 1867 when the Chicago & Northwestern came through to that point."[23]

The land distance from Omaha to the West Coast covered just over half of the nation's total coast-to-coast mileage. Ogden's C&NW, which would provide the rail link from Chicago to Omaha, equaled another 18 percent of the total; and in 1858 the first rail link between Chicago and New York City, the Pittsburgh, Fort Wayne and Chicago, had been established, closing the loop. Perhaps tellingly, that was the road Ogden had steered successfully through bankruptcy. So in fact, Ogden already had a large hand in the building of the first transcontinental railroad; he did not want or need the added pressure of the Union Pacific job.

Despite his misgivings, Ogden accepted the position.[24] He realized his name was needed atop the slate of officers during the railroad's crucial organizing period. It would give the new venture a better chance among potential investors. Henry Poor, who had long been active in Eastern railroading, was elected the railroad's secretary and Thomas Olcutt of Albany was named treasurer, completing the slate of officers needed to fulfill the terms of the Pacific Railway Act.

William Ogden understood railroads perhaps better than any other person in the country. He also understood how, why, and when major moneymen invested their capital. Knowing these things imbued him with special sense of what would be required to make the Union Pacific succeed. He was not fooled by the enthusiastic newspaper reports that followed the organizing meeting. His first speech after his election was full of cautionary notes; he believed many of the provisions of the railroad act were unsatisfactory, and that changes would be necessary "before capitalists will be glad to take hold of it," he said in his acceptance speech.[25]

"This project must be carried through by even-handed, wise consideration and a patriotic course of policy which shall inspire capitalists of the country with confidence. Speculation is as fatal to it as Secession is to the Union. Whoever speculates will damn this project," he said. Playing on Missouri senator Thomas Hart Benton's theme of finding a land route to India once a transcontinental railroad was completed, Ogden added, "Every New York merchant will prefer to get his goods in thirty days . . . rather than to run the risks of a nine-month Cape voyage." Once the meeting was over, much of the real work continued in the cigar smoke–filled rooms of the Tremont Hotel, where future alliances were forged over crystal tumblers of fine bourbon.

The Pacific Railway Act called for stock to be issued in thousand-dollar shares, of which one hundred thousand would be issued.[26] No person would be allowed to hold more than two hundred shares. Initial subscription sales were slow, despite early purchases by Ogden, Samuel Tilden, Henry Farnum, Brigham Young, and a few of the other commissioners. A one-thousand-dollar obligation was staggering to the average working man or farmer, and as Ogden had predicted, Eastern and international capitalists were not quick to subscribe, despite his position as president. The war too was an impediment; it scared common folks into hoarding what little cash they might have. On top of all that, war supply manufacturers offered investors a much higher rate of return on their money than the railroad could promise, often up to a staggering 30 percent.

Into this vacuum came Dr. Thomas Clark Durant.[27] A Massachusetts native, Durant had given up medicine to form a New York company involved in railroad promotion and development. His firm had been involved in the Michigan

Southern, the first Eastern railroad to link up with Chicago and with the Chicago and Rock Island and the Mississippi and Missouri lines. His railroad interests had made him a wealthy man, and unlike others of his ilk, he had a messianic fervor for the idea of a transcontinental railroad.

A cultured and educated man, Durant could be charming and worldly one moment and then inexplicably quick-tempered, curt, and arrogant the next. He was tall, lean, and hawkeyed, and his dress tended toward flamboyance, and he was known as a reckless spender. Even his very few good friends would have admitted that the man was an enigma. But nobody would ever deny that he could be tenacious when he set his mind to something.

Thomas Durant set his mind to convincing Eastern capitalists to buy Union Pacific stock. There seems to have been just one small flaw in Durant's plan: it was unorthodox at best and illegal at worst. Durant told his prospects that he was willing to advance them the cash to cover the necessary 10 percent down payment of any shares they purchased in their names. When the remainder of the subscription price came due, he told them, they could cover it and own the shares outright, or if they still regarded it as a bad investment, he would assume the ownership and pay off the debt. Durant advanced all the money and took all the risk, and under those circumstances, he was soon able to subscribe the required minimum of stock to get the company officially launched for business.

Durant and the Big Four of the Central Pacific Railroad—Stanford, Crocker, Huntington, and Hopkins—were the first of a new breed of railroad men. They were plunderers. Durant's plan was simply a ploy to get around the restriction in the law that nobody could own more than two hundred shares. When the next Union Pacific board meeting arrived in October 1863, Durant through his illegal maneuvers had underwritten three-quarters of the two million dollars in subscriptions required to formally organize the company.[28] Though his name was not on all those shares, he was in control of a formidable block of stock that would allow him to wield his influence at the shareholders' meeting to elect the company's first full board of directors. He accomplished his scheme and joined the other men he had anointed as a member of the first permanent Union Pacific board.

Ogden resigned the presidency of the Union Pacific at the meeting in order to spend more time building his Chicago and North Western line. With Durant's backing, John A. Dix became the new president, and Durant became vice president and general manager. Ogden was not complicit in Durant's bond-selling shenanigan, and it was a blessing for him that he got out when he did, although he continued to sit inactively on the board for a few more years. Having been the first president of the Union Pacific certainly added to the railroad lore surrounding him, but in fact his contribution to the building of the railroad was negligible.

In early 1864 Union Pacific board members Durant and Dix and a congressman named Oakes Ames bought a moribund firm, the Pennsylvania Fiscal Company, which was chartered to conduct a lending and contracting business. It was unique for the time in that the charter contained a provision limiting liability for the company's stockholders. The men renamed the company Crédit Mobilier and set it up to be the construction arm of the railroad. Through a shadowy exchange of stock, Union Pacific directors ended up owning the new company. They also liberally gifted many U.S. congressmen with shares of Crédit Mobilier, the same congressmen who supported all the legislation that made the scheme possible.

Once construction actually began, Crédit Mobilier wildly overcharged the Union Pacific for its work, in effect bleeding the railroad company dry. At the end of its first year of operation, Crédit Mobilier paid its first dividend to stockholders, an amount that equaled roughly three-quarters of their original investments. The stockholders—Union Pacific directors and their political lackeys—were delighted with the arrangement, while rank-and-file investors in the railroad lost almost everything. Within five years, the scam began to unravel. It resulted in a scandal that drove the Union Pacific into bankruptcy and ruined the political careers of many of its participants.

Ogden's reputation was untarnished by the scandal because he had sold his interest in the railroad at least five years before the scandal surfaced in 1872. However, as a board member for two years while the construction overcharges were occurring, he could have participated in the spoils during that period; but it is unlikely he did, as extant records do not show him as one of the owners of Crédit Mobilier. His initial warning that "whoever speculates will damn this project" had been prescient, but it had gone unheeded.

Historian Stephen Ambrose summed up the men who did build the railroad this way: "The men who founded the Union Pacific were like Lincoln's generals, some of them good, many of them bad, most of them indifferent. The wonder isn't how many things they screwed up, but how much they did right."[29] It would be seven weary and scandalous years before the Union Pacific and the Central Pacific joined their rails at Promontory Summit, Utah, on May 10, 1869. William Ogden did continue to serve the project by shipping much of the Union Pacific's equipment, ties, and rails on his Chicago and North Western to Council Bluffs, Iowa, where it was ferried across the river to the Union Pacific's terminus in Omaha.[30]

With the Union Pacific job out of his way, Ogden returned to his own railroad. He created the Kenosha Division by purchasing the seventy-two-mile Kenosha, Rockford and Rock Island through an exchange of stock. It was a short-line road that traversed the thriving farming communities of southeastern Wisconsin and northeastern Illinois. The little road had connections with both the C&NW and the Galena and Chicago Union in the rural areas.[31]

When the Kenosha consolidation was completed, the C&NW had 315 miles of track on its routes, a very significant system by 1860s standards. Already it was beginning to use its slogan, "The Best of Everything," to denote the quality and performance of its service. Its chief rival as a Midwest granger railroad, the Galena, had 545 route miles, including those they leased. Together, the two railroads would have been a Goliath of a system, on a scale never before seen in the United States. Of course, nobody ever thought of these two great railroads as one—it would have been inconceivable.

Except to one man. As historian William Downard wrote, "William Ogden did have a vision—beyond his own profit—and he carried it out. Chicago and the entire western Great Lakes region benefited from his labors."[32]

Despite his heavy involvement with railroads during the 1850s and 1860s, they were not the consummate businessman's only interest. At the same time he was forging one of the nation's largest railroads, he also had his fingers in real estate, land development, mining, and urban transportation. And as if all this were not enough, he also built a lumbering empire on a scale unrivaled for its time.

10

Building an Empire

U p until the time of the Great Fire in 1871, Michigan Avenue was Chicago's easternmost street south of the Chicago River. Across the river, on the north side, its extension was called Pine Street, and these two streets fronted Lake Michigan.

Today, the street is called Michigan Avenue along its entire length. However, the lakefront is now more than a half-mile further east of this grand thoroughfare, one of the most heralded avenues in the nation. All this new land—some of the most valuable real estate in the entire world—was created by accretion and landfill.

In 1857, while William Ogden was following his railroad dream, his real estate business continued to flourish, thanks in large part to the continued growth of Chicago and the emerging Midwest. Ogden, Fleetwood and Company, run by managing partner Stanley Fleetwood, continued doing a huge volume of investing for its clients. During this period, Ogden made a real estate purchase for his own portfolio that would have lasting significance, not only for him and his heirs but also for the city he had helped build.

The area then located on the north bank of the Chicago River, just as it emptied into Lake Michigan, was known as "the Sands."[1] Today, the area is the beginning of the "Magnificent Mile" of Michigan Avenue, one of the world's top shopping meccas. But in 1857 it was a slapdash mix of squalid shanties, gambling dens, and houses of prostitution, and its residents were a ragtag collection of society's castoffs: "the low saloon-keeper, the shoulder-hitter, the harlot, and the rest of the hideous caravan . . . they came down upon 'the Sands' as the housemaid deposits a pan of sweepings beside the alley fences,"[2] charged the *Chicago Tribune*.

As interesting as those denizens of the Sands were, the land itself had an even more fascinating story to tell.[3] Just a bit more than a quarter-century earlier, in 1830, the U.S. Army Corps of Engineers had proposed a plan to improve the

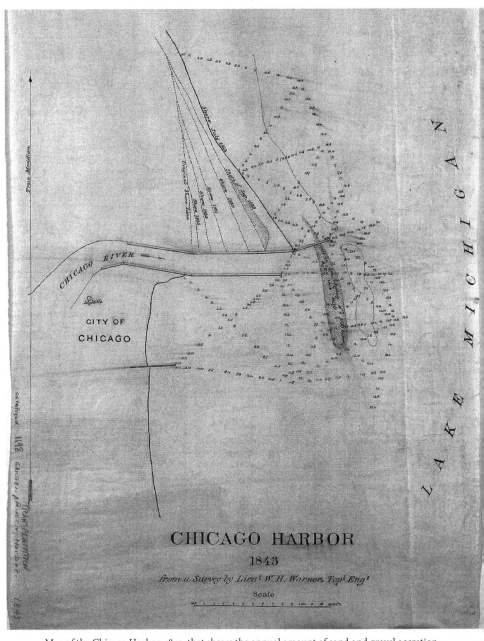

Map of the Chicago Harbor, 1843, that shows the annual amount of sand and gravel accretion where the Chicago River emptied into Lake Michigan, after the river's course was straightened and a pier was built into the lake in 1834. The area would come to be known as "the Sands." Chicago History Museum; ICHi-18072 (image cropped to show detail).

mouth of the Chicago River as it emptied into Lake Michigan. The intended purpose was to improve navigation by keeping the mouth of the river open and free of all the sand and gravel that the lake's wind and waves constantly deposited there. Their plan was to close the original mouth of the river and straighten its course so it would flow directly into Lake Michigan rather than making a broad loop and entering the lake a thousand feet further south. The plan also called for the construction of two piers into the lake, one just north of the new mouth of the river, and one just south of it. The work was accomplished by 1835, and while it did improve the flow of the river into the lake somewhat, it wasn't a perfect solution. On top of that, it created another situation in its wake.

In 1834 a man named William Jones purchased a large lot just north of the river, fronting on the lake, for $125. The next year, William Johnston purchased the lot just west of Jones's property on the riverfront; his lot did not have a lake frontage. Jones soon discovered he was the beneficiary of a natural phenomenon known as accretion. The lake's natural wind, wave, and current action had continued to deposit sand and gravel at the lake's shoreline, but the presence of the north pier's pilings caused this rubble to accumulate in front of his lot, in effect adding new land to his property. So for the next decade, while engineers continued to compete with natural forces to keep navigation open, Jones watched his valuable lakefront property expand further and further into the lake.

Jones began to develop the new land that fortune had provided him. He leased some of it to Sylvester Marsh, who opened a slaughtering and rendering establishment on the lakefront. Johnston, meanwhile, had been watching Jones's good fortune with increasing envy, and when Jones began to collect rent, Johnston took notice of this development. A little bit of accretion at the mouth of the river eventually worked its way upriver to Johnston's riverfront property and gradually formed a narrow, unbroken spit of land that connected with the larger lakefront accretion in front of Jones's property; as a result, Johnston concluded he was entitled to at least a share of that new lakefront land, whose property lines had never been determined. In July 1849, he filed a lawsuit against Jones and Marsh to eject them from the area of accretion and to obtain title to a portion of it in his name.

Unknown to any of the litigants at that time was that they had embarked upon a course of action that would eventually take five trials and more than eleven years to resolve; and during that entire time, Jones's land continued to get bigger and bigger, thanks to the accretion. The first trial was decided in favor of Jones and Marsh, but Illinois law allowed the losing party in this kind of case to request another trial, which Johnston did. In the second trial, Johnston prevailed; but then Jones and Marsh—now on the losing side—requested a new trial. At the third trial, Jones and Marsh lost again for "unlawfully withholding a part of" the accretion.

Attorneys for Jones and Marsh initiated an appeal to the U.S. Supreme Court. The case was accepted, and the appeal was heard in the December 1855 term. The Supreme Court found errors in the lower court's proceedings and reversed the decision, and it ordered that a new trial be held in the U.S. Circuit Court in Chicago.

By 1857, Jones had either tired of the whole mess or had decided to cash out his investment. The eastern lakefront portion of his property formed by the accretion had by this time acquired the name "the Sands," and a host of unsavory characters now made their homes there, squatting on the land. For one reason or another, it had become an untenable situation for Jones, so he decided to sell his choice piece of property—accretion and all.

William Ogden had long wanted to build piers, slips, and docks for his warehousing and shipping interests, so in April 1857 his Ogden, Fleetwood and Company purchased the Sands while the accretion matter was still in litigation. Once he held title, although it was encumbered due to the lawsuit, Ogden asked the undesirable residents of the Sands to vacate, offering them a fair price for their rude plank dwellings.[4] Most refused to budge. Vice was always a prosperous business in Chicago, despite the economy's ups and downs, and the Sands' inhabitants—many of them Irish and Catholic—had no interest in leaving. The city's feeble police force never patrolled the area, so the vice merchants were seldom hassled.

Ogden reported their refusal to vacate to his friend, Mayor "Long John" Wentworth, who was virulently anti-Irish and anti-Catholic. His honor the mayor developed a clever plan. He printed a number of handbills announcing that a dogfight, popular with the gamblers and grifters, would be held on the West Side, and he had them distributed in and around the Sands. Then he organized a posse of police and fire brigades and gallantly led them in a takeover of the Sands, which the *Chicago Tribune* said was home to "the most beastly sensuality and darkest crimes."[5] Wentworth's plan worked; most of the gamblers, pimps, and vagrants who might have put up a fight were heading for the make-believe dogfight, so most of the opposition came from the shady ladies who had remained behind. The few male residents who were present, held back by the police, "scowled and swore between their teeth." The women, however, "claiming a franchise of their sex, opened the vials of their wrath . . . swearing and howling and a cascading of tempestuous epithets," reported the *Tribune*.[6]

After warning them to vacate, Wentworth ordered the posse to pull down nine of the recalcitrant squatters' shanties with horse-drawn chains and hooks. Ogden got his land, and the vagrants, hookers, pimps, and gamblers simply relocated across the river to the south bank and were back in business within a week.

Ogden brought three other men into the enterprise as co-incorporators, his real estate partners Edwin Sheldon and Stanley Fleetwood, and a respected local attorney and judge, Van Higgins. He named his brother Mahlon president of the new company. On July 8, 1857, Ogden, Fleetwood and Company paid a one-hundred-dollar retainer to a young attorney from downstate named Abraham Lincoln.[7] He was retained to secure a charter for the new company in the state legislature and to represent it in the remanded accretion trial against William Johnston.

The new company that Ogden established to develop the land was initially named the Chicago Harbor, Pier and Dock Company. However, at some point during the litigation process, the name was changed to the Chicago Dock and Canal Company. Meanwhile, Lincoln secured an act of the legislature granting the new enterprise a special corporate charter, giving the company rights to "erect and construct, on their own lands and on the shore and in the navigable waters of Lake Michigan . . . wharves, docks, moles, piers, breakwaters and other such erections, protections, improvements and conveniences for the safety and accommodation of boats and vessels, and the security and advantageous use of their own property." It also granted broad rights to take additional land, by eminent domain if necessary, "as may be needful for the completion of the improvements hereby contemplated."[8]

It was an extraordinary piece of legislation, giving development powers to a privately owned company that would have normally been restricted to government use only. Lincoln had done an admirable job, but the remanded *Johnston v. Jones and Marsh* trial still loomed before him. In January 1858, after receiving a second one-hundred-dollar payment from Ogden, Fleetwood and Company, Lincoln began his involvement with the case.[9] It would be two more years before the extremely complicated case reached the courtroom, however, and in the meantime Lincoln became a likely candidate for president of the United States. However, he pledged to continue with *Johnston v. Jones and Marsh*—which by then had become known as the "Sandbar Case"—for as long as possible; and it would indeed end up being the last legal case Abraham Lincoln would ever try.

On April 4, 1860, the verdict was finally delivered. The jury, after deliberating for only five hours, found in favor of Jones and Marsh and against the plaintiff, William Johnston. Although Johnston again petitioned for a new trial, the court overruled the motion. It was finally over. Six weeks later, Abraham Lincoln won the Republican Party's nomination for the presidency.

William Ogden's immediate plans for the Chicago Dock and Canal Company had been forced into abeyance by the long trial, but this important parcel of land and his corporation's development of it would figure prominently in the future of Chicago, all the way into the twenty-first century. More will be said about this vital piece of real estate with its fascinating history in chapter 14.

With all of his enterprises turning nice profits—even during the Panic of 1857, the real estate business prospered, though at a slower rate—Ogden had become extremely wealthy. His friend J. Young Scammon said of him, "Mr. Ogden was a great, ambitious man; fond of acquiring wealth and power, and of availing himself of all their advantages."[10] But Scammon also pointed out that much of Ogden's wealth was used for the common good. "He was a public-spirited citizen, who found delight in public enterprises, especially those which developed that part of the country where he had made his home." Scammon concluded, "He could not forget that everything which benefited Chicago, or built up the great West, benefited him."

Two illustrations of what Scammon was saying were Ogden's involvement in the cemetery business.[11] In 1859 he and John H. Kinzie partnered in the development of Rosehill Cemetery on the North Side. Today, Rosehill, situated on 350 acres, is Chicago's oldest and largest nonsectarian cemetery. His second investment came the following year, when he and a number of other prominent men founded Graceland Cemetery, also on the North Side. Today occupying 119 acres, Graceland is the resting place of many of Chicago's Old Settlers. Eventually, Ogden and the other investors in the two cemeteries donated them to the city for incorporation into today's massive Lincoln Park.

Ogden was always on the lookout for new opportunities. In Chicago's shaky infrastructure—which was improving but still had a long way to go—he found one. Before the city emerged from the Panic of 1857, Ogden and four others organized the North Chicago City Railway Company.[12] The company started up at the same time as a second one, the Chicago City Railway Company, began servicing the city south of the river. The state legislature and the city's common council chartered both firms to construct horse-drawn railways on city streets.

Chicago's first public city transportation system consisted of horse-drawn wagons, called urban stagecoaches, which ran between the railway stations and the hotels.[13] It was largely unsuccessful because the muddy, rutted streets often left passengers stranded in the middle of giant mudholes. The city next tried the old plank-road technology, but the planks would not stay in place on top of the slippery, gooey mud. The answer, it seemed, was to install permanent rails in the streets, something that had been done two decades earlier in New York City. This new generation of "mass transit" was tried in Chicago in 1854, but the two partners ran out of money. In 1859 the two new competitors made it work.

In 1864 the two companies were authorized to connect their tracks, thereby making one continuous line of horse railway through the three divisions of the city.[14] Other ordinances allowed them to extend the railways to new streets, and by 1871 the North Chicago Railway Company was operating about twelve miles of track.

In 1867 Voluntine C. Turner was made president of the company. A lawyer by trade, originally from Saratoga County, New York, he had originally joined the company in 1859. Like men in leadership roles in so many of Ogden's enterprises, Turner had a familial relationship. He had married Eliza Smith, a granddaughter of Ogden's Uncle Daniel.[15] Just before leaving Walton in 1836, Ogden had been in business with Eliza's father, Henry Smith, in an ashery.

The horse railway was a great public convenience and a solid business investment for Ogden and the others until it was sold in 1886 to Charles Yerkes.[16] Although it had been the dominant transportation system in the North Side of the city since its inception, the company was inhibited from modernizing by laying cable to replace its dependence on horse power. The Chicago City Railway owned exclusive rights to trust patents in Chicago for the technology and would not share it. When Yerkes purchased the company, he overcame the patents by employing a new technology, and his new cable railway was very successful after solving some early problems. The system remained profitable until replaced by electric cars at the dawn of the twentieth century.

Historian Bessie Pierce described the periods in Chicago just before and after the Civil War as "a day when defalcations and malfeasance in office had become almost a habit."[17] Saying the same thing about state government, she added that stealing had become a fine art. Graft had become the primary de facto principle of government, and few successful businessmen did not take advantage of the loose business ethos.

William Ogden had been a large part of the national business scene for more than a quarter-century, and the strong Protestant ethic he had brought with him from Delaware County was being squeezed by the corrupt business practices that prevailed. His companies were succumbing to the easy money that was available to those with powerful allies, and although it is impossible to know if he was personally a part of these arrangements, it would be naive to imagine that his hands were clean. Ogden was, at his core, an honest man, but like many honest men, he often strayed. The stories of two business ventures provide good examples.

When Ogden's North Chicago City Railway sought the ordinance permitting a connection with the Chicago City Railway in 1864, Mayor Francis Sherman was offered ten thousand dollars in stock in the company as a bribe for pushing the ordinance through.[18] Although both parties to the agreement claimed the payment was made to Sherman because the new line would go right past a piece of property he owned, and thus damage his interests, that was obviously a smokescreen. A copy of the agreement between the two parties describing the payment was printed in the *Chicago Tribune* on July 14, 1864, and three years later in the *Chicago Times*.

In the second instance, the Chicago Dock and Canal Company was one of many enterprises granted special privileges by the state legislature.[19] These privileges, according to the *Chicago Tribune*, eventually gifted the company with twenty million dollars in city property. What the legislators received in return is not known, but for such a huge largesse—even by today's standards—it must have been significant.

Despite the "anything goes" ethos of the day, some of Ogden's business ventures still did not turn out well. Or perhaps it would be more accurate to say that some of those that prospered in the short term did not do so well in the long term. Such an operation was Brady's Bend Iron Works. In west central Pennsylvania, about fifty miles north of Pittsburgh, is the tiny village of East Brady. The village took its name from the famous Indian fighter, Captain Samuel Brady, and like its namesake, the village and its handful of residents have always been scrappy fighters.

Just west of the village, in the mid- to late 1800s, was located Brady's Bend Iron Company.[20] The "Bend" in the name comes from the huge horseshoe-shaped bend in the Allegheny River where the company was situated. Sugar Creek empties into the Allegheny almost at the western end of its bulge. Like its larger cousin, Sugar Creek twists, turns, and bends its way down the steep hills from Pennsylvania's rich iron country.

Along the creek's bends were located the various components that had made up the company's forerunner, the Great Western Iron Works: the rolling mill, the machine shop, the coke ovens, and the great brick blast furnaces. The coal and iron mines were dug into the hills on both sides of Sugar Creek. A little narrow-gauge railroad wound its way tortuously around the bends and up the creek. The Great Western had begun operations in 1839 and manufactured iron strap rails until it fell on hard times and shut its doors four years later.

The operation was reorganized the next year and renamed Brady's Bend Iron Company.[21] A second blast furnace was installed, and the company switched from strap rails to the more modern T-rails that most railroads had adopted. A company that gained little fame during its heyday, it did have the distinction of rolling the first T-rail west of the Alleghenies. The company was prosperous until 1858 when the owner passed away. It closed down completely for five years, letting the equipment gather rust while vines grew up the sides of the buildings and small children played hide-and-seek inside its massive walls.

In 1861 William Ogden led a group of investors in purchasing the moribund company and the surrounding five thousand acres of land.[22] Included in the group were Mahlon Ogden, Samuel J. Tilden, and another friend, Charles Canda, who, like the others, was a New Yorker. They capitalized their purchase at five hundred thousand dollars, and a clause in their charter permitted them to sell an additional two million dollars in stock if necessary. They set about rebuilding and expanding the facilities.

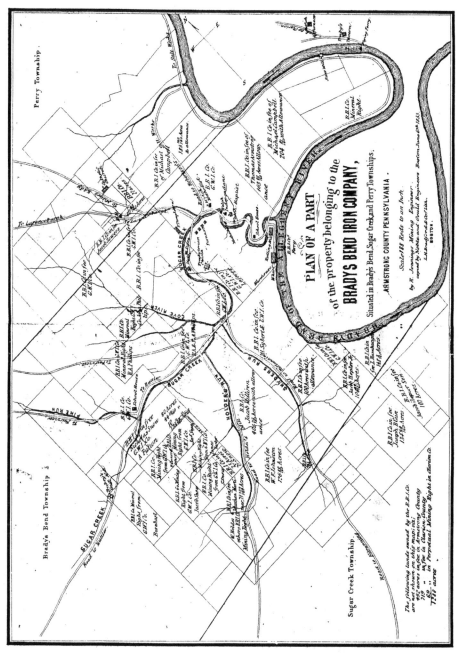

Plat map of Brady's Bend Iron Company's property in Armstrong County, Pennsylvania, 1855.
Armstrong County Historical Society.

By 1862 Brady's Bend Iron Works was back in full operation, employing some six hundred workers and turning out two hundred tons of rail a day.[23] The Pennsylvania and Illinois Central Railroads were two of its biggest customers. Another narrow-gauge railroad was built to supply the furnaces with coal and to haul the T-rails back down to the Allegheny River. There they were loaded onto keelboats and shipped downriver to Pittsburgh and then on to their final destination either by water or rail.

During the 1860s and the early 1870s, the operation prospered, and the workforce grew to fourteen hundred. The assessor's report for 1864 had valued the entire operation at $269,000, and by 1871—its production peak—at $1,292,700. An 1872 independent financial report listed all the company's assets at a healthy $7,575,900. By that time, it had also acquired another one thousand acres of land and held mineral and surface rights for the entire acreage.[24]

Another financial panic in 1873, however, decimated the operation, and it was forced to close down completely in October of that year. The following year, indicating the devastation that had been wrought on the company, it was assessed at only $282,663, and five years later, at a meager $27,500. By 1879 the plant had been completely dismantled and the machinery sold for scrap. The buildings were decaying, and a tall stone chimney was the only reminder of what once had been.

Another short-term business investment for Ogden occurred at about the same time he merged his C&NW Railroad with the Peninsula Railroad in Michigan's Upper Peninsula (discussed in chapter 12). The Peninsula had laid rails into the mineral-rich Marquette Iron Range that provided a cheap and easy way to transport iron ore and its by-products to Escanaba on Lake Michigan. Ogden's friend and adviser Samuel Tilden had invested in the iron mines a few years earlier and now convinced Ogden and one J. W. Foster to join him in another iron mine venture. On September 15, 1864, the three incorporated the Iron Cliffs Company, located near the town of Ishpeming.[25]

The company was incorporated with a capital stock of one million dollars, divided into forty thousand shares valued at twenty-five dollars each. The partners bought the St. Mary's River Ship Canal and forty thousand acres of mining land and opened the Barnum Mine. Soon they were also operating the Tilden, Ogden, and Foster mines, had erected a smelter, and began shipping charcoal pig iron. The company was the first to use dynamite in its operation.

In a November 17, 1864, letter from Tilden to the mine's executives, he laid out some of the men's responsibilities: "Col. Foster left Mr. Ray in charge of the Tilden and Foster Mines; Mr. Foote in charge of the Ogden; Mr. Curtis managing the accounts and finances, and Mr. Whitehead conducting explorations; and these gentlemen, all in the main, independent of each other . . . I shall be surprised if disorganization does not develop the want of a *head* to enforce accountability and to govern and direct."[26]

Ogden also had the C&NW's Peninsula Division lay a three-mile extension of the track directly to the Iron Cliff mines, at the railroad's expense.[27] Had that action ever come under close scrutiny, it might have raised eyebrows. However, it did provide excellent freight revenue for the railroad, undoubtedly more than compensating the company for the cost of the rail extension. However, it was this type of decision that often got Ogden in hot water, yet during his entire career he would never change his modus operandi.

Tilden continued to be involved in mining, on a much larger scale than Ogden, until his death in 1886. Ogden sold out his mining interests at a significant profit at some point in the early to mid-1870s.

Of all the businesses William Ogden was involved in during his Chicago years, none, save perhaps railroads, was closer to his heart than the lumbering business. His ancestors for many generations had been millwrights. His father, Abraham, had initially launched the family's humble fortune in lumber before the turn of the nineteenth century, and it was still in his son William's blood a half-century later. Ogden had originally visited Wisconsin in 1835 when it was still part of Michigan Territory, during his first trip to Chicago. At the time, he had been struck by the immense virgin pine forests he saw all around him. The lumberman in him saw opportunity, but it would be two decades before Ogden would return to take advantage of it.

In 1856—by then Wisconsin had been granted statehood—he purchased some timber acreage with two small sawmills on the swift Peshtigo River that flowed southeast to empty into Lake Michigan's Green Bay.[28] He bought controlling interest in the business—somewhere in the neighborhood of 80 percent—for $69,166 from the two owners, J. H. Leavenworth and Thomas Beebe. The north central Wisconsin timber area was among the most beautiful land in the Midwest, as one writer described: "In northern Wisconsin Autumn is the year's most beautiful season. Sumac forms splashes of scarlet on the hillsides. Maples and quaking aspen are transformed to pastel yellow. The oaks, retaining most of their leaves, join reluctantly in the autumnal carnival, their symmetrical outlines changing gradually from green to the color of blood against the sky. When the great pine forests abounded they formed a vast ocean of green that ignored the coming of fall. But in clearings where bushes and deciduous seedlings sprouted, the frosts of late September brushed the woods with color."[29]

Wisconsin's Oconto County contained five thousand square miles of forests, prairies, farms, and small towns.[30] Amid this beauty stood the small village of Peshtigo, with the cool, green pine forest marching right up to the town's front door. Some of the pines were over three hundred years old, stood one hundred and twenty feet high, and had trunks that measured a full three feet across. This was ancient old-growth forest. Just to the north of town were a number of small farms pleasantly situated in a maple grove called Sugar Bush. Here the

Peshtigo River gathered its headwaters from a number of small streams and then made its way through forest and town on down the hill toward Green Bay. About five miles before it reached its final destination, it began a convoluted series of seven squiggly bends, resembling an earthworm trying to avoid the angler's hook. In its last few miles, the Peshtigo widened considerably before emptying into the bay. There snuggled Peshtigo Harbor, a separate little town of seven hundred people, about eight miles downstream from Peshtigo proper. Due to its fall—eleven feet per mile—the Peshtigo River had bigger and faster rapids than any other river in Wisconsin, making it a natural sluice for running timber from the forest all the way to the edge of Lake Michigan. Except for the squiggles in the river—it is said that the eight-mile distance from Peshtigo to Peshtigo Harbor became at least sixteen miles on the river because of its topography—it would have been perfect.

When Ogden first surveyed the area, he knew it was the ideal spot for the extensive lumber business he planned to build.[31] By 1864 he was putting the finishing touches on this commercial empire. During one of his Wisconsin visits, he had met a man named Isaac "Ike" Stephenson, a Scots-Irish lumberman from Maine. Stephenson and his brothers owned a successful sawmill northeast of Peshtigo in the Marinette and Menominee area, twin towns that bordered the Menominee River, one in Wisconsin and the other just across the border in Michigan. Ogden and Stephenson decided to go into business together. Stephenson invested fifty thousand dollars that Ogden used to increase their timberlands. Ogden made Stephenson a minor stockholder in his Peshtigo Lumbering and Manufacturing Company, later renamed the Peshtigo Company, and named him vice president and general manager. When Ogden was finally finished, his lumber empire amounted to two hundred thousand acres of mostly pine forests, along with mills, warehouses, and a manufacturing plant in Peshtigo.

The town, like the surrounding area, was a beautiful little spot of around two thousand residents.[32] Four churches, two hotels, a gristmill, a sash-and-blind factory, two wagon shops, two livery stables, a foundry, and a wide assortment of retail stores served the community. So did a number of saloons and brothels. Peshtigo was a typical company town, with many structures and most of its employment controlled by Ogden's Peshtigo Company. About eight hundred of the area's citizens were employed in the company's forests, sawmills, and woodenware factory. The factory turned out many products that were shipped to Chicago and then around the world. One day's production included 600 common pails, 170 tubs, 250 fish kits, 5,000 broom handles, 50 boxes of clothes pins, 45,000 shingles, 96 barrel heads, 260 paint pails, 200 tobacco pails, and 200 kannakins (a type of bucket). There were also company-owned stores and housing.

The Peshtigo Company's woodenware factory, at one time a major employer in the small Wisconsin town. Courtesy Robert Couvillion, Peshtigo, Wisconsin.

Downriver at Peshtigo Harbor, the company operated a steam sawmill, the largest establishment of its kind in the West.[33] Here, for safety reasons, Ogden allowed no saloons. The Peshtigo Company also built the finest harbor on Lake Michigan, where a growing fleet of company-owned barges, tugs, and boats floated at anchor. At its peak, the company owned six barges and two tugs, plus steam dredges, pile drivers, dump scows, and sailing vessels, most built at the company's own shipyard near the harbor. Three of the barges had the capacity to haul seven hundred thousand board feet of lumber each, while the smaller ones could carry half that load. The larger tug could pull two barges, while the smaller pulled one.

A narrow-gauge railroad connected the towns of Peshtigo and Peshtigo Harbor.[34] Two trips a day were made between the two villages, and for years residents were allowed free passage between one and the other. In the early 1880s, the company had to assess a twenty-five-cent fare as the train was becoming so crowded it could no longer tend to its primary business. The company also owned a couple of handcars that the employees were allowed to use. Six seats lined each side of the handcar, so a dozen passengers could make the trip at once. This was a self-propelled vehicle, so the twelve people took turns pumping the handle, an arduous chore particularly on the trip uphill. It became a custom that the ladies were expected to take their turns at the pump handles, though they were normally allowed to work the downhill leg of the journey. It was such a popular mode of transportation that reservations had to be made days in advance and schedules worked out carefully so the handcar didn't encounter the train on its journey.

The Peshtigo Company's steam-driven lumber mill in Peshtigo Harbor, circa 1875. Courtesy Robert Couvillion, Peshtigo, Wisconsin.

Ike Stephenson, in his autobiography, remembered one incident at the harbor. In the early days, horses were carried on the decks of the barges to do the hoisting of lumber onto the ship. "In a gale, when footing was uncertain," he recalled, "the poor animals were thrown and lashed to the decks."[35] The invention of the "donkey" engine solved the problem. A small, steam-powered engine, it replaced the use of horses on the deck and greatly facilitated the handling of the lumber. "William B. Ogden purchased thirteen of them at an auction at Corry, Pennsylvania," Stephenson recounted, "and sold them to contractors who used them for driving piles at Chicago and other ports on the lakes." At its peak, the lumbering operation's sawmills had a combined capacity of fifty to sixty million board feet of lumber a year.[36] The Peshtigo Company was a lumbering enterprise on a scale never before seen in the United States.

By the mid-1860s, right after the Civil War, Chicago was booming, and the hunger for building materials was insatiable. The farmers who had taken over the tallgrass prairie were also desperately in need of lumber to build their homes, barns, and fences. The company was shipping about forty million board feet of lumber annually down the lake to Chicago, where it was stored in massive Ogden-owned lumberyards by the lake on both the north and south sides of the river. The price of lumber had risen dramatically after the war, and the company was generating staggering profits.

Rare photo of Ogden's Peshtigo Company lumber mill, which gives an indication of the scope of the enterprise at the town of Peshtigo. Courtesy Robert Couvillion and Jeff Kohrt, Peshtigo, Wisconsin.

The Peshtigo Company had an enviable reputation of being honorable in its dealings with customers and eminently fair to its employees.[37] Despite his sometime questionable tactics when dealing with competitors, William Ogden was a benevolent employer. His people were ensured year-round employment, not just seasonal jobs, as in most lumbering operations in the northern timberlands. In its thirty years of operation, the mill had only one small worker walkout, which was resolved to the employees' satisfaction within ten minutes. But employee-conscious management did not end there. Laborers built their own homes out of lumber and supplies furnished by the company at no cost, on company-owned land, which they were allowed to occupy rent-free for ten years. Thereafter, they were charged a very nominal rate for rent. Employees were also furnished with free fuel, delivered to their homes, and with free ice during the summer months. There was also a reasonably priced company store; and for single men, a large, three-story boardinghouse that was described as "equal to any hotel," with accommodations for 200 to 250 men, a butcher shop, bakery, two kitchens and dining rooms, and two chambermaids.

Once, the company's general manager was taking an inspection tour and saw that the two highly paid millwrights employed at the harbor were chatting idly. He asked why one of them could not be cut from the payroll since there didn't seem to be enough work for both of them. The superintendent told him it was of no great concern, and although it made no sense to the general manager, he let

it pass. On his next trip to the mill, he found out there had been a mechanical
breakdown and the entire crew of 150 men were sitting idly on the lawn around
the mill. The superintendent pointed to the two millwrights, who were busily
making repairs to the machinery. After the repairs had been completed and
the mill was back in operation, the superintendent said, "Mr. Ellis, which is
the most profitable, to have two men loafing and 150 men working, or have 150
men loafing and two men working?"

"You win," Ellis said.[38] As a descendant of generations of millwrights, William Ogden always got a hearty chuckle out of that story and loved to repeat
it to his friends.

Shipping Ogden's lumber from Peshtigo Harbor—roughly halfway down
Green Bay—to Chicago via Lake Michigan was a long and chancy proposition.
From Fort Howard, which was situated thirty miles further down the bay,
the trip was even longer. Ships carrying lumber and minerals from northern
Wisconsin through these ports were disadvantaged because they had to sail or
steam all the way up Green Bay to enter Lake Michigan, then turn south, and
cover the same distance a second time on their way to Chicago, Milwaukee, or
Detroit, adding up to two hundred miles to the trip. Earlier, local Indians had a
better solution: they simply portaged from the bay to the lake at Sturgeon Bay,
roughly the midpoint of the seventy-five-mile-long Door County Peninsula,
which is created by the bay knifing through the mainland. Sturgeon Bay already
cut about halfway through the peninsula's landmass, so it wasn't a difficult
portage for the Indians.

When Joseph Harris arrived on the scene in 1855 as the editor of the *Door
County Advocate*, he immediately began pushing for a canal to be cut through
the remaining landmass so there would be a water connection between the
bay and the lake.[39] By the mid-1860s, the Peshtigo Company was running at a
full head of steam. The canal idea, which hadn't progressed too far, sounded
like a wonderful idea to Ogden, whose company would be one of the primary
beneficiaries of the waterway. Ogden and other area businessmen formed the
Sturgeon Bay and Lake Michigan Canal and Harbor Company as a private,
for-profit enterprise. Ogden was appointed president, a position he held until
his death.

The first step was to obtain state approval. On April 2, 1864, the legislature of Wisconsin approved an act granting a charter to the company.[40] It was
authorized to construct a canal between the head of Sturgeon Bay and Lake
Michigan and granted the powers necessary for that purpose, including the
power to collect tolls and to borrow money on mortgages. However, the sandy
ridges through which the canal must pass belonged to the federal government,
so an attempt was launched to get congressional approval of a bill to donate the
land. William Ogden was in familiar territory here.

In 1866 Congress granted to the state two hundred thousand acres of public land for the purpose, and in 1868 the state passed legislation accepting the grant and passing it along to the company.[41] However, the company only then undertook a study to determine its costs and discovered that the proceeds of the sale of the land would be insufficient to build the canal. They went back to Congress requesting an additional two hundred thousand acres of land. While awaiting the results of the second request, they began removing all the trees along the right-of-way.

In 1870 a four-page pamphlet was sent to all members of Congress urging them to approve the pending act to double the land grant acreage and outlining the reasons for building the canal: First, because the completed canal would shorten voyages on each round trip by up to two hundred miles. Second, because it would allow shipping to avoid the treacherous *Porte des Mortes* Strait—"Death's Door"—at the north end of the peninsula, where an average of six ships and their cargos were lost annually. Third, because the breakwater that would be built on the lake would allow for the construction of a much-needed harbor on the west shore of Lake Michigan. The pamphlet went on to say that the canal would be only one and a half miles long, and not less than one hundred feet wide nor less than fifteen feet deep. Total cost was estimated to be five hundred thousand dollars.[42]

Congress refused to act on the second request. Writing on the history of the canal in 1918, one historian said, "This situation embarrassed the enterprise from the beginning."[43] Despite the setback, in July 1872 construction began.[44] The state act had mandated that the company would receive its first allocation of the land Congress had granted only after one-quarter of the canal was dug. As the entire canal was destined to be only one and a half miles long, it didn't sound like an overwhelming objective. However, because the land was mostly soft sand and gravel, the sides of the canal had to be sloped from top to bottom and the entire waterway lined with pilings or masonry below the waterline.

It would be ten long years before the job was completed.[45] It was plagued by bad weather and money shortages, and work was actually halted for a two-year period when bond sales slumped badly. Through many of the worst times, money to keep the project afloat was advanced to the canal company by the Peshtigo Company. Finally, in 1880, shallow draft boats were able to begin using the canal. As it was nearing completion in 1882, Congress approved building a lighthouse on the north breakwater at the lake. Despite all the hardships, the Sturgeon Bay and Lake Michigan Canal and the adjoining harbor on the lake would prove to be a boon to the lumbering and mining interests of central and northern Wisconsin, although William Ogden did not live to see the project completed. The federal government eventually purchased the ship canal from the company in 1893, and it has been operated by the U.S. Army Corps of Engineers ever since.

The final piece of the Peshtigo puzzle was to be a rail extension. Product was moved to Chicago exclusively by barge or steamer, a very unsatisfactory method of transportation for an enterprise as large as the Peshtigo Company. In the winter, the lake could be clogged with ice; year-round, Lake Michigan weather was unpredictable and dangerous, and shipwrecks were commonplace. And lake transport was both slow and expensive.

The extension of the Chicago and North Western Railway from Fort Howard to Michigan's Upper Peninsula and its vast mining region was already part of Ogden's grand scheme. Taking one small step by laying a rail from Fort Howard to Menominee would fit right into that plan and would allow immediate rail freight service for Peshtigo Company's lumber and woodenware products. It seemed like such an inconsequential step in the larger plan, but as we will see, this one small step would wreak more death and destruction that Beelzebub himself could have engineered.

Once the Peshtigo Company was operating at peak efficiency, Ogden wanted someone to oversee the entire operation for him from Chicago. Ike Stephenson and the men he had appointed were doing a fine job managing things on site, but Ogden no longer wanted to function as the operation's chief executive. For that job, he found a candidate of impeccable credentials. Naturally, he was also family.

William E. Strong had been born in New York but raised in the wilds of Wisconsin.[46] He had just been admitted to the bar when the Civil War broke out, and he immediately joined the Union Army. He participated in some of the war's earliest battles as a member of the Army of the Potomac under General George McClellan. Promoted to major, Strong was reassigned to Grant's Army of the Tennessee, where he served with distinction in every battle of that army until the end of the war. He was brevetted brigadier general in March 1865 for his gallant and meritorious service.

After the war, he moved to Chicago and was soon hired by Ogden as president of the Peshtigo Company. In 1867 Strong married Mary Bostwick Ogden, a daughter of Ogden's brother Mahlon from his first marriage. Whether Strong was hired before or after his marriage to an Ogden remains unclear, but given William Ogden's proclivity for hiring family, it's probable the marriage took place first, or at least its promise.

Although he was a confidant of presidents, friend of lords and ladies, and a leader of the emerging nation's super-rich entrepreneurial class, William Ogden still retained a childlike streak that had been a part of him since his earliest days in Walton, New York. A story that appeared in the *Green Bay Advocate* in 1858, not too long after Ogden initially acquired his Peshtigo lumbering interests, clearly shows that he hadn't lost that characteristic. It seems that during a visit to the Peshtigo mills, he decided to gather a party of friends and key employees and treat them to a cruise from the harbor to the town in a new steamboat he had purchased. Such a boat had never navigated *up* the swift-running, narrow, winding, and tree-lined Peshtigo River before, so everyone knew they would be in for a white-knuckle ride. An unnamed newspaper reporter, who joined the cruise, captured the frivolous nature of the event for his story:

It was a "right merry company" on board the *Aquila*. Col. Ogden [a pet name he had acquired in Peshtigo due to his earlier paramilitary service in Walton], he was commodore . . . Hiram Barney of New York and Judge Wheeler of Chicago, they were the first and second mates. Pomeroy of the Horicon [Wisc.] *Argus* was along; he was the poet laureate for the occasion . . . then there [was] Capt. Brooks, who had command of the boat when nobody else did.

It was late when we reached the mouth of the Peshtigo . . . so it was deemed advisable to lie by until morning, as the night promised to be very black, and the river ahead was crooked enough. The mills were five miles further on, as the crow flies, but as the river runs, some ten or fifteen or other indefinite number . . . at this juncture a portion of our party deserted us. They fled to the mills in a two horse wagon.

Early in the morning we started up the steam. It took some time for the *Aquila* to get the hang of the river. She had a perverse way of driving into the banks when rounding the bends, and would persist in swinging her stern into overhanging trees so as to sweep away her frail upperwork. The commodore had bought the boat, however, and paid for her, and rather enjoyed the fun. The mills hove into sight about ten o'clock. There was a flag hoisted on the staff; the blacksmiths were firing a gun; the people were all out there to welcome the strange visitor, and it was quite a gala day. A dinner was prepared for the guests at the large hotel or company house, and after a stay of a couple of hours the hoarse whistle of the *Aquila* called all aboard, and we started on the homeward trip.

Going down stream the *Aquila* behaved better. We should have stated that during the stop at the mill Col. Ogden and Judge Wheeler had so combined their inventive and mechanical powers as to produce the most remarkable apparatus to regulate the course of a boat which it has ever been our fortune to witness. It was a sort of cross between a steering oar and a rudder, and was rigged on the bow of the boat. Judge Wheeler retired to the upper deck and reposed upon his laurels. Not so the commodore. He presided at its operation during the whole downward passage. . . . down we went, rounding the sharp turns like a shot, past Fiddlers Elbow, past Hemlock Bend . . . out into the bay.

. . . Col. Ogden knows how to manage and carry out the luckiest and happiest excursion of the season.[47]

For the "Colonel," who loved a good time with friends, the trip must have been reminiscent of his happy-go-lucky days steering a lumber-laden raft down the Delaware River to Philadelphia.

11

An Overgrown Gawk of a Village

During the pre-panic years of the early to mid-1850s, while William Ogden was cobbling together his Chicago and North Western Railway system, Peshtigo Company lumbering monolith, real estate empire, and Pennsylvania iron mines and smelters, the remainder of Chicago's citizenry also prospered. When the Panic of 1857 hit, they demonstrated the same resilience that had carried them through previous hardships.

The Pittsburgh, Fort Wayne and Chicago Railroad opened its final extension into Chicago in 1858, completing the first rail link between Chicago and New York City. There was now both a land link and a water link—the Hudson River–Erie Canal–Great Lakes corridor—between America's two most important cities. It meant the handwriting was on the wall for other major inland cities: henceforth they would play second fiddle to Chicago. Philadelphia, which for years had been the country's second most important city, recognized its plight, evident in this report made to the president of the Pennsylvania Railroad: "In a survey of the map, the eye of the observer is naturally drawn to Chicago, and all the investigation he may give it will only strengthen the first impression, that it is destined to become a place of such magnitude as to leave Philadelphia no alternative in a commercial view but to obtain a direct railroad to it. The stake is too large in bulk and value to be permitted to pass wholly and forever through more northern channels, whither it is now tending, because it has no outlet leading towards sunrise."[1] The report went on to say that Chicago would no longer be "an agency post on main routes passing through her. It will perform the functions of a commercial city, and not the secondary part of a station-house agency." The report summarized, "In a word, Chicago is an independent city, and will trade with the Atlantic ports as the Atlantic ports trade with each other." These were bitter words for Philadelphia, Baltimore, and Charleston and words of warning to St. Louis, New Orleans, Cincinnati, and other major river ports.

Despite the grand words, Chicago was not without its hardships: poverty and vice, corrupt police and an inefficient fire department, abysmal public health and crushing infrastructure problems, rampant immigration and ineffective public service. Much of what muckraking journalist Lincoln Steffens wrote of the Chicago of the 1890s would have also been apt to the Chicago of the 1850s and 1860s: "first in violence, deepest in dirt; loud, lawless, unlovely, ill-smelling, irreverent, new; an overgrown gawk of a village, the 'tough' among cities, a spectacle for the nation."[2]

Unlike many mushrooming cities of the period, where rich and poor developed their own enclaves completely separate from one another, Chicago was a hodgepodge. The homes of the wealthiest citizens were on the North Side and the South Side, but those were also sites where the deepest poverty and degradation were found. The West Side was home to industrious workers "with their tens of thousands of labor-bought homes."[3]

The South Clark Street area, primarily Italian, was like most of the other poverty-stricken neighborhoods in the city, as Chicago historian Joseph Kirkland described it: "Emerging on a second-story balcony at the back of one of these Italian houses one comes upon a long vista of house rears and tumble-down back-sheds, squalid beyond conception. Neighboring windows are filled with faces peering out with interest and amusement at the stranger. Here and there are bits of rope stretched from one nail to another—from house to shed, from fence to banister, from window-sill to door-post—carrying forlorn arrays of washed clothing. Each is the effort of some lowly woman to preserve a little cleanliness in the garments of herself and her household."[4]

It was not as if the wealthy did not attempt to succor the poor; they certainly did, but there were simply too many of them. For example, prior to the Great Fire the city directory listed hundreds of benevolent organizations, including fifty-seven hospitals and asylums, twenty-eight free infirmaries and dispensaries, forty-one missions, sixty temperance societies, and thirty-seven full columns of secret benevolent associations, lodges, circles, and so on.[5]

The amazing thing about nineteenth-century Chicago was that it continued to grow and prosper despite its problems. The men who ran the city found it easier to ignore the major problems and concentrate on smaller, more manageable issues, ones that could show immediate results and—always a central factor—not interfere with business. Still, some of those causes they launched resulted in the establishment of institutions that have had tremendous long-term benefit for present-day Chicago.

Historical Society
Chicago, April 2, 1856
Dear Sir:

A Meeting of twenty or more gentlemen of this city, will be held at the Office of J. Y. Scammon, Marine Bank Building, on Thursday Evening next, at 7 1-2 o'clock, for the purpose of organizing a Historical Society. You are respectfully invited to attend.

Yours, &c.

I. N. Arnold

J. D. Webster

W. Barry

J. J. Kinzie

Mason Brayman[6]

The "twenty or more gentlemen" who received this letter included almost all of the founding fathers, the so-called Old Settlers of Chicago: Will and Mahlon Ogden, Ezra B. McCagg, Walter Newberry, Gurdon Hubbard, and others. Most, like the Ogden brothers, were literary sorts and felt the important story of the founding of the city should be recorded for posterity. That their names would be a prominent part of the history that was to be preserved was not lost on any of them.

Reverend William Barry, a retired Unitarian minister from Massachusetts, was the guiding light behind the idea for the organization, and when one meeting proved to be insufficient, he called a second one a short time later.[7] The Historical Society was organized at that second meeting, and officers were elected: William H. Brown, president; W. B. Ogden, first vice president; J. Young Scammon, second vice president; William Barry, recording secretary and librarian; and C. H. Ray, corresponding secretary. William Ogden retained the position of first vice president for many years, relinquishing the post only when he moved back to New York.

In an April 28, 1856, letter to a friend, William Barry wrote, "Mr. Ogden gives us rooms for the present time in the 3rd story of his fine building, corner of Clark & Lake Sts., & the Soc. have put upon myself their charge."[8] That last part meant that Barry, who had a great passion for the project despite having lived in Chicago for only three years, would be responsible for gathering the material that would form the basis for the society's collections. Ogden's pledge of free office space was not totally benevolent; it was proffered in the hope that when the permanent facility was built, it would be located near his home on the North Side.[9]

Isaac Arnold was then a member of the Illinois House of Representatives, and he sponsored the new society's charter through the legal channels.[10] Meanwhile Barry began combing the city, county, and state for appropriate materials to include in the new library the society planned to build. Fund-raising immediately got under way for the building. When the society's first president, William Brown, passed away, Walter Newberry was named to replace him in

1861. Newberry, like Ogden, wanted the building to be located on the North Side, and it was his promise to be a major benefactor that landed him the prestigious position.

Both Newberry and Ogden pledged generously.[11] When the fund-raising stalled, Ogden pledged an additional five thousand dollars and challenged Newberry to do the same, saying he would match Newberry's pledge even up to the entire cost of the building. With that challenge, others upped their contributions as well, and the new building was completed by fall of 1868.

Barry did an admirable job filling the library. A report at the end of the first year of operation recorded that the library had amassed 3,577 bound volumes and newspaper files, 4,966 public documents, reports, pamphlets, and broadsides, and 101 charts in bound volumes or single sheets. It was a promising beginning for an organization that has served the city admirably ever since.

November 19, 1868, was a surprisingly mild evening.[12] William Ogden may have decided to walk to the gala—it was only two short blocks down the street from his house—or he may have ordered out one of his carriages for the short trip. He walked less these days; perhaps it was a touch of gout, or maybe just the creeping specter of old age. When he did walk, he invariably used a fine silver-tipped cane he had acquired.

Either way, he would have headed east down Ontario Street, past Cass and Woolcott and the mansions of his neighbors, until he saw the beautiful new home of the Chicago Historical Society at the corner of Ontario and Dearborn. Tonight was the gala opening of the facility, and it was hard to believe it had been a dozen years since he and the others had launched the project.

Approaching the building, Ogden would have seen the golden reflection of the light from dozens of gas lamps radiating through the glass roof that covered the center courtyard. It was a beautiful building. Burling and Company, the builders, had done a grand job, and Ogden and his neighbors must have enjoyed watching the construction progress every day as they passed by. The entire second story was devoted to the library, and as the guests alighted from their coaches they could see the large skylights that would provide natural light for that room during the day. Handsome horse-drawn Victorian buggies, with their liveried coachmen sitting high atop on their upholstered boxes, lined up in front of the building, disgorging Chicago's wealthiest and most influential citizens.

Inside, the new librarian William Corkran from New York City greeted the guests. Many of the Old Settlers were disappointed that William Barry had taken ill and had to resign his post. Many of them, probably including Ogden, didn't like the new fellow; he was haughty and regarded Chicago as a disagreeable place, an opinion he was quick to share with anyone who would listen.

Ogden handed his coat and hat to a man standing outside the main office, which this evening served as an impromptu cloakroom, and was directed up the stairs where the reception was under way in the library. As the leaders of Chicago society, business, and politics climbed the stairway and entered the library, they must have noticed, hanging on the walls between the handsome walnut bookcases—all crammed with wonderful volumes of Chicago and Illinois history—were portraits of the society's chief benefactors. Perhaps Ogden felt pride at seeing his own portrait among them, a beautiful painting done by George P. A. Healy.

Despite the luminous occasion, the crowd was strangely subdued. Word had just been received that Walter Newberry, the society's president, had died while on his way to Europe. Ogden could recall that he and Newberry had first met on the Lake Michigan steamship when he was returning from his first land-buying trip to Wisconsin in 1835, and they had worked together on many business and civic projects since. The night that had begun with so much promise was now spoiled for many in the room, particularly the Old Settlers whose number seemed to be dwindling with each passing year.

J. Young Scammon rose to speak to the assembly, filling in for Newberry. He talked about the sudden death of their first president, William H. Brown, and now the unexpected departure of the second. "Such events should deeply impress upon the minds the necessity that those of us who desire . . . to labor for this and similar institutions . . . should at once do something to endow the public institutions and the great charities which we owe to the City of Chicago . . . which has made us what we are."

Like most of Chicago's booster-elite, Ogden's civic activities continued unabated, despite the pressures of his far-flung business enterprises. One of the most far-reaching institutions he participated in founding was the University of Chicago.

The college was originally chartered in 1857 by the legislature of Illinois and held its first classes the following year. From then until it was forced to cease operations briefly in 1889 due to financial problems, it was known as the "first" or "old" University of Chicago. In the period after its reorganization with funds provided by men like Marshall Field, John D. Rockefeller, and William Ogden, it was known as the "second" or "new" University of Chicago.

Stephen A. Douglas was the first president of the college's board of trustees, and he contributed the land the college was built on. At his death in 1861, William Ogden was named to replace him, a post he held until 1874, when he moved back to New York.

While he was the president, Ogden had an occasion to address the Board of Trustees. Of Ogden's speech, Henry Hurlbut wrote in 1881, "The first suggestion we think on record . . . by a Chicagoan . . . for the establishment, in each of our Collegiate Institutions, of a Professorship to occupy 'a Chair of Integrity,' for the teaching of that ancient and important accomplishment *honesty*, now so rare in our public men or officials, . . . was contained in an address by the late Hon. Wm. B. Ogden."[13] Despite the flaws in his own character, Ogden still realized the importance of virtuous qualities and even deplored their passing. Being highly intelligent, he could easily spot the backsliding morality of others, but at the same time he was naively oblivious of his own similar conduct.

Ogden's dedication to the University of Chicago culminated in a significant bequest from his estate (detailed in chapter 15). He also threw his financial support behind the McCormick Theological Seminary, the Chicago Nursery and Half-Orphan Asylum, the Erring Women's Refuge, Bell's Commercial College, and the Dearborn Seminary, to name but a few of the civic and charitable organizations for which he was a major benefactor.[14] The good works of the booster-elite also included Chicago's churches. Ogden had attended church with the town's small Episcopalian congregation from the time he first arrived in 1835, when they met in whatever open building space they could requisition on a Sunday morning.[15] The local congregation had been organized by Juliette Kinzie, wife of John H. Kinzie, who arranged for an Episcopal clergyman to be sent to the town in 1834. By 1837 the square, brick St. James Church had been built on the North Side, on land donated by the Kinzie family, with funds raised through pew sales and bazaars put on by the Ladies Sewing Society.

In the early decades, the church served a heterogeneous population. The fine, large homes of the wealthy were on the North Side, but so were the more humble homes of the new immigrant class and of many poor people. When he was in town, Ogden was frequently seen in the neighborhood carrying a large basket of fruit and flowers from his orchard and greenhouse that he passed out to the less fortunate and left on the doorsteps of the North Side's sick and elderly.[16]

From 1849 until 1865, Dr. Robert Clarkson served as rector of St. James. Under his leadership, the congregation expanded enormously. The church made a number of additions to the building and installed new pews and ornate stained glass windows. However, it soon became obvious that the congregation needed a larger church. Julian Rumsey was appointed chairman of a building committee, with included Ogden, John H. Kinzie, and a number of other prominent men. Money was raised, and soon a magnificent church, with seating for twelve hundred people, arose only two blocks from the old church. Its new neighbors were the large wooded estates of William Ogden, Walter Newberry, Isaac Arnold, Dr. Daniel Brainard, and Ezra McCagg.[17]

Ogden and Dr. Clarkson became fast friends during the sixteen years the rector remained in Chicago. In 1865 he was elected missionary bishop of the Nebraska and Dakota Territory, and he left Chicago. Years later, he traveled from Nebraska to New York City to officiate at the funeral of his good friend Will Ogden.

Carl Abbott, in a book about economic thought in the antebellum Middle West, wrote of those years: "Far from growing lazy and satisfied with the free gifts of railroads, Chicagoans in the 1850s undertook a vast array of projects. Demonstrating the same forcefulness that had previously characterized the city, they adopted a variety of methods for achieving their goals, often combining private, public and quasi-public actions on the same issue. The result was an entrepreneurial symbiosis in which Chicago saw to those institutional and physical needs that outsiders ignored."[18]

Chicagoans loved grand ceremony. Whether it was a simple store opening or the dedication of a significant edifice, the population turned out in great numbers. The Prince of Wales, who would become King Edward VII on the death of his mother, Queen Victoria, in 1901, visited Chicago as a nineteen-year-old lad in 1860 and received a warm welcome. Mayor "Long John" Wentworth had convinced the prince to visit Chicago when they met at the Prince of Wales Ball in Montreal some time earlier.[19] Along with Mayor Wentworth, William Ogden was a member of the three-man committee selected to provide reception and entertainment for the prince.

Wentworth was described by one Chicago historian as "another of those ambulatory Chicago caricatures who seem to have been invented by a novelist with an oversized imagination."[20] His Honor weighed in at over three hundred pounds, and for this occasion he was dressed to the hilt in high leather boots, a swallow-tail suit with brass buttons, and a tall beaver hat.[21] The prince, the mayor, and Ogden drove down Michigan Avenue in an open coach, leading a procession of landaus and phaetons filled with the city's leading men and women. A cheering crowd of thousands lined the street, exuberantly proclaiming their welcome for the young prince. That evening the leading citizens hosted a great banquet and ball to honor their royal guest.

Even while Chicagoans were celebrating the royal visit, somber war clouds hung heavily over the entire nation. On March 4, 1861, Abraham Lincoln, Illinois's favorite son—at least among Republicans—was sworn in as the country's sixteenth president. In the fall of that year, William Ogden was honored with an invitation to take tea with the president at the White House. A handwritten note from the president to his chief personal secretary, John Nicolay, read:

I wish Mr. Nicolay would invite the following gentlemen to tea at my home at 5 P.M. tomorrow.
Mr. Schenck

Mr. Piati

Mr. Carter

Mr. Ogden

Mr. Philips

Mr. [illegible]

Mr. Dubois

Mr. Nicolay—himself

Saturday, Nov. 3

Lincoln[22]

Lincoln's papers in the Library of Congress contain a number of letters to and from William Ogden during the president's four-plus years in office. Although not a close personal friend of Lincoln's, Ogden had gotten to know him well through Illinois politics and Lincoln's legal assistance with the establishment of the Chicago Dock and Canal Company, and he had vigorously supported Lincoln in his run for the presidency. Ogden also advised the president a number of times on the matter of a transcontinental railroad. However, two issues would eventually drive a wedge between the two of them. The first was Ogden's belief that President Lincoln exceeded his constitutional authority when trying to balance his war powers and citizens' rights to civil liberties. The second was on the issue of slavery.[23]

The two men were of one mind on the slavery question: it was morally reprehensible. However, as the Civil War raged on, a difficult dilemma faced the nation's antislavery faction. The question was, what should be done with the black population if slavery were abolished? Today the solution seems obvious: assimilation, or amalgamation as it was then called. But in the years leading up to the war and during the conflict itself, assimilation of the black population was a very frightening prospect to many white Americans. The two races, they felt, were simply too dissimilar to live together in harmony. And the feeling was shared by many members of both races.

It should be remembered that the only cross-cultural experience many white Americans and their ancestors had ever had was with the Indians, and it had convinced them that mass assimilation of a "primitive" (i.e., non-European) race was unworkable, so they saw no reason to believe that blacks could assimilate into the white world any better than the Indians had done.

Abraham Lincoln's early solution-of-choice was colonization, although he had always been opposed to compulsory deportation.[24] William B. Ogden was also firmly on the colonization bandwagon. Under this plan, the freed black population would be allowed to emigrate—or be forcibly deported, according to many advocates like Ogden—to some far-off place where they would live free. Liberia was one option; others were countries in South America, Central America, the Danish West Indies, and even Texas. As early as 1839, the Chicago Colonization Society was operating as an auxiliary of the Illinois Colonization Society, which in turn was a part of the national Colonization Society, which had been around since 1816.[25] William B. Ogden served as second vice president of the Chicago group almost from its inception, indicating that his belief in colonization had deep roots.

But as the Civil War progressed, President Lincoln changed his position on colonization. He came to realize it was impractical, and he reconciled himself to a program of amalgamation. Ogden's strong alliance with Lincoln began to unravel because he felt Lincoln was wrong in abandoning his position on colonization. According to Ogden's good friend Isaac Arnold, Ogden paid a price for his views: "These considerations brought Mr. Ogden into political antagonism with many of his old personal and political friends in Chicago."[26]

Less than six weeks after Lincoln's inauguration, the Confederate army fired upon Fort Sumter in the Charleston harbor, and the bloodiest war in American history began. The following day, the streets of Chicago were thronged once again, but this time there was no celebration. People were indignant, dazed, and frightened. Many were on their way to their churches, meeting halls, and other places where they hoped to find answers to the troubling questions of war. On Monday, April 16, 1861, when Governor Richard Yates called out the Illinois state militia, its ranks were already swollen with hundreds of eager volunteers.

A week later, the *Chicago Tribune* proclaimed, "The streets were alive all day with the movement of volunteers. Everything gives way to the war and its demands. Workmen from their shops, printers from their cases, lawyers from their offices, clerks and bookkeepers from counter and counting-room, are busily drilling, and the enlistments are marvelously rapid."[27]

Throughout Chicago, men and women began gathering to discuss the city's support for the war effort.[28] On April 18, two well-attended meetings were held, one at Bryan Hall, officiated by Mahlon Ogden, and the other at Metropolitan Hall, to discuss how to equip and arm their volunteers. Business and civic organizations of the community selected delegates to represent them. William Ogden and two other men were chosen to represent the citizenry at large. Over thirty-six thousand dollars was pledged for the effort.

As the war progressed, Chicago's muddy streets and wooden sidewalks were filled with the hustle and bustle of women, children, and old men. Almost entirely absent were the young men, except for the occasional hollow-eyed veteran hobbling along on crutches with one pant leg pinned up at thigh level, or an empty sleeve hanging limply at his side.

Before the war began, but while it still loomed ominously on the horizon, William Ogden decided to seek a seat in the Illinois state senate in the November 1860 election. He would win that election and be reelected in November 1862, thus serving throughout the war years from 1861 through 1865. It's hard to understand why he sought the position, since politics was anathema to Ogden, something to be avoided if at all possible. He may have been motivated by a sense of civic responsibility, or by his business interests, or perhaps both. With war looming and the nation still in the throes of the Panic of 1857, Ogden may have seen it as his duty to assist his Republican Party. It was certainly a trying time for Northern Illinois Republicans, and he may have believed that his presence in the general assembly would help the party withstand the challenges of antiwar Democrats. In any event, these two state senate terms would be William Ogden's last foray into politics.

As for his business interests, both railroading and real estate issues often came before the legislature. One biographer of Chicago leaders wrote that Ogden entered the election to encourage railroad development in the state during this crucial period, and that probably was his primary motivation; but fulfilling what he saw as his civic responsibility during the nation's crisis cannot be completely disregarded either.[29]

The war years not only brought about civil unrest throughout Illinois but also political unrest. Illinois was a border state, and many in the population, particularly in the southern part of the state, were sympathetic to the South. Republicans wanted victory at all costs, the total elimination of slavery, and the preservation of the Union. The Democrats, while they too wanted to preserve the Union, were more willing to compromise with the Confederacy to achieve it, and they sought an armistice to end the fighting. Many southern counties were even secession strongholds, and radical antiwar Democrats, called Copperheads, were willing to go to almost any length to end the war. As a state divided, Illinois's support of President Lincoln and the war effort was contentious. One newspaper put it in context, writing that "the Confederacy . . . allows no divisions among her people, no factious mass meetings to distract public opinion."[30] That was certainly not the case in Illinois.

Republicans, probably because they controlled most state offices in Illinois at the beginning of the war, felt the Democrats should be content to simply sit on the sidelines until the conflict was over. It was not a time for party politics, they preached. But that did not happen. In the 1860 elections, the Illinois electorate had approved the drafting of a new state constitution.[31] In an 1861 election to select delegates for the constitutional convention, forty-five Democrats and only twenty-one Republicans were seated. The Democrats used their superior numbers to attempt to usurp the legislative authority of the Republican-led general assembly; and although it succeeded for a brief time, the ploy did not last. Eventually this dissident faction drew up a new governing document for the state, replete with restrictive conditions against business and against their Republican counterparts. That new constitution, however, failed to muster enough support to pass in a special June 1862 referendum. But the Democrats would not give up, as we will see.

Before the war had progressed very far, Ogden received a letter from Samuel J. Tilden urging him to use whatever influence he had with President Lincoln to avert a widening of the conflict: "Your situation may enable you to be of great service to your country and to mankind." Tilden believed Lincoln to be "a frank, genial, warm-hearted man," but he feared the president was leaning toward all-out war. He begged Ogden to use his most persuasive skills to induce Lincoln to be "the Chief Magistrate of the whole country," instead of just "half a country. . . . The reality of the *danger* of disunion cannot be doubted. A statesmanlike policy would be to aid the formation of that minority [those in the Southern States opposed to war]—to strengthen it that it may become a majority, to create, to hasten, to swell the reaction for which we hope. . . . We must imagine ourselves in their position, in order to form a policy adapted to their case."[32] Unfortunately for the nation, Tilden's well-meaning words were too little and too late to avoid the calamitous events that had already been set in motion.

Very early in his first term in the senate, Ogden introduced a bill to protect banks that were failing due to the panic from being foreclosed.[33] Eventually that provision would be incorporated into a broader bank law that was passed. He was also appointed to head a committee to organize the chartering of the Chicago and Alton Railroad.[34] This was a highly desirous route. Alton was just across the Mississippi River from St. Louis, and the state had been trying for years to strengthen the position of their southern cities against rivals like St. Louis and Cincinnati. When—and if—the line were ever built, it was supposed to shadow the Illinois and Michigan Canal down the state.

This was not the first time the small road had gone to the well.[35] The Illinois legislature had originally chartered the Springfield and Alton Turnpike Company in 1841, but amid great optimism, backers could never generate enough subscriptions to meet the charter's requirement. They tried again, and on February 27, 1847, received another charter as the Alton and Sangamon Railroad. Again they failed. After one more aborted attempt in 1850, the line went into dormancy, where it stayed until the 1861 legislature decided to give it one final try. Under Ogden's leadership, the Chicago and Alton Railroad was chartered in February 1861, the fourth corporate name in the company's history.[36] From that point on, although it had to withstand some legal battles caused by its earlier failings, the railroad prospered, until the Baltimore and Ohio gobbled it up in the twentieth century.

As the November 1862 state elections neared, Illinois state senator Lyman Trumbull, in a letter to President Lincoln, issued a warning: "The Democrats are organizing for a party contest this fall," he wrote, pointing out that many Democratic Party leaders sympathized with the South. "If they get control of the State, Ill[inois] which has done so much and so nobly for the Union in this struggle, will be paralyzed."[37] President Lincoln's issuance of the Emancipation Proclamation only two months before the election only served to lather up the Democrats even more; and at election time they captured control of the Illinois house by a count of 54–32, and the senate by a count of 13–12.[38] The work of Senator William Ogden and other Republican general assembly members took on a new futility. However, Ogden had more serious problems.

At some point around mid-1862, Ogden was struck down with an unidentified illness. We learn of this because of his ongoing absences from state legislative sessions: "The continued absence of Mr. Ogden, Senator from Cook, is very much regretted by the Republicans and there is some talk of calling upon him to resign, or come on and take his seat," the *Chicago Tribune* wrote in early 1863.[39] A few weeks later, Ogden did return, and although the nature of his illness was never disclosed, the severity of it was obvious from the *Tribune's* next general assembly report: "Mr. Ogden looks in better health than I expected, judging from the unfavorable accounts his physicians and others gave of his disorder. He walks quite lame, however, and has lost a good deal of flesh."[40]

Ogden had returned just in time for the fireworks that resulted from the Democrats' taking control of the legislature. In a number of states, but more so in Illinois that in most others, the new legislatures began pressing resolutions and initiating bills calling for compromise or an armistice with the Confederacy, threatening the war effort. The most odious of those bills in Illinois was one known as a "Black Law," which legalized slavery on Illinois soil. Although it was repealed in two years, the law also provided for the sale of black men, women, and children and legalized whipping them.[41]

But those actions produced an unexpected backlash against the antiwar Democrats. Military regiments that had been raised in Illinois—composed of members of both political parties—were incensed. Many threatened to return home to "crush the treason" if it continued. Mark Neely, in *The Union Divided*, wrote, "The resumption of normal party activity in the Illinois Legislature nearly provoked an armed revolution among the Illinois soldiers."[42]

Another strange twist also occurred: Ogden was occasionally voting *with* the Democrats, although not on the Black Law. One of the Democratic state senators had passed away in office, which now meant there was a 12–12 tie vote on most issues. When Ogden crossed over, it threw those issues back into Democratic control. The first of those situations was a Democrat-sponsored resolution opposing taxation to pay for emancipation of slaves in the border states.[43] The next one involved opposition to a resolution calling for the U.S. Treasury to allocate money for the same purpose. One explanation for this crossover vote could have been Ogden's strong feeling about colonization and the fact that Lincoln had abandoned the idea. In any case, Ogden's fellow Republicans were irate over his abandonment of party causes.

The staunchly Republican *Chicago Tribune* wrote, "It will be no more surprising to your readers than it was to your correspondent to find Mr. Ogden, who was sent here *to represent the Republican district of Cook County by a Republican majority of nearing 5,000 votes* to desert his party and *every principle* of liberty and humanity" (italics in original).[44] Over the next few months, Senator Ogden took positions on enlarging the Illinois and Michigan Canal, building more branch railroads within the state, and imploring President Lincoln, on freedom of speech grounds, to rescind an order suppressing publication of the antiwar *Chicago Times*.[45]

Finally, fed up with the misadventures of the Democrat-controlled general assembly, Governor Yates, a Republican, used an extreme measure to forestall a direct confrontation.[46] He invoked an obscure statute to prorogue both houses of the 1863 state legislature, putting a temporary end to the Democrats' attempts to stop the war. But still these voices would not be silenced. They let loose a barrage of protest against Lincoln for his war actions and against Yates for proroguing the general assembly. The president finally responded by declaring a national emergency and taking steps to silence the dissent, and the U.S. Congress affirmed his right to suspend the rights of individuals in order to serve the greater good.

Dissent continued anyway, but by the following year the tide of the war had swung in favor of the North. In the November 1864 elections, Illinois Republicans regained control of the general assembly. More significantly, Congress passed and ultimately ratified the Thirteenth Amendment to the U.S. Constitution, which stated:

> Section 1. Neither slavery nor involuntary servitude, except as a punishment for crime where of the party shall have been duly convicted, shall exist within the United States, or any place subject to their jurisdiction.
> Section 2. Congress shall have the power to enforce this article by appropriate legislation.

Despite its contentious past, on February 1, 1865, Lincoln's home state of Illinois became the first of the required three-quarters of the states to ratify the Thirteenth Amendment. Two months later, Robert E. Lee surrendered to Ulysses S. Grant (who hailed, incidentally, from Galena, Illinois) to end the war.

Five days later, on April 14, 1865, Abraham Lincoln was assassinated.

In many ways, Illinois was a fortunate state during the Civil War. Not a single battle was fought on its soil, and only in the southern part of the state, on its borders with Missouri and Kentucky, did it come within cannon shot of the conflict.[47] But Illinois was certainly impacted. The state sent 259,092 of her sons into the Union Army, and nearly 35,000 of them made the supreme sacrifice. Chicago sent her fair share of those young men into battle and shared proportionately in the casualties. The 82nd Illinois, a regiment raised principally in Cook County, fought in the Fredericksburg, Gettysburg, Chattanooga, and Atlanta campaigns. The 23rd Illinois, also raised in Cook County, campaigned not only in Missouri but also in the major Eastern campaigns, ending its war service at the Battle of Appomattox Court House.

Newspaper correspondent Noah Brooks witnessed one sad by-product of the war during his 1864 Chicago visit: "There are 11,000 rebel prisoners at Rock Island [in northwestern Illinois], and 8,000 in the city at Camp Douglas, making quite a formidable corps, were the whole 19,000 under arms and marching on Chicago. These prisoners are well cared for at Camp Douglas, and look sleek and comfortable—enjoying themselves much more at ball playing, foot racing, etc., than when fighting Yankees or raiding in Kentucky and Tennessee."[48]

Brooks's comments did not reflect the true conditions at Camp Douglas. It was the worst of the North's detention camps and is often mentioned by Civil War historians in the same breath as the South's infamous Andersonville Prison in Georgia. The prison was located at 31st Street and Cottage Grove Avenue. Prior to the war, the camp—named after Stephen A. Douglas, from whose estate the land was donated—was the largest military training camp in Illinois. The first Confederate prisoners arrived in 1862, over eight thousand of them, who had been captured at Fort Donelson, which straddled the western border of Kentucky and Tennessee. Camp Douglas was quickly transformed from a training facility into a maximum-security prison. During the war, it housed over eighteen thousand prisoners-of-war, including over twelve thousand at one time in late 1864.

Journalist Henry M. Stanley, who later gained fame as an African explorer when he found the lost Dr. David Livingston, was a prisoner at Camp Douglas. He described what he saw: "crowds of sick men who had fallen prostrate from weakness, and had given themselves wholly to despair, and while they crawled or wallowed in their filth, they cursed or blasphemed as often as they groaned."[49] He also witnessed corpses, rolled up in their blankets, being loaded into wagons on a daily basis, "piled one upon another, as the New Zealand frozen mutton carcasses are carted from the docks." It has been estimated that as many as six thousand prisoners died from disease, starvation, and exposure to cold weather in the period from 1862 through 1865 at Camp Douglas.

Although the citizens of Chicago had nothing to do with what went on in the prison, it was still a black mark against the city. Suspiciously, all the camp records disappeared after the war, so the sadistic commandant, Colonel Benjamin Sweet, was never called to answer for his misdeeds.

During the Civil War, more railroads made connections in Chicago than in any other place in the world. That insured that, war or not, the city would be the pivotal spot for commerce in the future. In some ironic ways, Chicago benefited by the war. The city's railroad network was used to fill government contracts for salt pork for the Union Army, and grain moved freely from the city to government bakeries to the battlegrounds.

The congregation at Chicago's St. James Church established a Tower Fund in order to erect a fitting monument to the men from the congregation who had nobly served in the war.[50] Seventy men had served, and ten gave their lives for the cause. Ezra McCagg and Edwin Sheldon were in charge of raising the necessary funds. Fifty-five hundred dollars was raised, and a monument designed by Vaux, Withers, and Olmstead of New York was built and installed. It was a beautifully carved Victorian memorial. However, when the monument was finished, the church found itself thirty-eight hundred dollars in the hole. McCagg and Sheldon personally made up the bulk of the deficit; and then they, along with their brothers-in-law William and Mahlon Ogden, donated another twenty-five hundred dollars to fireproof the floor and ceiling of the vestibule where the monument stood. In the Great Fire of 1871, the memorial withstood the flames and the heat, thanks to those precautions. It is still inside the church.

Once the war was over, Chicagoans returned to doing what they did best: build and prosper. The railroads had sparked a significant change in the city by 1864 that led to the building of the infamous Union Stock Yard. The meat packing business had a very unassuming beginning. In 1829 Gurdon Hubbard drove a large herd of hogs to Chicago to have them slaughtered and packed into barrels so he could send them east by steamboat. But a brutal winter kept the boat carrying the barrels from arriving, and Hubbard's meat sat on the frozen riverbank until spring.[51]

From that humble beginning, Chicago quickly went on to become the pork capital, then the beef capital, of the nation.[52] During this time, however, small independent stockyards were scattered haphazardly across the entire city. As the railroads gained traction as the primary carriers of livestock into the city and dressed meat products out of the city, it began to make sense to consolidate the small stockyards into one giant facility. In the fall of 1864, the Chicago Pork Packers Association and nine railroads jointly proposed a giant yard on a half-mile square of land just southwest of the city. A charter was gained and the company capitalized for one million dollars, of which all but seventy-five thousand was subscribed by the railroads. The Union Stock Yard opened the following year.

Packingtown, as it became popularly known, was a small city in itself with thirty-one miles of sewers, seven miles of wood-paved alleys, and three miles of drinking troughs supplied from deep artesian wells.[53] For the nine railroads there were nearly two miles of platforms where the highly agitated animals were forced down chutes into holding pens. Despite the hundreds of jobs Packingtown provided, it was a gruesome, abhorrent place. "The only open space in this squalid pile of meat mills and acid-eaten houses was the 'hair field,' where the hair of hogs and the skin of cattle were spread out to dry, drawing great clouds of bluebottle flies," wrote historian Donald Miller.[54] It was not until Upton Sinclair's stomach-churning 1906 book *The Jungle* exposed the vile practices at the Union Stock Yard that federal legislation forced changes throughout the food industry.

Into this milieu in 1875 came Gustavus Swift from Sagamore, Massachusetts, and Philip Danforth Armour from Stockbridge, New York. The two men revolutionized the meatpacking business and became staggeringly wealthy in the process. Swift was a dour man and an audacious risk-taker, dedicated to his work, while Armour was an adventurer. He had traveled to the California gold fields at nineteen, riding a stolen mule part way and then walking when the owner reclaimed his purloined mule. Armour returned to Milwaukee, where he opened a business and gained his first fortune in pork during the Civil War. In 1862 he married Malvina Belle Ogden, a distant cousin of William Ogden.[55] Armour and his sons who followed him in the business built the company into the largest concern of its kind in the world. While Gustavus Swift, an avowed skinflint, held tightly to his first dime, Armour became a free-spending philanthropist and a latter-day Chicago booster-elite.

At the opposite end of the aesthetic and cultural spectrum from Packingtown was the Chicago Academy of Science. A young naturalist, Robert Kennicott, and a few other amateur and professional scientists were concerned about the disappearance of native plants and animals due to the population explosion in the Midwest. They began collecting specimens and information about these vanishing species and looking for a home for their collection. William Ogden and a group of concerned citizens put up the money, and Chicago's first museum was built. Though the academy's original building would be one of many victims of the Great Fire six years later, museums from all over the world would send it new specimens, and today it houses more than a quarter-million specimens, including an unparalleled butterfly house.

Although the pall of war hung over Chicago in the early 1860s, those who remained behind carried on the city's social life. In 1861 Ogden and a dozen other men launched the Dearborn Club, the city's first social club, with Ogden as its first president.[56] The group first met in the top story of the Portland Block at the corner of Dearborn and Washington, but after two years they were forced to close. Five years later, in the spirit of the old Dearborn Club, the Chicago Club was founded by many of the same members. By that time, however, Ogden was spending more time in his New York home and did not rejoin the group.

By the mid-1860s Chicago had become a much more livable city than it had been only a decade earlier. Historian and writer Henry M. Flint visited the city on a number of occasions while writing a treatise on American railroads. He had not been a complete stranger to the earlier Chicago either; his biography of Illinois native Stephen A. Douglas, published in 1860, had caused him to visit many times during the previous decade. He wrote a keen analysis of the city as it was in 1866:

> At the present time, Chicago has a population of nearly two hundred thousand; its streets are well-paved, and well-lighted at night, and it has an admirable system of drainage. Its commerce amounts to two hundred and fifty millions of dollars annually; its harbor is one of the finest and most capacious in the west, and is constantly crowded with vessels; and it is the largest grain market, pork market, and lumber market in the world; many of its churches and public buildings, and private dwelling-houses, are equal to, if they do not surpass, any similar buildings in New York or Philadelphia.[57]

For a number of years, it had been necessary for William Ogden to travel frequently between Chicago and New York City. As he got older, those trips became more difficult. A portrait of Ogden painted at this time shows him sporting a smart silver-tipped cane; so it is probable he was having more trouble moving about. He decided to enlarge and remodel his Chicago home, Ogden Grove, and buy a second home close to New York City. He could reduce his travel time and perhaps even begin to ease into retirement, he reasoned.

Samuel Gouveneur Ogden, William Ogden's distant cousin, was another descendant of the esteemed New Jersey founder, John Ogden.[58] A successful New York City merchant, owner of a fleet of merchant ships, and head of a number of French commercial concerns, Samuel Ogden was also a very prolific husband to his two wives, giving to the first fourteen children and to the second four more. Julia Gabriella Ogden was his eighteenth, born on June 7, 1829.

Most of Samuel Ogden's children married well, and the family traveled in the very highest New York society. In 1846, the youngest, Julia, married a gentleman named J. Kennedy Smythe, a Canadian by birth.[59] Of Smythe, little is known, save one thing: he too was extremely wealthy. At some point in his career, he had purchased a handsome Gothic villa called Boscobel at Fordham Heights, Westchester County, New York.

William Ogden almost certainly knew the Smythes, through family or business, or more likely both. In 1866 when Ogden decided to purchase his New York home, Smythe was in a selling mood. William Ogden bought Villa Boscobel.

The property was 110 acres and had a frontage of a half-mile on the Harlem River where it flowed into the Hudson. The picturesque home was situated high on a rocky hill overlooking both waterways. The grounds included a conservatory, stables, and greenhouses and sloped gently down to the Washington Bridge. The bridge was referred to as "Highbridge," because it had been built very high to allow for the passage of tall-masted ships. Today, it is the oldest operating bridge in New York City.[60]

Immediately after purchasing the property, Ogden began to make plans for personalizing it. The fruit trees he enjoyed experimenting with at his Ogden Grove estate would have to be duplicated at Villa Boscobel, and the huge flowerbeds his mother had so lovingly tended would have to be planted. He began to seek somebody to whom he could entrust the work. As usual, he turned to family.

William Ogden Wheeler was the oldest child of William's sister Emily and Judge Nelson Knox Wheeler.[61] Born in 1837, young Wheeler's health had been described as "delicate," and in his youth he had to forego the rough-and-tumble sports he so loved. When he was about twenty years old, he had been installed as manager of his parents' farm, Laurel Bank, in Delaware County, New York, but it was not a job he enjoyed. He left his Deposit, New York, home and moved to Chicago, where he found employment with his Uncle Will. It was to Wheeler that Ogden turned when he was seeking someone to oversee the work at Villa

Villa Boscobel, William Ogden's New York estate, at the confluence of the Harlem and Hudson Rivers. Walton Historical Society.

Boscobel, and Wheeler gladly accepted the assignment. "Mr. Wheeler found this work thoroughly congenial, and his natural taste for landscape gardening was fully gratified in seeing the results of his own planning develop into the thing of beauty which 'Boscobel' became," as Wheeler's own 1907 Ogden genealogy, *The Ogden Family in America*, tells it.

When his work at Villa Boscobel was completed, Wheeler traveled the world for the next few years. Upon his return, he moved into the estate with his Uncle Will, where he remained until 1882.[62] At that time, and with some of the money he inherited from his uncle, he purchased a beautiful home in Sharon, Connecticut, which he named Sterling Elm. Here he devoted the remainder of his life to researching and writing the Ogden family genealogy mentioned above.

Over the winter of 1866, Ogden decided to take another vacation to Europe. His sister Emily and her twenty-seven-year-old daughter Julia, then still unmarried, accompanied him. It is not recorded where they visited, but toward the end of the trip they took an apartment in Rome for a time. Ogden's other sister Eliza Butler and her daughters Emily, twenty-six, and Anna, twenty-three, were vacationing on the continent at the same time and were expected to join Ogden's party in Rome.

Anna's health was not good. In his autobiography, her father, Charles Butler, wrote, "Her health had long been delicate, and it was hope for restoration that had been the motive for the residence in Europe ten years before."[63] On this later trip, Eliza and her two daughters spent seven months in Divonne-les-Bains, France, overlooking the Jura Mountains, a location reputed to have restorative powers. Charles Butler wrote to his daughter Emily during their stay:

> I think you will carry away with you from Divonne many pleasant
> recollections. The mountain scenery that you have had before you there
> is probably unrivaled, and you have gazed so long and so often on Mount
> Blanc and his fellow mountains, that you will form a pleasant picture in
> your memory. To have seen them so much during the winter is, I think, a
> great privilege; and how familiar you will have become with the geography
> of that country. Nyon, Coppet, Ferney and Geneva will be as familiar to you
> as Scarsdale and the region round about. I cannot give you any useful hints
> about your journey south to Italy. . . . I hope you will go directly to Rome,
> and find there good apartments and your cousins, Julia and Emily and Will
> Ogden. How happy I should be to be there with you!
>   With love to dear mother and Anna and yourself, each a portion,
>   I am, your affectionate father.[64]

Butler's belief in the healing powers of travel, particularly in France, had its origins thirty years earlier, at a time when he was a weak, sickly young man.[65] Soon after he moved to New York City, a number of prominent doctors told him he would not live for more than a few years because of his consumption [tuberculosis.] As a last resort, he decided to seek an alternative opinion on the continent and set sail for Europe in 1838. The voyage itself gave him considerable comfort, and he underwent inhalation therapy in Paris. At the end of twelve months, he returned home completely cured, by his own admission. That he lived to be ninety-five must be considered some sort of endorsement for his cure. It was only natural that when his children became sickly, he advised the same treatment for them.

Back home in Chicago in late 1866, Ogden continued to entertain family whenever possible. His niece Anna, Mahlon's daughter, then about ten years old, later recounted her life as a child amid the large, extended Ogden family. "A mist of happiness and content seems to envelop my childhood days," she wrote. "A large and devoted family circle, constantly intermingling, is the background. Doubtless, we took meals alone, but I can never remember doing so, and always several guests staying."[66] Recalling her Uncle Will's Chicago home, she wrote:

> The flowering shrubs were in bloom and the square between Russ and Cass, Ontario and Erie, was a delightful spot to wander in. Not the least interesting thing was the smoke house where the[y] cured their own hams, &c. The rooms were large and high and always when I recall them filled with guests. His [Uncle Will's] great friendship with Gov. Tilden leads me to include it among the family experiences. If the older members of the family were out, how we children used to dread seeing Uncle Will with Mr. Tilden appear upon the scene of an afternoon, for one of us must then go in and give the two gentlemen their tea. Many an afternoon have I sat patiently for them to finish which . . . didn't happen very soon, for Mr. Tilden was known to take as many as eighteen cups.

Another recollection she shared was of visits to "my aunt Mrs. McCagg" (Will's sister Caroline.) "Everyone sang or played some musical instrument. It is here I remember my Uncle William Ogden sitting at the piano both playing and singing his favorite airs 'Guide Me, O Thou Great Jehovah' to 'Martha' and 'Rise My Soul, Stretch Every Nerve, Thy Better Portion Trace,' being most prominent among them."[67]

William Ogden could not deny that he was getting old. Stoking the fires of ambition that had burned for so long in his soul had become difficult; he had no more to prove to himself or to others. But in his moments of quiet reflection, he could vividly recall how much fun his last great challenge had been. It had been, after all, only two years earlier that he had shocked the entire nation with one of the most important railroad announcements ever made.

12

The Minnow Swallows the Whale

William Ogden visited New York City in the fall of 1862 or 1863. The city's trees were just beginning to put on their mantle of autumn colors—blazing reds and golden yellows, joyfully mingling on nature's palette with the last of the fading emerald greens. He had come to check on the work of his nephew, William Wheeler, who was landscaping Ogden's estate, Villa Boscobel, on the banks of the Harlem and Hudson Rivers. Wheeler's work was exemplary, as Ogden knew it would be. After giving his approval, he ordered his coach driver to take him downtown, to the office of his attorney and friend, Samuel J. Tilden, with whom he had an appointment.

Ogden may have gone by way of 5th Avenue so he could check on the progress Frederick Olmsted was making on his unprecedented Central Park project. The grounds were still relatively barren, with only a few hundred trees dotting the massive landscape; but to men of vision, it was easy to see what a wondrous place it would someday be. Previously it had been nothing more than swampland—much like the North Side of Chicago had once been, Ogden knew—yet he was able to imagine what it would eventually become. Ogden loved New York; it was still in his bones. As business forced him to make more trips to the city and the state, the lure to return permanently had taken root. His fabulous new estate would be a welcome respite, but he thought often about returning for good.

If his appointment took him further south, to the very tip of Manhattan where Fort Amsterdam once stood, he would have been on the same ground trod by his ancestor John Ogden, the leading founder of the English colonization of New Jersey.[1] Here, at the extreme southern tip of the island, John Ogden and his brother Richard also built the first permanent stone church on Manhattan Island in the early 1640s. It's doubtful that William Ogden was even aware of this, but if he were, it would have filled him with tremendous family pride.

Samuel Tilden greeted his friend at the office door and ushered him in. They had only recently concluded the purchase of Brady's Bend Iron Works in Pennsylvania with a few other men, and they would likely have discussed the progress made modernizing their mines and smelters. Tilden knew Ogden was a man with a sweeping railroad vision; he had attended the fiftieth birthday party where Ogden unveiled his plan for the Chicago and North Western Railway system. But even he would have been surprised at the scheme Ogden outlined that afternoon.

Railroad mergers and consolidations were not new; in fact, so many of them had taken place during the most recent financial panic that they weren't even newsworthy any longer. But all past railroad mergers met one of two criteria: either the takeover of a small, struggling, short-line railroad by a much larger and wealthier line, or the merger of two small granger, or farmer, railroads hoping to cut costs and gain traction by joining hands.

What Ogden described to Tilden that afternoon was something entirely different. His plan called for his large but financially struggling Chicago and North Western Railway System to absorb the larger and very profitable Galena and Chicago Union Railroad.[2] The minnow would swallow the whale. The merger of giant industrial companies in the twenty-first century does not even raise eyebrows, but in the 1860s it was unprecedented.

The merger, as Ogden outlined it, would add the Chicago and North Western's 315 route miles to the 545 owned or leased by the Galena and Chicago Union, creating an 860-mile monolith that would be the largest railroad in the nation. But Ogden's bold plan did not end there; he envisioned covering the entire midcontinent, just as he had outlined at his birthday party more than a half-dozen years earlier. Then, Tilden had likely believed it was just one man's idle dream; now, with the plan Ogden unveiled, he could see it was a real possibility.

As surprising as this was to Tilden, it became even more audacious when Ogden began laying out the details. As lawyers, both men realized the legality of the plan they formulated was questionable, but given the loose business ethics of the day for such things, Tilden was all in favor of it. Thus the two men began laying the groundwork.

The plan was deceptively simple.[3] Ogden still held a large block of shares in the Galena and Chicago Union, as did many of his friends and associates, and he was held in high regard by the hundreds of smaller stockholders who had initially funded the company. He was confident he could find a number of these individuals who would sign over their proxies to him for the purpose of voting at the annual meeting. Also, some who sat on the Galena and Chicago Union board were good friends: William Larrabee, whom he had hired as his assistant in the real estate office when he first arrived in Chicago; Benjamin Raymond, Mark Skinner, and William Brown, to mention only a few. Since the Civil War was raging throughout the country, not many men would leave their homes to travel to a meeting in Chicago anyway, so gaining enough proxies to control the election of directors was assured.

The second step would also be easy. It involved the board of the Chicago and North Western, of which Ogden was president. Enough men on this board were also his friends—Ogden had personally selected most of them—and they would go along with the idea, he was sure. Each of the C&NW men selected to participate would purchase one share of Galena and Chicago Union stock, perhaps even from Ogden's own portfolio, so that when the wheels were set in motion they, as stockholders, would become eligible to be elected directors of that company's board.

Ogden and Tilden selected the Galena's annual meeting of June 1, 1864, to make their play. On that day, the C&NW board members who were participants in the scheme, now also stockholders in the Galena, appeared at the annual meeting; and with the proxies that had been prearranged, were elected directors of the Galena and Chicago Union. Later during the same meeting, the issue of consolidating the two railroads was brought before the new board, and with the new directors in place, easily passed. It was agreed that for each share of common stock held in the Galena and Chicago Union, stockholders would receive in the new company one share of common stock, one share of preferred stock, and three dollars in cash to account for the superior financial condition of that company. C&NW stockholders would simply convert their stock in the old company, share for share, for stock in the new.

A meeting with the old C&NW board had taken place a few days earlier. The merger was financially a sweet deal for the smaller railroad, so it had passed easily there. When the two meetings were concluded, the consolidation was a fait accompli, or so Ogden and Tilden believed. There had been no hitches; the plan had worked out exactly as the men had anticipated, and the first president of the consolidated Chicago and North Western Railway Company was William B. Ogden. Sitting on the sixteen-man board with him were his brother Mahlon, brother-in-law Charles Butler, and extended family member Henry Smith.

The *Chicago Tribune* lauded the consolidation: "These two influential companies have consolidated, and will henceforth form one company, acting in diverse directions, yet with one aim, subject to one controlling power, and achieving results which singly they could not have accomplished." The story went on to describe the vast array of products that would henceforth flow into Chicago from across the Midwest and commended the plan's architect, crediting the "fertile brain of William B. Ogden, the king of western railroads. With some men this concentration of power would be dangerous, but we think there is little fear that Mr. Ogden will use the power he has acquired in any other way than to benefit the community."[4]

The new company wasted no time; on June 20, 1864, it released a report to its combined shareholders outlining the reasons the consolidation was a wonderful idea for stock- and bondholders of both railroads:

Much of the territory traversed by these roads was so situated as to induce injurious competition between them.

The union of both gives greater strength and power, favoring more advantageous and extended connections, and better relations with other railroads built and to be built, and will aid to prevent the construction of such roads as would only serve to create injurious competition, without any adequate increase of the aggregate earnings of the roads competing. Decided economy, material reduction of expenses, and increased and more profitable service of engines and cars, will also be the result of co-operation in the place of competition, and of one management of both Roads.

In explaining why the consolidated company chose to retain the name of the smaller, weaker railroad, the report noted, "The principal reason for dropping the pioneer name of Galena & Chicago Union Railroad Company in the consolidation will be apparent, when it is observed that no portion of either of the consolidated roads touches Galena."[5]

The report, written by Ogden himself, was prescient. All the good things predicted did come to pass in years to come. Still, the "Great Consolidation," as the newspapers called it, was not popular with some directors and stockholders of the Galena and Chicago Union. "It was talked about from the banks of the Atlantic to the slopes of the Missouri River, and opinions were as varied about it as were the people that gave them," one railroad biographer noted.[6]

We were robbed! was the most common complaint by Galena stockholders, and given the comparative financial health of the two companies at the time of the merger, it was a legitimate concern. The first angry bellow came from an unexpected source, Ogden's friend, ex-mayor "Long John" Wentworth.[7] He was a large stockholder in the Galena and Chicago Union and a member of its board, and he resented the absorption of the strong, profitable line into the smaller, debt-ridden Chicago and North Western.

Another stockholder, Julius Wadsworth, took more direct action.[8] He charged that the merger was illegal because of the way in which the consolidation meeting was called and conducted and the interests of stockholders not properly protected. On January 13, 1865, the attorney for the Galena and Chicago Union, Elliott Anthony, filed suit against the new company in Wadsworth's name in the U.S. Circuit Court for the Northern District of Illinois. Indicating the importance of the issue, David Davis, a former senator from Illinois and a current justice of the U.S. Supreme Court, was selected to preside over the case.

Wadsworth's suit asked for a financial review of the new company and an injunction prohibiting it from using the track and property of the Galena. It was a complicated filing, requiring "102 pages of foolscap," but Anthony's arguments were basically these: (1) Several of the men who had been elected directors of the Galena and approved the merger were not bona fide directors but had stock transferred to them for the mere purpose of making them directors. (2) This was not, in effect, a merger but was instead a sale of the Galena to the C&NW. (3) Since many of the men were directors of both railroads at the time of the so-called merger, it became a sale by themselves to themselves. (4) Ogden and Tilden had obtained the proxies by which they accomplished their scheme by fraud, not telling stockholders the real reason their proxies were being solicited. (5) The original charter of the Galena specified exactly how and where the railroad was to serve, and the areas served by the combined railroads did not meet that charter requirement. (6) There was an overissue of between two and three million dollars in stock in the new company, the proceeds of which were used to pay off stock- and bondholders of the two separate entities. (7) The addition of the Peninsula Railroad of Michigan to the merger in October 1864 brought substantial debt to the consolidation, thus watering down the value of the new company to debt-free Galena stockholders.[9]

The lawsuit specifically mentioned the men who had been "fraudulently elected" as directors of the Galena at the annual meeting. These included William B. Ogden, Mahlon Ogden, Edwin Sheldon (the Ogdens' brother-in-law), A. C. Coventry (apparently a member of the Ogdens' extended family), Samuel J. Tilden, and John Bice Turner. All these men, along with a number of others, it was charged, were at the time of the election also connected with the C&NW Railway.

Despite the lawsuit, which was progressing through the court during the early part of 1865, the Illinois legislature approved the consolidation on February 15, 1865, a fact that played a key role in the court's final ruling. Wadsworth's motive in filing the lawsuit is unclear. According to the *New York Times*, he held only three shares in the Galena, so he had no financial stake in the matter to speak of. He asked other Galena stockholders to join him in making it a class-action lawsuit, but not a single one did, not even the complaining Wentworth.[10]

Other lawsuits, more limited in scope, also followed. In one, for reasons impossible to determine, a few stockholders in the old C&NW Railway also filed suit to stop the consolidation, but they were unsuccessful.[11] When word got out that a few of the minority stockholders of the old Galena were planning to elect a new board of directors, the consolidated company filed an injunction in Superior Court enjoining them from doing so. That bill was dismissed, so it is possible they went ahead with their election; but if so, it became moot when the decision was handed down in the Wadsworth case.

Most Northern Illinois Circuit Court records were destroyed in the Great Fire of 1871, so we know of the court's findings only through the newspapers. On July 9, 1865, the *Chicago Republican* carried a story under the headline "The Great Railroad Case." It said, "The United States Circuit Court . . . yesterday refused the injunction prayed for by a portion of the stockholders in the Galena and Chicago Railway Company, to restrain the consolidation of that road with the North Western Railway Company, and for the appointment of a receiver. . . . the consolidation will not be disturbed or set aside."[12]

In arriving at their decision, Justices Davis and Treat declined to decide upon the merits of the case. However, they found the consolidation, which by now had occurred more than a year earlier and which had been approved by the legislature five months earlier, should not be tampered with because that would "disturb a system of railways, and overthrow a series of financial and commercial operations affecting the property and business of thousands of people who were in no way connected with the consolidation."[13]

The court did find, however, that Galena stockholders had not been treated fairly in the merger and that "non-consenting stockholders should be made whole as to the value of their property on the day the consolidation took place." The newspaper account opined that it would cost the railroad somewhere between fifty and eighty thousand dollars to satisfy the condition. The railroad subsequently made the necessary corrections for former Galena stockholders. One historical source of questionable veracity says Wadsworth was paid thirty thousand dollars. Since he held only three shares, if he was paid that much money it must have been in return for his agreement not to appeal the decision to the U.S. Supreme Court.

At the time of the merger, the Peninsula Railroad of Michigan's Upper Peninsula was not part of the C&NW; but later in 1864, it too was merged into the parent company and was included in Wadsworth's lawsuit.[14] Samuel J. Tilden was the legal representative of the bondholders of that railroad and arranged the merger with Ogden.[15] The road began at the mouth of Green Bay in Michigan's Upper Peninsula and continued northwesterly into the rich mining land that Ogden had long hoped to penetrate with rails. The sixty-two-mile-long road eventually became the Peninsula Division of the C&NW. There was an open stretch of seventy-five miles from the C&NW's Fort Howard terminus to the southern terminus of the Peninsula Railroad, running right up Green Bay's western shore, and Ogden knew they would eventually lay rails along that entire open stretch. But in the meantime, they were not going to miss a chance to cash in on the lucrative transport of the Upper Peninsula's iron and copper to Great Lakes ports. The C&NW either bought or leased three large ships and carried iron and copper ore and passengers between the Peninsula Division's terminus and other Great Lake ports. When ice kept the ship from traversing the lakes, the company began a stagecoach service for the passengers.

Even after the Wadsworth lawsuit was out of the way, the Great Consolidation's critics were not quelled. By far the strangest objection to the consolidation came in the form of a seventy-six-page pamphlet published by journalist James

Parton.[16] Parton was born in Canterbury, England, and came to the United States when he was five years old. He studied in New York City and White Plains and was a schoolmaster in Philadelphia and New York. He became a journalist and the most popular biographer of the day, writing books on Horace Greeley, Aaron Burr, Andrew Jackson, Benjamin Franklin, and a host of other nineteenth-century luminaries.

It is uncertain what connection Parton had to the financial world, if any, before he wrote his 1866 booklet on railroads, *Manual for the Instruction of "Rings," Railroad and Political, with a History of the Grand Chicago & North Western "Ring," and the Secret of Its Success in Placing an Over-issue of Twenty Millions, with a Margin of Three Millions in Three Years.* The booklet was an all-out attack on what Parton saw as a grand conspiracy between leading railroad executives and political leaders to manipulate stock, misappropriate funds, and commit fraud upon an unsuspecting public. Chosen to exemplify his conspiracy theory were the C&NW Railway, its president William B. Ogden, "the Grand Concoctor," and trustee Samuel J. Tilden, "the Grand Legalizer."

According to Parton, "A railway 'Ring' is a partnership among the managers, for the acquisition of personal advantages from the Stockholders or the public without their knowledge and without rendering an account of an equivalent."[17] Combining heavy analyses of financial statistics with his own skepticism, Parton's booklet is written in an almost tongue-in-cheek tone, a how-to manual for creating and using a "ring." It could easily be taken as parody if not for the thinly veiled and serious accusations it made. What is most obvious is that Parton saw inherent evil in monopolies and the power they bestowed on those in charge.

As specifically related to the Great Consolidation, Parton accused Ogden and Tilden of taking over a strong road—the Galena and Chicago Union—by manipulating stockholders and issuing shares beyond the assets of the new, combined road. He also accused Ogden of using the railroad to enrich his lumber, iron, and coal investments, a charge similar to one made against Ogden when he resigned from the old Galena's board. On that earlier charge, Ogden had prevailed in court.

Tilden got wind of the booklet and obtained an injunction against its distribution and supplied funds to have the copies in New York City and elsewhere purchased and destroyed.[18] But a few copies had already been put in circulation, and the *Chicago Republican* reprinted it in its entirety. Ogden did his best to quell the newspaper's publication but was only able to get them to admit in print that many of Parton's figures were inaccurate and faulty. On the whole, however, Parton's charges were simply a rehash of the charges in the original Wadsworth lawsuit. The booklet caused no more than a temporary flap, although it must have been of considerable concern to Ogden and Tilden, given the extent of their attempts to control its distribution.

Chicago historian William Downard put the happiest possible face on the entire mess: "The whole affair was an example of the excesses of 'the age of railroad combinations.' Certainly Ogden was not a 'robber baron' in the sense of Daniel Drew, James Fisk, or Jay Gould. He was a businessman, and a good one, and he knew how to maneuver for profit."[19] This may be true, but Ogden realized when he first began planning the details of the consolidation that his strategy involved a great deal of artifice. He had taken perhaps his largest step on a very slippery slope. Although his railroad vision was unquestionably the most farsighted of any American railroad pioneer, Ogden's railroad ventures from this period forward would slip deeper and deeper into the muck and mire of the postwar business ethos.

The charges against Ogden's Great Consolidation made one thing clear: building railroads had become an extremely profitable enterprise by the 1860s. Stewart Holbrook, in *The Story of American Railroads*, described railroad promoters' typical business plans in the mid-nineteenth century.[20] First they organized a stock company and named their railroad, often naming it after the principal towns or regions it would pass through, or possibly only the two terminal cities.

> Next came a charter involving land grants of alternate sections along the line of the proposed road. Next the railroad boys would incorporate a land company, owned by the directors of the railroad, to develop and peddle the lands. With the proceeds of the land sales, to which cash subsidies from federal, state, or even city sources often were added, plus the sale of mortgage bonds in Europe, actual construction of the railroad was begun. Construction, however, was not done by the railroad company, but by a separate concern, also owned by the railroad's directors, which commonly paid off handsomely, although the grade was made and the rails laid at stupendous cost to the holders of the railroad's stocks and bonds. A considerable number of American railroads were financed by methods that cost the railroad's directors not a penny of their own in actual cash.[21]

Buying non–land grant real estate ahead of demand and before public disclosure of the railroad's exact route was another easy method of profiting for those on the inside.

William Ogden's first railroad venture, the Galena and Chicago Union, was not built in the manner described by Holbrook. Ogden fronted much of the money himself when he was unable to secure financial support from Chicago or Eastern investors, European bonds, or government subsidies. Similarly, when beginning to cobble together his Chicago and North Western Railway, he went into personal debt for one and a half million dollars when other money sources were not available. Most notably, neither of these railroads received land grants, except for a small one for the Wisconsin and Superior Railroad.

In the case of Ogden's later railroad ventures—the consolidated Chicago and North Western and the Northern Pacific Railroads—the practices Holbrook outlined had become standard industry procedure. However, it is difficult to discern Ogden's attitude toward the unseemly practices, even though he seemed to be a willing participant. One historian, speaking of Ogden's latter-day railroad endeavors, aptly described him as a shadowy character, working mainly behind the scenes. That, plus the absence of records of such conduct in all but the most flagrant examples, makes it particularly difficult to flush out the extent of Ogden's profiteering. However, there is little doubt that he enriched himself from such practices for the rest of his railroad days.

During the remainder of Ogden's time at the helm of the Chicago and North Western and the years following until his death, the railroad that he built through extraordinary vision, hard work, and occasionally a touch of chicanery continued to grow and prosper. For the decade after the consolidation, the company paid handsome dividends of between 5 and 10 percent each year to stockholders and enjoyed good profits. And the C&NW continued to add track. In 1866 it added an important link to Milwaukee through the perpetual lease of the Chicago and Milwaukee Railroad.

By the time the consolidation was completed, the Civil War was exerting a crushing impact on the U.S. Post Office.[22] The increase of official government mail and servicemen's personal mail had ground the system almost to a halt. President Lincoln's assistant postmaster general, George B. Armstrong, had a solution: traveling post offices on rails that could deliver mail in a fraction of the time presently required by the use of stagecoaches and mounted postal carriers. He received authorization to field-test his idea, and he selected the Chicago and North Western Railway to help him. The nation's first railroad mail run occurred shortly thereafter, from Chicago to Clinton, Iowa. The idea worked. Within a couple of years, specially equipped cars had been built for the task, and the C&NW carried the mail to Omaha for its transcontinental delivery when that rail system was completed.

When Ogden resigned from the presidency of the nascent Union Pacific Railroad, he believed he could be more useful by connecting that railroad's eastern terminus in Omaha with leading Midwestern and Eastern cities. When the C&NW's first passenger train made the 488-mile trip from Chicago to Council Bluffs, Iowa, directly across the Missouri River from Omaha, in February 1867, he proved his point. The *Council Bluffs Nonpareil* wrote of the event, "The arrival of the first regular passenger train was marked by a joyous celebration. Cannon were fired and a long procession of wagons, artillery and citizens marched to the station to greet the train."[23]

The C&NW immediately put a railcar ferry in service across the Missouri River so construction materials and manpower could be carried without interruption from Chicago to the Union Pacific track where work was under way.[24] Before that connection, mule teams had to haul the materials from the river's edge to the worksite, a distance of many miles. This connection was of inestimable value to the Union Pacific and hastened the completion of the road by many months, if not years.

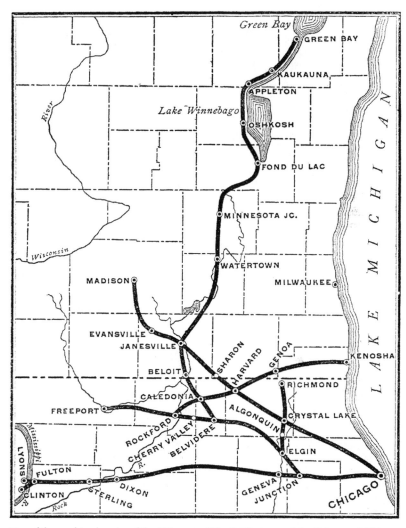

Map of the combined routes of the Chicago and North Western and the Galena and Chicago Union Railroads just after the Great Consolidation in 1864.

Chicago and North Western Railway passenger depot on Chicago's North Side, circa late 1860s. Union Pacific Historical Collection.

Later that same year, the company built a large, ornate stone freight house at the South Branch in Chicago at a cost of ten thousand dollars.[25] The next year, the C&NW became the second railroad to build a bridge across the Mississippi River, following a lawsuit filed against the first one, the Rock Island Railroad.[26] The U.S. Supreme Court in that case ruled that bridges were not an impediment to river travel and were therefore legal.

The C&NW also became embroiled in another issue that had just begun to raise its head in the United States, the labor movement.[27] The hours were long, the work was hard, and the pay was low for the vast majority of unskilled and semi-skilled labor, and by the 1850s and 1860s many of those jobs were held by immigrants. But workers in even more skilled positions also became restless. As early as 1856, railroad mechanics and engineers began to discuss their problems, which led to the formation of the Brotherhood of Locomotive Engineers. Wildcat strikes began to occur, but none were too serious. Jobs were fairly plentiful in Midwestern cities like Chicago, although workers were often trammeled by low pay, layoffs, and harsh working conditions, but when the Panic of 1857 struck, that was no longer the case.

The coming of the Civil War put an end to the unemployment problem, as there were again jobs for everyone, even if many of them were in military service. But at war's end, the old problems reappeared. In 1864 the General Trades Assembly was formed in Chicago to coordinate the activities of more than a dozen unions in the city. Finally, it was decided to make the eight-hour workday—instead of the normal ten hours—the linchpin in the unions' fight for better conditions and pay. An Illinois state law was even passed in 1867 calling for an eight-hour day for all mechanical trades and arts, the first in the nation.

But management responded decisively. The C&NW and Rock Island Railroads threatened to change pay from a per-day to a per-hour basis, nullifying the effect of the new law, or to bring in unemployed workers from other cities to fill the jobs, or even to move their mechanical shops to Iowa where there was no eight-hour-day law. The unions struck. However, only a week later, the labor opposition crumbled; men had to eat and feed their families, so they slunk back to their ten-hour-a-day jobs. Naturally, this was only the first salvo in labor's attempt to win fair treatment for its members, but it provided one more level of aggravation to the men like William Ogden who ran the nation's businesses.

On June 4, 1868, at age sixty-three, William Ogden resigned as president and board member of the C&NW. His colleagues protested, but he told them he was tired and ready for retirement.[28] The truth was, just as he had resigned from the presidency of the Galena and Chicago Union and later the Union Pacific, he felt the challenge was over. He had a dream, a grand vision, for a railroad that would connect the Midwest and Great Plains with the rest of the nation, and when the dream was realized, he was ready to move on.

The C&NW board honored Ogden with a resolution: "*Resolved:* That William Ogden's connection with this Company, dating back for a period of twenty-one years, his disinterested labors in its behalf without fee or reward during the whole time, the benefit he has conferred upon it and the country, demand our grateful acknowledgements, and we hereby tender him our warmest thanks for his long service and our best wishes for his long-continued health and prosperity."[29]

The railroad Ogden left behind operated six divisions: Galena, Iowa, Madison, Milwaukee, Peninsula, and Wisconsin.[30] Its latest gross earnings totaled $12,614,846, and net earnings stood at $4,741,199. It was an impressive railroad property. By 1869 the C&NW had 1,156 miles of track, including its subsidiaries, and by 1874, 1,990 miles. It continued to add short-line railroads to the books whenever they provided a strategic fit. Table 12.1 shows the railroads added from the Great Consolidation through the end of the nineteenth century. By the time William Stennett wrote the first history of the C&NW in 1900, the railroad had 7,452 miles of track (see table 12.2). Its Midwest and Great Plains service area had indeed become what Ogden had envisioned from the very beginning. Meanwhile, gross earnings from traffic (freight and passenger) grew from $1.976 million the year before the consolidation to $74.176 million in 1910.[31]

Table 12.1

Additions to the Chicago and North Western Railway Company, after consolidation with the Galena and Chicago Union, before 1900

Railroad	Date Added
Baraboo Air Line	March 1871
La Crosse, Trempealeau and Prescott Railway	June 1877
Menominee River Railroad	July 1882
Escanaba and Lake Superior Railway	July 1882
Galesville and Mississippi River Railroad	March 1883
Rock River Railway	March 1883
Elgin and Stateline Railroad	June 1883
Chicago, Milwaukee and Northwest Railway	June 1883
Chicago, Iowa and Nebraska Railroad	July 1884
Cedar Rapids and Missouri River Railroad	July 1884
Maple River Railroad	July 1884
Stanwood and Tipton Railway	October 1884
Iowa, Midland Railway	October 1884
Ottumwa, Chippewa Falls and St. Paul Railway	October 1884
Iowa, Southwestern Railway	October 1884
Des Moines and Minneapolis Railroad	October 1884
Maple Valley Railway	May 1887
Janesville and Evansville Railway	May 1887
Sioux Valley Railway	November 1887
Iowa Railway	November 1887
Linn County Railway	November 1887
Sycamore and Cortland Railroad	June 1888
Northern Illinois Railway	June 1888
Iron River Railway	June 1889
Iron Range Railway	June 1889
Lake Geneva and Stateline Railway	June 1889
Toledo and North-Western Railway	June 1890
Junction Railway	June 1891
Paint River Railway	June 1891
Milwaukee, Lakeshore and Western Railway	August 1893
Wisconsin Northern Railway	September 1897

Note: Data were assembled by the author.

Table 12.2

Chicago and North Western track in Midwest and Great Plains states in 1900

State	Miles of Track
Wisconsin	1,826
Iowa	1,578
Nebraska	1,101
South Dakota	948
Illinois	685
Minnesota	650
Michigan	520
Wyoming	130
North Dakota	14

Source: Stennett, *Yesterday and Today*, 129.

The C&NW would enjoy a long and very prosperous life, suffering its ups and downs as all railroads did during the nineteenth and twentieth centuries. But it performed exactly as William Ogden had foreseen. Railroad historian H. Roger Grant summed up the great railroad in his book on the subject:

> The North Western grew into a robust carrier that truly could boast the "Best of Everything" credo. Enormously profitable from the mid-nineteenth century until the early twentieth century, it fashioned a major rail network in the Midwest and Great Plains during these years, creating an excellent physical plant and providing quality service. At times, the North Western was an innovator, and often it set standards for the industry.
>
> Under William Ogden, and Marvin Hughitt [president from 1887 to 1910] two of the most gifted railroad leaders of the nineteenth century, the company bolstered the growing strength of Chicago by funneling freight and passenger traffic to and from the metropolis and also advanced western settlement and town making.[32]

Anyone who believed William Ogden was going to retire from railroading following his resignation from the Chicago and North Western did not know the man. Railroads were in his blood, and he would continue to build them as long as there was life left in his body.

Ogden's final major railroad venture was another story of vision and perseverance, although he would not live long enough to see the work completed. In the sunset of his career, in 1867, while he was still the president of the C&NW, he was called upon to participate in building a second transcontinental line, the

Northern Pacific Railroad. Familiarity with this iconoclastic man leads to the conclusion that Ogden resigned from the presidency of the C&NW in order to tackle this final project, although no extant records verify this opinion.

When Congress first began considering a transcontinental railroad in the early 1850s, a number of different routes were considered. Congress finally decided on a route along the 38th parallel, which would run roughly through the center of the country. The proponents of a northern route at the 45th parallel, having lost the battle, sought and eventually gained in 1865 congressional approval of an alternate route to run from Lake Superior to Puget Sound. Thus was born the Northern Pacific Railroad.

Josiah Perham of Maine was the man most responsible for gaining the charter, and he and a group of his New England friends formed a company to build the road.[33] The act of Congress that created the charter provided for a massive land grant for the Northern Pacific. In the normal checkerboard pattern used for such grants, the railroad was given every other section (a square mile) of land in a band forty miles wide through the states of Wisconsin, Minnesota, and Oregon and eighty miles wide through the territories of North Dakota, Montana, Idaho, and Washington. It amounted to a staggering fifty million acres of land if all the terms of the charter were met; but the act withheld all rights for the company to issue government-backed bonds or obtain any other federal assistance. The general feeling in Congress was that one transcontinental railroad was sufficient; if private capital wanted to take on the challenge of a second one, that was fine, as long as it was done without federal money. Perham wasn't dismayed; he was confident the public would see the wisdom of his vision and throw their support and money behind him.

Perham did have a vision. He felt that a railroad taking the northern route ending at Puget Sound would be a perfect avenue for opening trade with China, Japan, Russia, and the remainder of the Far East.[34] Had he been successful, perhaps history would have remembered him as the man who finally opened the storied Northwest Passage that had been sought for five hundred years. As it turned out, however, he became only a footnote in American railroad history.

Despite his vision, when Perham died in 1868, no longer on the board of directors in the company he had created, his dream still hadn't made headway.[35] A second board was installed, and they too failed to garner sufficient financial support for the road. Finally, J. Gregory Smith took over as president. The former governor of Vermont and a veteran of Eastern railroad management, he had been president of the Vermont and Canada Railroad, which had provided him contacts within the Canadian railroad industry. Using those contacts, he immediately sought to form an alliance with Canada's Grand Trunk Railroad, which had just begun thinking about its own transcontinental road that would lead to Far East trade. However, the talks stalled, as they were premature for the Canadians.

Smith tried again to gain federal aid, and again he failed.[36] Then he came up with a new idea. He realized his board, composed almost exclusively of New Englanders, didn't have enough railroad experience or political clout to get needed government assistance. Most Eastern railroads were secondary lines, connecting one small New England village with another; so Eastern railroaders did not have the background for a project as far-reaching as the Northern Pacific. Smith decided to create "a great railroad syndicate embracing many of the leading railroads in the country"—a kind of Grand Masters company—to get the job done. His dream company, he hoped, would include the presidents of the country's leading railroads. Smith appointed another board member, Thomas Canfield, to carry out his plan.

Canfield's first stop was New York. He felt if he could interest William Ogden in the proposition, the others would fall in line. "Of all the great railway managers of that day he was the one whose indorsement and active support was of most value to the struggling, feeble Northern Pacific scheme," historian Eugene Smalley wrote in 1883.[37]

New York in January could be a forbidding place.[38] The winter of 1867 was a harsh one, and when Canfield arrived at Villa Boscobel for his early morning appointment with Ogden, he was already late due to the heavy, tangled carriage and sleigh traffic on the snow-clogged streets. Ogden greeted Canfield and led him to a large, warming fire in the library. Canfield shed his coat and briskly rubbed his hands together to warm them. He looked around the large, book-lined room with its dark paneled bookcases and masculine furniture and complimented Ogden on his good taste.

Once Canfield was warm, the two men sat across from each other at the hearth, and Canfield began pulling papers from his valise, including a copy of the charter he had had printed in pamphlet form. As soon as he began talking about the Northern Pacific and the work that had been done so far, Ogden became intrigued. Nobody loved a visionary railroad plan better that William Ogden, and Smith's "grand masters" scheme was just that. He told Canfield he believed most, if not all, of the railroad chief executives Smith hoped to engage in the firm's reorganization could probably be enticed to participate. Some, he warned, were probably too busy to take an active role but would gladly lend their names to the endeavor in return for some handsome consideration. Although Ogden had been giving serious thought to stepping away from the C&NW, he had not mentioned it to anyone yet; but as he listened to Canfield's pitch, the lure of an exciting new project began to take hold of him. The two men talked for fifteen hours, stopping only to take a couple of meals during the day.

That evening they wired J. Gregory Smith, who joined them in New York at Ogden's office on January 10, 1867.[39] A financial plan was drafted. Smith declared that $102,000 had been spent thus far in procuring the charter and keeping the company alive, so they decided the newly organized company would be divided into twelve shares, each worth $8,500, which would return the $102,000 to those who had advanced it.

Smith's idea succeeded on a grand scale. The *New York Times* of May 17, 1867, reported on the Northern Pacific's new directors; it was a virtual who's who of the railroad business:

> Wm. B. Ogden, of Chicago, President of the Chicago and North Western Railway; J. Edgar Thomson of Philadelphia, Penn., President of the Pennsylvania Central Railroad; Robert H. Berdell, of New-York, President of the Erie Railway; George W. Cass of Pittsburgh, President of the Pittsburgh, Fort Wayne and Chicago Railroad; W. G. Fargo, of Buffalo, Vice-President of New-York Central Railroad; and Thomas H. Canfield, of Burlington, Vt. These gentlemen, with Hon. John Gregory Smith, President of Vermont Central Railroad; Hon. R. D. Rice, President of Portland and Kennebeck Railroad; Hon. Onslow Stearns, President of Old Colony Railroad; and Benj. P. Cheeny, of Messrs. Wells, Fargo & Co., constitute a Board of the ablest railway managers in the country.[40]

The twelve shares of stock were initially allocated like this: J. Gregory Smith, for himself and his associates (primarily current board members who were being paid off so they would resign their posts), four and two-thirds shares; William B. Ogden, one and one-third shares; Robert Berdell, G. W. Cass, and Edward Reilly, one share each; and D. N. Barney and B. P. Cheeny; A. H. Barney and W. G. Fargo (of Wells, Fargo); and J. Edgar Thomson and associates, each group one share jointly.[41] Ogden was appointed to the board's executive committee.

The subscribers of the twelve shares received nothing tangible for their money; the company had no assets, only the extravagant land grant which would not come into play until construction was under way. In fact, the shareholders would be expected to dig back into their own pockets for funds to obtain from Congress the passage of a bill granting federal aid for the construction of the road and to meet other costs that would arise during the preconstruction phase. Obtaining this support was a huge gamble, so if ever there was a financial pig in a poke, the Northern Pacific Railroad was it. However, all these experienced railroad men recognized one hard, cruel fact of life: the opportunity to milk this new venture, should it succeed, would be huge.

For the next two years, Ogden and the other influential railroad men on the board lobbied the U.S. Congress for government support for their project.[42] Finally, in 1869, with the political clout the Northern Pacific had assembled, there was a breakthrough. It was not all they had asked for—they wanted financial support from the government, or a government guarantee of their bond issues—but they were given a charter amendment, dated March 1, 1869, permitting the public sale of their bonds secured by a first mortgage against the railway and telegraph property they had initially been granted.

The men got right to work. By mid-1869, Ogden was in New York City attending the annual meeting of the prestigious American Geographical and Statistical Society. As the meeting's keynote speaker, he was there to begin plugging the new railroad. His address, entitled "Origin and Progress of the Pacific Railroad," spoke glowingly of the project, and he promised "the great Northern Railroad from Lake Superior through Missouri and across the Plains to the Columbia river [will bring] us 800 miles nearer the Empire of Japan than the present Pacific Railroad."[43] He also announced that the board was close to concluding negotiations with Jay Cooke and Company of Philadelphia to become the financial agent for the sale of bonds and overseer of the construction of the road.

Jay Cooke and Company was the leading financier of the North during the Civil War and the nation's largest banking house. Earlier that year, Ogden and Canfield had met with Cooke at his home north of Philadelphia to invite his participation. Cooke promised to spend some time examining the plans, including making a reconnaissance of the proposed route. Over the next six months, he spent a great deal of time doing that; and at the beginning of 1870 he signed on to handle the bond sales and construction supervision. Jay Cooke was a pious man who took his strong religious beliefs very seriously, but he was also an astute businessman. He realized the task being assigned him would be a difficult one. Consequently, he had asked for and been given a liberal stake in the company and broad powers to exercise a great deal of control over the enterprise.

When the railroad received its charter, Congress had authorized bonds with a total face value of one hundred million dollars, to mature in thirty years and yielding 7.3 percent interest. As Congress had approved, the bonds would be backed by a mortgage against the railroad's land grant. Cooke was to sell the bonds at par (at their face value, without a discount) and retain 12 percent of the price as his commission, returning the other 88 percent to the company.

Despite Cooke's expertise, and the railroad board's extensive experience and clout, the company faced formidable challenges. This would be the first railroad built *ahead* of demand, not in response to it. The two-thousand-mile route would pass through millions of acres of unsettled, boreal land—valuable timberland, scattered deposits of important minerals, and some of the richest untouched farmland in the nation. Yet the area was also virtually unpopulated, except for random tribes of hostile Indians. There would be no people to provide passenger revenue and no farm or businesses to provide freight revenue. But there was the massive land grant.

Cooke put the immense scale of the grant and its potential bounty in perspective in one of his early sales brochures:

The amount of land granted to the Northern Pacific by its charter, original and as amended, exceeds 50,000,000 acres. This superb estate is larger by 10,000 square miles than the six New England states, or as large as Ohio and Indiana combined. There is room in it for ten states as large as Massachusetts, each of them with a soil and climate, and resources of coal, timber, ores of metals and perpetual water power. . . . The grant is nearly seven times as large as Belgium and more than three-and-one-half times as large as Holland.[44]

Cooke's first challenge was to sell bonds and to convince potential home-steaders that despite the wicked winter weather, hostile Indians, and dearth of people, this was a bountiful land and would be a great place to start a new life. To assist him, the railroad board allocated huge sums of money for advertising and promotion. Still, selling settlers on the idea of moving to these extreme northern climes was hard. Cooke launched an extensive nationwide advertising campaign. Smalley wrote, "Advertisements were published in the newspapers far and wide, including the country weeklies, and city dailies. Liberal payments for advertising . . . secured favorable editorial comments."[45]

Cooke also relied on a variety of other promotional techniques to woo set-tlers to the vast, hostile countryside.[46] The nation's first speakers' bureau was established, and lectures and sales pitches were made in hundreds of Eastern, Midwestern, and Southern population centers. European agents were hired to pump up sales overseas. Wagon train excursions were conducted to give pro-spective homesteaders a firsthand look at the land (in the summer, of course). Hired hands pitched tents, provided white-glove food service, and entertained the prospects during the journey. Outlandish promotions were staged, like enormous buffalo hunts, which had great appeal for European prospects. Inter-esting exhibits were built extolling the advantages of cheap land and placed in state fairs across the country. And land agents were employed to form colonies. This last tactic involved linking like-minded people together and transporting them as a group to establish new colonies in the wilderness. This is how so many pockets of Scandinavians, northern Europeans, and Slavic ethnic groups came to be in the territories.

Despite Jay Cooke's best efforts, there still wasn't much of an appetite in the investment community for another transcontinental railroad, nor for mortgage bonds backed by property along the barren 45th parallel, nor for settlement in the area. Nevertheless, with the little money that was raised, construction finally began in July 1870 simultaneously near Carlton, Minnesota, moving west, and Kalama, Washington Territory, moving east.

From the summer of 1870 through 1871, sufficient money came in through Cooke's efforts to keep railroad construction progressing. The company bought a controlling interest in a smaller railroad with some track already laid in the territory and continued to lay its own T-rails.[47]

Early on it became obvious to Jay Cooke that his biggest obstacle to success was going to be the Northern Pacific board of directors itself. J. Gregory Smith, the chairman, proved to be a capricious, ineffective leader who spent lavishly and wastefully. His right-hand man, Thomas Canfield, was even worse. An inept man, he had a wide streak of larceny in his soul that dictated most of his decisions. And other board members—including William Ogden—had taken a mostly hands-off policy as far as day-to-day management of the project was concerned, leaving Smith, Canfield, and Cooke to do pretty much as they pleased.

From the beginning, the construction companies hired to do the work were corrupt, funneling money back to their owners, who were mainly the railroad's board members.[48] The company hired to build the first section of track on the westward leg of the road was the Canda Company, owned by Charles J. Canda and his brother Ferdinand. A French immigrant, Charles Canda had been a partner with William Ogden and some other men in the early 1860s in Brady's Bend Iron Works; and for a time in the mid-1870s Ogden even appointed Canda a trustee for his estate, describing him as "my esteemed friend."[49] Information from that time period indicates that Canda, who became a widower in 1871, intended to marry into Ogden's extended family until something altered that plan.

These facts seem to indicate that William Ogden was not just a recipient of the corrupt largesse that flowed to Northern Pacific board members but also an engineer of some of it. One of Cooke's biographers wrote of the Canda Company: "The work . . . was entrusted to a construction company which it was said was composed of officers and employees of the railroad."[50] Later, the Canda Company would also be awarded a contract on the eastward leg of the operation.[51]

In early 1872, the Oregon Steam Navigation Company, which operated almost all the steamboats on the Columbia, Snake, and Willamette Rivers and in Puget Sound, became concerned at the impending competition and offered to sell out.[52] The Northern Pacific bought 75 percent of the company for one and a half million dollars, which included a half-million dollars in gold. Cooke was against the sale; he was the one who had to come up with the gold, and his sales were still slow. But the sale went through despite his objections, and the Northern Pacific held possession of almost all the transportation facilities in Oregon and Washington Territory.

Late that fall, the newly elected Northern Pacific president, General George Cass, executive committee member William Ogden, and four other board members traveled to the Pacific Coast to select a route for the railroad from the Columbia River to Puget Sound.[53] They were also to select future town sites to occupy their land grants and a location for the western terminus of the railroad. Cass and Ogden had made a similar trip two years earlier: a reconnaissance of the area to get a look at the West Coast and the problems the railroad might encounter. Ogden loved the journey. It was his first trip to the West, and he found Oregon and Washington Territory to be gorgeous, peaceful places where he felt completely at ease. Only a half-dozen years earlier, General James Rusling was steaming down the Columbia River and described a few of the bucolic scenes that so captivated Ogden:

> Puff! Puff! And so we went down the Columbia at last. How exquisitely pleasant, how cozy and delightful, our little steamer seemed. Occasionally rapids appeared, of a serious character; but as a rule the river was broad and deep, majestic in size and volume.
>
> On the banks were frequent Indian villages, with their hardy little ponies browsing around—apparently on nothing but sage-brush and cobble-stones. These Indians fancied spotted or "calico" horses, as the Oregonians called them, and very few of their ponies were of a single color. They [the Indians] eke out a precarious subsistence by fishing, etc.[54]

On this second journey, the Northern Pacific men had made their way up the Columbia River and were cruising Puget Sound aboard the steamship *North Pacific* to accomplish their final task, the selection of the railroad's western terminus. Just the anticipation of the railroad's arrival had already spurred skyrocketing land prices throughout the region. The *San Francisco Daily Evening Bulletin* wrote, "Parcels of land worth $1,000 two weeks ago, have advanced to $10,000. One hundred acres which sold two weeks ago for $2,000 changed hands for $5,000 and now is held at $10,000."[55] Such news came as no surprise to the railroad men, but it would certainly have gladdened their hearts, given the astounding size of their land grant.

Today Tacoma, Washington, is an energetic city of about two hundred thousand people, perched gloriously on the southeastern shore of Puget Sound. It is undergoing a renaissance of sorts, trying to shed its image as a blue-collar city and entice younger professionals into its midst. Thirty miles up the Sound sits Seattle, sophisticated, urbane, and white-collar, everything Tacoma would like to be. But at one time, the roles were reversed.

The selection of the Northern Pacific's terminus was proving to be a frustrating chore; the men found their choices limited, as there were only a few sawmill hamlets from which to select, most notably Seattle, Tacoma, Olympia, Steilcoom, and Mukilteo. They had been told about the small village called Seattle, named after the chief of the local Suquamish and Duwamish Indians, but when they arrived at the small landing below the village they discovered it was only "a petty lumbering place of, perhaps, two score of houses."[56] Actually, there were about eighteen hundred inhabitants in Seattle at the time, and it was the commercial center of the Puget Sound region. However, to the village's detriment, it did not have enough level land to accommodate a large railway yard.

The Northern Pacific men pushed off again and continued south down the Sound to another village that wasn't much more promising. It was called Tacoma. It did have a small bay—Commencement Bay—that the men thought might serve their shipping needs, and a local landowner named General Morton McCarver convinced them that the villagers—all one hundred of them—would work hard to help the railroad succeed. The village was level enough for their railway yard, and it contained a steam saw mill, a small public school, a public hall, a hotel, and a store.

The directors agreed that Tacoma was their place, and in November 1875 the town was officially incorporated. Another company was formed with a two-million-dollar capitalization to lay out a town and sell lots and wharf privileges in Tacoma. The town exploded as soon as the news was out that it had been selected as the Northern Pacific Railroad's western terminus. Within a very short period, it had "stores, restaurants, hotels, drinking and gambling saloons, churches, and a saloon/dance-house for the patrons of vile squaws."[57] Ogden and his fellow board cronies purchased additional land in the area *before* the news was made public, and the townspeople gifted them another eight hundred acres for selecting Tacoma.

The company's financial fortunes began to sour in early 1872 when bond sales fell precipitously, but the Northern Pacific's extravagant spending continued unabated.[58] Jay Cooke's failure to succeed wasn't from lack of effort or money. To maintain the appearance of a healthy market for the bonds, he bought back 90 percent of the bonds he sold. He eventually spent so much promoting the sale of the railroad's bonds that the northern route became known as Cooke's Banana Belt. Ultimately, Cooke spent his company into collapse, which was one of the fiascos that led to the financial panic that began on September 19, 1873. By this time, the road had advanced 450 miles from Lake Superior to Bismarck, in Dakota Territory, and from Kalama on the Columbia River, north of Portland, to Tacoma on Puget Sound.

The overextension of the Northern Pacific was just one facet of an entire economy gone sour. Banks closed, businesses failed, and thousands of people lost their jobs. Northern Pacific president Cass cut costs and took out loans in order to keep the company afloat, but in early 1875, it was forced to declare bankruptcy.[59] Cass resigned, and in April was appointed the railroad's receiver. Two years later, following the panic, the Northern Pacific was sold at auction to some of its bondholders, and the company was reorganized.

It is not clear when and how William Ogden departed the company. In March 1873, he was elected to another three-year term as a director.[60] A newspaper article dated May 14, 1875, states that when board member J. Edgar Thomson died on May 27, 1874, Ogden was named to replace him as a trustee for the railroad's first mortgage bonds. The article went on to say of Ogden, "He resigned," but provided no other details.[61] Finally, in Ogden's last will and testament, drafted on August 30, 1875, no mention is made of any holdings in the Northern Pacific.

Thus it can be deduced that Ogden resigned from the company at some point between March 1874 and May 1875.

One of Cooke's biographers, Ellis Oberholtzer, writing in 1907, states that Cooke had purchased one of the original twelve shares from Ogden in 1871.[62] That would indicate that Ogden's holdings in the company were just the remaining one-third share he retained. However, the booty he and the other board directors shared from the construction companies, the land sales, and other forms of graft would have still made the Northern Pacific a lucrative enterprise. But with the panic upon him, and his kidneys beginning to fail, Ogden had either sold his remaining stake, or more likely, lost it when the road went into bankruptcy.

Despite the Northern Pacific's early hardships, which were more a function of the economy's ups and downs than of the railroad's efforts, it did eventually prove to be the major factor in opening up and populating the area it traversed.[63] During the formative years when Ogden and Cooke were involved (1870–75), an average of nearly 140,000 acres of the land grant were sold per year. The period 1876 through 1884 saw that figure swell to more than 400,000 acres a year. By 1903, the company had sold more than half of its land grant. Population burgeoned along with the sale of land, and not just among American citizens. Irish, Germans, Danes, Norwegians, Swedes, Austrians, Poles, and Russians moved from their mother countries onto the once vacant landscape, undeterred by the frigid winters. By the early twentieth century, the Northern Pacific Railroad was on its way to a long and illustrious corporate life.

A story-within-a-story developed during the Northern Pacific's struggling infancy. President Smith had tried to get his foot in the door with the Canadians when he first became president of the road, but he was unsuccessful. Canada had the same relationship to its western lands as the United States at the time. It had yet to formally adopt British Columbia into the nation, but Canadians were thinking ahead to the vast open land and resources of their western regions.

Into this situation stepped two Canadian entrepreneurs, Alfred Waddington and William Kersteman.[64] Waddington had tried to promote the transcontinental railroad idea to both the Canadian and the English Parliament but with no success. The men now decided that perhaps enticing an American partner into the scheme might have advantages. They contacted George McMullen, another Canadian who had resettled in Chicago and owned the *Evening Post*, one of many short-lived journals that cropped up in Chicago at the time.[65] McMullen liked anything that had money attached to it, so he approached William Ogden about the idea. Ogden liked it too, and he brought in General Cass and moneyman Jay Cooke. Ogden and Cass had their hands full, so they allowed Cooke to take the lead. Cooke was a dreamer; he saw a joint American-Canadian transcontinental road that would operate in both countries but under American control. Canadians, meanwhile, weren't too keen on a joint road, preferring their own Canadian transcontinental road.

On June 17, 1871, Ogden wrote to Cooke. He outlined the land route the Canadian-Pacific had in mind and the financial and land grant terms that could be available to whomever was granted the charter. He explained to Cooke:

> This project seems to me so taking and strong and so dearly to belong to the Northern Pacific as a great auxiliary and strengthener if your financial plans are sufficiently promising or advanced to make it prudent and proper to take the preliminary steps to cooperate with or control this project. . . .
>
> Another reason for consideration of this matter now or early is, that if satisfactory alliance and cooperation is secured now before the matter is presented widely the chances of interference by other parties or with the [Canadian] Government will be lessened.

Ogden's letter to Cooke continued in a somewhat high-minded tone. While claiming no interest in personal profit—which was probably true at this point in his life—Ogden did restate his belief in the inevitability of Western expansion:

> Now I as in the past, have no desire personally to engage in this for financial gain, but have as great an interest as anyone that this great rich and as yet but partially known world would be promptly developed and brought to the knowledge of the ignorant and made to bless vast numbers of the less fortunate of the human family, and at the same time be made to swell the volume of commerce of the Great North West and the earnings and profits of the Northern Pacific R. Road to which it would seem legitimately to belong.[66]

Ogden and Cooke's plan for the joint American-Canadian line eventually failed when the Canadian Parliament decided on a Canadians-only policy of building their transcontinental railroad.

These two ventures, the Northern Pacific and the Canadian Pacific, were the last in the long, fruitful railroad career of William Ogden. A retrospective look at his forty years in the business illuminates one important fact: he was the *only* nineteenth-century railroad pioneer whose influence and career stretched from coast to coast. His early promotion and hard-hitting speech in the New York legislature in favor of the New York and Erie Railroad was a principal factor in getting that line started, and his involvement in the Northern Pacific Railroad in the twilight of his life helped that line ultimately become a reality. From the New York and Erie's terminus at Piermont on the Hudson River to the Northern Pacific's terminus at Puget Sound, his vision and influence spanned the continent.

Ogden's lumbering partner, Isaac "Ike" Stephenson, described Ogden's accomplishments in his own autobiography: "These were days of large industrial enterprise and men of great capacity and breadth of view were required," he wrote. "Towering above all of them physically as well as mentally, in energy, breadth of vision, and masterful enterprise, was William B. Ogden."[67]

Stewart Holbrook, whose book on American railroad history was cited earlier, was one of the mid-twentieth century's most prolific writers, historians, and social commentators. The ex-logger's three-dozen books offer perceptive insights into the forestry, lumber, and railroad industries and the people who built them. A frequent visitor to Chicago from his home in the Pacific Northwest, Holbrook loved the excitement of that city, especially its giant railroad yards and terminals, which were in their heyday during the 1930s and 1940s when he was visiting: "Railroad stations are alive, throbbing, dynamic, charged with the urgency of life," he wrote. "Little wonder Chicago and its galaxy of railroad depots stands alone as the champion railroad junction of the country, and hence America's most exciting city."[68]

Holbrook wrote often about late-nineteenth-century railroad tycoons like Daniel Drew, James Fisk, Jay Gould, Cornelius Vanderbilt, J. Pierpont Morgan, and John D. Rockefeller. He referred to them as buccaneers, rascals, and plunderers, He wrote more favorably of the earlier generation of builders—the true pioneers of the industry, he called them—men like William B. Ogden, John Alfred Poor, and J. Edgar Thomson. He reserved his highest praise for Ogden: "Chicago might not have become a tremendous railroad town so soon had it not been for a prophet and genius of the first mark. The pioneer roads all the way from Maine to Georgia were projected and built by all sorts of men, some of them able, some dismally unfit, but among them none . . . of whom one could say: Here was a true prophet and great genius of railroads. It remained for Chicago to present the first great railroad man. He was William Butler Ogden . . . and in 1947 is all but forgotten."[69]

13

The Gates of Hell

In 1868, while he was embroiled with both the Chicago and North Western and the Northern Pacific Railroads, William Ogden retired from Ogden, Fleetwood and Company. His partner, Stanley Fleetwood, retired at the same time. The firm's name was changed to Ogden, Sheldon and Company, and William's brother Mahlon and brother-in-law Edwin Sheldon became the two managing partners. The real estate firm had made William Ogden fabulously wealthy and had allowed him to play out his railroad fantasies. The business had been very good to him.

On June 15, 1870, Ogden celebrated his sixty-fifth birthday. Like many men his age, he had contemplated complete retirement, but his strong Protestant work ethic made the idea of life without work unthinkable. He was still involved with the Northern Pacific, and he continued to share his time and resources with a number of civic betterment organizations in Chicago. But even with those, he found he was missing more and more of the scheduled meetings. From the time he originally purchased Villa Boscobel in New York, five years earlier, he had been splitting his time between his two residences. He maintained a household staff at each estate, and travel between the two was much easier now that there was direct rail connection between New York City and Chicago. Still, his time in New York was growing while his time in Chicago was waning.

His Villa Boscobel fruit trees and grape arbor were now fully mature, and he spent hours pruning and grafting them. As in Chicago at Ogden Grove, he loved to have friends in for dinner. He was spending quite a bit of time with a lady named Marianna Arnot, twenty years his junior, the daughter of a good friend, John Arnot. Like Ogden a self-made man, Scottish by birth, Arnot had been involved in mercantile, real estate, mining, and railroad investments. He and his wife Harriet, son John Jr., and daughter Marianna, all of whom lived in Elmira, New York, were frequent visitors to Ogden's home, where Marianna would serve as hostess to his other guests. Here, as in Chicago, he entertained many of the era's famous and powerful people.

In June 1871, a frequent guest, Ralph Waldo Emerson, wrote in his journal that he considered Will Ogden along with Henry David Thoreau, Oliver Wendell Holmes, and John Muir the men he most admired.[1] Ogden's very good friend and co-investor in a number of projects, Samuel J. Tilden, was also a frequent guest. He won a seat in the New York legislature in 1872 on a platform of cleaning up the crooked William "Boss" Tweed ring in New York City, became governor in 1874, and ran for president in 1876.[2] With Tilden present, politics was often the topic of conversation. A popular reformer, he and Ogden had many political viewpoints in common. Naturally, the Butlers often came up from the city too, bringing along as many of their grown children and grandchildren as they could round up.

When Ogden wasn't entertaining or pursuing his hobbies at Villa Boscobel, he spent a great deal of time in his library. It did not match his Chicago library for breadth, depth, or quality, and he loved adding new volumes to the shelves whenever something caught his eye. He loved to read, and he loved to try things others had never tried before.

The 1870s were a newsworthy time for the Panama Canal.[3] France, buoyed by the success of its work on Egypt's Suez Canal, began maneuvering to get the job to build the Central American water corridor. William Ogden had been following these events since the mid-1850s when the Panama Railway had established the first overland link across the isthmus. Ogden's nephew, William Ogden Wheeler, who lived at Villa Boscobel at the time, stated that Ogden became deeply interested in the canal project and took steps toward the formation of a syndicate to undertake its building.

Information on Ogden's plan—indeed, any information on these early years of planning for the canal's construction—is scant. However, a single sentence in his obituary in the *Chicago Tribune* years later does at least confirm his interest. A New York City friend and attorney, Charles Canda, would briefly manage Ogden's estate in the mid-1870s, according to the article, which went on to say that Canda had been "one of the partners of Mr. Ogden in his new canal enterprise."[4] Of course, it was not until long after his death that the United States became involved in the canal, so Ogden unfortunately never saw it built.

Another project that, according to Wheeler, Ogden spent a great deal of time on during this period was the New York City subway. Boston would not build the first U.S. subway until 1897, and New York City's subway didn't break ground until 1900. Yet London had opened one in 1863, and Ogden visited it on one of his European trips and saw great potential for the idea in Manhattan. Once, when Anna Ogden, Mahlon's eleven-year old daughter, was visiting her Uncle Will at about this time, he shared a dream with her. They were outside in one of the gardens overlooking the Harlem River, sitting side by side in a lawn swing. What about a *different* kind of train, her Uncle Will asked her, one that ran beneath the ground in a dark tunnel? Anna had trouble envisioning such a thing, but her uncle patiently explained exactly what it would look like.[5] Wheeler states that Ogden had had plans prepared for just such a project, a subway under Broadway, years earlier, which, Wheeler said, were still (as of 1900) in the possession of the Ogden family.[6] Wheeler was undoubtedly referring to the New York City Central Underground Railroad, a company Ogden helped found and for which he served as president from 1868 until 1871.[7]

By the 1860s, New York was desperately in need of mass transit of some kind.[8] The city's population had grown to nearly three-quarters-of-a-million people, and far too many of them were clustered together on the south end of Manhattan. Most large cities were able to grow out in many directions as population increased; but New York's business center was at the tip of a narrow island, forcing all growth into a slim corridor that ran northward. The population density was staggering, and streets were clogged with pedestrians and horse-drawn vehicles. It was obvious that something had to be done.

Early public transportation had been provided, as in Chicago, by omnibuses and street railways. But by the late 1860s, mass transit solutions in New York had boiled down to only two practical alternatives: elevated railways or underground railways. Each alternative had its fervent promoters and its angry detractors; and like all public improvements in New York at that time, politics played a prominent role. A leading underground project, championed by Alfred Beach, did have a novel twist. The Beach Pneumatic Transit Company planned to propel their railway cars through the tunnel by literally blowing them down the track with a technology known as "atmospheric power."

In 1868 William Ogden received a charter for the New York City Central Underground Railroad (NYCCUR), and the following year a charter amendment altered the original route and added a few new directors. One of them was another of Ogden's New York attorneys and friends, Andrew H. Green. Another was Origen Vanderburgh, an ex-military man who had won some minor fame with the invention of a multibarreled "volley gun," which he sold to the Confederacy during the Civil War. Another prominent member of the organizing group was William E. Dodge, one of the "merchant princes" of Wall Street and a principal of mining giant Phelps, Dodge and Company.

The NYCCUR project proposed a route from City Hall to Harlem, east of Broadway, which steered it clear of the contentious fight for a route that would go right down Broadway itself.[9] That fight pitted the two alternative styles—elevated versus underground—head to head against one another. Yet, despite avoiding that conflict, the NYCCUR ended up having more than its share of in-fighting and political maneuvering.

A March 13, 1870, article in the *New York Times* revealed that Ogden had signed a contract with some English capitalists to fund the construction of the

NYCCUR with a ten-million-dollar security, and that it was expected to begin the following June.[10] However, trouble soon erupted. In a second *New York Times* article seven years later, Vanderburgh explained what had occurred, at least his version of it: "The prominent and wealthy men who were concerned in it were all more or less occupied with their own business affairs, and the management of the company fell into the hands of two or three persons. They seemed to have learned from experience that they could manage affairs to their own advantage without disclosing to their associates any more of their transactions than they wished to disclose."[11]

Vanderburgh went on to describe how the few had misled the many, before getting to the real kernel of his anger and resentment. It seems that he had devised a way to overcome one of the most dangerous problems arising from an underground railroad, venting the buildup of gasses in the tunnel. His method was deceptively simple: build two tunnels side-by-side for the two trains traveling in different directions, rather than have both travel within one enclosed tunnel. And it did indeed seem to resolve the problem. However, credit for the idea was claimed by the project's contractor, Francis Byrne, a man whom Vanderburgh described as " a man of straw, without resources." Charges and countercharges followed, and of course lawsuits, and the NYCCUR would never get built. To New Yorkers, who had been inured to controversy and scandal by Boss Tweed and his Tammany Hall Gang, it was just more of the same.

Ogden resigned the presidency in early 1871, and both he and Green resigned from the board.[12] Thus they missed most of the fireworks and scandal that followed, but whether by blind luck or astute anticipation cannot be deduced. Perhaps the most prophetic quote about *all* these underground railroad projects was uttered by railroad man Cornelius Vanderbilt when asked if he wanted to participate: "No! I shall be underground a d——d sight sooner than this thing."[13]

If there was one constant in William Ogden's professional life, it was the courtroom. His broad and deep involvement in real estate and railroads, two of the most litigious businesses in the mid- to late nineteenth century, insured he would sue or be sued on a constant basis. The railroad lawsuits he was involved with were usually lengthy, complex corporate cases and were handled by a battery of attorneys.

In-house lawyers or attorneys Ogden maintained on retainer often settled the real estate lawsuits, and some dragged on for years. Ogden was a very careful, precise man, and he could afford the best legal representation in the country when trouble did arise, so he won more of the lawsuits than he lost. He also had many influential friends, a fact that aided his cause. One type of litigation that was especially troublesome to his real estate firm was the dower claim.

Going back hundreds of years, the dower claim granted to a wife the right to one-third of her husband's landed property at the time of their marriage.[14] She also had the right to approve or disapprove of the sale of her equity in the property during her husband's lifetime and to have any agreed-upon sale deeded separately for her and for her husband. Out on the Chicago frontier, most of the requisite formalities were ignored, which resulted in a plethora of dower lawsuits over the years against those most involved in the buying and selling of real estate, men like William Ogden. Although many were fraudulent, they all acted as a great hindrance to the purchase and sale of land.

Another problematic area was the accretion lawsuits, like the sandbar case discussed in chapter 10. Over the years, Lake Michigan deposited a significant amount of sand and gravel accretion at the shoreline, in effect reshaping and creating new land. Who owned this valuable new lakefront property? Those who owned the land adjoining the accretion claimed they did; after all, the accretions had robbed them of the lakefront status their land had previously enjoyed (until the accretions appeared). But on the other hand, property that had been surveyed and recorded *before* the accretions delineated property lines very precisely, and the new land was not a recorded part of the property. To-day, under the legal Doctrine of Accretion, accretion and its opposite, erosion, carry the boundary of the landowner along with the change; but not so in early Chicago. It was a thorny legal issue. Ogden was even involved in one lawsuit against the widow of one of the Kinzie clan that involved *both* legal situations at once: a dower claim involving accretion land. Ogden eventually won that claim, and the North Side accretion land became part of the Chicago Dock and Canal Company property that is discussed in chapters 10 and 14.

At nettlesome as these business-oriented legal situations were, they paled in comparison to one legal entanglement that Ogden would have loved to sidestep had it been in his power. It provides an example of how a small peccadillo can grow into a damaging weakness if one is not careful. The matter didn't even involve a lot of money but something much more important to Ogden: his reputation and his integrity.

To begin the story at the end, a man named William Hildebrand shot himself in the head in the suburbs of New York City in 1876.[15] In his pocket he carried a note that said, "Please call William B. Ogden. . . . He can identify me. He is the ruin of my familie [*sic*] and the fault of my suicide. He keeps me from my money wrongfully." Ogden was in failing health at the time, and the police did not speak to him; but his Villa Boscobel servants told them that Hildebrand was a frequent and unwelcome caller at the estate.

This squalid tale had its beginning more than a quarter-century earlier, in Chicago, when young Hildebrand, his wife, and their first three children arrived in the city from Germany. After a couple of years of hard work, he had saved enough money to buy a home, and they purchased a lot from Ogden and built a house on Lake Street. According to one of the newspaper stories that related this event, "Mr. Ogden seemed to have become much interested in Hildebrand, and twelve or fourteen years ago [1862–64] he set him up in a glove and buckskin factory."

The business prospered, but after some years Ogden suddenly dissolved the partnership and sold the business. Hildebrand had invested years of hard work in the enterprise, and he demanded thirty thousand dollars as his share of the sale. Ogden rebuffed him. "This demand was resisted by Mr. Ogden for a long time, but in the end he acknowledged the debt, and paid one of a number of promised installments," the newspaper story said. This payment was finally made, according to Hildebrand and his wife, as hush money. "Mrs. Hildebrand had borne her husband eleven children, but was still a comely woman," the story continued, leaving little doubt as to its implications. When Hildebrand discovered the indiscretion, he attempted to extort the thirty thousand dollars from Ogden in "a forcible way of reminding him of the inconvenience of exposure." That's when Ogden began to pay, the story claimed.

Somewhere in the middle of this sordid mess there was a lawsuit, a mysterious new business opportunity in New York for Hildebrand, and two years later his entire family's relocation to that city, although "Hildebrand did not scruple to renew family relations." But he claimed to have received no further relief from Ogden's debt after the first payment was made. So in 1874 Hildebrand filed another lawsuit, this time for criminal misconduct, seeking damages of one hundred thousand dollars against accused philanderer Ogden, who he claimed, "seduced his wife . . . and desolated his domestic hearth." "Social Naughtiness," the *Brooklyn Eagle* called the second lawsuit, saying that the offense was committed in 1871 in Ogden's Chicago home, Ogden Grove.

The lawsuit was postponed in the Brooklyn courts a number of times, probably due to Ogden's failing health, the last time providing the impetus for the cuckolded Hildebrand's suicide. Mrs. Hildebrand claimed that because of Ogden's refusal to meet his obligation, her family had "experienced direst penury." Her husband had been unable to obtain work and was on the verge of blindness, she said. The only saving grace for Ogden in this indelicate matter was that he was only a few months from death himself when it was finally exposed, so he probably did not accord it a great deal of importance.

Since he wasn't completely retired, Ogden did devote some time to his primary business enterprises.[16] In September 1871, he and William Strong took a trip to northern Wisconsin to visit the Peshtigo Company. The trip had three purposes. First, they wanted to visit with Ike Stephenson and make sure all was well with their core Wisconsin business, lumbering and woodenware manufacturing.

Second, Ogden wanted to see first-hand how the Chicago and North Western Railway was progressing toward Menominee. Finally, they wanted to visit their thousand-acre cranberry marshes located west of Peshtigo Harbor.[17] The company owned the land the bog occupied, and Ogden believed they could harvest the cranberries, pack them locally, and ship them via the new rails that were being built to Chicago and thence to markets across the country. This new industry promised to employ at least five hundred more people from the area, which would produce an economic boom in northern Wisconsin.

The C&NW's tracks were scheduled to follow a path from Fort Howard around the southern end of Green Bay and then head northeast along the waterfront to Oconto, a distance of about twenty-five miles. Then the tracks would proceed another fifteen miles in a small arc to Peshtigo. After crossing the Peshtigo River and passing through the town, the roadbed would again head northeast for another ten miles, cross the Menominee River, and arrive in the town of the same name in Michigan. From there it would join up with the C&NW's Peninsula Division tracks and head north to the rich iron mines of Michigan's Upper Peninsula.

Ogden and Strong had a positive meeting with Ike Stephenson. When they left his office, they may have walked the short distance to the river. Peshtigo was a company town, and everybody knew the two men. As the men strolled toward the river, every man and woman they passed would have greeted Ogden with a cheery, "Mornin', Mr. O," the familiar nickname most of the Peshtigo people called him. Ogden must have felt a real sense of pride in what he had helped build here; it would have reminded him so much of the early days in Walton when his dad was building his own lumbering enterprise, though certainly not on the immense scale of the Peshtigo Company.

Peshtigo was a beautiful little village. Reverend E. J. Goodspeed spoke glowingly of the beauty of the place:

> The site was well chosen for beauty as well as business; the river at this point runs through a slight bluff . . . before the stream escapes from the borders of the town. . . . a [water] mill was one of the first establishments in operation when the walls of the village began to rise. Below the mill the ground on either bank sloped gently into low, pebbly flats, which joined the water's edge a few rods from the centre of town. The business and residence streets were wide and well laid out, the houses prettily built and carefully painted, and little ornamental gardens were frequent.[18]

When they reached the river, Ogden and Strong would have noted that the C&NW's contractors had already sunk pilings for the bridge that would span the narrow, swift-running river.[19] Peshtigo's citizens were impatient; they were anxious for the rail line south that would end their isolation and allow then to join the more developed southern half of the state.

Laying the rails had already progressed about three-quarters of the distance from Oconto to Peshtigo. Stephenson drove Ogden and Strong in one of the company's carriages to the worksite, where workmen were still busily laying the heavy iron T-rails across oak ties. The land had been leveled and graded ahead of the rail crew, and chopped trees and brush had been pushed off to the side of the roadbed. The grass and undergrowth along the graded roadbed was burned and blackened, as this was standard procedure when clearing a road-bed. Still, it had been one of the driest summers in recent years, and the land was a tinderbox. Being an experienced lumberman and railroad man, Ogden may have sensed potential danger; but if he did, he did not vocalize it strongly enough to the contractors supervising the work.

A virgin forest is never without fire. Lightning strikes, sparks alight from distant sources, and uncrushed cigarette butts smolder. Generally, those fires remain small, perhaps even smoldering quietly beneath a deep humus bog for weeks. But then the rains come, or the small fires burn themselves out without damage, and life goes on in the forest. The September air in and around Peshtigo was grey and heavy, the smell of smoke permeating each breath the men took. But that too was a normal part of life in a lumbering forest, so nobody took much heed. A good rain would solve it, as it always had in the past.

Ogden and Strong returned to their homes in New York and Chicago respectively, confident of what they had seen on their visit and thoughtful about the new opportunities the railroad extension and the cranberry bog offered.

Sunday, October 8, 1871, was probably a quiet day for William Ogden. If he followed his normal routine, he would have attended a service that morning at the St. James Episcopal Church on Central Avenue in nearby Fordham. He enjoyed the sermons given by Reverend Blanchard, but mostly he enjoyed listening to the small choir as they sung from their leather-bound hymnals. When it was time for the congregation to join in, Ogden's lusty voice could be heard above all the others. After the service, the congregation milled about outside, under the shade of the trees that were in the midst of their annual autumn color show. The week's gossip was shared, words of greeting or comfort exchanged, and comments on local and national affairs bantered lightly about.

After church, Ogden probably spent the remainder of his day indulging in his pleasures. Perhaps he had company, perhaps not. Later in the evening, he retired to his study to do a little reading and then went upstairs to bed. His sleep, this night, was short-lived. His personal butler rushed into the bedroom without even knocking, which was unusual; but when Ogden saw the man's ashen face and shaking hands, he quickly forgot the minor breach. His man handed him three telegrams that had just been received in town and delivered immediately to Ogden's front door.

All three were brief: "All Chicago is on fire." "Chicago is burning." "A whirlwind of fire is sweeping over Peshtigo."[20] Ogden was stunned. Chicago on fire? How? Where? And Peshtigo? Is the entire Northwest ablaze? Ogden immediately dispatched his butler to the telegraph office to send hurriedly scribbled messages to his contacts in Chicago and Peshtigo asking for more information; but it is highly unlikely that any of the messages got through, or if they did, were answered. He dispatched another member of his staff to the train station in Fordham to make arrangements for his immediate departure for Chicago.

For Ogden, it must have seemed a very, very long trip, giving him plenty of time to think about the city he had had such a large part in building and to wonder what damages it had suffered. There were so many trees surrounding his own rambling home and those of his neighbors Isaac Arnold, Gurdon Hubbard, and his brother Mahlon. Would they be spared? He could have envisioned the limestone Water Tower and Water Works, the most prominent landmark on the North Side, now finally pumping clean water to the city's homes and businesses. What had become of it? And what of the railroads, ten of them at this time, many of which had expensive rolling stock on the miles and miles of rail sidings that dotted the North Side landscape?

On the South Side, the thought of the homes of other friends would also have been unsettling. The city's newer elite, the Armours, the Pullmans, the Fields, and the Scammons, were all located there, as were a score of burgeoning suburbs new to the growing city. On the lakefront sat a cluster of seventeen unpainted grain elevators, holding twelve million bushels of extremely flammable wheat. The State Street retail district was just beginning to develop, with Field and Leiter's giant department store surrounded by dozens of smaller, fledgling retail merchants.

Ogden's thoughts of the West Side would have brought particular panic. Here, tightly packed wooden homes and factories were stacked side by side like cordwood. And throughout the city stood massive piles of hound-yellow lumber, much of it his own, just waiting for sparks to ignite them. The mental images were horrific, and Ogden probably tried not to dwell on them until he reached Chicago and learned all the facts.

Peshtigo. He knew even less about what was going on there, so he tried not to speculate; but he likely could not stop recalling the tinder-dry conditions he had witnessed in the forest just weeks earlier.

Two days after arriving in Chicago, on October 11, Ogden posted a long letter to his brother-in-law Charles Butler in New York.[21] In it he gives his personal account of his first night in the city. It is one of only two personal Ogden letters known to exist. Ogden said he received dispatches along his trip on the progress of the Chicago fire: "On the cars I kept hearing of more and more dreadful things until I reached here. The truth cannot well be exceeded by statement or imagination."

The train came in on the route of the old Fort Wayne Road, entering Chicago from the south end of Lake Michigan and then curling up the lake through the South Side of the city. The train traversed the area where the fire had unleashed some of its greatest fury, and Ogden was literally choked by the devastation all around him. The courthouse, holding all the city's precious records, was gone. City hall, public buildings, churches, banks, hotels, stores, warehouses, offices, houses—all were leveled, only charred, smoking ruins remaining.

The train crossed the river and stopped at the station, where Ogden's personal account picked up. "When I reached the depot it was quite dark, the burning district had no lamps, thousands of smouldering fires were all that could be seen, and they added to the mournful gloom of all around, and do so yet." Ogden saw nobody he knew, so "I hired a hack and started for my own house directing the hackman, who was a stranger, as well as I could."

The North Side, where Ogden had made his home since his arrival in Chicago thirty-six years earlier, was primarily residential except for a narrow industrial belt just north of the river.[22] Here was located McCormick's Reaper factory, Lill's Brewery, some grain elevators, a C&NW Railway depot, and the wholesale meat market. There was also a row of stores, other breweries, and the Waterworks. Most of the mansions of the Old Settlers were further north, along with the homes of an increasing population of German, Irish, and Bohemian immigrants.

One of the first areas Ogden inspected from his carriage was the industrial belt north of the river. Almost everything was gone. Writing in the aftermath of the fire, the *Chicago Tribune* said, "At Chicago Avenue, [the devastation in] the North Division is a little over a mile wide and is still wider further north, until at Fullerton Avenue it is nearly two miles wide. This vast extent of territory is nearly as desolate and empty as it was 50 years ago."[23]

In a strange twist of fate, hundreds of lives had been saved by the hard-nosed business decision Ogden had made years earlier. When he purchased the area known as the Sands along the waterfront, he and Mayor Wentworth had torn down all the shanties, gambling dens, and houses of prostitution that populated the area. Due to the resultant openness of the space and its proximity to the river, hundreds of people had sought refuge there during the fire and had been saved. Had the area still been clogged with flammable wooden shanties, it would have been a hell rather than a haven.

But wooden shanties weren't the only victims of the holocaust. "Stone, brick, or wooden structures fell alike, and with almost the same degree of rapidity, and it had now become apparent that the entire business portion to the lake shore was doomed," said the *Tribune*.[24]

Another fire story involved Lill's Brewery, once partly owned by Ogden.[25] The fire had first touched down on the North Side in the carpentry and paint shop at the brewery as early as 1:30 A.M. on Monday. The buildings stood on pilings near the lakeshore, just south of Chicago Avenue; but they were so isolated that the fire did not spread from there. It would be hours later before the full fury of the fire swept over the North Side from a different source.

One of the dispatches Ogden had received on the incoming train told him that his home alone had been spared when the fire roared through the North Side. Now he directed the carriage to Ontario Street to see for himself. His personal account continues: "Often I was lost among the unrecognizable ruins and could not tell where I was. . . . I threaded my way over fallen debris, and past the pale blue flames of the Winter's stock of Anthracite coal, burning in almost every cellar, until I came to the ruined trees and broken basement walls—All was blackened, solitary, smouldering ruins around—all that remained of my more than 30 years pleasant home . . . gloomy beyond description, and telling a tale of woe that words cannot."

Driving through the debris-filled streets, Ogden was a witness to the horrible scenes of personal tragedy that the *Tribune* recorded: "In the terror and confusion which prevailed hundreds of women with their broods of children were seen wandering about in a state of hopeless bewilderment." And it reported, "Women would go by with dogs in their arms—their pets being all that they had saved from the ruins of their homes."[26]

Ogden learned that the spared home was that of his brother Mahlon, further north, and it indeed was the only one left standing on the North Side of the river.[27] He and his driver toured the remainder of the North Side and found everything in ashes. The *New York Times* said, "The North Side—but stay, there is no north side, and everyone wonders as they look from Lake-street across a blank treeless plain . . . three miles distant, at what has become of the 75,000 people who one week ago had their homes and businesses North of the Chicago River."[28] The North Side, the hardest hit part of the city, had simply ceased to exist.

When Ogden approached the home of his best friend and personal attorney, Isaac Arnold, it too was gone. Only later did Ogden learn of the miraculous escape of Arnold and his family and the devastating loss of his library, one of the greatest and most comprehensive private collections of history and literature in the nation. Arnold's home was a large brick mansion, and with its grounds it occupied the entire block bounded by Erie, Huron, Pine, and Rush Streets.[29] The grounds were luxuriant with shrubbery and trees and completely surrounded by a flowering lilac hedge. Virginia creeper hung heavily from the massive elms and covered the piazza and summerhouses. A large greenhouse and barn constituted the other out-buildings.

But it was within the house where the true treasures lay. A man of taste, wealth, and culture, Arnold had a law library and a general library of between seven and eight thousand books. First editions of famous English literature; leather-bound novels by Scott, Cooper, Irving, and others; ten large volumes of original handwritten manuscripts from the Civil War in the hand of McClellan, Grant, Sherman, Chase, and others; and ten years of speeches, writings, and letters of Abraham Lincoln. Arnold had a virulent hatred of slavery and had been a staunch supporter of Lincoln, whom he knew very well.[30] He had been the initiator of the resolution that called for an amendment to the U.S. Constitution ending slavery in the country. The House of Representatives rejected the "Arnold Resolution" proposing the Thirteenth Amendment in February 1864. However, it passed in the Senate, and the House passed it on its second try nearly a year later. The amendment was ratified and added to the U.S. Constitution in December 1865. Arnold had also penned one of the earliest biographies of Lincoln, *The Life of Abraham Lincoln and the Overthrow of Slavery*, in 1866.

"The failure of Mr. Arnold to save any thing, was the result of a most determined effort to save every thing, and his too confident belief that he could succeed," said noted nineteenth-century historian Elias Colbert, writing almost immediately after the fire occurred.[31] Mrs. Arnold left early on with their eight-year old daughter, while Arnold, his three older children, and the servants stayed to fight the fire. At about three in the morning, despite having a hose attached to the fire hydrant in front of the mansion, it became obvious they were losing the battle. As Arnold fought on, young Arthur called to his father, "The barn and hay are on fire!" "The leaves are on fire on the east side!" cried the gardener. "The front piazza is in a blaze!" screamed another. "The roof is on fire!" "The water has stopped!"

Finally, Arnold gave up hope, ran inside and gathered up a bundle of papers, and led the flight away from the house. However, by now there were flames on three sides, and their only escape was eastward toward the lakeshore. Leading his family, servants, horses, and a cow, Arnold miraculously made it to the Sands, where hundreds of others had already assembled. Still unsure of their safety, he searched for a better place to go. His good friend William Ogden had recently constructed a long pier of rocks and stones out into the lake, which had not yet been planked over. It was a hard road to travel, but Arnold and his small group—now minus the livestock—worked their way to the end of the pier and in a small rowboat crossed to the lighthouse. There they joined a few others who had sought refuge in the same place, and from this vantage point they watched as the city, the ships in the harbor, and the immense grain elevators blazed brightly throughout the night.

For twelve hours, the small party shivered in their refuge. On a number of occasions, burning boats and barges drifted toward their isolated spot, threatening to engulf them in flames. Finally the tugboat *Clifford* approached and beckoned them aboard, and they decided to take their chances on the water, hoping to run the gauntlet up the burning Chicago River to the safety of the West Side. Threatened by burning debris, fallen bridges, and charred flotsam on all sides, they picked their way up the narrow channel, ultimately reaching safety.

Right next door to the charred remains of Arnold's home, Ogden looked upon the smoldering ruins of the Chicago Historical Society, the organization and grand building he had so lovingly aided since its birth. A book published in 1956 celebrating the centennial of the Chicago Historical Society offers two versions of the attempt made to save the three-year old building and its contents from the ravages of the fire.[32] One version is by the librarian, William Corkran, written a month after the disaster, from New York City. It seems that nobody knew the whereabouts of Corkran during and after the fire; he had simply vanished. But many rumors had him acting in an unseemly fashion, so much so that the society's board later voted to censure him. From an attractive new position he had apparently secured in New York at the Astor Library, he penned his account of the event.

His letter tells of his heroic efforts to save the building and its collections at great personal risk and loss to his own person and property. "I had now lost everything, with the exception of my overcoat," he lamented. "My coat, trousers, vest, were burned off my back, and I had to borrow all around for a change." As proof of his fidelity, he asked that the charred remains of the deceased janitor, who he claimed had toiled unselfishly at his side, be used as a grisly witness to the truth of his account.

The second account was by Samuel Stone, the assistant librarian. Stone wrote that he saw Corkran when he himself first arrived at the scene, but that Corkran disappeared soon thereafter. His account—without all Corkran's self-glorification—told of how he attempted to secure the building from those attempting to enter its supposedly fireproof interior. He spoke of trying unsuccessfully to save some priceless Lincoln memorabilia and then making his last-minute escape: "At this moment a great blast of wind and smoke, seemingly a blaze of about 200 to 300 feet in length, perhaps 150 feet in height, passed nearly over me . . . pouring the entire volume [of flames] over two entire blocks [and] into the top of the spire of the Church of Holy Name." He added, "There were moments I could see buildings appear to melt down from three to five minutes. Such sights I never saw before." He continued: "While I was on the high stone steps on Erie St., I saw the entire west side of the Society building in one great sheet of blaze burning apparently every brick."

We can never be certain which account is the more truthful; but what is certain is that the young organization lost a huge collection of irreplaceable historical materials.

The fire had burned north until it reached raw prairie, just beyond the newly established area of Lincoln Park; then it stopped abruptly. There was simply nothing left for the voracious flames to consume.

Late that night, having worked his way further north, Ogden located his brother's house.[33] It stood alone, as if saved by some miracle, amidst the smoldering ruins where a few hours before had stood the homes of seventy-five thousand people. He approached the house and was halted by an armed guard, one of many Mahlon hired to keep looters away. Ogden gave his name and was passed through by William Strong. This became his base of operations for the remainder of his stay in Chicago.

Mahlon told his brother the extraordinary story of how his home came to be still standing. It was a story of incredible luck, without a doubt, but also one of neighbor helping neighbor. The best account of the Mahlon Ogden family's good fortune is found in an eight-page manuscript, "Reminiscences Dealing Largely with the Great Chicago Fire of 1871," written by Mahlon's twelve-year old daughter Anna a few years later.

"The day of October 9th, 1871 began for us about one in the morning, when the watchman roused my Father, telling him the fire was spreading rapidly, thinking he might like to go to his office before it was too late," she wrote. Mahlon left at once, returning from his Lake Street office with a buggy full

Home of Mahlon Ogden, the only North Side house left standing after the Great Fire. Chicago History Museum; ICHi-22617.

of important books and papers, being the last person to cross the Rush Street bridge before it collapsed.

"Later," she remembered, "I opened the front door to see what was going on outside. The vestibule was a large one, and on either side of the door stood a good sized arm chair. In these Mr. and Mrs. M. Scudder were discovered sitting, crying bitterly and holding each a bird-cage."

Mahlon went to the nearby home of his sister Caroline and her husband, Ezra McCagg, who were in Europe at the time; but he quickly determined there was nothing he could do stop the inferno from taking the house. "Mr. McCagg's house was burned, but his greenhouse was uninjured," the *Tribune* later reported.[34] Mahlon collected McCagg's elderly mother and her daughter and returned to his own house. Miraculously, he did all this on foot; his horses would not venture into the wall of flame.

By then the entire neighborhood was ablaze.[35] Taking some sound advice, Mahlon sent his wife Frances and the children to safety in a lumber wagon he commandeered—at a hefty price—as it rumbled hastily past his house. His expansive front lawn was crammed with friends and neighbors who had sought refuge in the large open space. They were surrounded by livestock, personal items, and furniture that fleeing residents had thrown over the fence, hoping to reclaim later.

Together, the large gathering of people—now being isolated and having no place else to flee to—attacked the fire around the Ogden house with buckets, brooms, wet blankets, and anything else they could lay their hands on. It was as if, having lost their own homes, they were determined to make a final stand against the cruel fire that had robbed them of everything. When the flames got closest to the house, the wind died down, as if the fire were granting the crowd this one small consolation prize. And so the grand home of Mahlon Ogden was spared. (Today, the city's most prestigious reference library, the Newberry, founded by friends of Walter Newberry, sits on the site of Mahlon Ogden's former home.)

That night, William Ogden would have slept fitfully, if at all, but the next morning he was greeted with more devastating news. More intelligence had arrived regarding Peshtigo, and the news couldn't have been grimmer. The fire, the telegraph related, had resulted in utter destruction of Ogden's immense lumber enterprise, but worse, casualties were very high, including a great number of Peshtigo Company employees.

Ogden was appointed a member of the Chicago relief committee by Mayor Roswell Mason, another railroad man; and for the next four days, he and hundreds of men and women, the prominent and the humble side by side, worked tirelessly in the Chicago relief effort. Ogden's efforts were neither greater nor less than those of anyone else. It was a time for heroes and heroines to step forward, and Chicago had both in abundance. Ogden and the others on the committee traveled to Springfield to request three million dollars in state aid, which was immediately granted.

Two days after the fire, the *Chicago Tribune* was publishing again. "Cheer up! In the midst of a calamity without parallel in the world's history, looking upon the ashes of thirty years' accumulations, the people of this once beautiful city have resolved that Chicago Shall Rise Again!"[36] The *New York Times* praised the publisher of the *Tribune* for getting back on the street so quickly at its city's moment of greatest need: "Hon. Joseph Medill . . . who is one of the heaviest sufferers, leas[ed] a brick building on Washington-street. . . . He also purchased two single cylinder presses, and has telegraphed East for paper and type."[37]

The final toll of the Great Chicago Fire was staggering, with but one consolation: out of a population of 334,000 people, less than 300 were killed, an incredibly low number given the intensity and range of the fire. The damage on the South Side was 450 acres burned, including 3,600 buildings. Gone were the customs house, the *Chicago Tribune* plant, Crosby's Opera House, Field and Leiter's department store, and Booksellers Row, to name only a few of the more prominent structures.[38]

On the North Side, 1,300 acres were burned and more than 10,000 buildings destroyed. Gone were dozens of the city's most prestigious homes, as well as the McCormick Reaper Factory, the Chicago Historical Society, and Lill's Brewery. On the West Side, 194 acres were burned, and about 500 buildings lost.[39] Among the homes destroyed here was that of Mrs. Patrick O'Leary, in whose barn, so the legend goes, the Great Fire began.[40]

View of the South Side of Chicago after the fire.

The fire had also taken a very heavy toll on Ogden's North Chicago Railway Company. Lost in the blaze was the stable with all its livestock, car-houses located throughout the North Side with all their rolling stock, blacksmith shops, and the general office. In his letter to Charles Butler, Ogden attempted to describe the intensity of the blaze that rampaged through the city, and why it had been so devastating: "How it could be that neither Buildings, Men, or any thing could encounter or withstand the torrent of fire, without utter destruction, is explained by the fact that the fire was accompanied by the fiercest Tornado of Wind ever known to blow here, and it acted like a perfect blow-pipe, driving the brilliant blaze Hundreds of feet with so perfect a combustion that it consumed the smoke, and its heat was so great that fire-proof buildings sank before it almost as readily as wood—Nothing but Earth could withstand it." Nevertheless, Ogden's account of his visit to the city ended on a thankful note. "Aid and sympathy comes to us from all quarters, with a will that touches our hearts to the core, and serves us wonderfully in our hour of need, but the great loss and ruin remains."[41]

In the days immediately following the fire, thousands of Chicagoans scrambled simply to survive. They got their water, tainted as it might be, from the river and the lake and camped by the thousands in every available park and open space that had not been decimated. "The people are being fed in the remaining churches, school-houses, in sheds, and by the road-sides," the *New York Times* wrote. Although cold weather haunted the homeless, "the people are praying earnestly for more rain, so fearful are they of a continuance of the flames." Of the hardest-hit North Side, the *Times* added that "fifty thousand men, women and children huddled together like so many wild animals . . . and in other places, helpless children [could be seen] asking for bread. A German said . . . 'This a second Sodom and Gomorrah, and the curse of God is on it.'"[42]

Exhausted and heart-broken after four days in Chicago and Springfield, Ogden felt his place now was in Peshtigo. He boarded a lake steamer and began the journey north to Green Bay, accompanied by William Strong.

Once again, as he steamed up the lake, his imagination probably ran wild. He had received a number of reports about the Peshtigo fire, and each succeeding one had painted a grimmer picture as new details unfolded. He had learned for the first time that on September 25 William Ellis, the Peshtigo plant supervisor, had suspended all operations in the lumbering mills and manufacturing plant because of the increasing intensity of the omnipresent forest fires.[43] He heard how the inferno had developed from the hundreds of small fires that had been burning for weeks. One account of the fire reported that "The cyclonic storm front served to make the main fire a veritable monster. The persistent surging and whirring rendered each obstacle in its path yet another opportunity to create more violent wind, which in turn created another vortex, which in turn strengthened the wind, which in turn fed the atmospheric turbulence—until the sky and the ground and everything in between was ablaze. . . . Oconto County, Wisconsin, . . . had become a roaring ocean of fire."[44]

Other reports were so gruesome they left strong men sick to their stomachs. One told of hundreds of people who took to the river to avoid the flames. Struggling, screaming, fighting for breath and for a handhold to keep them afloat, men, women, and children joined domestic and forest animals in the swift water. But the fire was not finished with them. Burning trees crashed down on them, and the main bridge across the river collapsed under the weight of other escaping townspeople, dumping dozens more into this unforgiving, fiery cauldron that eventually swallowed most of them in its fury.

One of the best eyewitness accounts of the fire was provided by Reverend Peter Pernin, a Catholic priest who was on a ministerial mission to the Sugar Bush, a collection of farms near Peshtigo. When the inferno threatened to consume everyone, Pernin was one of the leaders urging people to jump into the river. He related that while they shivered in the water, a three-story factory store sitting right at the river's edge was completely ablaze and threatened to tumble down on them. Burning tubs and broom handles exploded out of the inferno and pelted the river all around them, he said. Despite the cold water, the people in the river were forced to keep ducking their heads under to keep from being incinerated. Pernin wrote that there was a strange absence of smoke; the powerful wind currents apparently were lifting it away. He also remarked about how little noise the people were making; no screaming or talking, just the continual splashing as people tried to ward off burning debris. After five and a half hours, Pernin and the few others who were still alive were finally able to drag themselves from the river.[45] Ike Stephenson related another incident that brought home the intensity of heat generated by the firestorm: "In our store were sixty dozen of axes which had run together in an incongruous mass."[46]

On Saturday, October 14, Ogden and Strong disembarked from the steamer at Menominee, fearing that if they went directly to Peshtigo Harbor they might not be able to get to Peshtigo because of the fire damage. They hired a wagon and driver who took them by road the eight miles to the town. As they neared Peshtigo, the men saw that all the trees had been completely denuded, and twisted, grotesque black stumps spiraled choking gray smoke into the thick, still air. Here and there, small fingers of fire flared up from the charred tree trunks and then just as suddenly died away. The wagon climbed a small rise, and Ogden and Strong saw the small village lying below them. Of Peshtigo, including the homes and stores, the company's mills, and the manufacturing plant, nothing remained. Ogden and Strong probably gasped at the total devastation before them as they walked the last few hundred feet into town.

Although cleanup had been going on for four days, there were still many burned and bloated bodies at the river's edge. Miraculously, Peshtigo Harbor, eight miles downriver, had been untouched, they were told; but the Peshtigo Company still suffered heavy financial casualties there. "One of my large Barge Vessels burned and two others and the Steamer that towed them are missing as yet since the Storm, with a Million [board feet?] of lumber on them," Ogden wrote.[47]

Under the direction of the onsite managers at Peshtigo Harbor, the company was milling lumber as quickly as possible and sending it upriver to build coffins. "It is an act of God," Ogden said. "We will rebuild this village—the mills, the shops—and do a larger winter's logging than ever before." It was exactly the message the grief-stricken residents of the town needed to hear. More than at any time in his long career, William Ogden proved what kind of man he was. "With the energy of early manhood," Isaac Arnold wrote, "he took off his coat, and went to work to restore what was gone. He remained all through October, November, into December, superintending and directing the work. At daylight in the morning, he was up, and worked with the men till dark; constantly exposed to the rain and sleet and snow."[48]

After dark, Ogden went by mule cart the eight miles to Peshtigo Harbor where, working with his assistants and clerks, they drew plans and sent letters and telegrams to Chicago and New York requesting that money, supplies, and aid be sent. Ogden was always cheerful, despite the weight that must have been on his shoulders, and it is said he inspired everybody with courage and faith in the future.

Of this period, Ogden's constant companion William Strong later wrote: "He possessed many of the qualities of a great and successful general, viz.: unflinching courage, coolness in times of danger, rare presence of mind in emergencies, decision, a constitution of iron, great physical strength . . . and faith in his own judgment and plans."[49] Ike Stephenson was less generous in his praise of Ogden's assistance, perhaps wishing to receive more of the credit for himself in the aftermath of the fire. "His moral support was of great value to me, but he had little practical knowledge of the kind required by such a situation and I was left to my own resources in directing the work of rehabilitation," Stephenson wrote in his autobiography.[50]

Despite the possible culpability of the railroad in starting the fire, Ogden knew the railroad was now more vital than ever to restart the area's economy.[51] He offered his contractor a seventy-five-thousand-dollar bonus if he could finish laying the rails to Menominee by year's end. On December 27, the men spiked the final rail to its tie in Menominee, Michigan.

One story from the aftermath of the fire shows Ogden at his best. A man named Frank Jacobs had lived in Peshtigo for eighteen years and had worked much of that time for the company. He, like most employees, called Ogden "Mr. O," and had a great deal of respect and admiration for the man. When the fire broke out, Jacobs's two-year-old son Frankie was in the care of a relative who, like many others, had taken to the river. The lady drowned; however, there was no word of young Frankie's fate.

A few days later, a woman returned to town who had escaped the fire on a lake steamer headed for Fort Howard. Yes, she told Jacobs, she had seen his son on the same boat. He was in the charge of a man who said he was heading to Chicago. Jacobs immediately appealed for help to the only person he knew in Chicago, "Mr. O." Ogden took the time to write a lengthy letter on Jacobs's behalf that was printed in the *Chicago Tribune*. It said the boy could speak only one word, the name of his favorite uncle, Ike. "Frankie wore on the night of the fire a black and white checked flannel shirt, a red flannel dress and red, brown and checked apron," Ogden wrote. Unfortunately this poignant story ends here, as history did not record if Frankie was ever found.[52]

The company's Peshtigo Harbor mill worked night and day milling the lumber that was used to rebuild Peshtigo. A well-to-do resident, Nicholas Cavoit, had owned a sawmill and a few pieces of rental property in the town, which were all destroyed along with his home. He received his supply of boards from the Peshtigo Harbor mill—free, as they were to everybody—grabbed a hammer, and went to work. When his new house was finished, he nailed a sign on it proclaiming it was the first house built after the fire.[53]

As it turned out, the woodenware factory was never rebuilt. For a while, some citizens complained that Ogden had gone back on his word by not rebuilding the factory. Stephenson, in his autobiography, wrote that the factory had never made a profit and probably never could. "Construction of factories . . . had brought us no return," he recounted. "The market for woodenware appeared to be glutted and in some instances we were forced to sell our product at a loss."[54] Given that, it's probable that Ogden simply decided to cut his losses and concentrate on the mills where he knew he could keep his people gainfully employed and make a reasonable profit. There was enough timber to be salvaged even in the region's stricken condition to make it worthwhile to send out crews of lumberjacks and continue the milling operation at Peshtigo Harbor.

The second week after the fire, the foundry and machine shop at Peshtigo resumed operations. During the ensuing winter, the men built a water mill on the west side of the river, and it was used exclusively in the future as a sawmill. A flourmill and the sash-and-door factory were never replaced.

The Peshtigo fire was much larger than anyone had originally believed. It burned from the foot of Green Bay up both sides of the water at the same time. On the west side of the bay, it burned north for nearly ninety miles, going as far as fifty miles inland, sweeping through Oconto, Peshtigo, Marinette, Menominee, and dozens of smaller villages. On the east side of the bay, it swept up the Door Peninsula for forty miles, burning all the way east to Lake Michigan, until it finally lost its fury at Sturgeon Bay. In all, the holocaust destroyed 1.28 million acres. The death toll was never accurately recorded, though years were spent trying. One respected book puts the number at a minimum figure of 1,125. Peshtigo was the hardest hit. Six hundred victims of the fire are buried there, but the total number of Peshtigo residents to lose their lives is probably much higher. With only about 2,000 residents in the town at the time, it's not unreasonable to estimate that as much as half of the town's population died in the blaze. It is still the greatest human toll taken by a forest fire in North American history, by far.[55]

At the time of his death in 1877, according to his will, Ogden still retained majority ownership of the Peshtigo Company, which included "extensive tracts of wood lands, and saws and other mills upon and contiguous to the Peshtigo river, together with ships and other property."[56] The company continued to operate quite profitably for many more years. In 1891, William Strong, who had continued in his role as president of the Peshtigo Company, died during a visit to Florence, Italy. The following year, the Ogden estate trustees sold the company to Isaac Stephenson and D. L. Wells Jr. But its days were numbered, and in 1895, the mills closed for good and became only a relic of the glory days of American lumbering.[57]

The story of the Great Fire of Chicago is well known to most Americans. Far less well known is the story of the Peshtigo fire of the same day, although it destroyed more acreage and claimed at least three times as many lives. Rain began falling on northern Wisconsin on October 9, twenty-four hours too late to be any help. As if the damage to Chicago and northern Wisconsin were not enough, the same Midwest drought that made those fires so devastating also led to the fiery destruction of nearly two million acres of timber on the Lower Peninsula of Michigan.

As the tiny town of Peshtigo struggled to rebuild, the Midwest's largest city did the same. Exactly one week after the most devastating urban disaster in America, the people of Chicago proved their resilience. On October 15, 1871, the *New York Times* lead story reported:

> This city is settling down to much like its former self in the tone of its people and restored quiet.
>
> Nothing can exaggerate the individual sufferings of the burned-out people, but Chicago has passed already beyond the stage of paralyzed terror into a business activity that is the best antidote to grief and dismay.
>
> Reconstruction is rapidly going forward. On every side there is activity. The ruins will be cleared more rapidly than is usual after city fires, for such was the fierceness of the unchecked heat that everything combustible was consumed.

Nothing remains but crumbled brick, mis-shaped iron and shattered stone. Already the architects and builders are busy beyond all comparison in building annals in this country, first for temporary structures for the merchants, whose new stocks are already underway. . . . The Chamber of Commerce has struck their first blow and will restore a massive exchange building to their corner of LaSalle and Washington Streets. The Illinois Central Railroad Company has already taken measures for a million dollar building expenditure on their depot grounds . . . the work on the new Palmer House has been ordered forward.

I have canvassed carefully the state of feeling in Chicago. It is strong, earnest and intelligent, with a recognition of the grave difficulties to be overcome. Those best familiar with the facts believe in the solid future of Chicago.[58]

Ogden immediately ordered the rebuilding of the Nixon Building at 162 Lake Street at LaSalle, where the headquarters of many of his business enterprises were located. All the firms' business records had been stored in a steel vault and were spared from the fire. The huge Field and Leiter department store, which was leased from Potter Palmer, would also be rebuilt on its original site.

Estimates of William Ogden's losses on October 8, 1871, range from two to six million dollars, depending upon the source. Splitting the difference, at four million dollars his loss in 2008 dollars would be equivalent to sixty-five million dollars. A Dun and Bradstreet credit agent's estimate of Ogden's wealth done just over a year later placed his remaining net worth at eight million dollars, which would suggest that he lost about one-third of his net worth in the Chicago and Peshtigo fires.[59] More than the money, however, was what the twin calamities took out of the man himself, both physically and emotionally. His best friend, Isaac Arnold, said later, "This terrible strain upon him, and overwork, for a man of his years, probably shortened his life."[60]

Six years later, on the occasion of his funeral, the Right Reverend Robert Clarkson, bishop of Nebraska and a good friend from earlier days, said of Ogden, "Though Mr. Ogden was always theoretically a believer in Christianity and a generous supporter of its institutions, it was not until late in life that he acknowledged publicly before men his allegiance to the God who made him and the Savior who redeemed him."[61] The terrible mental stress of the two fires, coupled with the emotional pain of feeling that some blame lay with him for the Peshtigo fire, probably drove Ogden closer to his spiritual beliefs. It would be perfectly understandable.

In his autobiography, Isaac "Ike" Stephenson echoed the sentiments that both he and Ogden felt: "In our efforts to better our position [by building the railroad] we unwittingly paved the way for disaster. When work on the railroad was begun fires were started to clear the right of way. The contractors carelessly allowed these to spread and they ran through the country with startling rapidity."[62] The railroad contractors did accept the blame for the Peshtigo fire and approved taking a much-reduced fee for their work; but that did not assuage the feelings of complicity that both Ogden and Stephenson carried to their graves.

However, Ogden was a man conditioned to looking forward, not backward; it was one of his strongest traits. He was overwhelmingly grateful that he had not lost any family members in either fire; however, the loss of so many loyal employees of the Peshtigo Company scarred him deeply. He still had plenty of money, so the loss of worldly goods was not painful; but the loss of a lifetime's collection of personal treasures at Ogden Grove was. Ogden's nephew, William Ogden Wheeler, described one loss: "For several years before his death, William B. Ogden had interested himself in genealogy, intending to trace his family back to the original immigrant. Being a very busy man it was more in the nature of recreation with him than otherwise; yet his wide acquaintance gave him an advantage that enabled him to gather a mass of genealogical information, only to be lost forever at the burning of his Chicago home. . . . A few notes, mostly made from memory, were all that remained."[63]

Beginning with those few notes, Wheeler dedicated the remainder of his life to uncovering and telling the story of the genealogy of the Ogden family, from its roots in America in 1641 right up to the time before his own death in 1900. The result of his work is a massive, two-volume tome that has been quoted often in this book and has served as a genealogical lifeline for thousands of members of this extraordinary extended family, one of the most distinguished lines in America.

Mahlon Ogden was not as fortunate financially as his brother after the fire.[64] Since joining William in the real estate business, he had become a wealthy man. But he suffered heavy losses in the fire and worse, the shrinkage of real estate values in the subsequent Panic of 1873. He held investments in Ohio, too, and his entire real estate portfolio had been heavily mortgaged, a lesson in hubris he should have learned from his brother. In 1878, a year after William's death, Mahlon was forced to liquidate his estate, losing his home in Chicago. A large residence in Elmhurst, in Chicago's western suburbs, became the new home for him and his family, and less than two years later he passed away suddenly and unexpectedly of pneumonia.

14

Out of the Ashes

About a month after the Great Fire, Chicago's municipal elections were held. This was a very important election; the city had to select the men they believed could best lead them through the troubled times ahead. Some candidates banded together and formed the Fireproof Party, which they claimed would be nonpolitical and dedicated solely to leading the city out of the chaos and ruin of the Great Fire.

The *Chicago Tribune's* managing editor and part owner, staunch Republican Joseph Medill, was the Fireproof Party's candidate for mayor. The paper said of the election, "The city demanded then, if at any time, an honest local government; then, if at any time, party interests were a secondary consideration, and the general good a primary necessity. . . . men of honesty and integrity were needed."[1]

Medill was swept into office, and days later in his inaugural address he discussed Chicago's situation and his prophecy for its future:

Of the total property in Chicago created by labor and capital, existing on the 8th of October, more than half perished on the 9th. Such a tremendous loss cannot befall the people at large without seriously affecting their municipal affairs. The city, as a corporation, has lost in property and income precisely in the same proportion as have individuals. . . . I am not discouraged. Our municipal losses, like those of the citizens, will soon be repaired, and by judicious management of our city affairs, the people will soon recover from their losses.

The fire-fiend came like a thief in the night and caught our municipal government living in excess of its income, with a loose discipline in some departments, inefficiency in others, and extravagance in all. It will be no easy matter to reform the luxurious tastes and expensive habits of the past. . . .

Happily there is that left which fire cannot consume;—habits of industry and self-reliance, personal integrity, business aptitude, mechanical skills, and unconquerable will. These created what the flames devoured, and these can speedily re-create more than was swept away. . . . the rise will astonish mankind even more than the fall of Chicago.[2]

From its earliest days, Chicago had been a hodge-podge of design and construction. Most early buildings were built in the so-called balloon frame style, where small standardized timbers, similar to today's two-by-fours, were strung together and joined with basic mortise-and-tenon joints. The roof was similarly a system of small rafters nailed together. Then the flimsy wooden skeleton was covered by clapboard. It was a simpler, more economical method than the old heavy-timbered buildings that preceded it, and it was ideal when construction speed was important, as in early Chicago. Another building style that had become popular in the 1850s and 1860s was the iron frame.[3] In constructing large railway terminals, giant meeting halls, and other wide-span enclosures, it was necessary to cover the buildings without intermediate supports. The result was giant "balloon sheds," a huge vault of wrought iron ribs carrying a shell of glass or iron.

So Chicago architecture had been driven primarily by function. About two-thirds of its buildings were wholly made of wood, with the remainder having substantial wooden portions. This, and the fact that so many buildings were packed tightly together, was an invitation to disaster. "For the past thirty years," the New York Times said, "it has been the pernicious practice of Chicago to save its old-timed wooden structures to be moved again and again to temporary leaseholds. This has caused the squares . . . west of the river to be thickly impacted with frame buildings, one behind the other on the same lot, filling many of the blocks so that a cat could scramble on the closely-ranged roofs from one street front to the other."[4] In addition, the buildings sat at different heights, because some had been raised above the mud while others were still sunk down in it. All in all, Chicago was a visual nightmare. But the Great Fire created a virtually empty canvas, and talented architects would seize the opportunity to paint an entirely new picture.

The New York Times wrote: "The architects who came together in Chicago following the fire of 1871 included men of rare creative talent who had no formal education in architecture but who had a remarkable capacity for learning their craft through direct attack on the problem of large-scale commercial building. . . . in little more than a decade after the fire they had invented and mastered the modern technique of riveted steel framing and were thus able to develop the office building, hotel, and apartment block as we know them today."[5]

Paradoxically, one of the greatest unsung contributions William Ogden made to Chicago was his home, Ogden Grove, which he lost in the fire. It was the first building in Chicago designed and built by an architect, John Mills Van Osdel, whom Ogden had brought to Chicago and then courted to stay after the home was completed. Van Osdel did return to New York City, his original home, for brief stints as an editor for *American Mechanic* and then *Scientific American* magazines but returned to Chicago in 1841 for good.

Van Osdel was the city's first architect.[6] He was also the builder of Greek Revival Chicago. From his office on Clark Street, he designed a seemingly endless stream of hotels, public buildings, and private homes. Before the fire, he designed many of the city's landmark buildings, including the Tremont House, the Courthouse, and the Palmer House. His third Palmer House design, executed after the fire, would be the first hotel in the city with electric lights, telephones, and elevators when it opened in 1875.[7] He also partnered with Elisha Granger in a foundry and machine shop to manufacture cast-iron building fronts, one of the first architectural styles that was uniquely Chicago.[8] On Lake Street, both east and west of State, a four-block length of the street was solidly lined on both sides with nicely harmonized cast-iron facades.

John Van Osdel, Chicago's first professional architect, one of the leaders in rebuilding the city.

Van Osdel was working on another idea that held great promise when the fire struck. On a building on Lake Street at State, his iron structural elements had been encased in hollow terracotta tile, a fireproofing experiment that proved its merit when it withstood the heat of the fire. This process was carried forward by the new wave of architects that came later, and it became a staple in Chicago's commercial buildings.

Another significant building that was about 95 percent complete at the time of the fire was William Ogden's Nixon Building on the northeast corner of Lake Street at LaSalle. He planned to headquarter his Ogden, Sheldon and Company and Ogden and Scudder Company in the new building when it was completed. In *The Chicago School of Architecture*, Carl Condit says the Nixon Building was "a remarkable example of indestructibility and the most advanced work of building technique in the city at the time of the fire."[9] Designed by Otto Matz, almost all of the Nixon Building's primary structural elements—exterior walls and inner framing members—survived the fire intact.[10] After the fire, the walls were cleaned, the flooring, roofing, and exterior fixtures were installed, and the building opened by year's end. That Ogden's building survived so well was not an accident. It had been designed with maximum fireproofing, with heavy masonry walls and with columns and girders of cast iron covered by plaster or concrete. Concrete was virtually unknown in Chicago at the time, and this was the first building to use the product, then called "artificial stone."

John Van Osdel and Otto Matz were joined by other architects and builders, men of tremendous talent and vision like John Wellborn Root, Louis Sullivan, Daniel Burnham, Frank Lloyd Wright, Owen Aldis, and William LeBaron Jenney, and over the next quarter-century they created a "New Chicago" that would forever change the look of the onetime frontier village. The creativity and originality of these individuals gave the nation its first skyscraper city and a union of science, technology, and art that Condit calls "the structural-utilitar-ian-aesthetic unity of the best Chicago buildings."[11]

While this feverish commercial activity began all across the city, those who had lost their homes in what had become known as "the burnt district" had to get by as best they could. Mahlon Ogden's daughter Anna wrote years later in her diary of the challenges of the extended Ogden family. They had been more fortunate than most, as they were a wealthy family; and since Mahlon Ogden's large house was still standing, the family had a place to congregate:

> But there was our home, our yard full of piano legs, and eighteen cows that had taken refuge in our gardens. These same cows rather appalled us at first, but in the end, they proved our salvation for no one claimed them until spring.
>
> We had forty people in our house that winter. All the servants of the various members of the family who slept on mattresses laid in rows on the floor in the large rooms in the basement. Upstairs my Uncle Edwin H. Sheldon and his son and daughter, Uncle William Ogden as he came and went, Mr. And Mrs. Voluntine Turner, General and Mrs. William E. Strong, nurse and baby, Mr. McCagg for part of that time are some of those that come to mind. You may imagine the difficulties of providing for such a family, with every bridge between us and either the west or south sides gone. Our nearest neighbors were four or five miles away. The only method of reaching a shop of any kind was by way of the LaSalle Street tunnel. It was pitch black and the horses were really afraid to go through it, so it seemed quite an adventure to undertake it.
>
> We were under martial law in the city and I can remember the men going out with their guns to keep watch every night for a time. This being the more neces-sary, as it seemed there was some ill feelings about our house not having been burned. This was especially the case after we had achieved many new neighbors in the hastily run up barracks with which Washington Square was soon filled.

Later on, smallpox developed among them, so I image my elders were much relieved when one night towards spring these buildings, having served their purpose, were set afire and burned to the ground.[12]

Although the fire had destroyed much of the city, the spirit of Chicago was unscathed. Rebuilding began immediately. One writer pointed out that a good deal of construction was begun while the bricks were still warm, and to a large extent that was true. It was as if the same feverish activity that had built the city in the first place was now unleashed a second time. While there may have been advantages in that, there was also a downside. Had the post-Fire rebuilding activity continued unabated, the "new" Chicago would have been simply a rehashed version of the "old" Chicago. The same unplanned, hodge-podge appearance would have risen from the ashes, and the city would have missed its opportunity for greatness.

As fate would have it, the intervention of yet another financial panic saved the city from itself. By late summer of 1872, a European financial downturn found its way to the United States. A few strategic U.S. financial firms failed, and in the normal domino fashion that such things followed in the nineteenth century, the six-year Panic of 1873 began. The same panic that would save Chicago from itself also put an end to Reconstruction in the South.

New construction in the city essentially ceased during this period, which turned out to be a blessing in disguise. It allowed the new wave of architects to study the situation, analyze the needs of the city, and formulate an architectural vision of what Chicago could become. Historian Ross Miller said, "Ironically, the city's subsequent economic misfortunes, coming less than two years after its aborted destruction, provided a welcome corrective to the city's manic desire to put things right instantly."[13]

What resulted from this period of creative reconsideration became known as the Chicago School of Architecture. It combined some of the pre-Fire theories of Van Osdel and Otto Matz with fresh thinking about the relationship between form and function of the "new wave" architects. This new school of thought also took the idea of the skyscraper and perfected it in Chicago. By the mid-1880s, when the city's rebuilding was essentially completed, an entirely new place had risen from the ashes, one unlike any city before it.

A year after the fire, Mayor Medill's *Tribune* ran a long follow-up story. It was less an update and more an inspirational message about how well the city had coped in the face of overwhelming odds. It applauded the candidates who had won office on the Fireproof Ticket and then lived up to their pledge to put the city first: "Men who . . . before had held themselves aloof from petty wranglings of local politics . . . have done all in their power to secure good government, and the city affairs have never been better or more honestly administered. . . . The experiment was a triumphant success." The story also congratulated the citizens who were hardest hit by the fire: "A year ago nearly 80,000 persons were mainly dependent on the generosity of the outside world for their maintenance. . . . Today these unfortunates are again earning their daily bread."[14]

As Chicago rebuilt, it became obvious the time was right for younger men to take charge. Chicago's original builders, men like William Ogden, the Kinzies, Gurdon Hubbard, and Walter Newberry, had passed away or were old and tired and content to let the new wave take over. The fire had taken more out of these men than most; they had watched as the city they had poured their souls into went up in flames. Ogden's friend Isaac Arnold indicated that Ogden was never a resident of Chicago again: "As soon as he could set his affairs, demanding personal attention in the West, in order and promising activity . . . [he] became only a citizen of New York."[15]

Arnold added that Ogden's interest in Chicago and the Northwest remained, but that he was content to allow the new generation to succeed without him. In a

William B. Ogden as an older man, circa mid-1870s.
Chicago History Museum; ICHi-32561.

very rare personal letter from William Ogden to his niece Julia Wheeler in New York, extracted in the diary of Anna Ogden West, we see those sentiments, and how much Chicago meant to Ogden and the other Old Settlers who built it. The letter was written just after the fire, when Ogden was in Springfield with other relief committee members, soliciting state aid for his devastated city:

> Chicago will be built up again in good time and will continue to expand in busi-ness, wealth, and numbers—perhaps in ten years may contain 500,000 people, but a great many of the old citizens who have assisted to build it up and lived to enjoy it thus far in peace and great prosperity and happiness, will never, I fear, be able, in their more advanced period of life, to regain their former positions, but will be obliged to give place to new-comers with money, and leave to others the City they have assisted so much in creating, and the beauty and extent of which creation they have been so proud of and until now loved and enjoyed so much.
>
> I feel as if I should be entirely willing, so far as I am personally concerned, to give all I have left, and to live and die a poor man, if by so doing, I could see the City I have loved, enjoyed, and toiled for so long and with such hope and realiza-tion and joy, restored to the beautiful and happy position it occupied previous to its recent unparalelled [sic] calamity, indee[d], I might well give the remnant of life that is left to me to that end if it would avoid anything, but it will not. So far as I am concerned, I have all I need left and much more than I shall need personally, but with many of my friends and neighbors this is not the case.

Ogden discussed the purpose of the committee's visit to Springfield and its suc-cess in gaining state aid. Then as his letter continued, again in a more personal tone, we see clearly the grief he felt for his city:

> Don't misunderstand me as in the least desponding or as pining or unhappy on account of all that happened here so far as it concerns me personally, for that would be very wide of the fact. On my own account not an hour's grief or unhap-piness should I suffer, but be just as thankful as ever for my lot and path in life is strewn with so many friends and flowers. But for the loss of the beautiful City I spent the best and almost the majority of the years of my life in assisting to build, and which gave me such pleasure to labor for and the growth, expansion, strength, and beauty of which it was such a joy to see—I do grieve. . . . Never before was a large and very beautiful and fortunate City built by the generation of people so proud, so in love with their work, never a City so lamented and grieved over as Chicago. For this I do weep with those who have far greater oc-casion to weep than I.[16]

Ogden's continued commitment to Chicago is exemplified by his financial participation in rebuilding the Chicago Historical Society. When the society con-structed its original building in 1868 for sixty thousand dollars, it was proclaimed to be "a perfectly fire-proof structure." Of course, that claim proved inaccurate. It was estimated that the society lost—based on an 1868 inventory of its collection—more than fifteen thousand bound volumes, seventy-two thousand pamphlets, seventeen hundred newspaper files, forty-seven hundred manuscripts, twelve hundred maps and charts, and thousand of other pieces, the loss of the printed collection totaling in excess of one hundred thousand pieces.

Ogden, his brother Mahlon, and brothers-in-law Edwin Sheldon and Ezra McCagg were all declared Life Members of the Society.[17] Sheldon became one of the organization's largest benefactors among the next generation of boosters and served as its president for many years.

Throughout the early to mid-1870s, Ogden made a number of trips to the city from his home in New York. He may have built a second home in Chicago, more modest than the first, for those visits, but that has not been verified. On his visits, he toured the city, admired the progress being made, and met with the men overseeing his business enterprises. He also made trips north to Peshtigo to rally the people in their recovery work. The diary of an unnamed railroad man, in the collection of the Peshtigo Historical Society, states in a May 26, 1876, entry that "Mr. Ogden, his wife and General Strong are at Peshtigo."[18] Assuming the accuracy of this entry, Ogden would have been very frail by this time. No doubt he was most content when it was time to return home. The fires in Chicago and Peshtigo had taken their toll on the old man, and it was as if the inner flame that had driven him to such amazing heights had been extinguished along with the other two blazes.

Anyone who assumed that the Great Chicago Fire and the following financial panic would put an end to the growth of Chicago, or at least hinder it, would be sorely mistaken, as table 14.1 indicates.

Just as Chicago was rebuilding after the Great Fire, so was Peshtigo, although on a much smaller scale.[19] Reverend Peter Pernin, who had been a hero in the conflagration, was offered a new church in a more peaceful environment, but he refused. He elected to return to Peshtigo to rebuild his parish there. By the early 1880s, the town was completely rebuilt. An 1873 edition of the *Wisconsin Assembly Journal of Proceedings*, as recorded in Peter Leschak's book on the fire, listed the following destruction: "27 schoolhouses, 9 churches, 959 dwellings, 1028 barns and stables, 116 horses, 157 working cattle, 266 cows and heifers, 201 sheep, and 306 hogs."[20]

William Ogden and his partners had purchased forty acres of land on the Lake Michigan shore, just north of the river, in 1857. (His purchase of the area known as the Sands was detailed in chapter 10.) The planned development of the harbor area had been stalled, first by a lawsuit and the financial panic and then by the

Table 14.1

Population of Chicago

1835	3,265	1850	28,268	1865	178,900
1836	3,820	1851	34,437	1866	200,418
1837	4,179	1852	38,733	1867	220,000
1838	4,000	1853	60,652	1868	252,054
1839	4,200	1854	65,872	1869	273,043
1840	4,479	1855	80,028	1870	298,977
1841	5,752	1856	84,113	1871	334,270
1842	6,248	1857	93,000	1872	364,377
1843	7,580	1858	90,000	1873	465,650
1844	8,000	1859	95,000	1874	475,000
1845	12,088	1860	112,172	1875	500,000
1846	14,169	1861	120,000	1876	525,000
1847	16,859	1862	138,835	1885 (est.)	1,000,000
1848	20,023	1863	160,000	1911 (est.)	2,000,000
1849	23,047	1864	169,353		

Source: Balestier, *Annals of Chicago*, 34.

Civil War; but it had finally gotten under way, as the *Chicago Tribune* reported on May 31, 1867:

A MAMMOTH ENTERPRISE
PROPOSED SYSTEM OF DOCKS AND CANALS
IN THE NORTH DIVISION

It is reported that there is a scheme on foot for building a magnificent system of docks, on the Lake Shore, several hundred feet from the shore immediately north of the present pier. The plans are understood to include the fencing in with piles of the whole lake front, from the pier as far north as Huron street, a distance of eight blocks. . . .

We need scarcely say that William B. Ogden, Esq., is the gentleman whose name is mentioned most prominently in connection with this scheme. . . . the improvement would not only be a great advantage to the city, in itself, as furnishing a system of dockage, which will soon be imperatively demanded by the extension of our commerce, but that the benefit received by the harbor would more than warrant the appropriation of the lake shore to their use.

The improvement would cost from five to seven millions of dollars.

The plan, put forth by company president Mahlon Ogden, was called the North Shore Dock Plan, but it eventually became known as the Chicago Dock and Canal Company. It called for the construction of breakwaters, piers, slips, docks, canals, warehouses, and manufacturing facilities on the property to both facilitate the Ogdens' many enterprises and to serve the growing needs of the city. This would eventually become William Ogden's most enduring real estate legacy to the city he loved.

The *Tribune's* laudatory announcement followed by only three and a half months other stories in which they had excoriated the passage of the bill before the Illinois legislature that granted the company its powers.[21] "A Magnificent Fraud," one headline called it, while another said it was "A Stupendous Fraud on the People of Chicago." Both stories were referring to the right granted to the company to take public lands, but what caused the newspaper's complete flip-flop on the issue is not explained.

Five years after the *Tribune* announced the plan, after the Great Fire and just on the cusp of another financial panic, the newspaper ran another story headed "REAL ESTATE. Abandonment of the North Side Dock Project." The story described how Ogden had decided to abandon his original plan, saying he was instead "operating in harmony with the other owners of property on the shore south of Whitney street, who have unanimously agreed to extend the Lake Shore Drive from Whitney street . . . down to Indiana street."[22] Ogden had not abandoned the building project altogether in the five-year period between the two newspaper articles. Only one slip had been built, the Ogden Slip, also called the Michigan Canal; but many of the other plans had been abandoned or postponed when business did not develop as quickly as the partners had envisioned, due to the fire and the financial panic.

In an 1871 letter to his brother-in-law and largest client, Charles Butler, just after the Great Fire, Ogden wrote, "Everything but the two buildings mentioned [buildings at the end of their north pier] is swept from our Dock and Canal property and the new Wharves are considerably injured—I don't know that you have a paying lease left." He continued, "We have some Water lots and Wharves, but cannot count upon any receipts from here for some time to come."[23]

With these structures destroyed, his decision not to immediately rebuild could have evolved from any number of factors: problems with federal government approvals, trouble securing the necessary financing, or the Great Fire of 1871. It was most likely the latter, combined with his retirement from active business life, that caused him to change his plans for the harbor and waterfront area.

As it turned out, the 1872 *Chicago Tribune* story was not accurate. The company did rebuild, and the area boomed. At the dawn of the twentieth century, the North Pier Terminal Building was constructed, the largest combined warehouse and docking facility in the world. The Municipal Pier, today known as the Navy Pier, was constructed and then sold to the city for three hundred thousand dollars. For the next half-century, the Chicago Dock and Canal Company experienced financial highs and lows, but stayed the course; and the Ogden family maintained their financial interests in it. Finally, in the early 1960s, taking advantage of a new federal law, the company was reorganized into the Chicago Dock and Canal Trust, a real estate investment trust.[24]

Ogden, Sheldon and Company, whose roots went back to its founding by William Ogden in 1836, managed the company until its 1961 conversion to a trust, at which time management passed to another company. The company was dissolved in 1998, more than 160 years after it was founded.[25] Like Ogden, Sheldon and Company, the Chicago Dock and Canal Trust eventually passed on as well. In 1997 the trust's real estate portfolio was sold to a large, privately held Chicago real estate development firm.

Although Ogden's north shore land company ceased to be a corporate entity, it left a lasting legacy in many of the buildings that today occupy the land it once owned. These include the NBC Tower office building, the 1,200-room Sheraton Chicago Hotel and Towers, the 450-unit Cityfront Place apartment building, and the 440-unit CityView condominium project. There is also the fifty-story North Pier Tower condominium complex, and a complex known as River East, a late nineteenth-century warehouse that has been converted to offices and retail. Finally, there is a massive mixed-use complex that includes an Embassy Suites Hotel, a twenty-one-screen AMC movie theater, a bowling alley, a fifty-story condominium project, one hundred thousand feet of retail space, and parking for twelve hundred cars. Two additional projects included residential and retail space. There were additional land sites totaling between six and eight acres still to be developed, and the 3.5-acre DuSable Park is under construction. And finally, the seventy-story, 800-plus-unit Lake Point Tower condominium building situated between Lake Shore Drive and Navy Pier sits on land leased from Chicago Dock and Canal Trust in the 1960s.[26]

Not a bad legacy for a man who, at first glance at the north side of the Chicago River, declared it "a stinking swamp."

Although Ogden was slowing down and spending little time on business by the mid-1870s, both the place of his birth, Delaware County, New York, and his adopted home of Chicago still remembered him fondly. His business contemporaries held him in high regard by as well. During this period, he was invited to be a special guest at two separate celebrations.

The first event occurred in Delhi, New York, in late August 1873.[27] Ogden and two celebrated artists were invited to ride the town's new railroad, the first one to pass through Delhi. The New York and Oswego Midland Railroad, affectionately called the "Midland," had begun construction in 1868 to travel northwest across the state, reaching those unserved towns and villages that had put up the money to build it. They were justifiably proud of their new road, but it would soon enter into bankruptcy. It would live on, however, as the Ontario and Western Railway well into the twentieth century.

Joining Ogden in the celebration were "two fashionable ladies," Charlotte Cushman, one of the leading actresses of the day and an early feminist, and her companion, Emma Stebbins, a noted sculptress. The three were picked up at the Delhi Depot after their train ride and enjoyed a pleasant carriage ride to the Edgerton Hotel, where they participated in a lively community banquet. It's difficult to imagine what a threesome with such high national profiles would be doing visiting backwoods Delhi, but there they were. It is reported that Cushman so admired the beautiful team of horses that led them on their carriage ride that she purchased them from the hotel on the spot. It is interesting that through the years many of William Ogden's female friends were early feminists. He had few if any personal prejudices based upon religion, ethnicity, or gender; he simply liked to surround himself with interesting people who were passionate about their beliefs.

The second celebration Ogden attended was one of his last grand public appearances. He was invited to be the guest of honor at the opening of the Baltimore and Ohio Railroad when it reached Chicago on October 10, 1874. An invited-guests excursion up the river to an elegant hotel was followed by a "bounteous lunch . . . [and] music furnished by the popping of champagne corks." A toast was offered to "the health of William B. Ogden, which was drank amid hearty applause," the *Chicago Tribune* reported.[28]

Governor William Bross rose to speak, and like the good politician he was, he added a little rhetorical fuel to the competitive railroad fires that existed: "The Directors of the New York Central have watered its stock again and again, till the 8 percent it now divides on its nominal value probably realizes 40 to 60 percent on its actual cost. Jim Fisk and Jay Gould issued millions on millions of bonds, and stole the proceeds and the earnings of the road for years." The speech reflected the sad fact that the day of mostly honest entrepreneurial railroad men like William Ogden had passed. Railroads were in the hands of a new generation of men, often referred to as robber barons and plunderers, men like Fisk, Gould, Vanderbilt, and others to whom railroad building was done solely for profit, not progress. As William Ogden listened to the governor's speech, there can be little doubt that he raised a silent prayer in gratitude that he was of an earlier era.

On Tuesday, February 9, 1875, William Ogden married his longtime friend Marianna Arnot. He was approaching seventy, and as his friend Isaac Arnold said, "the only mistake about the marriage was that it did not take place twenty or thirty years earlier."[29] Between the broken heart he had suffered as a young man and his frenzied business career, he had wasted so many years being alone.

He had built his life around family and friends, so he was never lonely; but it was unfortunate that a man with so much to give had never had a life's partner with whom to share it.

The *Chicago Tribune*, republishing an article from the Elmira, New York, newspaper, reported on the event: "No one was present but the immediate families of the parties concerned. Miss Arnot is the eldest daughter of the late John Arnot, of this city [Elmira], a man of great wealth, and from whom she will inherit at least $1,000,000." The bride, it said, "is a magnificent-looking lady, with a very handsome face and stately carriage, and by training and nature is fitted to adorn the highest station in life." The story concluded, "Mr. And Mrs. Ogden left for quite an extended Southern trip."[30] Marianna was twenty years younger than Ogden.

In his obituary in the *Chicago Tribune* a few years later, another fact would be revealed that is unverified by any other source: "He was afterwards [after his arrival in Chicago in 1836] engaged to another lady in the West, but the marriage never came off. This lady is still living."[31]

Other than his own wedding, the highlight of 1875 for the family-oriented Ogden was the golden wedding anniversary celebration of his sister Eliza and her husband, Charles Butler.[32] The event was held on October 10 at the couple's Fox Meadow estate in Scarsdale, New York. The day of the celebration was clear, bright, and beautiful. The rooms were decorated with flowers and autumn leaves, and the house and lawn was crowded with family and friends. William Allen Butler read a poem, and guests sang *Auld Lang Syne* to the couple.

To Eliza Butler and Will Ogden, the highlight of the celebration was having so many immediate family members together again in one place and at one time. Their brother Mahlon and his wife, Frances, were there, as were sisters Emily and Caroline and their husbands, Nelson Wheeler and Ezra McCagg. Sadly, their youngest sister Frances had died five years earlier at only forty-six years of age. A multitude of children of the five Ogden siblings were also in attendance, as well as many of their grandchildren. Eliza and Will must have realized that there would not be too many more events like this in their lifetimes, and they enjoyed every second of it.

Somewhere in this period, Emily and her husband Nelson moved from their home, Laurel Bank, in Deposit, Delaware County, into a home close to Ogden's Villa Boscobel.[33] Having family nearby again would have been a tremendous pleasure to the aging man in his final years. Ogden's obituary in the *Chicago Tribune* states that because of failing health he had not visited his office in the National Park Bank Building in New York City since the beginning of 1877.[34] His affairs were completely in the hands of his partners and attorneys by that time. He was not bedridden, however, the story reported, because he had taken daily carriage drives up until a few days before he died.

On July 23, 1877, only a few days after Ogden's death, his niece Anna, Eliza and Charles's youngest daughter, also passed away.[35] She was only thirty-four at the time and had never married. It was her delicate health that had prompted at least two restorative journeys to Europe, trips that must have provided temporary relief at best. Will Ogden's remaining siblings would all outlive him: Eliza passed away in 1878, Mahlon in 1880, Emily in 1884, and Caroline in 1885. Eliza's husband, Charles Butler, would live to the ripe old age of ninety-five, leaving an enviable legacy of philanthropy and public service in New York City.[36]

15

A Whole-Souled Man

_____

On Friday, August 3, 1877, at 2:00 A.M, William Butler Ogden passed away quietly at his Villa Boscobel home in High Bridge. His death did not come as a surprise to his wife, his brother and sisters, his many friends and admirers, nor even to himself, as his health had been failing for nearly three years. "His physicians informed him his death was at hand—not more than a few hours. The dying man received the last sacrament of the Church, and quietly awaited his end. The last scene was very peaceful, the venerable honored citizen passing away without a struggle," the _Chicago Inter Ocean_ solemnly observed.[1]

Ogden's death certificate listed the official cause of death: "First (Primary), age & paralysis," and "Second (Immediate), Brights Disease." Bright's disease, or kidney failure, was the immediate cause of death.[2] The funeral service was held in the Gothic chapel of St. James Episcopal Church on Central Avenue in Fordham, New York.[3] According to his obituary in the _New York Times_, most of the mourners met first at Villa Boscobel and then traveled to Fordham on the 3:30 P.M. train. There, carriages provided by the family met the mourners and delivered them to the church.

"The services were characterized by the utmost simplicity," the _New York Times_ reported, "and a simple cross of roses was the only floral adornment of the coffin."[4] Many prominent men served as pallbearers. There was Andrew H. Green, who handled most of Ogden's business and personal legal affairs during the latter part of his life. Green, often called the "Father of Greater New York," was the mastermind behind the five-borough concept that defines New York City today. He also helped create the American Museum of Natural History, Central Park, New York Public Library, and the Washington Bridge, among other prominent institutions and landmarks.

Gouverneur Morris Jr., whose father was a Revolutionary War hero and a framer of the U.S. Constitution, was a Bronx neighbor and a railroad pioneer. Park Godwin was a poet and essayist. Oswald Offendorfer was a German American journalist, politician, and philanthropist from New York City. Franklin Edson was an ex-New York congressman and future mayor of New York City.

The eulogy was given by the Right Reverend Richard Clarkson, whose praise for Ogden and his accomplishments was soaring: "The master-builder of the City that is the lasting marvel of these days. . . . all these [qualities] made him as great a benefactor as the railroad or the city he brought into existence. . . . a generous, honest, high-toned, true-hearted, whole-souled man."[5] Only about twenty family and friends attended the service, and only immediate family were invited to the graveside service. The obituaries mention no Chicago friends in attendance, which, if true, seems odd. Ogden was interred in nearby Woodlawn Cemetery in the Bronx, in a heavy but plain rosewood casket bearing a silver plate with his name and date of death.

The *Chicago Tribune* also added words of praise for the man who contributed so much to building that city. "He was the contemporary of Webster, Clay, Calhoun, Benton, Douglas, and Lincoln," the paper noted, and it referred to him as one "of the ablest men the nation has ever produced. . . . William B. Ogden was the peer of the wisest and the best of them."[6]

From the dozens of obituaries that ran in newspapers throughout the country, the simplest, yet most accurate assessment of Ogden's life was published by the *Chicago Inter Ocean*:

> To recount his history is in large measure to chronicle the prominent events in the material progress made by the Northwest in the last forty years. During the two score years a wilderness has been converted into a fruitful field, villages have grown to the proportion of cities, and the chief city has taken the form and character of a great metropolis, and it is but simple justice to declare that to the energy, enterprise, and foresight of William B. Ogden, more than to any other single individual, country and city alike owe their rapid advance in wealth and prosperity.[7]

In an article three days earlier, upon first being notified of his death, the *New York Times* had this to say:

> The life of WILLIAM B. OGDEN . . . has been closely identified with some of the most important industrial developments of the last half century. His observing eye took in the future development of the great North-west while as yet the Indian paddled his canoe on Lake Michigan and the traveler had to pass through tribes of red men to penetrate into Wisconsin or to reach the banks of the Mississippi.
>
> In the development of the railroad system of the country, Mr. Ogden has been one of the foremost and most potent of coadjutors . . . the most censorious criticism cannot deprive him of the credit of being one of the most enterprising and far-seeing of the railroad magnates who have opened up the virgin lands of the continent to the settler.

In him an American has passed away of a type which the present generation does not produce and to which future generations will yield a degree of homage that we are but partially able to appreciate.[8]

William Ogden's last will and testament had been drafted on August 30, 1875, two years before his death.[9] In it, he named as executors and trustees his wife Marianna, brother-in-law Edwin Sheldon, nephew William Wheeler, and Charles J. Canda. Canda was described by Ogden as "my esteemed friend . . . who resides in the City of New York"; he had been a partner in a few earlier enterprises, including the Northern Pacific Railroad. In a codicil to the will dated January 6, 1876, Ogden added the name of Andrew H. Green as an executor and trustee. In a second codicil dated December 8, 1876, he revoked the executor and trustee status of Charles Canda and substituted William Strong of Chicago, the husband of Mahlon's daughter Mary and president of the Peshtigo Company.

Canda unsuccessfully contested his removal as a trustee. The only hint offered as to why he was dropped is a couple of lines in the *Chicago Inter Ocean* a few weeks after Ogden's death: "It is said that Canda's exclusion from the executorship arose, not so much from Ogden's feelings towards him as from the failure of certain proposed connections by marriage between the families of Ogden and Canda."[10] To his last breath, William Ogden never wavered from his strong commitment to his family.

The will was probated on September 7, 1877. The property and assets to be distributed through the will were significant. If the Dun and Bradstreet estate estimate of eight million dollars from about five years earlier was accurate, the estate should have grown, making wealthy people of many of the heirs, if they were not already so. The estate consisted largely of real estate in New York, Illinois, and New Jersey, and the executors were given broad latitude to sell or hold the properties, at their discretion. The *Chicago Tribune* obituary stated that "[Ogden] owned a large estate in New Jersey, where his ancestors came from."[11] His great-grandparents, David and Elizabeth Ogden, had left the family home of Elizabeth, New Jersey—which David's great-grandfather, John Ogden, the Pilgrim, had founded in 1665—and resettled in Hanover Township, Morris County, New Jersey, sometime prior to 1740. At some point after 1755, David, Elizabeth, and their seven children moved to nearby Morristown. Their oldest son, John Ogden, inherited the family land. This estate then passed, in whole or in part, to William Ogden's father Abraham, and at some point, William gained the estate through inheritance, purchase, or a combination of both.

There were certain direct bequests made in the will, and after those bequests were met, everything that remained was to be divided into twenty equal shares.[12] The direct bequests included Villa Boscobel and all its lands and contents, which went to his wife Marianna. Common and preferred shares of stock in the Peshtigo Company went to William Strong and his wife, the North family of Walton (discussed in chapter 3), and a number of other relatives and Walton, New York, friends. For support and maintenance, Marianna Ogden was provided with ten thousand dollars a year, and sister Emily Wheeler with five thousand dollars a year.

The remaining twenty shares were divided among a large group of his relatives: his wife Marianna, who received 25 percent of the shares, his sisters, his brother, their spouses, and their children. Significantly, he left one and a half shares, or 7.5 percent, of the estate to charity. Trustees Marianna Ogden and Andrew H. Green were given the latitude to determine when and to what organizations the money should be given. They also had the power to use those proceeds for the benefit of any of the heirs who may in the future have found themselves in need. Finally, the will held that after the death of the two charitable trustees, any assets still remaining in the charitable trust were to be divided among the remaining beneficiaries according to a rather elaborate scheme.

In January 1891, as the "new" University of Chicago was struggling to get off the ground, the new president Dr. Harper received a letter from a business acquaintance in New York: "I have read with much gratification your plans for the scope and work of the new University." The letter requested Harper to agree to meet with an unidentified man "who takes a strong interest in the new University, to confer in reference to the possibility of an endowment, on certain terms, for scientific studies."[13] Dr. Harper quickly agreed, and less than a week later he was sitting across the table from Andrew H. Green, one of the two trustees of Ogden's charitable trust.[14] Harper was aware of William Ogden's commitment to the university, as Ogden had been chairman of the "old" university's Board of Trustees for thirteen years. Still, he was stunned by Green's proposal. Green explained that he and Mrs. Ogden had decided to endow the new university with 70 percent of the remaining amount in the charitable trust, something between $300,000 and $500,000. The money, if accepted, was to be used for a scientific school "to be named by the donors."

Thus was born the Ogden Graduate School of Science at the University of Chicago.[15] The first payment on the endowment, made in 1893, amounted to $246,000. From that point on, payments continued to be made from time to time for twenty-one years, the aggregate amount being nearly $600,000, the equivalent of $10 million by 2008 standards. By the dawn of the twenty-first century, that school had become the Division of Physical Sciences and the Division of the Biological Sciences, with the Ogden name no longer appended to it. However, the University of Chicago does still award a William B. Ogden Distinguished Service professorship every year.

At the time the University of Chicago grant was being considered, about $51,000 had already been distributed from the charitable trust, according to a *New York Times* article.[16] Of that amount, $20,000 was given to the town of Walton, with $13,500 of that sum being used to build the William B. Ogden Free Library in the 1890s.[17] Another $25,000 was given to the trustees of a hospital to be under the management of the Institution of Protestant Deaconesses, a hospital training school for nurses that claimed Florence Nightingale as its most famous alumna. Reverend W. A. Passavant, a well-known leader of the German Lutheran Church, had founded the school.

Later in 1891, in a move that would have wounded William B. Ogden deeply, a group of his heirs, headed by Charles and Eliza Butler's unmarried daughter Emily, went to court in New York to have the charitable trust declared void and its remaining funds divided up among the other heirs.[18] In a complex legal case, the trust was declared void, but only as far as the holdings of William Ogden's New York property and its income were concerned. Other property and its income in Illinois and New Jersey were not affected by the New York court's decision.

The decision by Emily Butler to challenge the charitable provision of the will is odd. It's unlikely she was motivated by greed, as there wasn't that much left in the trust by that time. Too, Ogden's will stated, in granting to Emily and her sister Anna a smaller share than that granted to most others, that "this apportion [1.25 percent each] I fix for my said nieces . . . in view of the estate which will descend to them from their father, whereby after his and my decease, they will come into the possession of probably a larger estate than I leave to any other of my nieces."[19] Their mother Eliza Butler followed William Ogden in death the following year, and Charles Butler died in 1897, at which time Emily did inherit the entire Butler estate, her last sibling Anna having died just ten days before their Uncle William's death. So we are left to wonder why Emily challenged her Uncle Will's final wishes.

The will also leaves another mystery to be considered, now more than one and a quarter centuries later. Paragraph 8 of Ogden's will provided that Ogden, his family, and the family of his long lost love Sarah North be interred together in the cemetery in Walton, in a large family plot he had purchased.[20] However, as his *New York Times* obituary accurately stated, he was buried in Woodlawn Cemetery in the Bronx. Paragraph 8 says that Ogden could designate another burying place, but that it must be done in writing. However, no codicil is attached to his will designating this change, so we are left to wonder how it came to pass. It might be expected that once he married another woman, Ogden would be sensitive to the will's language requesting that he be interred next to the long lost love of his youth. However, the will was drawn in August 1875, six months *after* his marriage to Marianna Arnot, so that was not the case.

Adding to the mystery, Sarah North and her family, whom Ogden had designated should be buried in *his* family's plot, are interred in their own family plot in the Walton cemetery, not in the Ogdens.' However, Ogden's mother's parents, the Weeds, are interred in the Ogden plot along with his father, Abraham, his mother, Abigail, and a host of other Ogdens.

One possible explanation to both parts of the mystery is that when the North descendants declined Ogden's offer to have their family members disinterred and then reinterred in his plot, he was so disappointed he would not have his eternal rest next to Sarah North that he decided to be buried closer to his home.

Marianna Ogden never remarried.[21] She lived in Villa Boscobel for a number of years but eventually moved to a home on Madison Avenue in New York City. From that period to her death, she divided her time between the Madison Avenue estate, a summer home in Lenox, Massachusetts, and a "cottage" in Newport, Rhode Island. She subdivided the Villa Boscobel property at some point in the 1880s, as her own 1904 will stated that the home then occupied only 18 of the original 110 acres.

The major portion of Villa Boscobel that she sold was broken up into fifteen hundred individual lots, and in a historic four-day sale, the lots were auctioned off by Joseph P. Day.[22] It was the largest partition sale in the history of New York City up to that time. Following the sale, in 1884 or 1885, the property was surveyed and laid out with city streets and parkways by prominent engineer Louis Risse. On the property was built the Sedgwick Houses, a very early New York housing development.

Marianna (nee Arnot) Ogden died on September 28, 1904, at seventy-nine years of age. According to the *New York Times*, she left an estate valued at twenty million dollars, enormous for the times. The remainder of the Villa Boscobel property, along with all the buildings and contents, was left jointly to her sister and brother.

December 20, 1881, was a fairly typical Chicago winter evening. A light snow had fallen off and on during the day, and the temperature was chilly. Winter weather, however, was seldom a deterrent to hearty Chicagoans who were used to venturing out of their homes in much more severe conditions.

The hall of the Chicago Historical Society was filled with prominent citizens and the few surviving Old Settlers, who had come to pay homage one last time to the man who, as much as any other, had built Chicago.[23] Seated at the dais were many men and women of great note in Chicago and Illinois: Hon. Elihu B. Washburne, U.S. congressman, former secretary of state and ambassador to France in the administration of Ulysses S. Grant, and confidant of Abraham Lincoln; John Dean Caton, former chief justice of the Illinois State Supreme Court, first lawyer to set up shop in Chicago, and an early manufacturer of tele- graph instruments; and Judge Thomas Drummond. Also seated at the dais were seven ex-mayors of Chicago: B. W. Raymond, Isaac L. Milliken, John C. Haines, Julien S. Rumsey, Roswell B. Mason, Joseph Medill, and Thomas Hoyne.

Edwin H. Sheldon, Ogden's brother-in-law, trusted partner, and friend, was the evening's first speaker, and he set forth the purpose of the gathering: "The Chicago Historical Society, some months since, passed a resolution requesting Mrs. Ogden, the widow of the late William B. Ogden, to give to the Society a portrait of her late husband, who had been one of its founders, and always during his life, a liberal benefactor. The resolution referred to Mr. Ogden, in appropriate terms, as one of the founders of the City, and as one who had projected and largely aided the execution of many great enterprises, the benefits of which the people of Chicago, and the North-West, are reaping in such full measure today."

Based upon the resolution, Marianna Ogden had commissioned the great nineteenth-century American portrait artist and Ogden friend, George P. A. Healy, to paint a portrait of Ogden to hang in the Historical Society. Healy had painted Ogden on a number of occasions, but all the works had been lost in the Great Fire. For this occasion, he painted Ogden's portrait from a photograph taken just before the fire and from his own personal recollections of his subject.

After the portrait was formally presented to the Historical Society—renamed the Chicago History Museum, where it still hangs—two of Ogden's best friends, Isaac Arnold, then president of the society, and J. Young Scammon read papers before the assembly describing their relationships with, and recollections of, William B. Ogden. These two talks were later published as a seventy-two-page booklet that today provides much of the personal information we have about William Ogden. A lengthy handwritten letter from Charles Butler about his early exploration of Chicago and Ogden's role in that event was also read. That letter is now held among Butler's papers in the National Archives in Washington, D.C. The Chicago History Museum, still maintains a portfolio containing a great deal of Ogden's business papers; but like so many other precious early records of the city and the people who built it, his personal papers were all destroyed in the fire.

Despite its horrendous ramifications, however, not even the Great Fire of Chicago could destroy the legacy of this man who meant so much to the city of Chicago, the nation's railroads, and the settling of the American West. The Ogden name continues to carry on in Chicago in such place-names as the Ogden Dam, the Ogden-Wentworth Canal, Ogden Street, Ogden Park, Ogden Plaza Park, Ogden School, and Ogden Slip. In Elmira, New York, the Arnot-Ogden Medical Center also carries his name. A major grant from Marianna Ogden, after Ogden's death, established the 250-bed hospital and medical center, which is an independent, not-for-profit institution.

In his adopted home at Villa Boscobel, which is today part of the Bronx, there is an Ogden Avenue and a Boscobel Avenue. But it is in the town of his birth, Walton, New York, where we find his most lasting legacy. The William B. Ogden Free Library carries on in his name, and it is a splendid small-town library from every perspective.[24] A massive arched bluestone fireplace anchors one end, and high windows, ceiling beams, golden-hued oak bookcases, and handsome wooden pillars invite closer inspection.

The William B. Ogden Free Library, in Walton, New York, circa 1910, built in the 1890s with funds from Ogden's charitable trust and now on the National Register of Historic Places. Walton Historical Society.

Right across the street from the library, also on Gardiner Place, is the small, tidy Christ Episcopal Church, the oldest church building in Walton.[25] With few changes, it appears outwardly much as it did when construction was completed in 1832. Within the small church are nine glorious floor-to-ceiling stained glass windows. When the sunlight plays through them, the interior of the church is bathed in brilliant color. One of the windows has been dedicated to the North family; seven others are dedicated to William Ogden, his mother and father, Abigail and Abraham, and his siblings Mahlon, Eliza, Emily, Caroline, and Frances.

Church archives indicate that the interior of the building was completely remodeled in the early 1880s, including replacing the multipaned opaque glass windows. In 1883 new stained glass windows were donated to the church for that purpose, but the records do not indicate who endowed them. There is little doubt that Marianna Ogden, and perhaps the other families of William's siblings, funded the magnificent windows.

On July 6, 1961, a fire almost completely gutted the interior of the tiny church, according to Walton historian Helen Lane. However, the windows, legacies to a man who did so much for so many, and for his immediate family, whom he loved, honored, and looked after until his death, were undamaged. Their survival is a humble testament to a towering figure in nineteenth-century America who is today virtually a forgotten man.

Christ Episcopal Church, Walton, New York, built in 1832, features nine magnificent stained glass windows in remembrance of the Ogden family. Author's photo.

NOTES
BIBLIOGRAPHY
INDEX

NOTES

Newspaper Abbreviatons

AA	Albany Argus
BE	Brooklyn Eagle
CA	Chicago American
CJ	Chicago Journal
CD	Chicago Democrat
CIO	Chicago Inter Ocean
CPT	Chicago Press-Tribune
CR	Chicago Republican
CTI	Chicago Times
CTR	Chicago Tribune

DCA	Door County Advocate
DCG	Delaware County Gazette
GBA	Green Bay Advocate
MS	Milwaukee Daily Sentinel
NYDT	New York Daily Tribune
NYH	New York Herald
NYT	New York Times
SFB	San Francisco Daily Evening Bulletin
WSR	Wisconsin State Register

Preface

1. Arnold and Scammon, *William B. Ogden*, 25; Holbrook, *Story of American Railroads*, 133; Stephenson, *Recollections*, 163.

1. Prelude

1. B. North, "North Family Records."

2. Lynch, *Epoch and a Man*, 58, 235.

3. Holland, *Life and Political Opinions*, 221–23.

4. H. Alexander, *American Talleyrand*, 309–10.

5. There is no discoverable primary source evidence that a meeting such as the one described in this chapter actually took place for the purpose stated. A few mentions in secondary sources state that Charles Butler, at his brother Benjamin's bidding, approached Ogden to run for the New York Assembly in order to promote the building of the New York and Erie Railroad. However, Benjamin Butler was a leader in Martin Van Buren's Albany Regency, his law partner, and eventually his attorney general; so it is a near certainty that Ogden's candidacy was Van Buren's idea. Also, as the narrative relates, and as Van Buren scholars attest, his reputation for obfuscation and secrecy would have naturally precluded any recording of a meeting he might have attended to discuss a controversial regional topic such as the New York and Erie Railroad. Although he was not literally in hiding in the Hudson River valley during the summer of 1833, the sparsely settled region would have made him feel secure in attending such a gathering. Finally, Van Buren's support of Ogden's effort in the legislature is clearly evidenced by the fact that Ogden's entire speech was published in the *Albany Argus*. Van Buren was a major owner of the newspaper, and the editor of that paper was also a leader in his Albany Regency. For these reasons, I am confident in writing that this meeting took place for the purpose I have stated.

6. Background on American railroads is discussed more fully in chapter 2.

7. *American Railroad Journal*, March 7, 1835, as quoted in Ward, *Railroads and Character*, 23–24.

8. *AA*, March 21, 1835.

2. The Little Railroad That Could

1. Wormser, *Iron Horse*, 7.

2. Arnold and Scammon, *William B. Ogden*, 11.

3. Wendt, *Swift Walker*, 344.

4. For a description of technology changes in American society in the 1830s and their effects on the growth of cities, see Johnson, *Birth of the Modern*, 875–79.

5. Wormser, *Iron Horse*, 1–2; Gerstner, *Early American Railroads*, 830.

6. George W. Ogden, Personal Diaries, 1832–35.

7. Dickens, *American Notes*, 61–63.

8. Hungerford, *Men of Erie*, 15–16.

9. Frey, *Railroads in the Nineteenth Century*, 115.

10. Lord, *Historical Review of New York & Erie*, 10.

11. Frey, *Railroads in the Nineteenth Century*, 115.

12. *AA*, March 21, 1835.

13. *AA*, March 30, 1835.

14. Lord, *Historical Review of New York & Erie*, 39.

15. Hungerford, *Men of Erie*, 112–20.

16. Ibid., 120–21.

17. Holbrook, *Story of American Railroads*, 66.

3. Stately Edifices and Lofty Spires

1. Arnold and Scammon, *William B. Ogden*, 8.

2. Both letters are quoted extensively in chapter 13.

3. D. L. Miller, *City of the Century*, 92.

4. *NYT*, August 4, 1877.

5. Harpster, *John Ogden*, 38.

6. Wheeler, *Ogden Family*, 200. A family history book such as Wheeler's would not ordinarily be used extensively as a credible source in a biography like this one. However, Wheeler was William B. Ogden's nephew, was in his employ for many years, and lived with him for a time. Ogden had been a genealogy hobbyist himself, and it was his work that Wheeler took up after Ogden's death. Wheeler also had virtually unlimited access to Ogden's knowledge, his life, and his friends. Thus I believe that Wheeler's knowledge of Ogden and his life, as portrayed in the family history, ranks as firsthand, reliable information. For more on Wheeler's life, see chapter 11.

7. Gould, *History of Delaware County*, ch. 7.

8. Ibid.

9. Miles, "History of Cannonsville," 2.

10. Wheeler, *Ogden Family*, 200.

11. *Book B of Deeds*, 287–88.

12. Murray, *Centennial History*, ch. 3 (on Walton), p. 32.

13. Lane, *Story of Walton*, 21.

14. Gemming, *Wool Gathering*, 38–39.

15. Marvin, "History of Walton to 1875," 6.

16. Wheeler, *Ogden Family*, 201.

17. Munsell, "Town History: Walton," in *History of Delaware County.*

18. Wheeler, *Ogden Family*, 201.

19. Ibid.

20. Bennett, *Old Golden Rule Days*, 9.

21. Arnold and Scammon, *William B. Ogden*, 6–7.

22. Ibid., 43.

23. Ibid., 201.

24. Ibid., 4.

25. Lane and Lane, *Walton Yesteryears*, 104.

26. Wheeler, *Ogden Family*, 200.

27. A. W. North, *Founders*, 45.

28. *DCG*, Advertisement, October 10, 1825.

29. *Index of Mortgages*, Delaware County, N.Y.

30. Munsell, "Town History: Walton," in *History of Delaware County.*

31. Arnold and Scammon, *William B. Ogden*, 44.

32. Wheeler, *Ogden Family*, 201.

33. *DCG*, March 4, 1828.

34. Wheeler, *Ogden Family*, 203.

35. Ibid., 320.

36. Munsell, "Town History: Walton; Church History, Christ Church," in *History of Delaware County.*

37. Arnold and Scammon, *William B. Ogden*, 27–28.

38. B. North, "North Family Record."

39. "Last Will and Testament."

40. Wheeler, *Ogden Family.*

41. Haven, *Inland Navigation.*

42. Murphy, *Erie Canal*, 36.

4. Go West, Young Man

1. Wheeler, *Ogden Family*, 318.

2. On Charles Butler's fight for farmers and his friendship with Arthur Bronson, see Stoddard, *Life and Letters*, 114–20.

3. "Talk by Charles Butler," William B. Ogden Papers, box 1, folder 12, Chicago History Museum.

4. Butler, Talk before Chicago Historical Society, December 17, 1881, typescript folder, Charles Butler Papers, box 3, reel 3, Library of Congress.

5. Gale, "Chicago as It Was and Is."

6. For Butler's description of the trip he and Bronson made to Chicago, see Stoddard, *Life and Letters*, 132–36; and Butler, Talk before Chicago Historical Society, Butler Papers.

7. Butler, Talk before Chicago Historical Society, Butler Papers.

8. Ibid.

9. B. L. Pierce, *As Others See Chicago*, 57.

10. Butler, Talk before Chicago Historical Society, Butler Papers.

11. Haeger, *Investment Frontier*, 48.

12. Wheeler, *Ogden Family*, 199.

13. Ibid.

14. *DCG*, February 25, 1835.

15. Stoddard, *Life and Letters*, 149.

16. Butler, Talk before Chicago Historical Society, Butler Papers.

17. Stoddard, *Life and Letters*, 149.

18. *Francis B. Nicoll v. William B. Ogden et al.*, Supreme Court of Illinois 29 Ill. 323 (1862).

19. Stoddard, *Life and Letters*, 151; Wheeler, *Ogden Family*, 203.

20. For information on the history of the Chicago area, physical description of the Chicago River and the Chicago Portage, see Cronon, *Nature's Metropolis*; D. L. Miller, *City of the Century*; Quaife, *Checagou*; and Hansen, *Rivers*.

21. Cronon, *Nature's Metropolis*, 33.

22. Danckers and Meredith, *Early Chicago*, 37.

23. D. L. Miller, *City of the Century*, 59.

24. Murray, *Centennial History of Delaware County*, "Letter from Rev. Scott."

25. *Niles (Mich.) Register*, June 6, 1835, cited in Danckers and Meredith, *Early Chicago*, 46.

26. Danckers and Meredith, *Early Chicago*, 37–45, passim.

27. Ibid.

28. Lewis, *John S. Wright*, 31.

29. D. L. Miller, *City of the Century*, 57.

30. Poole, *Giants Gone*, 18.

31. Butler, Talk before Chicago Historical Society, Butler Papers.

32. Ogden to John Sullivan, June 10, 1836, in Ogden Papers, box 1.

33. Andreas, *History of Chicago*, 2:569.

34. Martineau, *Society in America*, 259–60.

35. *CTR*, September 8, 1872.

36. Baird, *Life in Territorial Wisconsin*, 242.

37. Danckers and Meredith, *Early Chicago*, 310; Arnold and Scammon, *William B. Ogden*, 60.

38. Danckers and Meredith, *Early Chicago*, 271; Arnold and Scammon, *William B. Ogden*, 60.

39. Danckers and Meredith, *Early Chicago*, 274.

40. For information and description of Potawatomi dance, see Beckwith, *Illinois and Indiana Indians*.

41. Of Abraham Ogden's siblings who had joined him in New York, Daniel died in 1835. William, only eleven years old when he joined his brothers in Walton, married a local girl, Ann Gregory, and they had two sons. William earned a medical degree, and was a practicing physician in Walton for many years, as was his nephew, Daniel and Phebe's son Thomas Jefferson Ogden. William died in 1850. Of Jacob, nothing is known; he seems to have vanished without a trace. He was seventeen when he arrived in Walton with his brothers, so it is probable that he simply moved on to find his own place in another town. Isaac Ogden is discussed in chapter 2. Wheeler, *Ogden Family*, 199.

42. Burhans to Ogden, October 21, 1835, Ogden File, Walton Historical Society.

5. The Benevolence of the Butcher

1. Historian and academic Edward Wolner, writing of Chicago's early years, cited five factors responsible for the rapidity of the city's growth: geography, frontier cycles, democracy, technology, and civic leadership. Wolner, "City Builder," 3.

2. Gates, *History of Public Land*, 171.

3. Ibid., 173.

4. Haeger, *Investment Frontier*, 110.

5. Gates, *History of Public Land*, 173.

6. A. Smith, *Wealth of Nations*, para. 1:82.

7. McCarthy, *Noblesse Oblige*, 53.

8. B. L. Pierce, *History of Chicago*, 1:xv.

9. Sandburg, "Chicago," in *Chicago Poems*.

10. Arnold and Scammon, *William B. Ogden*, 12.

11. McIlvaine, introduction to *Reminiscences of Early Chicago*, iv.

12. Haeger, *Investment Frontier*, 110.

13. B. L. Pierce, *History of Chicago*, 1:151.

14. Ogden to John Bailey, June 7, 1836, Ogden Papers, box 1.

15. Ogden to John Sullivan, June 10, 1836, Ogden Papers, box 1.

16. Schultz, "Businessman's Role," 21–22.

17. Halvorsen, "Newberrys," 3:1–4.

18. Haeger, *Investment Frontier*, 108–9.

19. Ibid., 164–65.

20. Ogden to Cogswell, December 26, 1838, Ogden Papers, box 1.

21. Haeger, *Investment Frontier*, 164–65.

22. For information on nepotism, its history, and practices, see Bellow, *In Praise of Nepotism*, 320–23.

23. Ibid., 317.

24. Cromie, *Great Chicago Fire*, 48.

25. Ogden to A. N. Wheeler, August 29, 1839, and Ogden to F. S. Kinney, June 15, 1840, Ogden Papers, box 2.

26. Gerstner, *Early American Railroads*, 481.

27. Ogden to Bushnell, November 24, 1840, Ogden Papers, box 3.

28. For the story of Michael Hoffman and Ogden's support, see Andreas, *History of Chicago*, 2:519.

29. Ogden to R. Stewart, February 7, 1838, Ogden Papers, box 1; McLear, "Galena and Chicago Union," 286.

30. Ogden to S. Hobbie, November 12, 1840, Ogden Papers, box 2; B. L. Pierce, *History of Chicago*, 1:68–69.

31. Ogden to Butler, December 8, 1840, Ogden Papers, box 3.

32. Hoyt, *One Hundred Years*, 21.

33. Arnold and Scammon, *William B. Ogden*, 12.

34. Ibid., 24.

35. Ibid.

36. Schultz, *Church and the City*, 29, 39.

37. Arnold and Scammon, *William B. Ogden*, 10–11.

38. See "New York State Legislature" (news release).

6. Mister Mayor

1. T. W. Goodspeed, *Biographical Sketches*, 39.

2. Ahern, *Political History of Chicago*, 20, 102.

3. Wendt, *Swift Walker*, 371–72, 374.

4. Ahern, *Political History of Chicago*, 93.

5. Merriner, *Grafters and Goo Goos*, 25.

6. Two of the three of the men Ogden joined would also serve as Chicago's mayors in the future. Sherman, who in later years owned the Sherman House, was elected mayor in 1841, 1862, and 1863, and Wentworth in 1857 and 1860.

7. D. L. Miller, *City of the Century*, 74.

8. Andreas, *History of Chicago*, 1:177–78; Cromie, *Great Chicago Fire*, 48–49.

9. *CA*, April 29, 1837.

10. Ibid.

11. Andreas, *History of Chicago*, 1:177.

12. Cromie, *Great Chicago Fire*, 49.

13. Andreas, *History of Chicago*, 1:177–78.

14. *CIO*, May 3, 1878, 8.

15. "Chicago Common Council Proceedings," May 3, 1837.

16. B. L. Pierce, *History of Chicago*, 1:28–31.

17. *CPT*, August 3, 1860.

18. See McGrane, *Panic of 1837*.

19. "Chicago Common Council Proceedings," May 17, 1837.

20. Ibid., May 9, 1837.

21. Ibid., May 11, 1837.

22. Ibid., May 22, 1837.

23. Ibid., June 9, 1837.

24. Ogden to Seely & Porter, July 5, 1837, Ogden Papers, box 1, folder 1.

25. "Chicago Common Council Proceedings," May 3, 1837.

26. Ibid., October 10, 1837; October 9, 1837; February 5, 1838.

27. Hoyt, *One Hundred Years*, 21, quoting from Moses, *History of Chicago*, 1:105.

28. T. W. Goodspeed, *Biographical Sketches*, 41–42.

29. Ogden to James Allen, January 15, 1840, Ogden Papers, box 1.

30. Andreas, *History of Chicago*, 1:444.

31. Descriptions of the repudiation meeting, the various speeches, and Ogden's remarks to the crowd are in Andreas, *History of Chicago*, 1:444; Downard, "William Butler Ogden"; and Arnold and Scammon, *William B. Ogden*, 47.

32. *CIO*, August 4, 1877.

33. On Ogden's episode with Raymond, see *CTR*, September 8, 1872.

34. McIlvaine, *Reminiscences of Early Chicago*, 86.

35. Ogden to Charles Butler, May 18, 1837, Ogden Papers, box 1.

36. McLear, "William Butler Ogden," 289.

37. Ogden to Hinckley, August 19, 1839, Ogden Papers, box 2.

38. Ogden to Charles Butler, May 18, 1837, Ogden Papers, box 1.

39. McLear, "William Butler Ogden," 290.

40. Ogden to Coster, June 1, 1840, Ogden Papers, box 2.

41. For description of Ogden's participation in the beer brewery, see Skilnik, *History of Beer in Chicago*, 3–5.

42. Ogden to Townsend, September 1, 1840, Ogden Papers, box 2.

43. Ferris, *Grain Traders*, 2.

44. For a description of the arrival of the grain steamer *Illinois* and Ogden's speech welcoming it, see Arnold and Scammon, *William B. Ogden*, 16–17.

45. B. L. Pierce, *History of Chicago*, 1:377.

46. Andreas, *History of Chicago*, 1:144.

47. Danckers and Meredith, *Early Chicago*, 106; Balestier, *Annals of Chicago*, 1.

48. McCarthy, *Noblesse Oblige*, ix.

49. Arnold and Scammon, *William B. Ogden*, 26.

50. Grant, "William Butler Ogden," 293.

51. Arnold and Scammon, *William B. Ogden*, 25.

52. B. L. Pierce, *History of Chicago*, 1:207.

53. Ogden to North, November 1840, Ogden Papers, box 3.

54. Ogden to H. Moore, January 25, 1841, Ogden Papers, box 2.

55. Haeger, *Investment Frontiers*, 179.

56. T. W. Goodspeed, *Biographical Sketches*, 43–44; Andreas, *History of Chicago*, 1:433.

57. Gerstner, *Early American Railroads*, 483.

58. *CD*, April 23, 1848.

59. Andreas, *History of Chicago*, 1:169.

60. Grant, *North Western*, 4–5; T. W. Goodspeed, *Biographical Sketches*, 43–44.

61. Hubbard and Hamilton, *Life of Gurdon Hubbard*, 39–40.

62. Arnold and Scammon, *William B. Ogden*, 22.

63. Einhorn, *Property Rules*, 52–53.

64. Chicago Dept. of Public Works, *Movable Bridges*, 4.

65. Ogden to Arthur Bronson, December 18, 1839, Ogden Papers, box 2.

66. Ahern, *Political History of Chicago*, 102; Chicago Dept. of Public Works, *Movable Bridges*, 5.

67. Arnold and Scammon, *William B. Ogden*, 45; Wheeler, *Ogden Family*, 326.

68. "Sheldon," folder 11, Ogden Papers; Ogden and Jones to Joseph Beer, September 14, 1847, Ogden Papers, folder 6.

69. McCarthy, *Noblesse Oblige*, 58.

70. Cathedral of the Holy Name, *100 Years*.

71. Ibid.

72. Danckers and Meredith, *Early Chicago*, 202, 300; T. W. Goodspeed, *Biographical Sketches*, 43.

73. Condit, *Chicago School of Architecture*, 16–17.

74. Danckers and Meredith, *Early Chicago*, 49, 83.

75. Wheeler, *Ogden Family*, 327; Arnold and Scammon, *William B. Ogden*, 38.

76. Arnold and Scammon, *William B. Ogden*, 38.

77. "Private Gardens of Chicago," *Prairie Farmer*, September 1847, 246–47.

78. Wolner, "City Builder," 15.

7. Harnessing the Iron Horse

1. Reprinted in Marshall, "Early History of Galena," 9–10.

2. Andreas, *History of Chicago*, 1:245–46; Gerstner, *Early American Railroads*, 499.

3. Marshall, "Early History of Galena," 123.

4. Ibid., 10–11.

5. Andreas, *History of Chicago*, 1:245–6

6. Marshall, "Early History of Galena," 23.

7. Ibid., 27, 42.

8. Proof that the meeting described here took place before the Rockford Convention is offered in Marshall's scholarly master's thesis: "A study of the personnel of the Chicago delegation, the active part its members took in the convention, the preparation they had made for their part, and their later activity in reviving the old company is evidence that they had come to Rockford with a definite plan of action." (Marshall, "Early History of Galena," 38–40.)

9. Danckers and Meredith, *Early Chicago*, 191.

10. Ibid., 346.

11. Wendt, *Swift Walker*, 371.

12. Holbrook, *Story of American Railroads*, 133–34.

13. Casey and Douglas, *Pioneer Railroad*, 42.

14. McLear, "Galena and Chicago Union," 21.

15. Arnold and Scammon, *William B. Ogden*, 63–64.

16. Wendt, *Swift Walker*, 405.

17. Lord, *Historical Review of New York*, 36.

18. Stennett, *Yesterday and Today*, 11.

19. Marshall, "Early History of Galena," 38–39.

20. Ibid., 40, 43.

21. Ibid., 31.

22. "Chicago Common Council Proceedings," online, 1847.

23. T. W. Goodspeed, *Biographical Sketches*, 45; B. L. Pierce, *History of Chicago*, 1:283–84.

24. McIlvaine, *Reminiscences of Chicago*, 113–14.

25. Arnold and Scammon, *William B. Ogden*, 67.

26. T. W. Goodspeed, *Jonathan Young Scammon*, 340.

27. *Boston Daily Atlas*, July 10, 1847.

28. Andreas, *History of Chicago*, 1:248.

29. Young, *Iron Horse and Windy City*, 23.

30. Stennett, *Yesterday and Today*, 15.

31. T. W. Goodspeed, *Jonathan Young Scammon*, 341.

32. Marshall, "Early History of Galena," 60–62.

33. Ibid., 62.

34. Arnold and Scammon, *William B. Ogden*, 64.

35. *Prairie Farmer*, "Galena & Chicago Union Railroad" (editorial), September 1847, 269.

36. Moore and Crabb, "Young People's Story," ch. 5.

37. Hansen, *Rivers*, 42.

38. Cromie, *Great Chicago Fire*, 64.

39. T. W. Goodspeed, *Biographical Sketches*, 45; D. L. Miller, *City of the Century*, 93–94.

40. Andreas, *History of Chicago*, 1:247.

41. Musich, "John Van Nortwick," 415.

42. Galena and Chicago Union Railroad Co., "Report of William B. Ogden."

43. Casey and Douglas, *Pioneer Railroad*, 36.

44. Grant, *North Western*, 11.

45. Musich, "John Van Nortwick," 416; Frey, *Railroads in the Nineteenth Century*, 416.

46. Musich, "John Van Nortwick," 390.

47. McLear, "Galena and Chicago Union," 24.

48. Casey and Douglas, *Pioneer Railroad*, 59.

49. Howard, *Great Iron Trail*, 73.

50. Andreas, *History of Chicago*, 1:248.

51. Gale, "Chicago as It Was and Is."

52. McIlvaine, *Reminiscences of Chicago*, 116–17.

53. Grant, *North Western*, 123.

54. Andreas, *History of Chicago*, 1:249.

55. Arnold and Scammon, *William B. Ogden*, 46.

56. Dickens, *American Notes*, 63.

57. Stover, *American Railroads*, 44.

58. Lewis, *John S. Wright*, 116.

59. Casey and Douglas, *Pioneer Railroad*, 51.

60. Wheeler, *Ogden Family*, 200, 111, 326.

61. Downard, "William Butler Ogden," 54.

62. On the board's ouster of Ogden as president and his resultant lawsuit, see Arnold and Scammon, *William B. Ogden*, 20–22.

63. Marshall, "Early History of Galena," 65.

64. Arnold and Scammon, *William B. Ogden*, 21.

65. Andreas, *History of Chicago*, 1:249–51.

66. Downard, "William Butler Ogden," 54.

67. Young, *Iron Horse and Windy City*, 75, 77–78.

68. Andreas, *History of Chicago*, 1:237.

69. Casey and Douglas, *Pioneer Railroad*, 72.

70. Young, *Iron Horse and Windy City*, 110.

8. The First Businessman

1. For background on Robert McCormick and his inventions, see McCormick, *Century of the Reaper*, 14–15.

2. Ibid., 26.

3. Casson, *Cyrus Hall McCormick*, 74.

4. McCormick, *Century of the Reaper*, 28–29; B. L. Pierce, *History of Chicago*, 1:143.

5. D. L. Miller, *City of the Century*, 104.

6. Casson, *Cyrus Hall McCormick*, 75.

7. McCormick, *Century of the Reaper*, 29.

8. Arnold and Scammon, *William B. Ogden*, 46.

9. Poole, *Giants Gone*, 141.

10. Ferris, *Grain Traders*, 9.

11. Peyton, *Over the Alleghanies*, 325–29.

12. B. L. Pierce, *As Others See Chicago*, 99, 106–7.

13. Ibid., 107.

14. Arnold, *Reminiscences of Illinois Bar*, 12.

15. B. L. Pierce, *As Others See Chicago*, 107.

16. Johannsen, *Stephen A. Douglas*, 210–11.

17. Hansen, *Rivers*, 144.

18. See "Chicago Portage Historical Site," http://www. chicagoportage.org/chicago-portage.htm.

19. B. L. Pierce, *As Others See Chicago*, 133, 135–36.

20. Ibid., 136.

21. Boorstin, *Americans*, 115–19.

22. Knox, *History of Banking*, 25.

23. Ibid., 76.

24. Ibid., 719–23.

25. Ibid., 726–88; Schultz, "Businessman's Role," 138.

26. Andreas, *History of Chicago*, 1:549, 2:626.

27. Schultz, "Businessman's Role," 139.

28. T. W. Goodspeed, *Biographical Sketches*, 37.

29. Buettinger, "Economic Equality in Early Chicago," 413–18.

30. Arnold and Scammon, *William B. Ogden*, 46.

31. Stoddard, *Life and Letters*, 286–87.

32. Ibid., 287.

33. Arnold and Scammon, *William B. Ogden*, 49.

34. T. W. Goodspeed, *Biographical Sketches*, 47.

35. Duis, *Challenging Chicago*, 29.

36. *CTR*, March 12, 1854. The unidentified black substance was probably crude oil.

37. Ogden to Scripp & Bross, January 8, 1854, Ogden Papers, box 3.

38. West, "Reminiscences," 7.

39. On the sinking of the *Arctic*, see Othfors, "Arctic, 1850–1854."

40. Mead, journal, January 1, 1854.

41. Carbutt, *Biographical Sketches*, 33; Wheeler, *Ogden Family*, 326.

42. Arnold and Scammon, *William Ogden*, 26

43. B. L. Pierce, *History of Chicago*, 2:183

44. Cromie, *Great Chicago Fire*, 55–57.

45. *CTR*, March 3, 1856.

46. "Committee for Relief of Fugitive Slaves in Canada."

47. Mead, journal, December 1, 1856.

48. Duis, *Challenging Chicago*, 7.

49. B. L. Pierce, *As Others See Chicago*, 148–49.

50. D. L. Miller, *City of the Century*, 122–24.

51. Duis, *Challenging Chicago*, 7–8.

52. Leyendecker, *Palace Car Prince*, 41.

53. Ibid., 26.

54. *CPT*, February 28, 1859.

55. Leyendecker, *Palace Car Prince*, 33–34.

56. Ibid., 28–29.

57. Ibid., 35–36; Cleaver, *Early-Chicago Reminiscences*, 30.

58. Brooks, "Empire City of the West," 341–42.

59. D. L. Miller, *City of the Century*, 128–30.

60. Fehrenbacher, *Chicago Giant*, 212.

61. Merriner, *Grafters and Goo Goos*, 32–33; D. L. Miller, *City of the Century*, 131.

62. *CTR*, June 14, 1874, 4.

63. *CTR*, June 20, 1874, 2.

64. Fehrenbacher, *Chicago Giant*, 213–14.

65. *CTR*, June 20, 1874, 2; December 23, 1877, 4.

66. *CTR*, December 23, 1877, 4.

67. Duis, *Challenging Chicago*, 95; Sawyers, *Chicago Sketches*, 95–96.

68. *CTR*, May 4, 1902.

9. The Best of Everything

1. Robert T. Lincoln, *Report of the Secretary of War on Transcontinental Railways*, 29th Cong., 1st sess., 1883, 260. See Central Pacific Railroad Photographic History Museum, http://www.CPRR.org/museum/secty_war_report_1883pictures/260.html (accessed June 17, 2007).

2. Spearman, *Strategy of Great Railroads*, 196–204; Casey and Douglas, *Pioneer Railroad*, 69–72.

3. Duis, *Challenging Chicago*, 146.

4. Casey and Douglas, *Pioneer Railroad*, 71–82.

5. Galena and Chicago Union Railroad Co., "Report of William B. Ogden, 1848."

6. Flick, *Samuel J. Tilden*, 116; E. P. Alexander, *Pennsylvania Railroad*, 23–24; Arnold and Scammon, *William Ogden*, 53–55.

7. Bigelow, *Letters and Memorials*, 130.

8. T. W. Goodspeed, *Biographical Sketches*, 51.

9. Carbutt, *Biographical Sketches*, 6.

10. *MS*, October 15, 1855.

11. *NYH*, August 30, 1857.

12. Arnold and Scammon, *William Ogden*, 37.

13. T. W. Goodspeed, *Biographical Sketches*, 48–49.

14. Murray, *Centennial History*, 21.

15. Grant, *North Western*, 25–27.

16. Casey and Douglas, *Pioneer Railroad*, 76–81.

17. Ibid., 80; Andreas, *History of Chicago*, 1:257.

18. Casey and Douglas, *Pioneer Railroad*, 81.

19. Arnold and Scammon, *William Ogden*, 30–31.

20. *CJ*, September 22, 1858.

21. Howard, *Great Iron Trail*, 126.

22. Ibid., 127.

23. White, *History of Union Pacific*, 13.

24. McCague, *Moguls and Iron Men*, 62–63.

25. Howard, *Great Iron Trail*, 127–28.

26. Casey and Douglas, *Pioneer Railroad*, 116; Howard, *Great Iron Trail*, 133.

27. McCague, *Moguls and Iron Men*, 65–67.

28. White, *History of Union Pacific*, 18–19.

29. Ambrose, *Nothing Like It*, 83.

30. Casey and Douglas, *Pioneer Railroad*, 16–17.

31. Stennett, *Yesterday and Today*, 59.

32. Downard, "William Butler Ogden," 60.

10. Building an Empire

1. Merriner, *Grafters and Goo Goos*, 25–26; D. L. Miller, *City of the Century*, 136.

2. *CTR*, October 20, 1872, 7.

3. On the Sands, its early troubles, and Ogden's acquisition of it, see *"Johnston v. Jones and Marsh,"* in Stowell et al., *Papers of Lincoln*, vol. 3

4. McIlvaine, introduction to *Reminiscences of Early Chicago*, xx; D. L. Miller, *City of the Century*, 136.

5. *CTR*, July 3, 1865.

6. *CTR*, October 20, 1872, 7.

7. *"Johnston v. Jones and Marsh."*

8. "Chicago Dock and Canal Charter."

9. *"Johnston v. Jones and Marsh"*; Wolper, *Chicago Dock and Canal Trust*, 11, 13.

10. Arnold and Scammon, *William B. Ogden*, 72.

11. Wolner, "City Builder," 15.

12. Andreas, *History of Chicago*, 2:121.

13. Duis, *Challenging Chicago*, 10.

14. Andreas, *History of Chicago*, 2:121.

15. Wheeler, *Ogden Family*, 315.

16. Hilton, *Cable Car in America*, 240.

17. B. L. Pierce, *History of Chicago*, 2:290.

18. *CTR*, July 14, 1864; *CTI*, April 14, 1867.

19. *CTR*, March June 1867; B. L. Pierce, *History of Chicago*, 2:290.

20. Smith, *History of Armstrong County*, 1:569.

21. Ibid., 1:570.

22. Arnold and Scammon, *William B. Ogden*, 55–56.

23. Ibid., 56.

24. R. W. Smith, *History of Armstrong County*, 1:571.

25. Flick, *Samuel J. Tilden*, 509; Schuster, "Cliffs Shaft Mine," 7–8.

26. Bigelow, *Letters and Memorials*, 193.

27. Dobson, *Early History of a Mining Town*, 6–7.

28. Gess and Lutz, *Firestorm at Peshtigo*, 18; Rohe, *Ghosts of the Forest*, 138.

29. Wells, *Fire at Peshtigo*, 1.

30. Gess and Lutz, *Firestorm at Peshtigo*, 11; Burke, *I Lived at Peshtigo Harbor*, 2.

31. Gess and Lutz, *Firestorm at Peshtigo*, 11, 27.

32. Ibid., 8; Holbrook, *Burning an Empire*, 62; Arnold and Scammon, *William B. Ogden*, 55.

33. Burke, *I Lived at Peshtigo Harbor*, 18–20; Stephenson, *Recollections*, 166.

34. Burke, *I Lived at Peshtigo Harbor*, 19–20.

35. Stephenson, *Recollections*, 125.

36. Ibid., 166.

37. Rohe, *Ghosts of the Forest*, 141, 166, 147–51.

38. Burke, *I Lived at Peshtigo Harbor*, 23–25.

39. Ibid., 61; Nesbit, *Wisconsin*, 308.

40. Kraft, "History of Sturgeon Bay Canal," 1.

41. Ibid.; "Sturgeon Bay and Lake Michigan Ship Canal," 2.

42. *Proposed Ship Canal at Sturgeon Bay.*

43. Kraft, "History of Sturgeon Bay Canal," 1.

44. "Sturgeon Bay and Lake Michigan Ship Canal," 2.

45. Kraft, "History of Sturgeon Bay Canal," 4–5.

46. Wheeler, *Ogden Family*, 422.

47. *GBA*, November 11, 1858.

11. An Overgrown Gawk of a Village

1. Fernon, "Report to J. Edgar Thompson," 14.

2. Steffens, *Shame of the Cities*, 234.

3. Kirkland, "Among the Poor," 14.

4. Ibid., 8.

5. Ibid., 18.

6. Angle, *Chicago Historical Society*, 15.

7. Ibid., 15–16.

8. Ibid., 17–18.

9. Arnold and Scammon, *William B. Ogden*, 60.

10. Angle, *Chicago Historical Society*, 24.

11. Arnold and Scammon, *William B. Ogden*, 60; Andreas, *History of Chicago*, 2:410–11.

12. On the Chicago Historical Society's opening, see Angle, *Chicago Historical Society*, 43–47, 49–50.

13. Hurlbutt, *Chicago Antiquities*, 48.

14. Ibid.; Andreas, *History of Chicago*, 1:220; T. W. Goodspeed, *Biographical Sketches*, 52.

15. Schultz, *Church and the City*, 22, 26.

16. McCarthy, *Noblesse Oblige*, 58; Arnold and Scammon, *William B. Ogden*, 24.

17. Schultz, *Church and the City*, 50–52.

18. Abbott, *Boosters and Businessmen*, 139.

19. Fehrenbacher, *Chicago Giant*, 260n.

20. Merriner, *Grafters and Goo Goos*, 25.

21. Poole, *Giants Gone*, 37–38.

22. Lincoln to Nicolay, November 3, 1860, Abraham Lincoln Papers, Library of Congress.

23. Arnold and Scammon, *William B. Ogden*, 31.

24. For Lincoln's stand on colonization, see Klingaman, *Abraham Lincoln*; Blackett, "Lincoln and Colonization," 19–22; and Lincoln Institute, "Mr. Lincoln and Freedom," http://www.mrlincolnandfreedom.org.

25. T. W. Goodspeed, *Biographical Sketches*, 52; B. L. Pierce, *History of Chicago*, 1:244–45.

26. Arnold and Scammon, *William B. Ogden*, 31.

27. *CTR*, April 23, 1861.

28. Andreas, *History of Chicago*, 2:622–23.

29. T. W. Goodspeed, *Biographical Sketches*, 51.

30. Neely, *Union Divided*, 39.

31. Biles, *Illinois*, 111.

32. Bigelow, *Letters and Memorials*, 147–48.

33. *CTR*, January 10, 1861.

34. T. W. Goodspeed, *Biographical Sketches*, 51.

35. Glendinning, *Chicago and Alton Railroad*, 7, 12–14.

36. Ibid., 202.

37. Neely, *Union Divided*, 40.

38. Biles, *Illinois*, 112–13.

39. *CTR*, January 17, 1863.

40. *CTR*, January 23, 1863.

41. *CTR*, January 17, 1863.

42. Neely, *Union Divided*, 44.

43. *CTR*, February 6 and 7, 1863.

44. *CTR*, February 7, 1863.

45. *CTR*, February 11 and 12, June 5, 1863.

46. Biles, *Illinois*, 113.

47. Hicken, *Illinois in the Civil War*, viii, 166.

48. Brooks, "Empire City of the West," 348.

49. Sandburg, *Abraham Lincoln: The Prairie Years*, 630.

50. Schultz, *Church and the City*, 60–61.

51. D. L. Miller, *City of the Century*, 58–59.

52. Young, *Iron Horse and Windy City*, 110.

53. Poole, *Giants Gone*, 133–34.

54. D. L. Miller, *City of the Century*, 218.

55. Wheeler, *Ogden Family*, 442.

56. Andreas, *History of Chicago*, 3:390.

57. Flint, *Railroads of the United States*, 264.

58. Wheeler, *Ogden Family*, 155, 277.

59. Ibid., 208.

60. Ibid.

61. Ibid., 323.

62 Ibid.

63. Stoddard, *Life and Letters*, 346.

64. Ibid., 344–45.

65. *NYDT*, December 14, 1897.

66. West, "Reminiscences," 1.

67. Ibid., 3.

12. The Minnow Swallows the Whale

1. Harpster, *John Ogden*, 81–95.

2. Marshall, *Early History of Galena*, 65–6; Grant, *North Western*, 28–29; Casey and Douglas, *Pioneer Railroad*, 121–23.

3. Details of Ogden's merger plans are taken from the plaintiffs' arguments made in Anthony's "Treatise on Consolidation," so they present a one-sided view. However, what few facts are known support these allegations as to how the scheme was carried out.

4. *CTR*, June 4, 1864, 4.

5. "Circular to Stockholders," 3.

6. Stennett, *Yesterday and Today*, 46.

7. Fehrenbacher, *Chicago Giant*, 215–16.

8. Anthony, "Treatise on Consolidation."

9. *CTR*, January 15, 1865.

10. *NYT*, January 25, 1865.

11. *CTR*, February 12, 1865.

12. *CR*, July 9, 1865.

13.Ibid.

14. Stennett, *Yesterday and Today*, 23.

15. Buckman, *Samuel J. Tilden*, 8. Tilden's involvement with the Peninsula Railroad merger is just one of many perfidies he is accused of being involved with in a small, testy booklet called *Samuel J. Tilden Unmasked!* The self-published book, written in 1876 by New York City policeman Benjamin Buckman, claimed Tilden had wronged him in another stock deal. There are probably many truths in his story, but they are obfuscated by the author's angry, vindictive prose, making it impossible to tell fact from fiction.

16. Parton, *Manual*, 19.

17. Ibid., 17.

18. Downard, "William Butler Ogden," 57–58.

19. Ibid., 59–60.

20. Holbrook, *Story of American Railroads*, 154.

21. Ibid.

22. Henry, *Fascinating Railroad Business*, 340.

23. Stennett, *Yesterday and Today*, 70–71.

24. Ibid., 71.

25. Ibid., 70.

26. Young, *Iron Horse and Windy City*, 29.

27. For details of the growing labor problems for railroads, see B. L. Pierce, *History of Chicago*, 2:151–79.

28. A few historical references say Ogden was forced out of the C&NW by Wall Street moneyman Henry Keep, who had accumulated a large financial position in the railroad. Keep did follow Ogden as president for about a year before he died, but it's unlikely he engineered Ogden's departure.

29. Wheeler, *Ogden Family*, 204.

30. Frey, *Railroads in the Nineteenth Century*, 293.

31. Stennett, *Yesterday and Today*, 153.

32. Grant, preface, *North Western*.

33. Mercer, *Railroads and Land Grant*, 52–53; Jensen and Draffan, *Railroads, Clearcuts*, 3; Smalley, *History of Northern Pacific*, 116–18.

34. Smalley, *History of Northern Pacific*, 116–18.

35. Ibid., 134.

36. Ibid., 141–42.

37. Ibid., 143.

38. For information on Canfield's visit to Ogden, see ibid., 142; Renz, *History of Northern Pacific*, 24.

39. Smalley, *History of Northern Pacific*, 142–43.

40. *NYT* , May 17, 1867.

41. Smalley, *History of Northern Pacific*,143–45.

42. Lewty, *To the Columbia Gateway*, 5; Frey, *Railroads in the Nineteenth Century*, Introduction, xx.

43. *WSR*, May 29, 1869, in Gale Cengage Learning, "19th Century U.S. Newspapers."

44. Mickelson, *Northern Pacific Railroad*, 1.

45. Smalley, *History of Northern Pacific*, 171.

46. Mickelson, *Northern Pacific Railroad*, 16–23.

47. Smalley, *History of Northern Pacific*, 187–88.

48. *CIO*, September 12, 1877; Lubetkin, *Jay Cook's Gamble*, 58.

49. "Last Will and Testament."

50. Oberholtzer, *Jay Cooke*, 2:244.

51. Lubetkin, *Jay Cooke's Gamble*, 64.

52. Smalley, *History of Northern Pacific* 183; Lewty, *To the Columbia Gateway*, 8.

53. Lewty, *To the Columbia Gateway*, 13.

54. Rusling, *Great West and Pacific Coast*, 252.

55. *SFB*, December 11, 1871, in Gale Cengage Learning, "19th Century U.S. Newspapers."

56. Rusling, *Great West and Pacific Coast*, 193–94.

57. *SFB*, August 22, 1873, in Gale Cengage Learning, "19th Century U.S. Newspapers."

58. Ibid., 196; Frey, introduction, *Railroads in the Nineteenth Century*, xxi.

59. Smalley, *History of Northern Pacific*, 197; Lewty, *To the Columbia Gateway*, 14.

60. *NYT*, March 15, 1873.

61. *NYT*, May 14, 1875.

62. Oberholtzer, *Jay Cooke*, 2:244.

63. Mickelson, *Northern Pacific Railroad*, 126.

64. Berton, *Great Railway*, 60–62.

65. Ibid., 62–63.

66. Irwin, *Pacific Railways and Nationalism*, 164–65.

67. Stephenson, *Recollections*, 163.

68. Holbrook, *Story of American Railroads*, 133.

69. Ibid.

13. The Gates of Hell

1. Gess and Lutz, *Firestorm at Peshtigo*, 19.

2. A wealthy man, Tilden gained his greatest fame in the presidential election of 1876, the most controversial American election in the nineteenth century. Running for the nation's top office as a Democrat, Tilden won the popular vote over his Republican opponent Rutherford B. Hayes. But the results of the Electoral College vote were tainted when three states sent two sets of electoral votes to Congress, rather than the one set they were entitled to. A constitutional crisis appeared eminent. Congress appointed a fifteen-member Electoral Commission to decide the matter, composed of eight Republicans and seven Democrats. When all the members voted along party lines, Hayes won the election by one electoral vote.

3. Wheeler, *Ogden Family*, 208.

4. *CTR*, August 4, 1877.

5. West, "Reminiscences."

6. Wheeler, *Ogden Family*, 208.

7. Brennan, "Beach Pneumatic," ch. 7.

8. Ibid., ch.1.

9. *NYT*, April 18, 1868.

10. Brennan, "Beach Pneumatic," ch. 7; *NYT* , March 12, 1870.

11. *NYT*, December 29, 1877.

12. Brennan, "Beach Pneumatic," ch. 7.

13. Ibid.

14. *CTR*, November 22, 1874, 10.

15. For the story of Ogden and the Hildebrand family, see *CIO*, November 9, 1876; *CTR*, November 10, 1876; *BE*, January 15, 1874, and February 22, 1875.

16. Gess and Lutz, *Firestorm at Peshtigo*, 27.

17. Ibid., 28; Wells, *Fire at Peshtigo*, 7.

18. E. J. Goodspeed, *History of the Great Fires*.

19. Arnold and Scammon, *William Ogden*, 32.

20. Ibid.

21. All of Ogden's personal recollections of the Chicago fire are from Ogden to Charles Butler, October 11, 1871, Ogden Papers, box 1, Chicago Historical Society.

22. Cromie, *Great Chicago Fire*, 102.

23. *CTR*, October 11, 1871, 1.

24. Ibid.

25. Arnold and Scammon, *William B. Ogden*, 33.

26. *CTR*, October 11, 1871, 1.

27. *NYT*, October 15, 1871, 1.

28. Ibid.

29. Colbert and Chamberlain, *Chicago and the Great Conflagration*, 256.

30. Angle, *Chicago Historical Society*, 63–70.

31. For the account of the escape from the fire by Arnold and his family, see Colbert and Chamberlain, *Chicago and the Great Conflagration*, 256–61.

32. See the two accounts of the Historical Society's burning, in Angle, *Chicago Historical Society*, 68–74; and Arnold and Scammon, *William B. Ogden*, 33.

33. West, "Reminiscences," 4.

34. *CTR*, October 11, 1871, 1; Colbert and Chamberlain, *Chicago and the Great Conflagration*, 174–76.

35. Chamberlain, *Chicago and the Great Conflagration* 42–43; Casey and Douglas, *Pioneer Railroad*, 131–32.

36. *CTR*, October 11, 1871, 1

37. *NYT*, October 11, 1871.

38. Andreas, *History of Chicago*, 3:164.

39. Ibid.

40. More than 130 years after the Great Chicago Fire, the most definitive book yet written about the cause of the conflagration was published, Richard Bales's *The Great Chicago Fire and the Myth of Mrs. O'Leary's Cow*. Bales's conclusion is that while the fire did start in the O'Leary barn, neither Mrs. O'Leary nor her unfortunate cow started it. It was likely started accidentally by two neighbors who had stopped in her barn for a rest.

41. Ogden to Charles Butler, October 11, 1871, Ogden Papers, box 1.

42. *NYT*, October 11, 1871. There is much more to tell about this cataclysmic event, certainly one of the most devastating urban catastrophes in modern times; but it is not within the scope of this biography of William Butler Ogden to tackle the immense detail or the indescribable suffering of the Great Chicago Fire, except as it affected the lives of the Ogdens and those closest to them. However, dozens of excellent books have been written about the tragic event. One of this author's favorite contemporaneous accounts of the fire is Sheahan and Upton, *The Great Conflagration: Chicago, Its Past, Present, and Future* (1871).

Written by two *Chicago Tribune* editors, it contains very detailed information about the extent of the damages suffered, and it's full of great stories of loss and survival. It may be difficult to locate, but it is worth the effort to any student of Chicago history.

43. Gess and Lutz, *Firestorm at Peshtigo*, 32.
44. Pernin, *Great Peshtigo Fire*.
45. Ibid.
46. Stephenson, *Recollections*, 182.
47. Ogden to Charles Butler, October 11, 1871, Ogden Papers, box 1.
48. Arnold and Scammon, *William B. Ogden*, 35.
49. Gess and Lutz, *Firestorm at Peshtigo*, 188.
50. Stephenson, *Recollections*, 183.
51. Wells, *Fire at Peshtigo*, 225–26.
52. Ibid., 195.
53. Stephenson, *Recollections*, 174.
54. Ibid., 185.
55. Holbrook, *Burning an Empire*, 70–71.
56. "Last Will and Testament."
57. Wheeler, *Ogden Family*, 422; Rohe, *Ghosts of the Forest*, 171.
58. *NYT*, October 15, 1871.
59. McClear, "William Butler Ogden," 291.
60. Arnold and Scammon, *William B. Ogden*, 53.
61. *NYT*, August 7, 1877, 5.
62. Stephenson, *Recollections*, 175.
63. Wheeler, *Ogden Family*, 324.
64. Andreas, *History of Chicago*, 1:442.

14. Out of the Ashes

1. *CTR*, October 27, 1872.
2. "Chicago Common Council Proceedings," December 4, 1871.
3. Condit, *Chicago School of Architecture*, 7.
4. *NYT*, October 11, 1871.
5. Ibid., 11.
6. Lowe, *Lost Chicago*, 18.
7. Condit, *Chicago School of Architecture*, 175.
8. Ibid., 20.
9. Ibid., 23.
10. Ibid.
11. Ibid., 12.
12. West, "Reminiscences."
13. R. Miller, *Great Chicago Fire*, 83.
14. *CTR*, October 27, 1872.
15. Arnold and Scammon, *William B. Ogden*, 59.
16. West, "Reminiscences."
17. Chicago Historical Society, *Brief History*, 29.
18. Letter in the author's possession from the curator of the Peshtigo Historical Society, quoting from the diary of an unnamed railroad man.
19. Leschak, *Ghosts of the Fireground*, 263.

20. Ibid., 264.

21. *CTR*, February 12, 1867, 2, and February 15, 1867, 1.

22. *CTR,,* September 8, 1872.

23. Ogden to Charles Butler, October 11, 1871, Ogden Papers, box 1, Chicago Historical Society.

24. See Wolper, *Chicago Dock and Canal Trust.*

25. Ibid.; *Cyber Drive Illinois.*

26. Email from Charles Gardner, president and CEO of Chicago Dock and Canal Trust (retired), to author, November 28, 2005.

27. Raitt, *Ruts in the Road*, 107.

28. *CTR*, October 11, 1874.

29. Arnold and Scammon, *William B. Ogden*, 31–32.

30. *CTR*, February 10, 1875.

31. *CTR*, August 4, 1877.

32. Stoddard, *Lives and Letters*, 345–46.

33. Ibid., 91.

34. *CTR*, August 4, 1877.

35. Wheeler, *Ogden Family*, 319.

36. Ibid., 202.

15. A Whole-Souled Man

1. *CIO*, August 4, 1877, 2.

2. Certificate of Death, Wm. B. Ogden, Health Department of the City of New York, New York City Municipal Archives, New York, N.Y.

3. *NYT*, August 7, 1877.

4. Ibid.

5. Ibid.

6. *CTR*, August 4, 1877.

7. *CIO*, August 4, 1877, 2.

8. *NYT*, August 4, 1877.

9. "Last Will and Testament ."

10. *CIO*, September 12, 1877.

11. *CTR*, August 4, 1877.

12. "Last Will and Testament."

13. T. W. Goodspeed, *History of University of Chicago*, 173.

14. Ibid., 174.

15. Ibid.

16. *NYT*, November 26, 1891.

17. Arnold and Scammon, *William B. Ogden*, 62.

18. *NYT*, November 26, 1891.

19. "Last Will and Testament."

20. Ibid.

21. McNamara, *History in Asphalt*, 173.

22. Ibid.; *NYT*, October 7, 1904, 7.

23. Arnold and Scammon, *William B. Ogden*, 3.

24. Lane, *Story of Walton*, 208.

25. Ibid., 209.

BIBLIOGRAPHY

Archives and Depositories

Armstrong County Historical Society. Kittanning, Pa.
Central Pacific Railroad Photographic History Museum. http://www.CPRR.org/
    museum.
Chicago History Museum. Chicago, Ill.
Chicago Portage National Historic Site. http://www.chicagoportage.org.
Chicago Public Library. Chicago, Ill.
Delaware County Clerk's Office. Delhi, N.Y.
Delaware County, New York, Genealogy and History Site. http://www.dcnyhistory.org.
Historical Newspapers Database, Pro Quest Information and Learning Co. http://
    www.proquest.com.
Illinois Institute of Technology, Paul V. Galvin Library. Chicago, Ill.
Illinois Regional Archives Depository, Northeastern Illinois University. http://www.
    cyberdriveillinois.com.departments/archives/archives.html.
Library of Congress. Washington, D.C.
Newberry Library. Chicago, Ill.
New York State Historical Association Library. Cooperstown, N.Y.
Rock County Historical Society. Janesville, Wisc.
Walton Historical Society. Walton, N.Y.
William B. Ogden Free Library. Walton, N.Y.
Wisconsin Historical Society. Madison, Wisc.

Newspapers

Albany (N.Y.) Argus
Brooklyn (N.Y.) Eagle
Chicago American
Chicago Democrat
Chicago Democratic Press
Chicago Inter Ocean
Chicago Journal
Chicago Press-Tribune
Chicago Republican
Chicago Times
Chicago Tribune
Delaware County (N.Y.) Gazette
Door County (Wisc.) Advocate
Green Bay (Wisc.) Advocate
Milwaukee Daily Sentinel
New-York Daily Tribune
New York Herald
New York Times

Oneonta (N.Y.) Daily Star
San Francisco Daily Evening Bulletin
Wisconsin State Register (Madison)

Books, Articles, Papers, and Dissertations

Abbott, Carl. *Boosters and Businessmen: Popular Economic Thought and Urban Growth in the Antebellum Middle West.* Contributions in American Studies, no. 53. Westport, Conn.: Greenwood, 1981.

Ahern, M. L. *The Political History of Chicago, 1837–1887.* Chicago: Donohue & Henneberry, 1886.

Alexander, Edwin P. *The Pennsylvania Railroad: A Pictorial History.* New York: Bonanza, 1947.

Alexander, Holmes. *The American Talleyrand: The Career and Contemporaries of Martin Van Buren, Eighth President.* New York: Russell & Russell, 1935.

Ambrose, Stephen E. *Nothing Like It in the World: The Men Who Built the Transcontinental Railroad, 1863–1869.* New York: Simon & Schuster, 2000.

Andreas, A. T. *History of Chicago: From the Earliest Period to the Present Time.* 3 vols. Chicago: A. T. Andreas, 1884–86.

Angle, Paul M. *The Chicago Historical Society, 1856–1956: An Unconventional Chronicle.* New York: Rand McNally, 1956.

Anthony, Elliott. *A Treatise on the Law of Consolidation of Railroad Companies: Being an Argument in the Case of Julius Wadsworth of New York et al., versus Chicago & Northwestern Railway Company, William B. Ogden et al., in the United States Circuit Court for the Northern District of Illinois.* Chicago: Beach and Barnard, 1865.

Arnold, Isaac Newton. *Reminiscences of the Illinois Bar Forty Years Ago.* Springfield: Illinois State Bar Association, 1881.

Arnold, Isaac N., and J. Young Scammon. *William B. Ogden; and Early Days in Chicago.* Chicago: Fergus, 1882.

Arrington, Leonard J. "The Transcontinental Railroad and the Development of the West." *Utah Historical Quarterly,* Winter 1969.

Baird, Elizabeth T. "Life in Territorial Wisconsin, 1824–1842." *Historical Society of Wisconsin,* vol. 15, edited by Reuben Thwaites. Madison: Democrat Printing, 1900.

Bakeless, John. *Eyes of Discovery: The Pageant of North America as Seen by the First Explorers.* New York: Lippincott, 1950. Reprint, Mineola, N.Y.: Dover, 1961.

Bales, Richard F. *The Great Chicago Fire and the Myth of Mrs. O'Leary's Cow.* Jefferson, N.C.: McFarland, 2002.

Balestier, Joseph N. *The Annals of Chicago: A Lecture Delivered before the Chicago Lyceum, January 21, 1840.* Chicago: Fergus, 1876.

Beckwith, H. W. *Illinois and Indiana Indians.* 1884. Reprint, New York: Arno, 1975.

Bellow, Adam. *In Praise of Nepotism: A Natural History.* New York: Doubleday, 2003.

Bennett, Beatrice. *Old Golden Rule Days: One-Room Schoolhouses, Their History, Town of Walton, New York.* Walton, N.Y.: Walton Historical Society, n.d.

Berton, Pierre. *The Great Railway, 1871–1881: The National Dream.* Toronto: McClelland & Stewart, 1970.

Bigelow, John, ed. *Letters and Literary Memorials of Samuel J. Tilden.* New York: Harper & Brothers, 1908.

Biles, Roger. *Illinois: A History of the Land and Its People*. DeKalb: Northern Illinois University Press, 2005.

Biographical Review: The Leading Citizens of Delaware County, New York. Boston: Biographical Publishing, 1895. Online version at Delaware County, N.Y., Genealogy and History Site, http://www.dcnyhistory.org/bioindex.html.

Blackett, Richard. "Lincoln and Colonization." Organization of American Historians, *Magazine of History* 21, no. 4 (2007).

Book A of Deeds. June 24, 1797–June 6, 1804. Delaware County Clerk's Office, Delhi, N.Y.

Book B of Deeds. June 6, 1804–July 9, 1809. Delaware County Clerk's Office, Delhi, N.Y.

Book of the Fair (World's Columbian Exposition of 1893). Digital History Collection, Paul V. Galvin Library, Illinois Institute of Technology. http://www.Columbus.Gl.iit.edu/bookfair/ch2.html.

Boorstin, Daniel. *The Americans: The National Experience*. New York: Random House, 1965.

Bowen, Fred Q. *10,000 Vital Records of Western New York*. Baltimore: Genealogical Publishing, 1986.

Bragdon, Kathleen J. *The Columbia Guide to America Indians of the Northeast*. New York: Columbia University Press, 2001.

Brennan, Joseph. "Beach Pneumatic: Alfred Beach's Pneumatic Subway and the Beginning of Rapid Transit in New York." http://www.columbia.edu/~brennan/beach (accessed August 5, 2005).

Brief History of the William B. Ogden Free Library, 1899–1979. Walton, N.Y.: William B. Ogden Free Library, 1979.

Brooks, Noah. "The Empire City of the West: View of Chicago in 1864." *Journal of the Illinois State Historical Society* 56, no. 2 (Summer 1963).

Brown, Henry. *The Present and Future Prospects of Chicago*. Chicago: Fergus, 1876.

Buckman, Benjamin. *Samuel J. Tilden Unmasked!* New York: Self-published, 1876.

Buettinger, Carl. "Economic Equality in Early Chicago, 1849–1850." *Journal of Social History* 11, no. 3 (Spring 1978).

Burke, F. C. *I Lived at Peshtigo Harbor*. Peshtigo, Wisc.: *Peshtigo Times*, 1971.

Butler, Charles. Family File. Walton Historical Society, Walton, N.Y.

———. Papers, 1819–1929. Microfilm no.16,610. Library of Congress, Washington, D.C.

———. Talk before Chicago Historical Society, December 17, 1881. William B. Ogden Papers, Box 1, Folder 12. Chicago History Museum, Chicago, Ill.

Cahill, Marie, and Lynne Piade, eds. *History of the Union Pacific, America's Great Transcontinental Railroad*. New York: Crescent, 1989.

Carbutt, John. *Biographical Sketches of the Leading Men of Chicago*. Chicago: Wilson, Pierce, 1876.

Casey, Robert J., and W. A. S. Douglas. *Pioneer Railroad: The Story of the Chicago and North Western System*. New York: McGraw-Hill, 1948.

Casson, Herbert Newton. *Cyrus Hall McCormick: His Life and Work*. Chicago: A. C. McClurg, 1909.

Cathedral of the Holy Name. *100 Years: The History of the Church of the Holy Name, the Chapel That Became a Cathedral, and the Story of Catholicism in Chicago*. Chicago: Cathedral of the Holy Name, 1949.

"Chicago Common Council Proceedings." Illinois Regional Archives Depository, Northeastern Illinois University. http://www.cyberdriveillinois.com.departments/ archives/chicago_proceedings/proceedings_intro.html.

Chicago Department of Public Works. *The Movable Bridges of Chicago: A Brief History.* Chicago: Department of Public Works, Bureau of Engineering, 1983.

Chicago Dock and Canal Company Charter, February 12, 1857. Special Collections, Chicago Public Library, Chicago, Ill.

Chicago Historical Society. *A Brief History of the Chicago Historical Society: Together with Constitution and By-Laws, and List of Officers and Members.* Chicago: Fergus, 1881.

"Circular to Stockholders of the Chicago & North-Western R'y Company." June 20, 1864. Special Collections, Chicago Public Library, Chicago, Ill.

Cleaver, Charles. *Early-Chicago Reminiscences.* Fergus Historical Series, no. 19. Chicago: Fergus, 1882. Originally printed in the *Chicago Tribune.*

Colbert, Elias, and Everett Chamberlin. *Chicago and the Great Conflagration.* 1871. Reprint, New York: Viking, 1971.

"Committee for Relief of Fugitive Slaves in Canada." November 11–December 7, 1850. Zebina Eastman Papers, Chicago History Museum, Chicago, Ill.

Condit, Carl W. *The Chicago School of Architecture: A History of Commercial and Public Building in the Chicago Area, 1875–1925.* Chicago: University of Chicago Press, 1964.

Cooke, Jay, and Company. *The Northern Pacific Railroad Company: Its Land Grant, Resources, Traffic, and Tributary Country* (prospectus). Philadelphia, 1871.

Cromie, Robert. *The Great Chicago Fire.* Nashville, Tenn.: Rutledge Hill, 1958.

———. *A Short History of Chicago.* San Francisco: Lexikos, 1984.

Cronon, William. *Nature's Metropolis: Chicago and the Great West.* New York: W. W. Norton, 1991.

Cutler, Irving. *Chicago: Metropolis of the Mid-Continent.* 1973. 4th ed. Carbondale: Southern Illinois University Press, 2006.

Cyber Drive Illinois, Online Corporate Database, Illinois Secretary of State's Office. http://www.cyberdriveillinois.com.

Danckers, Ulrich, and Jane Meredith. *A Compendium of the Early History of Chicago to the Year 1835 When the Indians Left.* Chicago: Early Chicago, 1999.

DAR Patriot Index. Vol. 2: G–O. National Society, Daughters of the American Revolution. Baltimore: Gateway, 2003.

"Declaration of Trust, William B. Ogden to Sarah North and Others." 1860. Copy in the possession of the author.

Delaware County Statistics Extracted from Federal and State Census Records (1790–1845). Delaware County Clerk's Office, Delhi, N.Y.

Denton, Daniel. *A Brief Description of New-York.* London, 1670. Reprint, New York: Westvaco, 1973.

Dickens, Charles. *American Notes: A Journey.* Reprint, New York: Fromm, 1985.

Dobson, Robert D. *The Early History of a Mining Town: Ishpeming, Michigan, 1852–1920.* Negaunee, Mich.: Dobson, 2005.

Door County Advocate. "Sturgeon Bay and Lake Michigan Ship Canal, and Harbor of Refuge." Sturgeon Bay, Wisc., n.d. Wisconsin Historical Society, Madison, Wisc.

Downard, William L. "William Butler Ogden and the Growth of Chicago." *Journal of the Illinois State Historical Society* 75, no. 1 (Spring 1982).

Dufwa, Thamar Emelia. *Transcontinental Railroad Legislation, 1835–1862.* Arno Press Collection, the Railroads. New York: Arno, 1981.

Duis, Perry R. *Challenging Chicago: Coping with Everyday Life, 1837–1920.* Urbana: University of Illinois Press, 1998.

Eastman, Zebina, ed. *"Chicago Magazine: The West as It Is, Illustrated."* Chicago: Chicago Mechanics Institute, 1857.

Eckert, Allan W. *Gateway to Empire: The Winning of America Series.* New York: Little, Brown, 1983.

Einhorn, Robin L. *Property Rules: Political Economy in Chicago, 1833–1872.* Chicago: University of Chicago Press, 1991.

Fehrenbacher, Don Edward. *Chicago Giant: A Biography of "Long John" Wentworth.* Madison, Wisc.: American History Research Center, 1957.

Fernon, Thomas Sargent. "A Report to J. Edgar Thompson, President, Pennsylvania Railroad Co., Submitting Results of Observations Concerning the Tendencies of Trade toward the Seaboard through the West, Near the Ohio River." Philadelphia, 1859. American Cultural Series, microfilm reel 378. Ann Arbor: University of Michigan Microfilms, n.d.

Ferris, William G. *The Grain Traders: The Story of the Chicago Board of Trade.* East Lansing: Michigan State University Press, 1988.

Flick, Alexander. *Samuel J. Tilden: A Study in Political Sagacity.* New York: Dodd, Mead, 1939.

Flint, Henry M. *Railroads of the United States: Their History and Statistics.* Philadelphia: John Potter, 1868.

Fogel, Robert William. *The Union Pacific Railroad: A Case in Premature Enterprise.* Baltimore: Johns Hopkins University Press, 1960.

Frey, Robert L., ed. *Railroads in the Nineteenth Century.* New York: Facts on File, 1988.

Gale, Edwin O. "Chicago as It Was and Is." Address before the Illinois State Historical Society, January 31, 1908. Springfield: *Illinois State Journal,* 1909.

Gale Cengage Learning. "Nineteenth Century U.S. Newspapers." Digital collection. http://www.gale.cengage.com. Farmington Hills, Mich.

Galena and Chicago Union Railroad Company. *Ninth Annual Report to Stockholders.* June 4, 1856. Chicago History Museum, Chicago, Ill.

———. "Report of William B. Ogden, Esq., President of the Company, together with Reports of the Engineer, Secretary and Treasurer." Read at the annual meeting of stockholders, April 5, 1848. Newberry Library, Chicago, Ill.

Gates, Paul Wallace. *History of Public Land Law Development.* U.S. Public Land Law Review Commission. Washington: U.S. Government Printing Office, 1968.

Gemming, Elizabeth. *Wool Gathering: Sheep Raising in Old New England.* New York: Coward, McCann & Geoghegan, n.d. (1979?).

Gerstner, Franz Anton Ritter von. *Early American Railroads.* 1842–43. Translated by David Diephouse and John Decker. Palo Alto: Stanford University Press, 1997.

Gerwing, Anselm J. "The Chicago Indian Treaty of 1833." *Journal of the Illinois State Historical Society* 57, no. 2 (Summer 1964).

Gess, Denise, and William Lutz. *Firestorm at Peshtigo: A Town, Its People, and the Deadliest Fire in American History.* New York: Henry Holt, 2002.

Glendinning, Gene V. *The Chicago and Alton Railroad.* DeKalb: Northern Illinois University Press, 2002.

Goodspeed, E. J. *History of the Great Fires in Chicago and the West.* New York: H. S. Goodspeed, 1871.

Goodspeed, Thomas Wakefield. *A History of the University of Chicago: The First Quarter-Century.* Chicago: University of Chicago Press, 1916.

———. *Jonathan Young Scammon.* Chicago: Privately printed, 1923.

———. *The University of Chicago Biographical Sketches.* Chicago: University of Chicago Press, 1922.

Gould, Jay. *History of Delaware County and Border Wars of New York: Containing A Sketch of the Early Settlements in the County and a History of the Late Anti-Rent Difficulties in Delaware, with other Historical and Miscellaneous Matters, Never Before Published.* Roxbury, N.Y.: Keeny & Gould, 1856. Delaware County, N.Y., . Genealogy and History Site, http://www.dcnyhistory.org/goulds.html.

Grant, H. Roger. *The North Western: A History of the Chicago & North Western Railway System.* DeKalb: Northern Illinois University Press, 1996.

———. "William Butler Ogden." In *Encyclopedia of American Business History and Biography: Railroads in the Nineteenth Century,* edited by Robert L. Frey. New York: Facts on File, 1988.

"The Great Chicago Fire and the Web of Memory." Chicago Historical Society and Trustees of Northwestern University, http://www.chicagohs.org/fire/intro.

"The Great Fire of 1871." *Green Bay (Wisc.) Advocate.* Chicagology.com, http://www.chicagology.com/chgofire.htm.

Guernsey, Orrin, and Josiah Willard, eds. *History of Rock County and Transactions of the Rock County Agricultural Society and Mechanics Institute.* Janesville, Wisc.: The Society and the Institute, 1856.

Haeger, John Denis. *The Investment Frontier: New York Businessmen and the Economic Development of the Old Northwest.* Albany: State University of New York Press, 1981.

Halvorsen, Ralph H. "The Newberrys" (draft). 1990. 3 vols. Special Collections Reference, Newberry Library, Chicago, Ill.

Hansen, Harry. *Rivers of America: The Chicago.* New York: Rinehart, 1942.

Harpster, Jack. *John Ogden, the Pilgrim (1609–1682): A Man of More than Ordinary Mark.* Cranbury, N.J.: Fairleigh Dickinson University Press, 2006.

Haven, Janet. *Inland Navigation: Connecting the New Republic, 1790–1840.* American Studies at the University of Virginia, *Tocqueville's America* website, http://www.xroads.Virginia.edu/~hyper/detoc/transport/front.html.

Heath, Kingston. "Cast-Iron Fronts in Chicago: Case Study." M.A. thesis, University of Chicago, 1975.

Henry, Robert Selph. *This Fascinating Railroad Business.* Indianapolis: Bobbs–Merrill, 1942.

Hicken, Victor. *Illinois in the Civil War.* Urbana: University of Illinois Press, 1966.

Hilton, George. *Cable Car in America: A New Treatise upon Cable or Rope Traction as Applied to the Working of Street and Other Railways.* Berkeley: Howell-North, 1971.

History of the City of Chicago, Its Men and Institutions and Biographical Sketches of Leading Citizens. Chicago: Inter Ocean, 1900.

Hobbie, Selah R. "Address Delivered at the Funeral of Mr. Cyrus North, in Walton, on the 24th of August, 1825." Cyrus North Family Papers, Walton Historical Society, Walton, N.Y..

Holbrook, Stewart H. *The Age of the Moguls.* Garden City, N.Y.: Doubleday, 1953.

———. *Burning an Empire: The Story of American Forest Fires.* New York: Macmillan, 1952.

———. *The Story of American Railroads.* New York: Crown, 1947.

Holland, William M. *The Life and Political Opinions of Martin Van Buren.* New York: Hartford, Belknap & Hamersley, 1835.

"Homespun to Factory Made: Woolen Textiles in America, 1776–1876." North Andover, Mass.: Merrimack Valley Textile Museum, c. 1997.

Howard, Robert West. *The Great Iron Trail: The Story of the First Transcontinental Railroad.* New York: Putnam's Sons, 1962.

Hoyt, Homer. *One Hundred Years of Land Values in Chicago.* Chicago: University of Chicago Press, 1933. Reprint, New York: Arno, 1970.

Hubbard, Gurdon Saltonstall, and Henry Hamilton. *Incidents and Events in the Life of Gurdon Saltonstall Hubbard.* Chicago: Rand McNally, 1888.

Hungerford, Edward. *Men of Erie: A Story of Human Effort.* New York: Random House, 1946.

Hurlbutt, Henry H. *Chicago Antiquities: Comprising Original Items and Relations, Letters, Extracts and Notes Pertaining to Early Chicago.* Chicago: Self-published, 1881.

Index of Deeds: Delaware County, N.Y., 1797–1835. Delaware County Clerk's Office, Delhi, N.Y.

Index of Mortgages: Delaware County, N.Y., 1797–1835. Delaware County Clerk's Office, Delhi, N.Y.

Irwin, Leonard Bertram. *Pacific Railways and Nationalism in the Canadian-American Northwest, 1845–1873.* New York: Greenwood, 1968.

Jensen, Derrick, and George Draffan. *Railroads and Clearcuts: Legacy of Congress's 1864 Northern Pacific Railroad Land Grant.* Spokane, Wash.: Inland Empire Public Lands Council, 1995.

Johannsen, Robert Walter. *Stephen A. Douglas.* New York: Oxford University Press, 1973.

Johnson, Paul. *The Birth of the Modern: World Society, 1815–1830.* New York: Harper Collins, 1991.

Judgments from the Court of Common Pleas (1797–1808). Delaware County Clerk's Office, Delhi, N.Y.

Junker, Bruce C. "Brady's Bend Iron Company." Unpublished manuscript. Armstrong County Historical Society, Kittanning, Pa.

Kirkland, Joseph. "Among the Poor of Chicago." *Scribner's Magazine,* July 1892. Cornell University Library, Making of America Series, http://cdl.library.cornell.edu/moa/index.html.

Klein, Maury. *Union Pacific: Birth of a Railroad, 1862–1893.* New York: Doubleday, 1987.

Klingaman, William K. *Abraham Lincoln and the Road to Emancipation, 1861–1865.* New York: Viking, 2001.

Knox, John Jay. *A History of Banking in the United States*. 1900. Reprint, New York: A. M. Kelley, 1969.

Kogan, Herman, and Robert Cromie. *The Great Fire: Chicago, 1871*. New York: Putnam, 1971.

Kraft, Roa Iza. "History of the Construction of the Sturgeon Bay Canal." Typescript, 1918. Wisconsin Historical Society, Madison, Wisc.

Lane, Frank, and Helen Lane. *Walton Yesteryears*. Walton, N.Y.: *Walton Reporter*, 1985.

Lane, Helen, ed. *The Story of Walton, 1785–1975, by Many of Its People*. Walton, N.Y.: Walton Historical Society, 1975.

"Last Will and Testament of William Butler Ogden, with Codicils." August 30, 1875. William B. Ogden Free Library, Walton, N.Y.

Leschak, Peter M. *Ghosts of the Fireground: Echoes of the Great Peshtigo Fire and the Calling of a Wildland Firefighter*. San Francisco: Harper, 2002.

Lewis, Lloyd. *John S. Wright, Prophet of the Prairies*. Chicago: Prairie Farmer, 1941.

Lewty, Peter J. *To the Columbia Gateway: The Oregon Railway and the Northern Pacific, 1879–1884*. Pullman: Washington State University Press, 1987.

Leyendecker, Liston Edgington. *Palace Car Prince: A Biography of George Mortimer Pullman*. Niwot: University of Colorado Press, 1992.

Lincoln, Abraham. Papers. Series 2, General Correspondence, 1858–1864. Library of Congress. http://memory.loc.gov/cgi-bin/query/P?mal:7:./temp/~ammem_68GZ:: (accessed May 14, 2007).

Lincoln Institute. "Mr. Lincoln and Freedom," http://www.mrlincolnandfreedom.org.

Lord, Eleazar. *A Historical Review of the New York & Erie Railroad*. New York: Mason Brothers, 1855. American Cultural Series, microfilm reel 378. Ann Arbor: University of Michigan Microfilms, n.d.

Lowe, David Garrard. *Lost Chicago*. New York: Watson-Guptill, 2000.

Lubetkin, M. John. *Jay Cooke's Gamble: The Northern Pacific Railroad, the Sioux, and the Panic of 1873*. Norman: University of Oklahoma Press, 2006.

Lynch, Denis Tilden. *An Epoch and a Man: Martin Van Buren and His Times*. New York: H. Liveright, 1929.

Marshall, Ralph William. "The Early History of the Galena and Chicago Union Railroad." M.A. thesis, University of Chicago, 1937.

Martineau, Harriet. *Society in America*. 1837. Reprint, New York: AMS, 1966.

Marvin, Thomas. "History of Walton to 1875." Reprinted from a series of articles in the *Walton Chronicle*, 1886. Walton Historical Society, Walton, N.Y.

McCague, James. *Moguls and Iron Men: The Story of the First Transcontinental Railroad*. New York: Harper & Row, 1964.

McCarthy, Kathleen. *Noblesse Oblige: Charity and Cultural Philanthropy in Chicago, 1849–1929*. Chicago: University of Chicago Press, 1982.

McCormick, Cyrus. *The Century of the Reaper: An Account of Cyrus Hall McCormick, the Inventor of the Reaper; of the McCormick Harvesting Machine Company, the Business He Created; and of the International Harvester Company, His Heir and Chief Memorial*. Boston: Houghton Mifflin, 1931.

McGrane, Reginald Charles. *The Panic of 1837: Some Financial Problems of the Jacksonian Era*. New York: Russell & Russell, 1965.

McIlvaine, Mabel, ed. *Reminiscences of Chicago during the Forties and Fifties*. Lakeside Classics series. Chicago: R. R. Donnelley, 1913.

——. *Reminiscences of Early Chicago.* Lakeside Classics series. Chicago: R. R. Donnelley, 1912.

McLear, Patrick E. "The Galena and Chicago Union Railroad: A Symbol of Chicago's Economic Maturity." *Journal of the Illinois State Historical Society* 73, no. 1 (Spring 1980).

——. "William Butler Ogden: A Chicago Promoter in the Speculative Era and the Panic of 1837." *Journal of the Illinois State Historical Society* 70, no. 4 (November 1977).

McNamara, John. *History in Asphalt: The Origin of Bronx Street and Place Names.* Harrison, N.Y.: Bronx County Historical Society, 1978.

Mead, Eliza Ann Irene Ogden. Journal, January 1853–December 1858 (transcription of handwritten diary). William B. Ogden Free Library, Walton, N.Y.

Mercer, Lloyd. *Railroads and Land Grant Policy: A Study of Government Intervention.* New York: Academic Press, c. 1982.

Merriner, James L. *Grafters and Goo Goos: Corruption and Reform in Chicago, 1833–2003.* Carbondale: Southern Illinois University Press, 2004.

Mickelson, Sig. *The Northern Pacific Railroad and the Selling of the West.* Sioux Falls, S.D.: Center for Western Studies, Augustana College, 1993.

Miles, Hester Lane. "History of Cannonsville." Handwritten notes, 1887–92. Delaware County, N.Y., Genealogy and History Site, http://www.dcnyhistory.org/cannon.html.

Miller, Donald L. *City of the Century: The Epic of Chicago and the Making of America.* New York: Simon & Schuster, 1996.

Miller, Ross. *American Apocalypse: The Great Fire and the Myth of Chicago.* Chicago: University of Chicago Press, 1990.

——. *The Great Chicago Fire.* Urbana: University of Illinois Press, 2000.

Monroe, John D. *Chapters in the History of Delaware County, New York.* Delhi, N.Y.: Delaware County Historical Association, 1949.

Moore, Jean, and Richard Crabb. "Young People's Story of DuPage County," DuPage County Heritage Gallery, http://www.dupageheritage.org.

Moses, John. *History of Chicago, Illinois.* 2 vols. Chicago: Munsell, 1895.

Munsell, W. W. *History of Delaware County, New York: With Illustrations, Biographical Sketches and Portraits of Some Pioneers and Prominent Residents.* New York: Munsell, 1880. Delaware County, N.Y., Genealogy and History Site, http://www.dcnyhistory.org/munsell.html.

Murphy, Dan. *The Erie Canal: The Ditch That Opened a Nation.* Buffalo: Western New York Wares, 2001.

Murray, David, ed.. *Centennial History of Delaware County, New York: 1797–1897.* Delhi, N.Y.: William Clark, 1898. Delaware County, N.Y., Genealogy and History Site, http://www.dcnyhistory.org/murray17971897.html.

Musich, Gerald. "John Van Nortwick." *Encyclopedia of American Business History and Biography: Railroads in the Nineteenth Century,* edited by Robert L. Frey. New York: Facts on File, 1988.

Neely, Mark E., Jr. *The Union Divided: Party Conflict in the Civil War North.* Cambridge Mass.: Harvard University Press, 2002.

Nesbit, Robert C. *Wisconsin: A History.* 2nd ed., edited by William F. Thompson. Madison: University of Wisconsin Press, 1989.

"New Gateway Cities (1800–1860)." *U.S. History Resource Center*, database: America Eras. Gale Group, http://galenet.galegroup.com.

"New York State Legislature Asks Governor Pataki to Proclaim Isaac Newton Arnold Day." News release, August 25, 2005, Hartwick College, Oneonta, N.Y.

Nicoll, Francis B. vs. William B. Ogden et al., Supreme Court of Illinois at Ottawa, 1862. LexisNexis, no. 1841:24469641, http://www.lexis.com.

Niven, John. *Martin Van Buren: The Romantic Age of American Politics.* New York: Oxford University Press, 1983.

North, Arthur W. *The Founders and the Founding of Walton, New York.* Walton, N.Y.: Walton Reporter, 1924.

North, Benjamin. "North Family Record, 1864." Handwritten journal. Special collections, William B. Ogden Free Library, Walton, N.Y.

Oberholtzer, Ellis Paxson. *Jay Cooke, Financier of the Civil War.* 2 vols. Philadelphia: Jacobs, 1907.

Ogden, George Washington. Personal diaries, 1832–35, 1837–41. Rock County Historical Society, Janesville, Wisc.

Ogden, William B. File. Special collections. Walton Historical Society, Walton, N.Y.

———. Papers, 1829–81. Manuscripts, correspondence, and letterbooks. Chicago History Museum, Chicago, Ill.

Orsi, Richard J. *Sunset Limited: The Southern Pacific Railroad and the Development of the America West, 1850–1930.* Los Angeles: University of California Press, 2005.

Othfors, Daniel. "Arctic, 1850–1854." The Great Ocean Liners, Othfors and Ljungstrom. http://www.greatoceanliners.net/arctic.html.

Pacific Southwest Railway Museum. "Railway History." http://www.sdrm.org/history/timeline.

Parton, James. *Manual for the Instruction of "Rings," Railroad and Political, with a History of the Grand Chicago & North Western "Ring," and the Secret of its Success in Placing an Over-issue of Twenty Millions, with a Margin of Three Millions in Three Years.* New York: American News, 1866.

Pernin, Peter. *The Great Peshtigo Fire: An Eyewitness Account.* Library, Pamphlet Collection, Madison: State Historical Society of Wisconsin, 1999.

Peyton, J. Lewis. *Over the Alleghanies and Across the Prairies: Personal Recollections of the Far West, One and Twenty Years Ago.* London: Simpkin, Marshall, 1870.

Pierce, Bessie Louise. *As Others See Chicago: Impressions of Visitors, 1673–1933.* Chicago: University of Chicago Press, 1937.

———. *A History of Chicago.* 3 vols. Chicago: University of Chicago Press, 1975.

Pierce, Harry H. *Railroads of New York: A Study of Government Aid, 1826–1875.* Cambridge, Mass.: Harvard University Press, 1953.

Poole, Ernest. *Giants Gone: Men Who Made Chicago.* New York: Whittlesey House, 1943.

The Prairie Farmer: Devoted to Western Agriculture, Mechanics and Education. John S. Wright. ed. Chicago: Union Agricultural Society, 1847.

"Private Gardens of Chicago." *Prairie Farmer*, September 1847.

Proposed Ship Canal at Sturgeon Bay, Wisconsin, to Connect Green Bay with Lake Michigan and Open a New Harbor on the West Shore of the Lake (pamphlet). 1870. Wisconsin Historical Society, Madison, Wisc.

Putnam, James William. *The Illinois and Michigan Canal: A Study in Economic History.* Chicago Historical Society Collection, vol. 10. Chicago: University of Chicago Press, 1918.

Quaife, Milo Milton. *Checagou: From Indian Wigwam to Modern City, 1673–1835.* Chicago: University of Chicago Press, 1933.

"The Rail-roads, History, and Commerce of Chicago: Three Articles Published in the *Daily Democratic Press.*" 1854. Chicago History Collection, Chicago Public Library, Chicago, Ill.

Raitt, John E. *Ruts in the Road.* (Reprint of Bicentennial columns from the *Delaware County Times.*) Walton, N.Y.: Reporter Company, 1982.

Renz, Louis T. *The History of the Northern Pacific Railroad.* Fairfield, Wash.: Ye Galleon Press, 1980.

"Return of Jurors for the Town of Walton." 1798. Delaware County Clerk's Office, Delhi, N.Y.

Rockwell, Charles. *The Catskill Mountains and the Region around: Their Scenery, Legends and History.* New York: Taintor Bros., 1869. Online version, "Catskill Archive: A Treasury of Catskill Mountain History," http://www.catskillarchive.com/Rockwell/index.htm.

Rohe, Randall E. *Ghosts of the Forest: Vanished Lumber Towns of Wisconsin.* Vol. 1. Wisconsin Rapids: Forest History Association of Wisconsin, 2002.

Rusling, James Fowler. *The Great West and Pacific Coast; or, Fifteen Thousand Miles . . . ,* New York: Sheldon, 1877.

Sandburg, Carl. *Abraham Lincoln: The Prairie Years and the War Years.* 1925–26. Reprint, New York: Harcourt, Brace, 1954.

———. *Chicago Poems.* New York: Henry Holt, 1916.

Sawyers, June Skinner. *Chicago Sketches: Urban Tales, Stories, and Legends from Chicago History.* Chicago: Wild Onion Books, 1995.

Schultz, Rima Lunin. "The Businessman's Role in Western Settlement: The Entrepreneurial Frontier, Chicago, 1833–1872." PhD diss., Boston University, 1985.

———. *The Church and the City: A Social History of 150 Years at Saint James, Chicago.* Chicago: Cathedral of St. James, 1986.

Schuster, James. "Cliffs Shaft Mine, 1867–1967 (100 Years)." MBA term paper, Michigan Tech University, 2002. http://www.me.mtu.edu/~jdschust/cliffs/csmhistory.html (accessed May 23, 2007).

Sheahan, James W., and George P. Upton. *The Great Conflagration: Chicago, Its Past, Present, and Future.* Chicago: Union Publishing, 1871.

Skilnik, Bob. *The History of Beer and Brewing in Chicago, 1833–1978.* St. Paul, Minn.: Pogo, 1999.

Smalley, Eugene V. *History of the Northern Pacific Railroad.* New York: Putnam's Sons, 1883. (Microfilm.)

Smith, Adam. *An Inquiry into the Nature and Cause of the Wealth of Nations.* 1776. Liberty Fund, Library of Economics and Liberty, http://www.econlib.org/library/smith/smwn.html.

Smith, Robert Walker. *History of Armstrong County, Pennsylvania.* Chicago, 1883. Reprint, Evansville, Ind.: Unigraphic, 1975.

"Some Early History of Walton, N.Y." *Walton Reporter,* January–July 1935. New York State Historical Association Library, Cooperstown, N.Y.

Spearman, Frank H. *The Strategy of Great Railroads.* New York: Charles Scribner's, 1904.

Steffens, Lincoln. *The Shame of the Cities.* New York: McClure, Phillips, 1904.

Stennett, W. H. *Yesterday and Today: A History of the Chicago and North Western Railway System*. 3rd ed. Chicago: Winship, 1910.

Stephenson, Isaac. *Recollections of a Long Life: 1829–1915*. Chicago: Privately published, 1915.

Stoddard, Francis Hovey. *The Life and Letters of Charles Butler*. New York: Charles Scribner's, 1903.

Stover, John F. *American Railroads*. Chicago: University of Chicago Press, 1961.

Stowell, Daniel W., et al., eds. *The Papers of Abraham Lincoln: Legal Documents and Cases*. 4 vols. Charlottesville: University of Virginia Press, 2008.

Taylor, Charles Henry. *History of the Board of Trade of the City of Chicago*. Chicago: R. O. Law, 1917.

Torr, James D., ed. *Westward Expansion*. Farmington Hills, Mich.: Greenhaven, 2003.

Ward, James Arthur. *Railroads and the Character of America, 1820–1887*. Knoxville: University of Tennessee Press, 1986.

Wells, Robert W. *Fire at Peshtigo*. Englewood, N.J.: Prentice-Hall, 1968.

Wendt, Lloyd. *Swift Walker*. Chicago: Regnery, 1986.

Wertenbaker, Thomas Jefferson. *The Founding of American Civilization: The Middle Colonies*. New York: Cooper Square, 1963.

West, Anna Sheldon Ogden. "Reminiscences Dealing Largely with the Great Chicago Fire of 1871." 1877. Chicago Fire of 1871 Collection. Chicago History Museum, Chicago, Ill.

Wheeler, William Ogden. *The Ogden Family in America, Elizabethtown Branch, and Their English Ancestry: John Ogden, the Pilgrim and His Descendants 1640–1906, Their History, Biography and Genealogy*. Philadelphia: Lippincott, 1907. Facsimile ed., Pawtucket, R.I.: Quintin, 2003.

White, Henry Kirke. *History of the Union Pacific Railroad*. Chicago: University of Chicago Press, 1895.

Widmer, Ted. *Martin Van Buren*. The American President Series. New York: Times Books/Henry Holt, 2005.

Williams, John Hoyt. *A Great and Shining Road: The Epic Story of the Transcontinental Railroad*. New York: Times Books, 1988.

Winter, Katherine. "Early Days of Cannonsville." In *Cannonsville, New York, 1786–1956*. Originally published in the *Deposit (N.Y.) Courier Journal*, July 21, 1926. Online version, Delaware County, N.Y., Genealogy and History Site, http://www.dcnyhistory.org/cannonsville17861956hunter.html.

Withuhn, William, ed. *Rails across America: A History of Railroads in North America*. New York: Salamander, 1993.

Wolner, Edward W. "The City Builder in Chicago, 1834–1871." *Old Northwest* 13 (Spring 1987): 3–22.

Wolper, Gregg. *The Chicago Dock and Canal Trust, 1857–1987*. Chicago: The Trust, 1988.

Wormser, Richard. *The Iron Horse: How Railroads Changed America*. New York: Walker, 1993.

Young, David M. *The Iron Horse and the Windy City*. DeKalb: Northern Illinois University Press, 2005.

INDEX

accretion, 157, 158–59, 225
Albany Argus, 13, 15, 42
Albany Regency, 2, 4, 11
Aldis, Owen, 247
American Geographical & Statistical Society, 213
American Land Co., 46, 64, 91; description of, 60–61; Ogden and, 61; structure of, 65
Ampere, J. J., 128
antislavery issue, 134–36
Armour, Philip Danforth, 60, 191
Arnold, Isaac: and Chicago Historical Society, 178–79; and Chicago North Side home, 70, 181, 229; family of, escapes from Chicago Fire, 231–33; and Galena & Chicago Union Railroad, 98–99, 116–17; and Illinois & Michigan Canal, 87–88; as Lincoln biographer, 232; on Ogden, 7, 29, 35, 85, 126, 150, 184, 239, 242, 249, 255, 264; Ogden shares vision for railroads with, 144–46; at railroad convention, 101; speaks at Ogden memoriam, 264
Arnold, Ogden & Co., 72
Arnot, Marianna, 221, 256. *See also* Ogden, Marianna
Arctic, shipwreck of, 133

banking, 129–30
Bank of the United States, 129
Barry, William, 178, 179
Best Friend of Charleston locomotive, 9
Boorstin, Daniel, 128
boosterism, 61–62
Brady's Bend Iron Works, 164–65
Brainard, Dr. Daniel, 93–94, 134
Bridgeport, Ill., 68, 127, 139
Bronson, Arthur: meets C. Butler, 41; builds house in Chicago, 44; early visit of, to Chicago, 42–43; purchases land in Chicago, 46, 65; and Illinois & Michigan Canal, 45, 88; advises Ogden, 58; hires Ogden to handle real estate investments 86
Bronson, Frederick, 54
Brooklyn Eagle, 226
Buffalo, N.Y., 37, 43, 52, 56, 82, 83, 124, 127, 134, 212
Burnham, Daniel, 247
businessman, background of term, 128
Butler, Benjamin, 1–5, 46
Butler, Charles: and American Land Co., 60–61, 64; background of, 40–42; buys Bronson's land in Chicago, 46; celebrates golden wedding anniversary, 256; and Chicago & Michigan Steamboat Co., 69; and Chicago & North Western Railroad, 198; death of, 257, 262; describes Chicago, 43–44; discusses New York Assembly race with Ogden, 1–5; dispatches Ogden to Chicago, 46–47; early visit to Chicago, 42–43, 264; effect of Panic of 1837 on, 81, 86; European vacation of, 131–33; and Illinois & Michigan Canal, 45; and land reform, 40–41; marries Eliza Ogden, 40; Ogden as client of, 66; receives Ogden's letter about Chicago Fire, 229, 237, 253; relocates to New York, 58; and Rock River Valley Union Railroad, 146; shares railroad vision with Ogden, 144–46; visits Ohio, Indiana to study opportunities in, 45; writes to Eliza Ogden, 194
Butterfield, Justin, 87, 88, 97

California Gold Rush, 39
Camp Douglas, 189
Canadian-Pacific Railroad, 218–19
Canal Party, 84

301

Jack Harpster graduated from the University of Wisconsin with a bachelor's degree in journalism in 1959. He spent forty-three years working on the business management side of the newspaper industry in Southern California and Nevada before retiring in 2002. Harpster then began writing as a hobby. He currently has nine nonfiction books published in the biography and history genres, and more than forty essays and articles in journals and magazines. Harpster lives in Reno, Nevada.